20p.

SHAKESPEARE

SHAKESPEARE

the poet and his background

Peter Quennell

READERS UNION
WEIDENFELD & NICOLSON
London 1964

This RU edition was produced in 1964 for sale to its members only by Readers Union Ltd at Aldine House, 10-13 Bedford Street, London W.C.2 and at Letchworth Garden City, Herts. Full details of membership may be obtained from our London address. The book is set in 11 point Ehrhardt type leaded and has been printed by C. Tinling & Co Ltd at Prescot, Lancs. It was first published by Weidenfeld & Nicolson Ltd.

Ad Ajaiam Ajajam

CONTENTS

I CHILDHOOD AND YOUTH 17

II LONDON APPRENTICESHIP 41

III THE CLIMATE OF THE AGE 66

IV EARLY POEMS 95

V 'HIS SUGARED SONNETS' 120

VI ROMEO AND JULIET 141

VII ROMANTIC COMEDIES 166

VIII HISTORICAL DRAMA 196

IX THE FALL OF ESSEX 222

X A NEW REIGN 252

XI OTHELLO AND ANTONY 274

XII 'UNACCOMMODATED MAN' 298

BIBLIOGRAPHY 335

INDEX 339

ILLUSTRATIONS

facing page

1 Shakespeare's birthplace in mid-Victorian times (*Photo: Radio Times Hulton Picture Library*)   56

2 Rustic festivities, *c.* 1569. Painting by J. Hoefnagel. In the collection of Lord Salisbury (*Photo: Courtauld Institute of Art*)   56

3 Queen Elizabeth in procession. In the collection of Simon Wingfield Digby MP (*Photo: Royal Academy*)   56

4 The wedding masque, and other scenes in his career, of Sir Henry Unton. Painting by unknown artist. (*Photo: National Portrait Gallery*)   56

5 Miniature of Queen Elizabeth I in old age by Isaac Oliver (*Photo: Victoria and Albert Museum*)   56

6 English costumes about 1580. From Caspar Rutz, *Habitus Variorum Orbus Gentum*, 1581, in the British Museum (*Photo: John Freeman*)   57

7 Elizabethan chivalry: George Clifford, Earl of Cumberland. Painting by Nicholas Hilliard (*Photo: National Maritime Museum, Greenwich*)   57

8 An Elizabethan Court beauty: Mary Fitton. Portrait by an unknown artist. In the collection of Mrs C. G. Lancaster   104

9 An Elizabethan great house: Hardwick Hall, Derbyshire (*Photo: A. F. Kersting*)   104

10 Robert Devereux, Earl of Essex. Portrait by an unknown artist (*Photo: National Portrait Gallery*)   104

11 William Cecil, 1st Lord Burghley. Portrait by an unknown artist (*Photo: Bodleian Library, Oxford*)   105

facing page

12 Robert Cecil, 1st Earl of Salisbury. Portrait attributed to J. De Critz (*Photo: National Portrait Gallery*)   105

13 Sir Walter Ralegh and his son. Portrait by an unknown artist (*Photo: National Portrait Gallery*)   152

14 An important member of the Essex circle, Lord Mountjoy. Miniature by Nicholas Hilliard. In the collection of Sir John Carew-Pole (*Photo: By permission of the owner*)   152

15 Henry Wriothesly, 3rd Earl of Southampton, in his youth. Portrait by an unknown artist. In the collection of the Duke of Portland (*Photo: W. E. Middleton, Nottingham*)   152

16 Southampton during his imprisonment in the Tower. In the collection of the Duke of Buccleuch (*Photo: Tom Scott, Edinburgh*)   152

17 Southampton as a middle-aged courtier. Portrait by an unknown artist. In the collection of the Duke of Portland (*Photo: W. E. Middleton, Nottingham*)   153

18 A performance at the Swan Theatre. Contemporary copy of a drawing by Johannes de Witt (*Photo: Radio Times Hulton Picture Library*)   208

19 A reconstruction of a playhouse, *c.* 1595. From *The Globe Restored* by C. Walter Hodges   209

20 Seventeenth-century swordmanship. From *Académie de L'Esprée* by G. Thibault, 1628, in the British Museum (*Photo: John Freeman*)   209

21 Alphabet of rhetorical gestures. From *Chirologia* by John Bulwer, 1644, in the British Museum (*Photo: John Freeman*)   224

22 King James I of England and VI of Scotland. Portrait by Van Somer at Hampton Court (*Reproduced by gracious permission of HM The Queen*)   225

23 Triumphal Arch, erected for James I. From *Archs of Triumph* by Stephen Harrison, 1603, in the British Museum (*Photo: John Freeman*)   264

facing page

24   The opening page of a pageant-play staged on the Arch of
     Triumph to mark James I's arrival. From *Archs of
     Triumph* by Stephen Harrison, 1604, in the British Museum
     Photo: John Freeman)   264

25   Pages from the first Quarto of Hamlet, 1603. In the British
     Museum (*Photo: John Freeman*)   265

26   Ben Jonson. Portrait by an unknown artist (*Photo: National
     Portrait Gallery*)   265

27   Five examples of Shakespeare's signature (*Photo: Radio Times
     Hulton Picture Library*)   312

28   The City and Bankside in 1647. Engraving by Wenceslaus
     Holler (*Photo: John Freeman*)   313

29   London Bridge, seen from Southwark. Engraving by Wences-
     laus Holler (*Photo: John Freeman*)   313

PREFACE

THIS BOOK, WHEN I wrote the first pages, was provisionally named *In Search of Shakespeare*; and, although that title has since been discarded, it sufficiently explains my purpose. Like many other students of English poetry, I was brought up to believe that there was something inescapably mysterious about the circumstances of Shakespeare's life, and that remarkably little information existed that helped us to understand his individual growth. But the more I looked into the existing records, the less tenable did such a belief appear. From the year 1592, when he was attacked by an unhappy fellow poet, we find constant references to his increasing reputation as a writer, accompanied by numerous allusions to his human qualities. If these allusions are separately examined, we may find it difficult to draw a detailed portrait; but, if what we know of Shakespeare himself is combined both with the evidence that his work affords us and with our knowledge of his social period, a recognizable impression very soon emerges. Here, without indulging in speculative licence, I have attempted to reach the poet at once through his work and through his times. My hero is the ambitious Stratfordian player. I have become firmly convinced that Shakespeare's plays and poems were produced, not by Derby, Oxford, Bacon, nor even by Christopher Marlowe after his supposed death, but by a middle-class writer born in Warwickshire in April 1564, and that all the current anti-Stratfordian theories involve some serious distortions of the facts.

It has been argued that William Shakespeare could not have composed the majestic works attributed to him, because his origins were relatively obscure: that only an aristocrat could have depicted aristocrats, a statesman have described the doings of statesmen, or a cultured traveller have written of foreign countries. But then, Stendhal, Balzac and Proust were bourgeois novelists, who have left us vivid descriptions of the nineteenth-century upper class. They were also extremely imaginative artists; and Shakespeare's glimpses of courts and council-chambers were possibly as inaccurate and over-coloured as certain of their more romantic flights. Secondly, Shake-speare, to judge from the records, was a highly businesslike person, who accumulated landed property, lent small sums of money and was apt to engage in petty law-suits. Could a litigious landowner, we are asked, have written *Othello*, *Lear* or *Hamlet*? Well, Shake-speare was undoubtedly a man of the world, and apparently a typical citizen of his age. All the Elizabethans were interested in money and accustomed repeatedly to go to law. Shakespeare, despite his creative genius, followed the contemporary social pattern. Nor is it true to say that every great artist has been particularly scrupulous in his private conduct.

Finally, assuming that a formidable hoax—one of the most extra-ordinary ever perpetrated—was indeed engineered by some 'con-cealed poet', how precisely was it devised and carried out? Had Shakespeare lived in the present day, the operation might have been fairly simple. The real author, who preferred to remain hidden, could then have despatched his manuscript by registered post to the pretended author at his quiet London rooms or secluded country cottage, and Shakespeare could have retyped the material and dutifully handed it on to an unsuspecting actor-manager, who, know-ing little of Shakespeare's own talents, would not have been too much astonished by its splendid quality. But Shakespeare was a hard-working player and, like other players and almost all Eliza-bethans or Jacobeans, lived an exceedingly public life. Plays were often revised and rewritten, usually at short notice; and Shake-speare's fellow players, if he had been a commonplace hack, would soon have perceived that between the original text and the additions he made on the spot there was a startling discrepancy. The Eliza-bethans were talkative people, notably jealous and cantankerous; and they would have pointed out that, whereas the Shakespeare they knew was a vulgar and ungifted drudge, he possessed a strange knack of dashing off tragedies and comedies that brought him in a large profit. Yet both Heminge and Condell, who prepared, or helped to prepare, the First Folio, and who had been prominent members of

Shakespeare's company, acclaimed him as the genial author of the plays—each of these old acquaintances was remembered in the Stratfordian player's testament; while Ben Jonson, also a theatrical colleague—a poet, moreover, who had some motives for resenting Shakespeare's popular success—paid him an affectionate post-humous tribute, declared that he had 'loved the man' and spoke warmly of his 'open and free nature'.

Were Heminge and Condell Shakespeare's innocent dupes? Was Jonson himself engaged in this elaborate conspiracy? All the anti-Stratfordian theories raise many more problems than a whole-hearted acceptance of William Shakespeare's claim. Christopher Marlowe, for example, reputedly killed by a quarrelsome boon companion, but, according to an American enthusiast, really smuggled out of the country by his protector Thomas Walsingham, was the subject of a coroner's inquest in the year 1593. Lord Oxford, alleged director of a mysterious 'syndicate', said to have acted as a secret propaganda service, subsidized by the Elizabethan govern-ment, unquestionably died in 1604. Are we to assume that he left behind him an accumulation of unacted plays? Lord Derby survived until 1641, but must have laid down his pen after the publication of the First Folio.

Next, there is the question of the apocryphal plays. I have sug-gested here that Shakespeare may perhaps have had a hand in the composition of Fletcher's somewhat feeble tragi-comedy *The Two Noble Kinsmen*, but have not admitted that he was responsible either for *Sir Thomas More* or for that lively, though decidedly unpoetic, melodrama *Arden of Faversham*. This book, however, is intended for the general student of life and literature rather than for stern Shakespearian experts; and I hope that experts will not take it amiss when they see that, in the general reader's interest, I have relegated the names of living authorities to the accompanying foot-notes: there is always the danger that a biography of Shakespeare may become a treatise upon previous studies. The text I have employed is that of the new Cambridge Edition; and the system of chronology I have adopted is customarily that put forward by Sir Edmund Chambers. Among those who have encouraged and advised me, my thanks are due first and foremost to Professor Joel Hurstfield, who has consented to read through portions of the book that discuss political and social matters. But much of my typescript I have not troubled him with; and, where I have gone astray, the fault is mine alone. I am also grateful to my friend Robin McEwen, who has elucidated an important legal point; to Mr Anthony Wood, County Archivist of Warwickshire; to Miss Gillian Thompson, Mrs Yardley and Mrs Hutchinson for their patient work upon my long-hand draft; and to the Duke of Portland, the Duke of Buccleuch, the Marquis of Salisbury, Mrs C. G. Lancaster, Mr A. F. Kersting, the Trustees of the National Portrait Gallery and the Directors of the Victoria and Albert Muscum for permission to reproduce pictures.

London, 1963

CHAPTER I

Childhood and Youth

GREAT ARTISTS ARE frequently the product of an unhappy or ill-balanced marriage; and, although we cannot say whether the marriage solemnised, during the autumn months of 1557, between John Shakespeare, burgher of Stratford-on-Avon, and Mary, youngest daughter and joint-heiress of Robert Arden of Wilmcote, ran a particularly inharmonious course, at the outset, judged by a worldly standard, its prospects may have seemed discouraging. For, whereas John Shakespeare was a rustic tradesman, Mary belonged to a family that had made a considerable show in Warwickshire. True, Robert Arden was a descendant of the younger, less patrician branch; but until his death, which occurred towards the end of 1556, he had inhabited a substantial manor-farm and cultivated a large tract of his own land, while a pair of supernumerary farms were leased to industrious yeoman tenants. On one of these holdings, at Snitterfield, John Shakespeare had been born and brought up. About 1551, however, he left Snitterfield and settled down in Stratford. There, in Henley Street, he presently bought a house, with a garden and a croft, or paddock; there he began his married life and conducted his modestly profitable business, dealing in corn and malt, leather, hides and raw wool. He is also variously described as a glover and a retail butcher.

A gentleman he could not pretend to be, since he had inherited no armorial bearings. His wife, on the other hand, like the possessive matriarch portrayed in *Sons and Lovers,* was a decidedly 'superior soul', whose ancestors included a sheriff of Warwickshire, and whose maiden name recalled the ancient forest, lying to the north and west

B   17

of Stratford, that, as a remnant of the world's innocent, unspoiled youth, her eldest son later commemorated in a romantic and nostalgic comedy.[1] Robert Arden, moreover, was a devout supporter of the old religion, at a period when middle-class Stratford had generally accepted the Reformed Church. Like Lawrence's mother, Mary Shakespeare may sometimes have reproached her husband with his lack of social grace, and have reminded him of the privileges and opportunities that, through her marriage, she had been obliged to forfeit. Nevertheless, her family multiplied. Two girls, who expired in early childhood, were followed by William, born on April 22nd or 23rd, 1564, and christened on April 26th; and William was succeeded by Gilbert, Richard and Edmund, born in 1566, 1574 and 1580, and by two further daughters, Joan and Ann, of whom the last died when she was seven years old. Meanwhile John Shakespeare continued to increase his credit. An important and respected trades- man, he received a series of honourable civic appointments: as ale- taster in 1557, commissioned to appraise the quality of ale and bread; petty constable in 1558; borough chamberlain in 1561; alderman in 1565; and—his final dignity—bailiff in 1568. Ten years later, he enlarged his Henley Street property by acquiring two adjacent houses; and, about the same time, possibly to please his wife—'a daughter and heir,' he explained, 'of Robert Arden, a gentleman of worship'—he approached the Heralds' College in London and laid claim to a grant of arms.

That claim he did not pursue; for, suddenly and inexplicably, just as he seemed to be reaching the peak of his career, his fortunes under- went a gloomy change; and, when his eldest son was twelve, it became clear that they were rapidly declining. No doubt because he feared arrest, he ceased to take his place among the local Council, thereby losing the dignified rank of alderman, and also neglected to attend church.[2] Besieged at home by his creditors, he made desperate attempts to raise money, and was reduced to the awkward expedient

---

[1] Oliver: Where will the old Duke live?
Charles: They say he is already in the forest of Arden . . . They say many young gentlemen flock to him every day, and fleet the time carelessly, as they did in the golden world. *As you Like It* Act I Scene ii.

[2] In 1592, John Shakespeare is listed among those who had failed to come 'monthly to the church according to her Majesty's law'; but against his name and eight others it is noted that they were believed not to attend 'for fear of process for debt'.

of borrowing from his wife's relations; before long, much of Mary Shakespeare's Arden inheritance had been either sold or mortgaged. Finally, a crowning disaster, he committed some offence that involved him with the Queen's judiciary. How he offended, records do not reveal: there is no evidence that he was a recusant Catholic or adhered to any of the Puritan sects. But in 1580, having omitted to give security against a breach of the peace, and neglected to produce another culprit, at the London Court of Queen's Bench, he was fined no less than forty pounds—a fine that, if he paid it, must have hastened his complete ruin. Yet, so far as we can judge, John Shakespeare did not lose hope; and a seventeenth-century gossip told an acquaintance that he recollected having seen him in his place of business, 'a merry-cheeked old man' who, speaking of his distinguished eldest son, said that 'Will was a good honest fellow', with whom he never hesitated to crack a joke.[1] Obviously, the ruined alderman was not an alarming or depressing parent, or the kind of man who, having failed himself, likes to transmit his private sense of failure. Though he had lost his seat on the Council, he retained the affection of his former colleagues. At all events, they treated him leniently and seem to have forgiven him most of his unpaid dues.

Only writers who have themselves been happy in youth can afterwards recall the experiences of childhood, and the relationship between parent and child, without some trace of lingering bitterness. Despite his father's misfortunes and the effect they may have had upon his mother's character—that of a proud woman, living among memories of the past, which presumably became more magnificent as her husband's prospects and position declined—no such bitterness is discernible in the adult dramatist's pictures of childhood and boyhood; and he has left one tribute to the joys of early life, to the 'green paradise of infantile loves',[2] that appears to have been coloured by deep personal feeling. Here Polixenes, King of Bohemia, describes to Hermione, Queen of Sicilia, the schooldays that he had shared with Leontes, now her royal consort:

---

[1] This story recorded about 1657 by Thomas Plume, Archdeacon of Rochester, is quoted by E. K. Chambers in *William Shakespeare: A Study of Facts and Problems*, 1930, who suggests that it may incorporate 'some genuine reminiscence'.
[2] '. . . *le vert paradis des amours enfantines*': Charles Baudelaire, *Moesta et Errabunda*.

Hermione: You were pretty lordings then?
Polixenes: We were, fair queen,
Two lads, that thought there was no more behind,
But such a day to-morrow, as to-day,
And to be boy eternal.
Hermione: Was not my lord
The verier wag o'th' two?
Polixenes: We were as twinned lambs that did frisk i' th' sun,
And bleat the one at th' other: what we changed
Was innocence for innocence; we knew not
The doctrine of ill-doing, nor dreamed
That any did. Had we pursued that life,
And our weak spirits ne'er been higher reared
With stronger blood, we should have answered
heaven
Boldly 'not guilty' . . .[1]

Elsewhere, the dramatist writes of the laggard schoolboy, and of the jubilant hubbub with which a crowd of children, at length released from their classroom, tumble out into the street again.[2] Since we have no record of how William Shakespeare received his youthful education, some students have chosen to assume that he did not go to school at all, or that he was educated, not in his native town, but perhaps in the household of some cultured dignitary, while he served his master as a musical page. A quite unnecessary inference; for Stratford had an excellent grammar school close beside the ancient Guild Chapel; and the son of a prominent citizen would naturally have been enrolled there. Tuition was free; the Elizabethans, like the Victorians, were determined educationalists; and illiteracy, writes a recent historian of the period, during Shakespeare's lifetime was probably 'a good deal less prevalent than in early-nineteenth-century England, when the old social structure was crumbling under stress of the Industrial Revolution'.[3] Though John

---

[1] *The Winter's Tale* Act I Scene ii.
[2] My lord, our army is dispersed already:
Like youthful steers unyoked, they take their courses
East, west, north, south; or, like a school broke up,
Each hurries toward his home and sporting place
    Henry IV Part II Act IV Scene ii.
[3] A. H. Dodd: *Life in Elizabethan England*, 1961.

Shakespeare used a mark, this does not mean that he was unable to sign his name; and, as a member of the rising yeoman class which now aspired to gentlemanly rank, he would certainly have insisted that his eldest son should enjoy the advantages that a proper modern schooling offered. If William joined the school in 1571, the master beneath whom he sat was Simon Hunt; but Hunt, a Catholic sympathizer, was replaced in 1577 by Thomas Jenkins, a pedagogue of Welsh descent, whose odd accent the dramatist may possibly have recalled while composing *The Merry Wives of Windsor* and creating the character of Sir Hugh Evans; and in 1579 Thomas Jenkins gave way to a London scholar, John Cotton. From them William Shakespeare gained his first insight into the two great branches of Elizabethan learning—the *trivium* which embraced Latin grammar, logic, rhetoric, and the *quadrivium* which consisted of arithmetic, geometry and astronomy and music.[1] He was, no doubt, taught to construe Ovid and obliged to memorize selected passages of the *Metamorphoses*— a strange transition from the Christian psalms and prayers that had ushered in the day's work. Both physically and intellectually, it was a somewhat strenuous form of training. On summer days, he must have been at his desk by six—but then, every Elizabethan, young or old, was accustomed to leave his bed as soon as the sun had risen; and his lessons, with one or two breaks, continued for eight or nine hours.

Few distinguished artists have been exemplary schoolboys; yet Shakespeare acquired a basis of Latin that, although he could never pretend to genuine classical scholarship, he preserved throughout his adult life. His education is said to have been interrupted once his father touched the verge of poverty; and Nicholas Rowe,[2] the poet's earliest biographer, whose account appeared in 1709, relates that 'the narrowness of his circumstances, and the want of his assistance at home, forced his father to withdraw

---

[1] The curriculum of English grammar schools was to change very little for the next two hundred years. The young Samuel Johnson's daily routine at school was 'similar to that of a boy in Stratford in the sixteenth century'. J. L. Clifford: *Young Samuel Johnson*, 1955.

[2] Nicholas Rowe (1674-1718), author of such popular tragedies as *Tamerlane* and *Jane Shore*; while preparing his six volumes of Shakespeare's works, which appeared in 1709, he employed Thomas Betterton the actor to collect biographical material from the Stratford neighbourhood. The stories he collected, however, must be treated with some reservation.

him from school'—a different version of the tale already told by John Aubrey,[1] who reports that he had been informed 'by some of the neighbours' that, when William was a boy, he had assisted John Shakespeare in the butcher's trade, and that, as often as he slaughtered a calf, 'he would do it in high style and make a speech' above the lowing victim's head. Yet evidently he was not a self-taught writer; nor was Stratford a remote and backward town in which literacy was under-valued. With its population of about two thousand souls, it was an interesting, eventful borough, unquestionably far more eventful than a modern township of the same size. Meadows encircled it; the river bordered it, sailed by ruffling fleets of swans; and across the Avon strode Clopton Bridge, which a rich merchant, Sir Hugh Clopton, had built during the latter decades of the fifteenth century, when he had also erected New Place, 'a pretty house of brick and timber', since sold by the Cloptons and now lapsing into 'ruin and decay'. From the river-banks, three principal thoroughfares— Bridge Street, divided by a line of houses into Back Bridge Street and Fore Bridge Street, Sheep Street and Chapel Lane—ran up towards the centre of the town; and Bridge Street, of which Henley Street was a continuation, included the building known as High Cross, where the local glovers pitched their stalls, and thieves, vagabonds and loose women were exposed and corrected at the whipping-post. Citizens' houses were solid, half-timbered structures; and behind almost every house lay a pleasant garden and usually a high-walled orchard.

Even today, there is something peculiarly slumbrous, almost oppressively still and remote, about the English Midland landscape, its moist green fields and wandering hedgerows and long vistas of ancient rooky elms, that roll off towards a vague horizon beneath a softly dappled sky. Ninety miles of rough road separated Stratford from the capital; but Stratfordians often covered the distance on visits to their London friends; and in their own immediate vicinity they had a series of distinguished neighbours. Not far away was Kenilworth Castle, home of Robert Dudley, Earl of Leicester, the handsome, swaggering, ambitious favourite, whom the Queen called her 'Sweet Robin' and who had been the beloved companion of her

---

[1] John Aubrey, 1626-1697; author of brilliant personal portraits and indefatigable collector of literary and social gossip.

early years; his brother, the Earl of Warwick, lived in feudal state at Warwick Castle; while on the verge of Stratford, stood Charlecote, the red-brick mansion of Sir Thomas Lucy, with its impressive gate-house and many-chimneyed, steeply gabled roofs. The presence of these gentlemen naturally drew the Queen, who loved travelling, rustic sports and the splendid pageantry that her richer subjects provided. In 1565, she had visited Kenilworth; and, ten years later, when Shakespeare was eleven, she returned for a more extended visit, to enjoy what proved to be one of the most costly and dazzling entertainments staged by any Elizabethan courtier. Elizabeth was a difficult, capricious guest: already she had displayed extreme vexation because, on a 'marvellous hot day', her attendants could not supply a single 'drop of good drink'—only flagons of strong beer, whereas she demanded light ale; and, at Kenilworth, she briefly lost her temper, refusing to leave her apartment and admire an ingenious 'device of goddesses and nymphs', perhaps because she had discovered that the party included Leicester's mistress Lady Essex, a beautiful termagant, the former Lettice Knollys, with whom, much as he dreaded the Queen's jealousy, he was afterwards to contract a secret marriage. George Gascoigne, Leicester's poetic employee, thereupon received hasty instructions to produce a supplementary interlude; and a sylvan demi-god accosted the Queen and spoke at length of the universal mourning and lamentation now heard among the harmless dwellers of the forest, since the tragic news had reached their ears that 'her Majesty would shortly and too suddenly depart . . .' Sylvanus was followed by the personage of Deep Desire, emerging from an arbour to the sound of music.

At which, the Queen's irritation subsided; and there was no further talk of leaving Kenilworth until the festivities had reached their end. They continued three whole weeks. A succession of writers on the Elizabethan Age have described them in elaborate detail, pointing out that Shakespeare, his father and their kinsmen must almost certainly have swelled the crowd, and also drawing a comparison between one of the set-pieces and a passage in *A Midsummer Night's Dream*—Oberon's reference to the song he had heard sung by 'a mermaid on a dolphin's back'. At Kenilworth, beneath the parapet of a bridge, on which the Queen was placed amid her courtiers, a mermaid appeared, all tailed and finned, and a masked figure of Arion, seated on a buoyant dolphin. Arion had begun to deliver the usual complimentary discourse, when, like Snug the Joiner enacting the part of the lion that affrighted Thisbe, he snatched off his mythological mask and exultantly declared his name, announcing that he was no Arion but simple Harry Goldingham, a good, honest, true-born English subject—a gesture that greatly amused Elizabeth, who said that it had pleased her more than anything else in the entire display.[1] Otherwise contemporary accounts of the pageantry suggest the most aureate type of Elizabethan pastoral poem rendered into mime and song. Behind the sea-gods who breasted the pool and the five hirsute Tritons, 'all with grisly heads and beards of divers colours', who came splashing in to wind their conches, terraced islands, raised from an artificial sea, blossomed skywards with extravagant bouquets of fireworks; and 'fire-wheels, pikes of pleasure, and balls of wild fire' burned across the water or blazed along the banks. At dawn, the 'Princely Pleasures' of the night were replaced by the poetic amusements of the day; and the park and woodlands were filled with choirs of sylvan personages, reciting Gascoigne's fluent verse or chanting amorous hymns and catches.

An entertainment on so prodigious a scale was never again to be staged in sixteenth-century Warwickshire; but bands of London players, touring the provinces, very often found their way to Stratford; and, late in the 1560's, the Queen's Players and the Earl of Worcester's Players both arrived and held performances, being paid by the borough chamberlain the sums of nine shillings and one shilling respectively. Comedians took to the road when pestilence attacked the capital; travellers from London and other large cities frequently brought with them an epidemic of the plague; and a particularly severe outbreak had ravaged the town during the year of Shakespeare's birth. *Hic incipit pestis* wrote John Bretchgirdle, the learned parish priest who had christened him, against July 11th, 1564, in the pages of the parish register; and, before the year was out, the number of deaths he recorded, as compared with deaths for the previous six months, had been multiplied by more than ten. The summer months were an especially dangerous period; and, once the

[1] Elizabeth Jenkins: *Elizabeth and Leicester*, 1961.

disease was under way, nothing could restrain its spread. Perfumes, unguents, purges, powders, the regular watering of entries and house-doors, wormwood and rue strewn along window-ledges, huge bon-fires lighted in the streets—none of the remedies that physicians recommended could be relied on to avert the sickness; and, besides sternly prohibiting public assemblies, and ordering that stables should be cleansed, dunghills removed, and that no cats, dogs or pigs should henceforth be allowed to run abroad, the authorities en-deavoured to limit infection by imprisoning sufferers within their own houses. Bubonic plague had decimated the population of Strat-ford; in London, during the summer and autumn of 1593, the disease was to carry off over a thousand citizens a week; and there may be a link between these recurrent tragedies and certain aspects of the Elizabethan character—its fatalism and dark superstitious fears, its addiction to sudden bouts of melancholy, and the obsessive preoccu-pation so many poets reveal with fantastic images of decay and death.

Yet the English were a hardy, sanguine people, devoted to the transitory pleasures of existence, great lovers of music and dancing, whether they dwelt in town or country. Londoners still danced around garlanded maypoles—both Cheapside and the Strand pre-served their ancient phallic emblems; and on Shrove Tuesday, which heralded the beginning of Lent, apprentices were privileged to leave their shops and turn the City upside down. Among country-men, the Christian calendar incorporated numerous pagan feasts—May Day, Midsummer Day, the junketings that marked the con-clusion of the harvest, the decline of the Old Year and the triumphant ressurection of the New. Stratford itself, on Ascension Day, was in-vaded by a band of local mummers, who played the victory of St George over a canvas-and-pasteboard dragon which, once it had been vanquished and humiliated, they lugged in triumph through the town. All these festivities promoted amorous enterprise; and Robert Herrick, where he describes the May-day revels that followed the gathering of may-blossom, employs a catch-phrase he must pre-sumably have learned from his West-Country parishioners. 'Green gowns', he relates, were freely given and received:[1] high-spirited

[1] Many a green-gown hath been given;
Many a kiss, both odd and even . . . Robert Herrick: *Corrina's going a Maying*.
'Greengowns', a common phrase, was also used by Thomas Nashe in 1592.

girls, who had slipped away into the dusk but at length returned to join the party, often exhibited tell-tale grass-stains across the backs of their light-coloured dresses. Such an occasion—the time, we know, was August 1582—must have preceded a crucial development in the story of William Shakespeare's early life. He was suddenly thrust into marriage—not, however, by his own relations, but by a pair of well-meaning neighbours, loyally determined to see justice done. On November 28th, 1582, Fulk Sandells and John Richardson, 'husbandmen of Stratford', appeared in the consistory court of the Bishop of Worcester, and there, against a surety of forty pounds, promised to indemnify the bishop, should any legal complications arise, owing to 'pre-contract' or a forbidden degree of blood-relationship, from the forthcoming marriage of 'William Shagspere' and 'Anne Hathwey of Stratford', which was to be celebrated by special licence, with only 'once asking of the bans'. Both Sandells and Richardson were friends of a certain Richard Hathaway, husbandman of Shottery, a village adjoining Stratford, who is generally recognised as the bride's father; and it is evident that, on behalf of her injured family, they did their best to hurry on the marriage. Anne Hathaway had been pregnant since August; no doubt her burden was becoming visible.

The marriage licence, which either the prospective bridegroom or his officious neighbours must already have obtained from the bishop's court, has long ago completely vanished. But the register records that, on November 27th—the day before Sandells and Richardson agreed to 'hold the bishop harmless'—a licence was issued for the marriage of 'William Shaxpere' and 'Anne Whateley of Temple Grafton'. Did an idle, or overworked, clerk, his mind preoccupied with other papers, besides mis-transcribing the bride's name confuse two villages in the Stratford neighbourhood? That seems the most probable explanation. But Shakespeare's more speculative biographers advance a very different theory—that Anne Hathaway and Anne Whateley had rival claims on their too-impetuous lover, and that each, fearful of desertion, was doing her best to pin the young man down. Whatever the truth may be, it was Anne Hathaway of Stratford whom William Shakespeare made his wife. Where or when, remains an unsolved question. Perhaps because his parents disapproved, he was not married at Stratford parish church, but, according to an old story, at Luddington chapel, or conceivably at Temple Grafton; which, if he had informed the clerk that he was calling the banns there, might account for the deceptive entry. Still, married unquestionably the young man was—during his nineteenth year, to a woman eight years older than himself; and Anne duly gave birth to a daughter, christened Susanna on May 26th, 1583.

Apart from the fact that she bore him two further children, the twins Hamnet and Judith, and survived her husband until 1623, historical scholarship can tell us nothing of the life and character of Anne Shakespeare. We seek a portrait: we confront an empty frame, which a series of variously gifted writers have attempted to fill in with their own imaginings. For James Joyce, Anne Hathaway was a 'boldfaced' country girl, who, beneath a hedgerow or amid 'the acres of the rye', seduced a young and inexperienced lover—'if others have their will, Ann hath a way. By cock, she was to blame. She put the comether on him, sweet and twentysix.' Similarly, as the poet's wife, she has received some rather unkind handling; and a French biographer gives us his personal impressions of how she may have turned out: *c'était apparemment* (he writes) *une créature médiocre, de nature molle et passive . . . une femme commune et insignifiante . . .*[1] The description, of course, is entirely imaginative. Since Anne Hathaway was still unmarried at the age of twenty-five—in a period when girls, whether rich or poor, were accustomed to wed soon after they had reached puberty—we may deduce that she was neither very beautiful nor possessed of a particularly disturbing charm; but we have no excuse for assuming that she was insignificant or commonplace. Docile and long-suffering she may well have been; though Shakespeare often expresses his dislike of jealous, loud-voiced, scolding wives. If Anne scolded and protested, there was little else that she could do. Many Elizabethan women—Leicester's second wife, for example, and her daughter Penelope who married Lord Rich—were as fiery and energetic as the men they loved. Usually, however, these dominant females were members of the ruling class, or married to rich London merchants; and Anne Shakespeare was the daughter of a modest yeoman, who had wedded the son of a much-impoverished

[1] Louis Gillet: *Shakespeare*, 1930.

country tradesman. Her young husband could scarcely have afforded the expense of setting up a separate household; and no doubt she moved into Henley Street and shared the daily existence of John Shakespeare's family.

Thereupon darkness once again shuts down, in which, if it can be said that she has ever properly emerged, Anne Shakespeare disappears for good, and William's development is illuminated only by some meagre shreds of local legend. Thus we are told that, during his early manhood, he gained his living as a rustic school-master; while, on the evidence of the abstruse legal terms that he frequently uses in his plays and poems—often in an inappropriate context, but always with a highly expert air—it has been suggested that, after his marriage, he endured the humdrum routine of a lawyer's office. Yet he also displays a certain knowledge of soldiering; which has inspired a hope, among his martial readers, that, when Stratford and his family life began to weary him beyond endurance, with the help of its commander Robert Dudley he may have joined the English expeditionary force then campaigning in the Netherlands and seen service against the Prince of Parma's troops.[1] We have no real reason, however, to suppose that he had yet considered leaving home; and, as happens in the lives of many artists whose genius develops slowly but at a gradually increasing speed, he may first have passed through a difficult probationary period—years of arduous and ultimately fruitful, but apparently undirected, labour—until at last he heard the secret summons that would send him out along his proper path. Impossible to decide whether, facing the responsibilities he had shouldered, he was philosophic and acquiescent, or rebellious and resentful; but twice at least, with passionate emphasis, he would write of the miseries that attend an unsought marriage—first in *Henry VI, Part I*, which is among his earliest prentice works:

> For what is wedlock forced but a hell,
> An age of discord and continual strife?[2]

Then, in his latest and loveliest comedy, when Prospero, suddenly overcome by a transport of unmeaning violence, rounds on his

[1] See Duff Cooper: *Sergeant Shakespeare*, 1949.
[2] *Henry VI, Part I*, Act V Scene v.

blameless daughter Miranda and the virtuous young prince to whom her heart is given:

> If thou dost break her virgin-knot before
> All sanctimonious ceremonies may
> With full and holy rite be ministred,
> No sweet aspersion shall the heavens let fall
> To make this contract grow; but barren hate,
> Sour-eyed disdain and discord shall bestrew
> The union of your bed with weeds so loathly
> That you shall hate it both[1]

In the circumstances, so brutal a warning seems at once offensive and inapposite; but Prospero and the middle-aged Shakespeare are thought to have been closely linked—each a magician bidding farewell and preparing to discard his magic lore; and even an arch-magician may sometimes be troubled by the shameful sting of early memories.

Meanwhile, towards the end of January 1585, Anne Shakespeare gave birth to twin children—a son and a daughter, who were baptised on February 2nd and named in honour of two family friends, the baker Hamnet Sadler and his wife Judith. Anne Shakespeare was never to bear again: perhaps her husband had already left home; perhaps the last vestiges of a former passion had died, and he had now exhausted his remaining stock of matrimonial good will. Yet it was not the burdens of parenthood or an inharmonious marriage that finally decided him to pull up his roots in Stratford: according to a local tale, reported by Richard Davies, a bibulous seventeenth-century clergyman with literary inclinations, who lived at Sapperton in Gloucestershire, he had been 'much given to all unluckiness in stealing venison and rabbits', particularly from the local grandee Sir Thomas Lucy of Charlecote, 'who had him oft whipped and sometimes imprisoned', and at length 'made him fly his native country to his great advancement'. Nicholas Rowe repeats the story; Shakespeare, he tells us, continued to reside among his father's people 'till an extravagance that he was guilty of, forced him out of his country and that way of living . . . He had, by a misfortune common

---

[1] *The Tempest*, Act IV Scene i.

enough to young fellows, fallen into ill company; and . . . some that made a frequent practice of deer-stealing, engaged him with them more than once in robbing a park that belonged to Sir Thomas Lucy . . . For this he was prosecuted by that gentleman, as he thought, somewhat too severely; and in order to revenge that ill usage, he made a ballad upon him', which was 'said to have been so very bitter, that it redoubled the prosecution against him to that degree, that he was obliged to leave his business and family in Warwickshire, for some time, and shelter himself in London'.

Sir Thomas Lucy, a justice of the peace and a member of parliament, did not keep a deer-park, though his will mentions that he possessed a 'free-warren'; and, under the existing game-laws, he was not authorized to whip poachers. On the other hand, Mr Justice Shallow, whose deer Falstaff stole, would seem undoubtedly to have been a composite portrait of Sir Thomas and of a quite different, but equally opinionated and small-minded, magistrate;[1] and, just as the Lucy arms were *three luces hauriant argent'*, so Shallow bears a 'dozen white luces', which furnish Sir Hugh Evans, in the *Merry Wives of Windsor*, with a characteristic Elizabethan pun. Though the details of the anecdote may be fictitious, we need not question its historical basis. What is more probable than that a gifted young man, shackled to an uninteresting profession and condemned to the dull domesticity of his father's crowded household, should have at last burst out into some 'extravagance' that involved him with a Warwickshire justice of peace, and that, in a mood of disgust or despair, he should have chosen to desert his native county? But we need not assume that he left Stratford as a friendless fugitive. Offers of employment may already have come his way; the London players regularly visited his birthplace; and, during the year 1587, five companies, among which were Leicester's, the Queen's, Essex's and Stafford's, gave performances in the medieval Guild Hall. Alternatively, he had a useful link with the world of printers, publishers and booksellers; for Richard Field, a native of Stratford, whose father

---

[1] See T. Leslie Hotson: *Shakespeare versus Shallow*, 1931, where the author identifies Shallow with a rascally Surrey justice, William Gardiner, a great enemy of the playhouses, and Slender with his stepson William Wayte, who 'craved surety of the peace' against Shakespeare and others in November 1596. (*See* p. 164.) Gardiner's coat also included luces. A luce is the armorial name of that voracious fish the pike.

was a friend of John Shakespeare, had been apprenticed since 1579 to Thomas Vautrollier, a London printer, and in 1587 set up on his own account 'at the sign of the White Greyhound in St Paul's Churchyard'.[1]

It is also possible that Shakespeare had found a patron, who gave him advice or introductory letters. If so, a likely candidate is the Warwickshire landowner Fulke Greville, the courtier, poet and European diplomatist, afterwards raised to the peerage as the first Lord Brooke. Greville's family seat was at Beauchamp Court, Alcester, some seven or eight miles south of Stratford. School-fellow and devoted companion of Sir Philip Sidney, he had entered the Queen's circle, together with Sidney, in the year 1577 and, being both intelligent and personable, almost immediately became a favourite. He enjoyed 'the longest lease and the smoothest time without rub' of any of those on whom the Queen smiled; but Francis Bacon, a hypercritical observer, assures us that he had used his influence wisely and honourably, and, during his heyday, had 'done many men good'. Certainly, he appreciated the company of writers, wits and men of learning; and, in 1583, when the Italian philosopher Giordano Bruno visited England, Fulke Greville was his generous host. Moreover, he was rightly proud of his record; and, in later life, he would remark that he desired 'to be known to posterity under no other notions than of Shakespeare's and Ben Jonson's master, Chancellor Egerton's patron . . . and Sir Philip Sidney's friend'.[2] Exactly ten years older than William Shakespeare, himself drawn towards the art of poetry, he was well qualified to encourage a promising, attractive young man whose literary gifts had roused some local interest. He may, of course, have been Shakespeare's 'master' at a considerably later period of the poet's life; but by that time the author of *Venus and Adonis* had attracted the notice of another rich patron; and, as a neighbour, it was surely Greville's task to assist him along the earlier stages of his road, either with money and the loan of books or, once he had escaped from Stratford, by helping him to make his way in London.

[1] Like many Elizabethan tradesmen, Field married his original employer's widow.

[2] From David Lloyd: *Statesmen and Favourites of England since the Reformation*, 1665, quoted by E. K. Chambers, *op. cit.* Around his tomb, in the chapter-house of St. Mary's Church, Warwick, runs the following inscription: FULKE GREVILL / SERVANT TO QUEENE ELIZABETH / CONCELLER TO KING / JAMES AND FREND TO SIR PHILIP SIDNEY.

We do not know how Shakespeare reached the city; even the date of his arrival remains mysterious. But there can be no doubt that he was still at home during the spring of 1584, since Hamnet and Judith were born towards the end of January 1585; and a legal document, connected with a mortgage on his parents' ill-fated Wilmcote property, mentions him, as having agreed to a proposed sale, about the year 1587. Otherwise, until 1592, modern biographers can only proceed by guesswork. Some send him to London in 1586; some in 1587, when the five companies of players visited Stratford and Richard Field set up his own business; some in 1588. From an imaginative point of view, there is much to recommend the last suggestion; for then Shakespeare would have travelled to London— probably through Oxford and High Wycombe—beneath a heavy cloud of signs and portents. Living as they still did half in the Middle Ages, Elizabethan Englishmen were a deeply superstitious race; and 1588 appeared to have been marked out to produce catastrophes and great adventures. Scholars and scientists, who based their prophecies on *Daniel* and *The Book of Revelation*, had long been concerned with the 'strange events' that might be expected soon to overtake the world. The last cycle of human affairs, asserted the German humanist Melanchthon, had come to an end in 1518 when Martin Luther had defied the Pope; which left a period of ten times seven years—the period of the Babylonian captivity—before the Seventh Seal was opened. Such predictions, widely circulated in Spain and France, had perturbed the Holy Roman Emperor himself; and, though the Queen's government discouraged alarmist reports, they were taken up by various English writers, who referred to the ancient prophecies, 'now so rife in every man's mouth', and the perils of the 'present famous year . . . supposed to be the great, wonderful and fatal year of our age'.[1] News that Philip was preparing his Invincible Armada—a gigantic assemblage of ships and men, designed, wrote the exiled leader of the English Jesuits, 'to reduce our people to the obedience of Christ's Church, and deliver our Catholic friends from the damnable and intolerable yoke of heresy'—confirmed the gloomy prophets' worst forebodings.

By the end of July, the huge crescent-shaped formation of Spanish

---

[1] Garrett Mattingly: *The Defeat of the Spanish Armada*, 1959.

ships had been broken up and driven northwards. But it was now thought that the Duke of Parma might attempt a landing from the Low Countries; and, on August 8th, Elizabeth visited Tilbury to review her troops assembled there, and rode between their ranks 'like some Amazonian empress', the Earl of Leicester at her horse's head, before delivering one of those memorable speeches which only she knew how to frame. Parma's flotilla did not cross the Channel; and public rejoicings, in which Shakespeare must have taken part, with sacred music, religious exhortations, bonfires, dancing and sumptuous secular pageantry, continued through the autumn and winter months. Meanwhile Leicester had died, worn down by a chronic 'burning fever', at the age of fifty-six. Many years had passed since he had expected to marry the Queen and she was rumoured to have borne him a secret child; the dashing, insolent, aggressive youth had become a paunchy, bald-headed, rubicund counsellor. But Elizabeth had never forgotten her love, though she had long ago outlived her passion; and his disappearance brought to a sudden end an important chapter in the history of her life and reign. The way was open for a new favourite—a successor whom Leicester, growing tired and old, had himself selected. That favourite's rapid rise to power would coincide with the growth of Shakespeare's genius; Essex's fall was to launch the dramatist into the composition of some of his darkest tragedies.

1588, then, was a critical year, which left the English people free and confident, and London, the heart of the kingdom, full of prosperity and civic pride. No other metropolis in Northern Europe could claim so large a population; and before the end of the century, as suburbs expanded, London may have found room for three hundred thousand inhabitants.[1] Its nucleus was the ancient City, guarded by medieval walls and gates; and behind them emerged the towers and steeples of over a hundred venerable churches, with St Paul's, a blackened, time-scarred hulk, now shorn of its original spire,[2] but still enormous and majestic, standing high on Ludgate

---

[1] A. H. Dodd, *op. cit.* The population of England and Wales is thought to have been about five millions by the year 1603. See A. L. Rowse: *The England of Elizabeth*, 1950.

[2] It had been destroyed by lightning in 1561, when, early one afternoon, following a 'terrible hideous crack of thunder', a 'long and spear-pointed flame of fire' is said to have descended from the heavens. See John E. N. Hearsey: *Bridge, Church and Palace in Old London*, 1961.

Hill. At its feet, in St Paul's Churchyard, the home of booksellers and publishers, Shakespeare would have discovered Richard Field; and the cathedral itself was now one of the busiest centres of metropolitan comings and goings, crowded from dawn till dusk, the resort not only of talkers and idlers and beggars, but of businessmen, discussing their current affairs, and lawyers, who sat at the base of the columns holding conference and taking scribbled notes. Needy and hungry vagrants loitered round the south aisle; while the splendid, but dilapidated, Norman nave, which Londoners had nicknamed Paul's Walk, was thronged with men of military appearance—'stale knights and captains out of service, men of long rapiers and long breeches, which . . . turn merchants and . . . traffic for news'. Paul's Walk, wrote John Earle, might be called 'the land's epitome . . . The noise in it is like that of bees, a strange humming or buzz, mixed of walking, tongues and feet. It is a kind of still roar or loud whisper.'[1] Here new fashions were paraded, gossip or insults exchanged, quarrels begun or patched up. 'What swearing is there,' Dekker expostulates, 'yea, what swaggering, what facing and out-facing? What shuffling, what shouldering, what justling, what jeering, what biting of thumbs to beget quarrels,[2] what holding up of fingers to remember drunken meetings, what braving with feathers, what bearding with mustachios, what casting open of cloaks to publish new clothes, what muffling in cloaks to hide broken elbows?' The market-place of Verona, as Shakespeare imagined it, filled with blustering partisans of the Montagues and Capulets, must have presented much the same spectacle; and through the crowd, 'like so many white butterflies', skipped the band of surpliced cathedral choristers—at odd times, also boy-actors—licensed to claim a fine from any gentleman who entered the sacred precincts wearing spurs.[3]

Other centres of urban activity, just as interesting to an ambitious young writer, were situated beyond the City's limits. In 1588, besides

---

[1] John Earle: *Micro-cosmographie*, 1628. The 'walking, jangling, brawling, fighting, bargaining' that went on, even during services, had been criticised as early as the 1560's.

[2] Sampson: I will bite my thumb at them; which is a disgrace to them, if they bear it.
Abraham: Do you bite your thumb at us, sir?
Sampson: I do bite my thumb, sir. *Romeo and Juliet* Act I Scene i.

[3] Thomas Dekker: *The Gull's Hornbook*.

the City inns, the Bel Savage, the Bull and the Cross Keys, that leased out their spacious, galleried yards for scenic entertainments, London had three playhouses, the Theatre and the Curtain, opened in 1576, and the Rose, which the great theatrical speculator Philip Henslowe had acquired and rebuilt in 1587. Because the City magistrates harried and oppressed the players, whom they regarded as a dangerous social nuisance, all three had been built in the suburbs, whither the Lord Mayor's writ did not extend: the Theatre and the Curtain, near Finsbury, along the country road that ran from Bishopsgate; the Rose, amid the marshy fields bordering the river's south bank, a region famous for its Bear Garden, its prison, the Southwark Clink, and the cluster of much-frequented brothels that had sprung up around the Bishop of Winchester's residence. The Theatre and the Curtain were especially popular with London's tradesmen and apprentices; and it was the crowds they drew and the disturbance they caused that most alarmed the City Fathers, though the magistrates were also troubled by the vanity and immodesty of modern acting. Now and then, the concourse of playgoers provoked an ugly civil broil. In June 1584, for example, 'near the Theatre or Curtain, at the time of the plays, there lay a prentice sleeping upon the grass', and an impertinent stranger, one Challes, 'did turn the toe upon the belly of the same prentice'; at which the offended youth sprang up indignantly and engaged Challes in a fierce scuffle, and Challes and his companions, who 'were little better than rogues that took upon them the name of gentlemen', reviled the apprentices as 'but the scum of the world', their abusive language starting a general riot that spread towards the City's gates. The tumult was at length put down; but it had considerably alarmed the Lord Mayor and his aldermen; and they addressed an immediate petition to the government, asking for leave to demolish both theatres. This request, which the government evaded, was followed in course of time by many similar petitions. The playhouses increased their hold on the public; yet the 'harlotry players' were still a suspect caste, in theory liable to the same punishments as vagabonds, 'cozeners' and 'sturdy beggars'.

Happily, the Queen herself required their services; and, despite the antagonism they aroused in the City, elsewhere they gained enthusiastic friends—among great noblemen who allowed them to wear their liveries, thus enrolling them as privileged personal servants, and among the multitude of gifted young law-students who had their lodgings at the Inns of Court. Those four Inns—Grays Inn, Lincoln's Inn, the Middle Temple and the Inner Temple—together with the subsidiary Inns of Chancery, then formed, if we except the Queen's entourage, 'the liveliest, the most intelligent, and certainly the most influential society England could furnish'.[1] Composed of the sons of the landed gentry and the rising middle class, its membership, during the Elizabethan and the early-Jacobean ages, included a long succession of variously distinguished writers: Richard Hooker, theologian and renowned master of the art of English prose; Francis Bacon, who was to dedicate his volume of *Essays* 'from my chamber at Gray's Inn'; Walter Ralegh, whose literary achievements might be better known had his personal life been less extraordinary; John Davies, a brilliant minor poet; John Marston, author of *The Malcontent*; Francis Beaumont, the romantic dramatist; Arthur Golding, translator of Ovid; and the inimitable John Donne. Here young men pursued or neglected their studies in the heady atmosphere of a great and growing city; they made love to the citizens' amorous wives, and filled the theatres' more expensive seats: the lawyers, suggested a contemporary wit, should be grateful to the players 'for giving them something to do of an afternoon'.[2] At home, in their semi-monastic Inns, they celebrated public feasts by staging their own theatrical displays. On Twelfth Night in 1561, the society of the Inner Temple had produced a tragedy entitled *Ferrex and Porrex*, better known as *Gorboduc*, the work of Thomas Norton and Thomas Sackville, the first English dramatists to try the possibilities of blank verse; and it was later played before the Queen. Whereas the playhouses provided popular amusement—a type of amusement, however, that cultivated persons did not refuse to share —the Inns of Court were the chief stronghold of what the eighteenth century would call 'polite learning'; and, once Shakespeare had published *Venus and Adonis*, which reflected the fashionable Ovidian

---

[1] G. M. Young: *Shakespeare and the Termers*, Proceedings of the British Academy, 1951.
[2] G. M. Young: *op. cit.*

taste, their inmates were to provide him with some particularly enthusiastic readers.

All London's Inns of Court stood well beyond the City's gates, and formed part of the irregular ribbon of buildings that had sprung up along the river's northern bank and followed the main highway— Fleet Street and Strand conjoined—leading from the mercantile City towards Whitehall and Westminster.[1] On either side of the Strand, as a traveller, coming from Ludgate, approached the royal seat of government, rose the houses of noblemen and gentlemen whose duties kept them near the Palace: on the right, Drury House and Burghley House, the impressive residence of the Queen's Secretary; on the left, between the street and the river, a range of lofty battlemented mansions, Leicester House—subsequently re-named Essex House—Arundel House, Russell House, Durham House and York House, bordering the Thames or set behind spacious garden-terraces that shelved down to the water's edge. Having reached Charing Cross, the traveller turned south; and there, spanning the road to Westminster, its Abbey and its ancient palace clustered round Richard II's hall, lay Whitehall Palace, formerly York Place, which 'after his fall and ruin' the Crown had appropriated from Cardinal Wolsey. A vast Tudor-Gothic structure with endless galleries and courtyards, it embraced the Privy Garden, where the energetic sovereign during her stays in London took her daily exercise; the Tilt Yard, where she watched her courtiers show their mastery of horse and lance; Wolsey's Great Hall, the scene of theatrical productions; the Sermon Court and the Chapel, the latter distinguished by its almost popish splendour; and a library full of Greek, Latin, French and Italian books, in variously coloured, and often richly jewelled, velvet bindings. A foreign visitor, who recorded his impressions of the palace, admired its many decorative detals —not only the Queen's magnificent inlaid bed 'with quilts of silk, velvet, gold, silver and embroidery', 'two little silver cabinets' she used for writing-boxes, and the pearl-studded chest in which she 'keeps her bracelets, ear-rings, and other things of extraordinary value', but also 'a piece of clockwork, an Ethiop riding upon a Rhinoceros, with four attendants', which made their obeisance when it

[1] See John Norden: *Speculum Britanniae*, 1593.

struck the hour, a sundial and fountain combined that drenched the onlooker who came too close, and 'a small hermitage, half hid in a rock', finely wrought in carved wood.[1]

If St Paul's Churchyard and the suburban theatres were meeting-places of wits and poets, and the Inns of Court 'the third university of the realm', a finishing school for intelligent, well-bred youth, the Court itself, at Whitehall and elsewhere, has been described as 'a centre of education, in the arts of culture and manners, in worldli-ness and sophistication, intrigue and treachery'.[2] The Queen's personal magnetism and nation-wide influence could scarcely be exaggerated; and her court, despite all the difficulties, hardships and disappointments of an Elizabethan courtier's life, was the stage on which every adventurous young nobleman must aspire to play some striking role. Even subjects who could not mount that stage derived a vicarious satisfaction from the tragedies and comedies enacted there. For the Elizabethans had a keen dramatic sense, not uncon-nected with a sense of sin and an instinctive attraction towards ideas of death; and the vicissitudes of fortune, and the rise and fall of 'great ones', provided a spectacle that never lost its charm, whether it were presented on the boards of a playhouse, reported among items of court-gossip or exhibited on the public scaffold, when a traitor was beheaded and dismembered, or a broken favourite paid the last penalty. Confronted with such an example of human misfortune, the Elizabethan moralist, though unperturbed by the sight of bloodshed and cruelty, would very often shed tears. Spectators wept over the disgrace of Essex, whom they regarded as the almost perfect type of human grandeur brought low; and, later, when his greatest adversary succumbed, and it was Ralegh's turn to stand trial, the hostile judges delivered their sentence in an appropriately dramatic form, remind-ing him that he had 'risen like a star' and that, like a star, he must expect to drop from heaven. Thus the Court provided a multitude of themes that both moralists and poetic dramatists found equally enlivening. It was the fount of privilege, power and wealth, the nursery of elegance and fashionable culture; at the same time, it

[1] Paul Hentzner: *Travels in England*, 1844.

Hentzner, a native of Brandenburg, made a grand tour of Europe, as tutor to a young Silesian nobleman, between 1597 and 1600.

[2] A. L. Rowse: *op. cit.*

afforded lurid hints as to the ultimate vanity of human wishes, being a place, wrote a Catholic agent, Anthony Standen, 'whence all charity is exiled, and all envy and treachery doth prevail'. Ralegh himself, a life-long courtier, wrote of the poisoned atmosphere of the Court and its unhealthy phosphorescent glow;[1] and other critics, who had studied court-life only at second hand, drew a similarly depressing picture. Innumerable panegyrists celebrated the Queen's virtues, her beauty, grace and regal dignity; but no satirist could pretend to moral weight who did not bear down on the vices and follies that had their roots in her immediate circle.

For a young, country-bred poet, however, who had just reached London from his native town, the Court was as remote as the Americas, though like them a fruitful source of legend. His place was in the world of booksellers, versifiers, playwrights, actors and their kind—the Elizabethan equivalent of what, during the eighteenth and early nineteenth centuries, the Japanese would call 'The Floating World'. There are, indeed, some interesting resemblances between Queen Elizabeth's capital and the Shogun's Yedo. Each city had its artistic bohemia, frequented not only by arrogant gentlemen but by prosperous, cultivated tradesmen; in each, great nobles made their way through the streets accompanied by an armed retinue, and their bellicose attendants were sometimes apt to come to blows; each had its boastful, quick-tempered knights and its *ronin*, or desperate masterless men; and, finally, the Elizabethan stage and the *Kabuki*, or traditional Japanese popular drama, had evidently much in common—the plays they showed dealt with episodes of violence, treachery, intrigue, drawn from the historical or heroic past; and their method of presentation, rigorously stylized, found room for music and dancing and sword-play, feminine parts on each stage being invariably performed by male actors. There, of course, any resemblance ceases: the Elizabethan and Jacobean drama had a far less prolonged, but a far more various and active, life; when Shakespeare first appeared it had not yet achieved maturity; and it was

---

[1] Say to the Court it glows
And shines like rotten wood,
Say to the Church it shows
What's good and does no good.
  Ralegh: *The Lie.*

already moribund before the official closing of the theatres in the year 1642. During that brief period, besides its native vigour, one of its most notable characteristics was its astounding versatility. The Elizabethan playwright was, above all else, the servant of his public, concerned to please the crowd and swell the theatre's receipts rather than perpetuate an honoured tradition or develop new aesthetic forms; and the public's taste was inclined to change so rapidly that a play produced five or six years earlier was often 'thought too old to fetch an audience'.[1] A dramatist, therefore, must work against time and be constantly providing fresh material. Even established favourites needed regular revision—Ben Jonson was to receive the unenviable task of revamping the famous *Spanish Tragedy*; and the English theatrical world remained a battle-ground where rival companies and the poets they employed endlessly disputed for the public's suffrage. Into this stimulating, harshly competitive existence William Shakespeare's talents were very soon absorbed.

[1] see p. 235.

CHAPTER II

London Apprenticeship

HAVING REACHED THE threshold of the theatrical world, how did
Shakespeare step across it? Seventeenth- and eighteenth-century
memorialists, anxious to emphasize the poet's genius by dwelling on
his humble origins, assured their readers that he had first entered the
playhouse 'in a very mean rank',[1] perhaps as a 'servitor' working in
the theatre itself, even—Sir William Davenant's tale—as the attendant who held gentlemen's horses outside the doors of the Theatre or
the Curtain, a calling he exercised with such 'dexterity and care' that
he is said to have attracted 'a good deal of business . . .'[2] These stories
may well be romantic fiction; all that we know of Shakespeare's
professional beginnings is that by 1592 he had acquired sufficient
fame to arouse the antagonism of an unhappy fellow author; and that,
probably about the same period, he joined the company known as
'Strange's Men', which in 1594 was re-named 'the Chamberlains',
when Lord Strange (later Earl of Derby) died and the players, need-
ing a new protector, sought the interest of the Lord Chamberlain,
Henry Lord Hunsdon, a cultured and tolerant official, whose son
inherited his post and continued to protect the company.[3] Shakespeare may have gained some previous experience working with the
Queen's Men, and under their aegis both glimpsed the Court—in
three seasons they entertained the Queen and her courtiers on no less
than nine occasions—and travelled to and fro around the kingdom,

[1] Nicholas Rowe: *Life of Shakespeare*, 1709.
[2] Manuscript note, citing Davenant's authority, 1748.
[3] George Lord Hunsdon, who succeeded his father in 1596, was himself appointed
Lord Chamberlain in 1597.

from Kent, East Anglia, the Midlands and Lancashire to Gloucester-shire, Somerset and the Welsh Marches. The Chamberlain's, how-ever, was his final choice, and received the full benefit of his dramatic genius.[1] In his maturity, he wrote for them alone; and it was his assistance, no doubt, that helped them to outsoar their rivals. The Chamberlain's Men soon prevailed at Court; and during the Queen's reign they gave thirty-two command performances, as against a mere twenty given by their keenest competitors, who wore the Lord High Admiral's badge.

Not only did Shakespeare choose the right company; but, with the good fortune that would never afterwards desert him, he joined it at the right moment. In recent years, two sensational productions had revolutionized the native English drama, infusing it with new poetic enthusiasm, arousing fresh rivalries and suddenly quickening its rate of growth. Hitherto, perhaps because its origin was divided, its development had been slow and awkward: on the one hand, from the medieval morality plays, which besides personifying virtues and vices, included a number of traditional comic roles, and from the secular 'interludes' that had followed the moralities; on the other, from the pedestrian efforts of cultured addicts of the 'New Learning', who had studied Seneca, admired his horrific tragedies, and hoped to apply the Senecan method to subjects that would please a modern audience. Such was *Ferrex and Porrex*, mentioned in the previous chapter; but none of these antiquarian playwrights had yet evolved his own dramatic style. When, during the 1580's, the group of well-educated young men called the 'University Wits'—George Peele, Robert Greene, Thomas Nashe and Thomas Lodge—turned their intelligence to the production of popular plays, being first of all poets and scholars they did so with a slightly grudging air: they were reluctant, as Lodge announced, to tie their pens 'to a penny-knave's delight'. Simultaneously, John Lyly, whose novels *Euphues: the Anatomy of Wit* and *Euphues and His England* had been published in 1578, and 1580, was writing prose comedies for boy-actors. Castes were recruited from the choristers of St Paul's and the Children of the Chapel Royal; and a theatre was run up in the disused refectory of an ancient monastic house near Ludgate, just outside the Lord

[1] E. K. Chambers, *op. cit.*

Mayor's rule, which before the Reformation had been inhabited by a prosperous community of Black Friars. During the autumn of 1589, however, Lyly and the Paul's boys became involved in a political imbroglio—the strange affair of the Martin Marprelate tracts; the players, decided the Queen's Council, had 'taken upon themselves to handle in their plays certain matters of Divinity and of State unfit to be suffered . . .' Further performances at the makeshift theatre were thereupon prohibited; and Lyly's series of pretty, flimsy entertainments was brought to an abrupt end.

Meanwhile, about 1587, Thomas Kyd had composed his *Spanish Tragedy*, and, that same year, Christopher Marlowe had launched his tremendous *Tamburlaine the Great*. Each production took its audience by storm. Each seems to have induced in the Elizabethan spectator a kind of moral vertigo, as he gazed up at the heights of pride and passion, or looked down into abysmal depths of crime and guilt and human suffering. *The Spanish Tragedy* was particularly successful and had an extraordinarily long life; Ben Jonson, we know, was set to revise it; and half a century later it still retained its popularity. Kyd's fellow dramatists found it a heavy burden: although they laughed at many of its lines and very often parodied them, the griefs of 'old Hieronimo', the miseries of Bel-imperia and the villainous stratagems of the Machiavellian Lorenzo had established a dramatic precedent from which henceforward there was no escape. Its Ghost, too, who begins the action by entering in company with Revenge, after which the twin apparitions, like 'official observers', occupy privileged places on either side of the proscenium, was to beget a large and obtrusive family of revengeful Elizabethan spirits. Kyd's blank verse is fluent and vigorous; but his plot is almost as rambling and perversely complicated as the libretto of a nineteenth-century opera. For an Elizabethan audience, nevertheless, the play was the epitome of tragic feeling; they returned to it again and again, even more readily perhaps than modern playgoers return to *Hamlet*; and, despite the laughter of contemporary intellectuals, who especially ridiculed the old man's opening phrase, they continued to experience sensations of pity and terror when, his son Horatio having been stabbed to death in the arms of Bel-imperia his forward mistress, Hieronimo comes wandering on to the stage and discovers

the corpse of Horatio suspended from a 'pleasant bower', where the
lovers had taken refuge to enjoy 'delight and mirthful dalliance'.
Hieronimo carries a blazing brand, and his aged limbs are covered
only with a shirt:

> What out-cries pluck me from my naked bed,
> And chill my throbbing heart with trembling fear,
> Which never danger yet could daunt before?
> Who calls Hieronimo? Speak, here I am.
> I did not slumber; therefore 'twas no dream . . .
> But stay, what murd'rous spectacle is this?
> A man hang'd up and all the murderers gone . . .
> This place was made for pleasure, not for death.
> These garments that he wears I oft have seen:
> Alas, it is Horatio, my sweet son.

Edward Alleyn, with his 'bent brows', 'furious gestures' and
majestic pacings up and down the stage, was the actor who immortalized Hieronimo's role; and it was Alleyn, a famous interpreta-
tive artist but at the same time a far-sighted and hard-headed
business-man, who also gave life to the Scythian conqueror and,
mounted in Tamburlaine's chariot, cracked his whip over a team of
subject kings. That scene, which Marlowe reserved for his Second
Part, produced as decisive an effect, and was almost as eagerly taken
up, as Hieronimo's midnight lamentations. Since his services had
been secured by the Admiral's Men, the young dramatist was careful
to provide declamatory speeches that would suit their chief tragedian's thunderous style:

> Holla, ye pamper'd jades of Asia!
> What, can ye draw but twenty miles a-day,
> And have so proud a chariot at your heels,
> And such a coachman as great Tamburlaine . . .[1]

Yet, being a visionary projection of Marlowe's own 'aspiring
mind', Tamburlaine is occasionally allowed to forget his conquests
and triumphs, and that beneath his conqueror's robes he is still a
savage Scythian shepherd, and to speak of mankind's insatiable
thirst for knowledge and the poet's pursuit of an ideal beauty:

[1] *Tamburlaine the Great, Part II* Act IV Scene iii.

What is beauty, saith my sufferings, then?
If all the pens that ever poets held
Had fed the feeling of their masters' thoughts,
And every sweetness that inspir'd their hearts,
Their minds, and muses on admircd themes;
If all the heavenly quintessence they still
From their immortal flowers of poesy,
Wherein, as in a mirror, we perceive
The highest reaches of a human wit;
If these had made one poem's period,
And all combin'd in beauty's worthiness,
Yet should there hover in their restless heads,
One thought, one grace, one wonder, at the least,
Which into words no virtue can digest.[1]

Faustus, too, is an imaginative self-portrait; and, as the reward of his submission, he demands from the Tempter not only power but scientific knowledge—he would understand the mechanism of the universe; whereupon Mephistophilis proceeds to make it clear that Hell has rejected the novel Copernican theory—and not only the joys of ruling and knowing but the exquisite gratification of all his senses. Earlier, his fellow-magician Valdes has described the princely state they may expect to keep, once, together with their friend Cornelius, they have enlisted a supernatural retinue:

As Indian Moors obey their Spanish lords,
So shall the spirits of every element
Be always serviceable to us three;
Like lions shall they guard us when we please;
Like Almain rutters[2] with their horsemen's staves,
Or Lapland giants trotting by our sides;
Sometimes like women, or unwedded maids,
Shadowing more beauty in their airy brows
Than have the white breasts of the queen of love:
From Venice shall they drag huge argosies,
And from America the golden fleece

[1] *Ibid. Part I*, Act V Scene i.
[2] German cavalrymen.

That yearly stuffs old Philip's treasury;
If learned Faustus will be resolute.

Marlowe's appetite for life would never fail; it drove him headlong through his brief existence; and, as Shakespeare's exact contemporary, he stands in a significant relation to the greater, steadier,
much more cautious artist. While Shakespeare was to develop slowly,
but consistently and evenly, Marlowe emerges from his first drama
—written some five years before Shakespeare's earliest plays—as
already an adult poet, master of the 'mighty line' that transfigured
English blank verse. He did not live to consolidate his victory, or
achieve a uniform poetic style. *Edward II* is an ambitious historical
play; but *The Jew of Malta* and *The Tragedy of Dido* seem to have
been written with comparatively little zest, the former being designed
to afford Alleyn, as Barabas, the opportunity of plunging from a
treacherously contrived gallery into a heated cauldron placed beneath
the floor, a device that the Admiral's Men had just perfected; the
latter, where he was assisted by Nashe, a somewhat unexciting
revival of the familiar Virgilian story. Yet, in whatever Marlowe
produced, we can distinguish traces of his incandescent touch—in
Dido, for example, which opens with a picture of Jove paying impassioned court to Ganymede, now tearful and sulky because he had
been cuffed by Juno for spilling the wine at an Olympian banquet:

Jupiter: What, dares she strike the darling of my thoughts?

           . . .

           I vow, if she but once frown on thee more,
           To hang her, meteor-like, 'twixt heaven and earth,
           And bind her, hand and foot, with golden cords . . .
Ganymede: Might I but see the pretty sport a-foot,
           O, how would I with Helen's brother laugh,
           And bring the gods to wonder at the game!
           Sweet Jupiter, if e'er I pleas'd thine eye,
           Or seemed fair, wall'd in with eagle's wings,
           Grace my immortal beauty with this boon . . .

Only Marlowe could have written the penultimate line, or con-
densed so much melody and movement into a succession of eight
simple words. No less characteristic is the poet's bold approach to the

dangerous subject of homosexual love. Before he died, Marlowe had acquired a reputation as a pederast: 'that all they that love not tobacco and boys were fools' was among the many subversive statements credited to him. In this, and in his 'scorn of God's Word', he registered his protest against respectable society; unlike Shakespeare's slowly maturing genius, which worked by acceptance and assimilation rather than by rejection and revolt, the daemon that inhabited Marlowe was a restless, anarchic, self-destructive force, and flourished in the stimulating atmosphere of danger, violence and moral conflict. Each poet was the son of a modest country tradesman: Marlowe's father, a respected citizen of Canterbury, earned his living as a shoe-maker; but, while Shakespeare lingered on in Stratford until he was twenty-three or twenty-four, and his worst 'extravagances' were apparently concerned with the occasional theft of deer and rabbits, Marlowe went up to Corpus Christi, Cambridge at the age of seventeen, and before he had been granted his master's degree seems to have joined the English secret service, the elaborate system of counter-espionage managed by Sir Francis Walsingham, whose cousin, Sir Thomas Walsingham, was the poet's friend and patron. In this capacity, he is believed to have travelled abroad and, posing as a convert or sympathizer, collected intelligence about seditious groups of Papist exiles. His absences must have disturbed the University; for, during May 1587, the Privy Council issued an official statement, announcing that, whereas it had been reported that 'Christopher Morley was determined to have gone beyond the sea to Rheims . . . their Lordships thought good to certify that he had no such intent, but that in all his actions he had behaved himself orderly and discreetly, whereby he had done her Majesty good service . . . It was not her Majesty's pleasure that anyone, employed as he had been in matters touching the safety of his country should be defamed by those that are ignorant of the affairs he went about.' The interest of the august Privy Council in the fortunes of an obscure young scholar shows that he had been entrusted with some important task. Possibly Marlowe was a disciple of Machiavelli—the dreaded bugbear of Elizabethan England, whom he would afterwards bring on to the stage to speak the prologue of *The Jew of Malta*—and, having rejected the established moral code, was not averse from turning spy, a role that enabled him to wander through Northern Europe and 'know the cities and the minds of men'.

Equally significant was his association with Sir Walter Ralegh's so-called 'School of Night'. That ruthless soldier and unscrupulous courtier—by temperament 'damnable proud', but devoted to literature and the unselfish pursuit of knowledge—had gathered around him a circle of friends, who shared his philosophical and scientific studies: Thomas Harriot, the celebrated mathematician, accused by his contemporaries of cultivating the Black Arts, entertaining 'strange thoughts of the Scriptures' and undervaluing 'the old story of the creation of the world'; Lawrence Keymis, Fellow of Balliol, who was both a mathematician and a geographer and navigator; Northumberland, 'the Wizard Earl', scholar and artistic patron, but also a keen student of astrology and alchemy; Marlowe and his fellow poet George Chapman; besides Ferdinando Lord Derby and George Lord Hunsdon, whose connection with Shakespeare's fortunes has been noted on a previous page. All were men of speculative intelligence; some, like Ralegh, Marlowe himself and the 'devil Harriot', were often considered to be militant atheists. At 'Sir Walter Ralegh's school of atheism,' wrote Robert Parsons, the pious English Jesuit, 'both Moses and our Saviour, the Old and the New Testaments, are jested at, and the scholars taught, among other things, to spell God backwards.' Certainly, Marlowe propagated his agnostic views with a satirical hardihood that alarmed his hearers. Thus a suspected atheist named Richard Chomley had asserted, according to a government informer, Richard Baines, that the dramatist was 'able to show more sound reasons for atheism, than any divine in England is able to give to prove divinity, and that Marlowe told him he hath read the Atheist lecture to Sir Walter Ralegh and others'. He may have enjoyed some measure of official protection, thanks to the secret services he had already rendered; but the discovery of a fragmentary essay apparently disputing the Godhead of Christ, which his friend Kyd, then under arrest upon a different charge,[1] alleged that Mar-

---

[1] It is now known that this document was merely an extract from *The Fall of the late Arian*, a highly orthodox work published by John Proctor in 1549, in which the Arian case is set forth and then contraverted. Kyd was suspected of having been concerned in the dissemination of seditious libels against London's foreign residents. When his rooms were searched, this document came to light; and, after torture, he declared that it had been left behind by Marlowe.

lowe had left behind him in a room they had formerly occupied together, at length aroused the Privy Council; and in May 1593 he was summoned to attend them, to hear accusations and explain his conduct. Though he 'entered his appearance', he did not meet his accusers; that same month, in an unexplained struggle, the *poète maudit* lost his life, his brain pierced by a random dagger-thrust, which had penetrated the skull—making a wound 'of the depth of two inches and of the width of one inch'—just above the right eye.

Historians have suggested that Marlowe's killing was a case of political assassination; it occurred in the presence of three witnesses, each a somewhat shady character, including Robert Poley, probably the Robert Poley whom Walsingham had employed to worm his way into the secrets of the Babington Plot; and the fatal fray was preceded by a long and seemingly harmonious conversation, while the company dined and walked up and down the garden, from one o'clock 'until the sixth hour after noon'. Why had they met at the tavern on Deptford Strand? Witnesses declared that it was a casual friendly meeting; but that the inn-keeper's bill had caused an argument, which in turn provoked 'divers malicious words'; that Marlowe, who had stretched out on a bed, seized a dagger from the belt of Ingram Frezer, then seated with his back towards him, and inflicted a couple of trifling wounds; and that Frezer, as he wrestled for the weapon, dealt his opponent the unintentional blow of which 'the aforesaid Christopher Morley instantly died . . .'[1] Whatever its background, Marlowe's death provided Elizabethan moralists with the kind of anecdote they dearly loved: 'the manner of his death was terrible,' remarked Thomas Beard in his *Theatre of God's Judgements*; 'for he even cursed and blasphemed to his last gasp, and together with his breath an oath flew out of his mouth'; while Francis Meres, in *Palladis Tamia*, published five years after the affray at Deptford, asserted that 'Christopher Marlowe was stabbed to death by a bawdy servingman, a rival of his in his lewd love'. Such stories were evidently designed to ram home an obvious moral lesson; and there is little support for the theory that he was disposed of as a secret agent. It seems more credible that he fell a victim to his own hasty, uncontrolled temper.

[1] J. Leslie Hotson: *The Death of Christopher Marlowe*, 1925.

D

Other poets lamented the extinction of an artist who during the few years of his active literary life, between 1587 and 1593, had set a new poetic standard. He is the 'dead shepherd' quoted in *As You Like It*; a manuscript copy of *Hero and Leander* would appear to have encouraged the composition of *Venus and Adonis* and *The Rape of Lucrece*. Yet, for Shakespeare, Marlowe's early death was surely a providential stroke of fate, which enabled him to go his way un-challenged, following towards their poetic conclusion the demands of his very different nature. He was neither interested in 'the School of Night' nor concerned to advertise forbidden doctrines; and, when he sought a patron, he chose the opposite camp, and became associated with the aristocratic coterie headed by Ralegh's most determined foe. He mentions modern 'Natural Philosophers' only to deride their learning, and hints that to chart the heavens and name the separate stars may be a pedantic, unrewarding task.[1] Marlowe, writes a twentieth-century critic, had, 'not excepting Shakespeare or Chap-man, the most *thoughtful* and philosophic mind, though immature, among the Elizabethan dramatists'.[2] During the early stages of his professional existence, Shakespeare shows very little of Marlowe's speculative fire. To the workaday world as he found it, he was content to apply himself with systematic diligence, and, his world being that of the theatre, he devoted his intellect to carefully studying its prob-lems, becoming a highly expert technician, a capable actor and, before long, the general master of his trade.

These problems were often severely practical: the Elizabethan theatre was no place for a doctrinaire or dilettante artist. It was dominated by enterprising men of affairs—by efficient financiers like Philip Henslowe, who understood the public taste. In some respects, Henslowe was the typical Elizabethan—much more typical perhaps than any of the hard-pressed poets he employed—the industrious *entrepreneur*, with an eye to the main chance, steadily bettering his social and financial position, glad to turn his hand to any deal, whether it were small or large, that promised an immediate profit. He had begun life as a servant's servant, the humble employee of a bailiff named Woodward attached to the service of Lord Montague; but,

[1] *Love's Labour's Lost* Act I Scene i.
[2] T. S. Eliot: *Selected Essays*, 1932.

when Woodward died, Henslowe married the widow and took possession of his master's savings, which he laid out in landed property around his own suburban house at Southwark. Here he derived part of his income from the well-attended Bankside stews; but he was also concerned with the purchase of goat-skins, and went into business both as a dyer and as pawnbroker and moneylender. Despite his commercial interest in brothel-keeping, Henslowe was a solid citizen, a regular communicant every Sunday, a vestryman and churchwarden; and before he died, he had managed to collect some dignified minor court appointments. Meanwhile, in 1592, his stepdaughter, Joan Woodward, married the popular tragedian Edward Alleyn; and, with the help of Alleyn's professional experience, he set forth to conquer new markets. In 1594, for example, they bought a substantial share of Paris Garden, the Bankside resort where Londoners gathered to enjoy the pleasures of the 'Royal Game', the baiting of bears and bulls by ferocious English mastiffs, which always drew a huge appreciative crowd.

By then, the successful speculator had already purchased and rebuilt the Rose; and in 1592 he opened the business diary that he kept up until 1603, giving a list of plays performed, marking them down as new or old and recording the payments he had himself received and the loans and advances he had laid out.[1] Henslowe had an interest in every aspect of the business—the provision of properties and costumes and the labours of the players' hireling poets, to whose assistance, when their creditors troubled them, he contributed a few pounds or a few shillings. Yet, at least in his domestic existence, he was not an entirely unamiable personage; and, among his archives, he kept a series of letters that he and his daughter Joan exchanged with Edward Alleyn, while Alleyn was touring the provinces and the plague raged around his wife and family.[2] They give a vivid, sometimes endearing, impression of an Elizabethan actor's life. Thus, from his lodgings in far-off Bristol, on August 1st, 1594, Alleyn sends a letter to his wife Joan, whom he addresses as 'My good sweet Mouse', begging her to take wise precautions against the encroachments of the sickness:

[1] *Henslowe's Diary*, edited by Walter W. Greg, 1904.
[2] *Henslowe Papers*, edited by Walter W. Greg, 1907.

Therefore use this course; keep your house fair and clean, which I know you will, and every evening throw water before your door, and in your backside, and have in your windows good store of rue and herb of grace, and with all the grace of God, which must be obtained by prayers; and so doing, no doubt but the Lord will mercifully defend you.

Now, good mouse, I have no news to send you but this, that we all have our health, for which the Lord be praised . . . I have sent by this bearer, Thomas Pope's kinsman, my white waistcoat, because it is a trouble to me to carry it. Receive it with this letter, and lay it up for me till I come.

Alleyn is also concerned about his 'orange tawny stocking of woollen', which he wishes to have dyed 'a good black' that he may wear them in the winter months, and complains that he has received no news of his garden, reminding Joan that the spinach-bed should presently be re-sown with lettuce. His wife and his father-in-law then wrote back, signing themselves 'your loving wife till death' and 'your poor and assured friend till death', assuring him that they had duly taken charge of the white waistcoat and his lute-books and other items that he had sent home, and that his garden did 'very well, thanks be to God, for your beans are grown to high hedge and well codded'; though his tenants 'wax very poor' and, as long as the sickness lasts, can pay no rent. His household have strewn their windows with wormwood and rue, watered the doors and kept the house clean, thus so far avoiding the plague, which, 'within the city and without', had raised the death-rate 'to the number of seventeen or eighteen hundred in one week'. Later, Joan and her father protest that 'we cannot hear from you as we would do, that is when others do', and add that the spread of the plague had not yet slackened: their neighbours are falling right and left: and that their 'two wenches' have succumbed, but somehow contrived to make a good recovery. Alleyn at that time had joined Lord Strange's Players, and Shakespeare, it may be, was his travelling companion. No doubt, he too wrote to his wife and parents—less tenderly perhaps than Alleyn wrote to his beloved 'Mouse'; but his letter, like so many precious Shakespearian documents, have now vanished into night eternal.

Henslowe presumably was not a man who valued the theatre as a form of art; but in his appreciation of the trend of current taste he showed himself a sound psychologist. Play-going was no mere transitory vogue: Englishmen crowded the London playhouses both because they were a gregarious, pleasure-loving race addicted to every kind of public pageantry, and because the new drama, apart from its visual charm, fulfilled some of their most deeply rooted needs. Lovers of the language they spoke,[1] who enjoyed eloquence as much as they enjoyed music, they tended to dramatize human life and saw the world as a gigantic stage: 'this world', had remarked Thomas Wythorne in the 1560s, quoting a popular proverb, 'is but a scaffold for us to play our tragedies and comedies upon.'[2] They were always apt to think in terms of the theatre; and, while the ageing Queen would draw a parallel between the sorrows and difficulties of her last years and the well-known tragedy of *Richard II*, the fallen Essex was to voice a desperate foreboding that he might soon be represented by the common players. The drama, then, gave a poetic unity to the Elizabethans' view of existence; but at the same time, it gratified their passion for history and their consuming appetite for education.

The sixteenth century was an age of popularizers—of educationalists who believed that the enjoyment of knowledge should not remain the privilege of learned men. 'Besides the rascal multitude and the learned sages,' wrote John Dolman, the translator of Cicero, in 1561, 'there is a mean sort of men, which, although they be not learned, yet, by the quickness of their wits, can conceive all such points of art as nature could give.' A regard for the 'meaner sort', the 'vulgar people', inspired a multitude of writers to produce useful, popularly written books—translations from the Greek and Roman classics, collections of travellers' tales, 'books of manners' and moral treatises, as well as works of modern history. Thus Raphael Holinshed

---

[1] With prophetic insight, they felt that the English language might one day encircle the whole terrestrial globe:

> And who, in time, knows whither may be sent
> The treasure of our tongue, to what strange shores
> This gain of our best glory shall be lent,
> T'inrich unknowing nations with our stores?

Samuel Daniel: *Musophilus*, 1602

[2] *The Autobiography of Thomas Wythorne*, edited by James M. Osborn, 1961.

prefaced his *Chronicles* of the kingdoms of England, Scotland and Ireland, published in 1577, with the statement that his speech was plain and that he had disdained throughout 'any rhetorical show of eloquence, having rather a regard to simple truth, than to decking words'. The knowledge of history was considered to have an especially civilizing effect; and Barnabe Rich went so far as to declare that even the savage Irish, if they could be persuaded to read books —particularly historical volumes, 'wherein are reported the manners, conditions, governments, counsels and affairs of every country'— might soon become a tolerably cultivated nation.[1] Among the English middle classes, history was a favourite form of reading;[2] and those who were disinclined to read could spend their leisure at the playhouse, and follow the events of the historic past graphically rendered into verse and mime.

The Englishman's interest in history was also coloured by his patriotic feelings. Proud of the country he inhabited and of the vast metropolis that formed the kingdom's centre—its splendid mercantile streets, Cheapside and Lombard Street; Sir Thomas Gresham's elegant new Exchange; London Bridge, one of the marvels of Europe, which bore a double rank of shops and houses; and the Thames rushing through the arches of the bridge, a turbulent, unembanked stream, celebrated for its ships and swans[3]—he was no less proud of the historical past on which his present well-being seemed securely founded. Here the dramatist had an important duty to perform: he reminded his audience that English prosperity and peace had been achieved only at the cost of fearful effort, after a long period of ferocious civil strife, from which the Queen's grandfather, Henry VII, had finally rescued the half-ruined throne. It was not perhaps an entirely truthful picture; but it strengthened Elizabeth's dynastic legend and ministered to her subjects' national self-regard. Since the Armada year, English historical plays could be sure of a doubly appreciative audience; and, once Shakespeare had joined the

---

[1] *Alarm to England*, 1578.

[2] 'The vast influence of historical reading upon the rank and file of Tudor and Stuart Society cannot be measured, but clearly it was a potent factor in the intellectual progress of the citizenry.' Louis B. Wright: *Middle-Class Culture in Elizabethan England*, 1935.

[3] 'Our flood's-queen Thames for ships and swans is crowned . . .'
                                        Michael Drayton: *Idea's Mirror*, 1594.

London theatre and had begun to make his name, he went to work on a tragedy of *Henry VI*, which modern scholars believe he wrote unaided, whereas earlier critics often preferred to assume that he shared the task with several fellow-hacks.[1] Whatever their origin, the three parts of *Henry VI* are rough and immature plays, not so much imaginative constructions as attempts at popular dramatic serialization, in which a long and complex story is divided into a series of arresting episodes, with numerous opportunities for expert swordmanship, gun-fire, military music, endless alarums and resounding noises off. Few of their personages are distinctly characterized, though La Pucelle, the sorceress Maid of Orleans, and Jack Cade, rebel leader of the English peasants, possess a certain individual life. The blank verse is heavy and clumsy; and only here and there, in a single flash or in two or three isolated lines, does it rise above dramatic commonplace. Then briefly a voice is heard that seems recognisably to be the voice of Shakespeare, the adult poet who drew so many of his images from his contemplative affection for the watery element:

> Glory is like a circle in the water,
> Which never ceaseth to enlarge itself
> Till by broad spreading it disperse to nought

Holinshed's *Chronicles* were the dramatist's main source—he must have worked with his source-book lying ready on his table; and often he was content to hammer Holinshed's prose into rudimentary poetic shape. Both in his drawing of characters and in his development of the plot, he gladly follows the historian's guidance; and it is difficult to believe that any of his dramatis personae deeply stimulated his imagination—at all events, during the earlier stages of his work, while he was doggedly pushing through the story of the French wars, illustrating the genesis of the struggle between the partisans of York and Lancaster, killing off the notorious Pucelle or sending Talbot to a hero's grave.

Amid so dense a throng of villains and intriguers, lowering, threatening, gesturing, expostulating, arguing—

[1] Marlowe, Greene and Peele are names that have been put forward. Coleridge contended that no reader with a sensitive ear could believe that Shakespeare wrote the opening speech.

> Beaufort's red sparkling eyes blab his heart's malice
> And Suffolk's cloudy brow his stormy hate;
> Sharp Buckingham unburthens with his tongue
> The envious load that lies upon his heart . . .

there is very little scope for real portraiture. It is with relief that we enter Part III, and watch the fiendish crook-backed Duke of Gloucester beginning to out-distance his less accomplished enemies, a villain who is something of a poet himself, destined to become, if not a character, at least a magnificent melodramatic type:

> . . . I, —like one lost in a thorny wood,
> That rends the thorns and is rent with the thorns,
> Seeking a way and straying from the way,
> Not knowing how to find the open air,
> But toiling desperately to find it out
> Torment myself to catch the English crown:
> And from that torment I will free myself,
> Or hew my way out with a bloody axe . . .
> I'll drown more sailors than the mermaid shall;
> I'll slay more gazers than the basilisk;
> I'll play the orator as well as Nestor,
> Deceive more slily than Ulysses could,
> And, like a Sinon, take another Troy.

In this, as in later historical works, some authorities have credited Shakespeare with what one of them calls 'a steady political earnestness'[1], a grasp of affairs that distinguishes him from all his fellow Elizabethan playwrights. It is difficult to understand how they have reached that conclusion; the belief that Shakespeare was a deep political thinker, an impassioned student of statecraft, appears to have little solid basis; his 'ideas' were dictated by his theme and are for the most part fairly simple ones. Evidently he assumed—and who does not?—that civil strife spelt national disaster—

> Civil dissension is a viperous worm
> That gnaws the bowels of the commonwealth

—and that a firm central government guaranteed the kingdom against

[1] E. M. W. Tillyard: *Shakespeare's History Plays*, 1944.

1 Shakespeare's Birthplace in mid-Victorian times, before its drastic restoration

2 Rustic festivities (*c.* 1569). From a painting by J. Hoefnagel of Bermondsey. In the distance appears the Tower of London

3 (*opposite left*) Queen Elizabeth in procession: 'in her immediate circle, no Christian ruler has been more nearly deified'

5 Queen Elizabeth I in old age; unfinished miniature by Isaac Oliver

4 (*below*) The wedding masque of Sir Henry Unton (1557?-1596), soldier and diplomatist, and other scenes of his career. In the masque scene Sir Henry sits at table in his great chamber, attended by musicians, while a procession of comedians files up from the hall below

6 (*above*) English costumes about 1580: a rich merchant, a girl of noble birth, a woman of the middle classes and a fashionable youth

7 Elizabethan chivalry: the Queen's Champion, George Clifford, Earl of Cumberland

the endless bickering of ambitious nobles. Such is the gist of his so-called political message. His chief object was to 'fetch an audience'; and in the process he revealed, not extraordinary powers of thought, but an almost unequalled gift of adaptation and assimilation. *Henry VI* was followed by *Richard III*, where Gloucester continues his tremendous tirade, a monster who derives his monstrosity from his hatred of his own ugliness and his sense of moral solitude. He is a stock villain, who immediately explains his purpose:

> I am determined to prove a villain

But he is far more introspective, much less unimaginative, than most Elizabethan villains of a similar stamp; and now for the first time Shakespeare introduces the theme of individual loneliness and solipsistic isolation. Gloucester cannot escape from the prison of the Self; he is an ill-starred, misshapen Narcissus condemned to play with his own crooked shadow:

> Why, I, in this weak piping time of peace,
> Have no delight to pass away the time,
> Unless to spy my shadow in the sun . . .

On the verge of death, he is still tormented by the conflict between furious self-love and corroding self-hatred:

> Richard loves Richard; that is, I am I.
> Is there a murderer here? No—yes, I am:
> Then fly. What, from myself? Great reason why—
> Lest I revenge. Myself upon myself?
> Alack, I love myself. For any good
> That I myself have done unto myself?

This fatal conflict gives him a tragic dignity that lifts him high above his main rival. By comparison 'shallow Richmond', destined to found a new royal line and 'unite the white rose and the red', seems the epitome of insignificant virtue.

Although neither can be definitely dated, both these historical plays must have been written before 1594; and during that period of apprenticeship, which may have lasted six or seven years, Shakespeare displayed his opportunist talents in a variety of audience-catching media. *The Spanish Tragedy* having created a demand for stories of revenge and bloodshed, he dutifully produced his *Titus Andronicus*, a blood-boltered melodrama so strange and horrific that, besides captivating the audiences of the day, it maintained its vogue throughout his lifetime.[1] Since there was a market for comedies, he also tried his hand at comic subjects, and turned out *The Two Gentlemen of Verona*, *The Comedy of Errors*, *The Taming of the Shrew* and probably *Love's Labour's Lost*, a play that, as it has an important bearing on his personal progress, will be considered elsewhere. The others bear much the same relation to the comedies of his middle period as do *Henry VI* and *Richard III* to his most impressive tragedies. Each has a plot derived from the playwright's reading, *The Two Gentlemen* being based on a Spanish novel recently translated into French; *The Comedy of Errors* on Plautus' *Menaechmi*, which, as the earliest English translation did not appear until 1595, would suggest that he remembered something of his schoolboy Latin; and *The Taming of the Shrew*, in part at least, on Ariosto's *I Suppositi*, of which George Gascoigne had produced a rendering over a quarter of a century earlier.

Similarly, Shakespeare's comic technique is founded on well-established models. He does not disdain farce or knockabout fun and in *The Taming of the Shrew* he seems to throw away an admirable comic situation by adulterating high with low comedy. Petruchio is a splendid extravagant figure, whose strain of blustering eloquence is perfectly suited to his aggressive role:

Katharina: They call me Katharine that do talk of me.
Petruchio: You lie, in faith, for you are called plain Kate,
    And bonny Kate, and sometimes Kate the curst:
    But Kate, the prettiest Kate in Christendom,
    Kate of Kate Hall, my super-dainty Kate, . . .
    Take this of me, Kate of my consolation—
    Hearing thy mildness praised in every town,
    Thy virtues spoke of, and thy beauty sounded, . . .
    Myself am moved to woo thee for my wife.

[1] 'He that will swear *Ieronimo* or *Andronicus* are the best plays yet shall passed unexcepted at here as a man whose judgement shows it is constant, and hath stood still these five-and-twenty or thirty years . . .' Ben Jonson: *Bartholomew Fair*, 1614.

But, when he adopts a kind of primitive shock-treatment to break down Katharina's spirit, little by little our attention wanders and we find we are losing interest in his facile victory. Here as elsewhere, the effect is often mechanical—we imagine Shakespeare working against time, concerned to fill so many sheets a day; and, from Henslowe's accounts, we knew that the hireling dramatists, having first submitted a skeleton plot, would deliver a series of sheets for which he received advance payment, until he had completed the entire 'book'. Nevertheless, we feel that these early comedies were sometimes written with intense enjoyment; and again and again they include some lyrical allusions to a happy youth and its placid country background, to roast chestnuts puffing and spitting on the hearth—

> And do you tell me of a woman's tongue,
> That gives not half so great a blow to hear,
> As will a chestnut in a farmer's fire?

—or the laden hazel-branches among the Warwickshire lanes:

> Kate like the hazel-twig
> Is straight and slender, and as brown in hue
> As hazel-nuts and sweeter than the kernels.

Even *The Two Gentlemen*, though it has been described by a modern critic as having 'some claim to be considered Shakespeare's most tedious play',[1] does not lack a redeeming lyrical gusto. The intrigue itself may be dull and far-fetched; but the dramatist is able to bring on to the stage the earliest of his comic heroines, girls, as the story demanded, yet oddly boyish since they were played by boy actors, neither wholly grown-up nor yet entirely juvenile. Of these bold, sharp-tongued but disarming young women, Julia is the lively prototype. On one plane, when she is assuming male disguise, she jokes with her maid Lucetta about the provision of a proper codpiece—

> Lucetta: What fashion—madam—shall I make your breeches?
> Julia: That fits as well as, 'Tell me, good my lord,
>   What compass will you wear your farthingale?' . . .

---

[1] Derek Traversi: *Shakespeare: The Early Comedies*, 1960.

Lucetta: You must needs have them with a cod-piece, madam.
Julia: Out, out, Lucetta! that will be ill-favoured.
Lucetta: A round hose, madam, now's not worth a pin,
            Unless you have a cod-piece to stick pins on.

On the other, she compares her passion to a stream, smoothly hurrying her towards her lover's arms:

> The current that with gentle murmur glides,
> Thou know'st, being stopped, impatiently doth rage:
> But when his fair course is not hindered,
> He makes sweet music with th' enamelled stones . . .
> And so by many winding nooks he strays,
> With willing sport, to the wild ocean.
> Then let me go, and hinder not my course:
> I'll be as patient as a gentle stream,
> And make a pastime of each weary step,
> Till the last step have brought me to my love . . .

Like most writers, Shakespeare was frequently applauded for his clumsiest and most immature work: *Titus Andronicus* delighted the sensation-loving 'penny-knaves'; and *Henry VI*—particularly the Talbot episode—scored an immediate popular success.[1] 'How would it have joyed brave Talbot . . . ,' wrote Thomas Nashe in 1592, 'to think that, after he had lain two hundred years in his tomb, he should triumph again on the stage, and have his bones new-embalmed with the tears of ten thousand spectators at least . . . who in the tragedian that represents his person imagine they behold him fresh bleeding?' Apart from two mysterious passages, in Spenser's *Tears of the Muses* and *Colin Clout's Come Home Again*, that, under the names of 'our pleasant Willy' and the gentle shepherd 'Aetion', may conceivably denote Shakespeare—

> Whose Muse full of high thoughts' invention
> Doth like himself heroically sound

—this is the earliest extant reference to Shakespeare's growing

---

[1] It was performed at the Rose, where, on March 3rd, 1592, Henslowe's box-office receipts showed an increase of over fifty shillings. They reached the impressive total of £3 16s. 8d.

popularity. But, that same year, a different note was sounded—the hoarse valedictory outcry of a sick unhappy man of letters. Robert Greene had died at his London lodgings, broken by dissipation and incessant hackwork, the kind of proud, crapulous, cross-grained bohemian, described in the annals of every literary period, whose grudge against life goes with a loudly proclaimed contempt for younger, happier, more fashionable writers. The stage had disappointed him; and he had lately turned to journalism, 'yarking up pamphlets' in the space of a day and a night (as his friend Thomas Nashe would afterwards record) upon any topical subject likely to hold a lazy reader's interest. For a graduate of Cambridge, it was not a dignified calling; but it brought him in a fair income. He had a vigorous, highly coloured style; and his 'cony-catching' series— exposures of the London underworld, in which he wrote of card-sharpers and 'cross-biters' and similar metropolitan vermin, who pursued the unsuspicious rabbit—aroused so much excitement that the cony-catchers themselves soon felt obliged to take action; and 'fourteen or fifteen of them', Greene asserted, had 'beleaguered him about in the Saint John's Head within Ludgate' while he was sitting peaceably at supper, a situation from which he only escaped alive thanks to some 'courteous citizens and apprentices'. None of these successes had finally eased his problem. 'Glad was that printer,' wrote Nashe, 'that might be so blessed to pay him dear for the very dregs of his wit'; but Greene was always deep in difficulty; and some time during the early days of August 1592, he and Nashe and an acquaintance of theirs named William Monox, attended a banquet where they consumed an enormous meal of pickled herrings, washed down by tankards of strong Rhenish wine. At once he fell deadly sick—the robust dishevelled figure, with his long hair and his 'jolly long red peak'[1], was now in his middle thirties, but he must already have been ill and tired; and by the end of the month he understood at last that he was a dying man.

Then desperation descended and, with desperation, a sense of poignant remorse. He was alone in a plague-stricken city, from which all his remaining friends had fled. He owed his landlord ten pounds; his doublet, hose and sword had been sold for three shillings;

[1] A peak was a pointed beard.

he had left only a single shirt, and was obliged to borrow the land-lord's 'whiles his own was a-washing'; recently he had trudged the streets and begged for a 'penny-pot of Malmesy'. Unattended except by Mistress Isam, the good-natured woman of the house, his bastard son and the boy's mother, sister of the well-known criminal 'Cutting Ball' and, according to Gabriel Harvey, 'a sorry ragged quean'—true, a Mistress Appleby sometimes appeared, but 'as much to expostulate injuries with her as to visit him'[1]—he composed a pathetic message to the wife he had abandoned six years earlier:

Sweet wife, As ever there was any good will or friendship between thee and me, see this bearer (my host) satisfied of his debt . . . But for him I had perished in the streets. Forget and forgive my wrongs done unto thee, and Almighty God have mercy on my soul.

Greene died on September 2nd; and his hostess, that good and kindly woman, crowned the dead poet's brows with a garland of bays. She was presently interviewed by certain writers and journalists, among whom was Gabriel Harvey, once his bitterest foe; and, while Mistress Isam—'with tears in her eyes, and sighs from a deeper fountain (for she loved him dearly)'—told the gentlemen her sad tale, they profited by the occasion to pick up some interesting manu-scripts then scattered round the death-chamber. These manuscripts included an autobiographical fragment, which came into the pos-session of a writer named Henry Chettle, who copied it out, 'as sometime Greene's hand was none of the best', deleted 'what then in conscience I thought he in some displeasure writ', and presently published it under the title *Greene's Groatsworth of Wit, bought with a million of Repentance.*

Although Chettle announced that he had attempted to remove all the more hurtful and malevolent passages, he proved a somewhat careless editor: he did not delete Greene's ferocious diatribe on the state of the contemporary stage. Three dramatists were wildly apostrophised—Marlowe, Nashe and a playwright, himself driven 'to extreme shifts', who can probably be identified as Lodge. Mar-lowe comes in for especially stern reproof:

---

[1] These details we owe to Gabriel Harvey, who had a bitter grudge against Greene; they may therefore be somewhat over-coloured.

Wonder not . . . thou famous famous gracer of tragedians, that
Greene, who hath said with thee (like the fool in his heart) there
is no God, should now give glory unto this Greatness . . . His
Hand lies heavy upon me; He hath spoken unto me with a voice
of thunder . . . Why should thy excellent wit, His gift, be so
blinded, that thou shoudst give no glory to the Giver? Is it pesti-
lent Machiavellian policy that thou hast studied? . . . Defer not
with me till this last point of extremity: for little knowest thou
how in the end thou shalt be visited.

Greene's last sentence has a distinctly prophetic ring; but then,
having admonished his three misguided contemporaries, he proceeds to warn 'those gentlemen his quondam acquaintance, that
spend their wits in making plays', against the general dangers of a
playwright's life:

Base-minded men all three of you, if by my misery you be not
warned: for unto none of you (like me) sought those burrs to
cleave: those puppets (I mean) that spake from our mouths,
those antics garnished in our colours . . . Is it not like that you, to
whom they have all been beholding, shall (were ye in that case as
I am now) be at once of them forsaken? Yes, trust them not: for
there is an upstart crow, beautified with our feathers, that, with
his *Tiger's heart wrapped in a player's hide*, supposes he is as well
able to bombast out a blank verse as the best of you, and, being
an absolute *Johannes fac totum*, is in his own conceit the only
Shake-scene in a country. O that I might entreat your rare wits
to be employed in more profitable courses . . .[1]

From this invective, two things are clear—that Greene detested
the players, who, he had persuaded himself, had exploited and
betrayed him: and that he especially resented Shakespeare, whom he
accuses of opportunism and unscrupulous plagiarism, pinning down
his reference by a parody of a line in *Henry VI, Part III*, that every
playgoer would at once recognize.[2] But many of his readers were

---

[1] Some critics have claimed that both the *Groatsworth*, published on September 20th,
1592, and *The Repentance of Robert Greene*, published on October 6th, were ingenious
forgeries. If so, they are certainly good imitations of Greene's style and, as Professor
G. B. Harrison points out in *Elizabethan Plays and Players*, seem to have been written
with genuine feeling.

[2] 'O tiger's heart wrapp'd in a woman's hide' *Henry VI, Part III* Act I Scene iv.

indignant that a favourite dramatist should be so unjustly treated. Nashe, who was rumoured to have produced it, denounced the *Groatsworth* as 'a scald, trivial, lying pamphlet'; while Chettle, who had also been under fire, inserted a disclaimer in his *Kindheart's Dream*. He was sorry, he wrote, to have offended a living poet, 'because myself have seen his demeanour no less civil than he excellent in the quality he professes. Besides, divers of worship have reported his uprightness of dealing, which argues his honesty, and his facetious grace that approves his art.' Chettle may have been moved by instinctive generosity, or alarmed by the angry comments that Greene's book provoked. Too late, perhaps, he learned that 'divers of worship'—persons of solid social standing—were interested in the poet's welfare; and, although we cannot name them, one of the supporters who resented Greene's attack may have been the youthful Lord Southampton, to whom, in 1593, Shakespeare was to dedicate 'the first heir of my invention', *Venus and Adonis*. Persons of worship—and Southampton was a 'dear lover and cherisher of poets'—were useful friends but extremely dangerous enemies; and Chettle hastened to publish a retraction that he hoped would set the record straight. And then, of course, he may have been instantly disarmed by Shakespeare's good-humour and his open, winning manners.

Those manners were often commented on. For Greene, blinded by professional spite, Shakespeare was the impudently self-assured, maddeningly accomplished newcomer who, without benefit of genuine scholarship, now threatened to carry all before him; while Greene and his fellow scholars sank into obscurity or were reduced to exgurgitating trivial pamphlets. Chettle, however, having implied that, at the time when he was editing Greene's manuscripts, he had not yet encountered Shakespeare, hints that, as soon as they met, he had immediately been won round. The dramatist, he noted, was 'civil'—in other words, both civilized and courteous; and his tribute was to be echoed and re-echoed during the course of the next fifty years. There is a remarkable unanimity about such references: Shakespeare was 'friendly', 'gentle' and, according to Jonson's well-known posthumous tribute, 'honest, and of an open and free nature'. He was also 'sweet', which applies to the man himself and the honeyed quality of his early poems. Here, for the first time, an impression of a personal character emerges from the clouds of history. Shakespeare, we deduce, was essentially an amiable person, the kind of man who easily arouses affection, and repays affection with no less charm and ease. What is more, he appears to have been physically attractive. 'He was a handsome, well-shaped man,' John Aubrey learned, 'and of a very ready and pleasant, smooth wit'. Only two portraits—the frontispiece of the *Folio*, engraved by Martin Droeshout for his editors and one-time colleagues, and the Stratford bust, created by Gerard Johnson, or Janssen, which Anne Shakespeare must have esteemed a passable likeness—have any convincing claims to authenticity; and each shows us a good-looking face, in the bust somewhat coarsened and thickened, with a particularly large and lofty brow, arched nostrils, a slightly tip-tilted nose and firmly moulded cheeks and chin. He wore moustaches and a small tufted beard; the light-coloured hair rapidly receded, exposing an impressive cranium; and, in Droeshout's portrait, the finely formed lips—the lower lip more prominent than the upper—if we examine them very closely, seem to be touched by a faint ironic smile. A worldly face, sensual, sceptical, alert; Shakespeare was no visionary artist who shrank from distracting mundane pressures, but a man of the world who grasped the chances it offered and, shrewdly, perhaps a trifle cynically, made them serve his own creative ends. By 1592 he had already travelled far; and he owed his progress at once to his native genius and to the skill with which he had adapted his genius to the demands of the society in which he lived. Few writers have been so much a part of their epoch, yet have risen so high above its intellectual level; and we cannot understand his ascent until we studied the conditions that provided the background of his day-to-day existence. Although sometimes represented as an English Golden Age, the decade that witnessed many of his greatest triumphs was marked by increasing discord and confusion.

E

CHAPTER III

The Climate of the Age

EVERY LONG REIGN, before it reaches its end, is apt to become a little onerous: every century, as it approaches its conclusion, seems to bear a growing weight of trouble. When the sixteenth century entered its last decade, an elderly sovereign still occupied the throne she had held since 1558; and, between the defeat of the Armada and the old Queen's death, there was an interval, if not of decline, at least of anxiety and disenchantment. Yet, a few years earlier, hopes had been running high. Protestant Englishmen, who had believed that the execution of Mary Queen of Scots would introduce an era of universal peace, and who had danced through London's streets to the sound of pipes and tabors, welcomed the news that the Spanish fleet was scattered with a mixture of pious enthusiasm and profane rejoicing. The English, remarked a foreign observer, were now 'lords and masters of the sea and need care for no man'. In 1589, ninety-one rich Spanish vessels were reported to have been captured and brought into English havens; and during the autumn months of 1592 a syndicate of naval adventurers, among whom was the Queen herself, seized the gigantic seven-storeyed carrack named the *Madre de Dios*, largest and wealthiest of the Spanish ships then trading with the East Indies, and acquired a cargo that, despite much private pilferage, realized more than £140,000. But, while English sailors enjoyed these lucrative triumphs, English forces on land scored no corresponding victories. The Queen's intervention in the affairs of France, whither she had despatched a small contingent to aid the Protestant Henry of Navarre, proved a costly and inglorious business.

66

Before the decade was over, her incorrigible Irish subjects would once again break out in armed revolt; and amid their hills and bogs many English soldiers would lose both life and reputation.

Literally and figuratively, the skies were darkening; for, during 1594, 1595 and 1596, the variable English climate took a particularly malevolent turn. So cold and wet was each succeeding summer that the green corn rotted in the fields. 'One year,' a sermonist reminded his congregation, 'there hath been hunger, the second a dearth, and the third there was a great cleanness of teeth.' With hunger, unemployment grew; and beggars and vagrants—that 'rowsy ragged rabblement of rakehells', always a source of alarm to local magistrates and the Queen's Council—infested country roads and threatened the good order of towns and cities. But on the justices, whom they enjoined to pursue and punish vagabonds, the government at Whitehall laid another, much more serious charge—they were to hunt down outlawed Catholic priests, 'lewd and evil-disposed persons which do remain obscurely in secret places or else very secretly do go from place to place, disguised . . . either after the manner of servingmen or of artificers . . . and do, under that visor, in whispering manner hold and maintain her Majesty's subjects in superstition and error'.[1] Thus the Council had written as long ago as 1578; but the problem continued to engage them throughout the '80s and the '90s. Once the Papal Secretary, in 1580, had assured a deputation of English Jesuits that whoever should remove that 'guilty woman of England', with the purpose of doing God service, 'not only does not sin but gains merit', all Catholic missionaries, however devout and harmless, were regarded as potential regicides. Yet, undeterred by the prospect of martyrdom—torture, hanging, disembowelment—priests constantly arrived and travelled as they pleased around the kingdom. In 1587, William Allen, of the English Colleges at Douai and Rome, announced that over three hundred priests were still attached to the households of 'noblemen and principal gentlemen'; and, in 1592, a Spanish prisoner, recently released from custody, asserted that a multitude of Englishmen, rich and poor, looked forward to deliverance by Spanish arms: some

[1] The Council to the Justices of Surrey: *The Loseley Manuscripts*, edited by John Kempe, 1835.

did not avow themselves Catholics because they feared to lose their houses and their goods; others declared that they would stand firm and die in the faith they had inherited.

Every Catholic plot, real or alleged, heightened the severity of the persecution; but in 1601, though they seem to have changed their disguises, devoted Catholic emissaries, were still moving on their dangerous rounds—Father Blackwell, for instance, the arch-priest, who governed the English secular priesthood, 'about fifty years of age, his head brownish, his beard more black, cut after the fashion of a spade . . . decently attired in black silk'; or the Jesuit Father John Gerard, who had already suffered imprisonment and torture, but had escaped from the Tower of London by swinging hand over hand along a rope across the moat, 'of stature tall, high-shouldered, especially when his cope is on his back, black-haired and of complexion swarth, hawk-nosed, high-templed, and for the most part attired costly and defencibly in buff leather, garnished with gold or silver lace, satin doublets and velvet hose of all colours, with cloaks correspondent, and rapiers and daggers gilt or silvered.'[1] Both priests survived to die as exiles—Gerard, who had escaped in 1597, did not leave England until 1606; and their survival shows the strength of the opposition that co-existed with, and defied, the Protestant government.

A second powerful opposition was provided by the aggressive Protestant left wing. That, too, bred its zealots and devotees, notably Peter Wentworth, an influential member of parliament and an agitator of 'whet and vehement spirit', with his bold defence of free speech and his conviction, freely expressed, that, sweet as was the name of liberty, 'the thing itself has a value beyond all inestimable treasure'. In 1588, the 'Martin Marprelate' tracts—a series of fiercely satirical pamphlets by unidentified writers, who campaigned under that pseudonym—struck at the foundations of episcopal rule. 'Martin's' printing-press was at length discovered and destroyed; and Wentworth, whose *Pithy Exhortation to her Majesty*, begging her to nominate a successor, had been adjudged even more offensive than his animadversions against the rule of bishops, was cast into a London gaol. Yet the Puritan movement, though temporarily checked, never

[1] Informer's report to Sir Robert Cecil: *Salisbury Papers*, August 27th, 1601.

lost its vital impetus; and it had many supporters, not only in the City and the House of Commons but in the circle round the throne, who despised and resented the Established Church, a product of political compromise which, according to keen-eyed reformers, still incorporated numerous popish relics. The Queen's own practice was not above suspicion: 'enormities of idolatry', gold ornaments and embroidered vestments, were freely exhibited in the royal chapel, and the elaborate services that the Court attended were (Puritans alleged) scarcely distinguishable from the hated Mass. An autocrat by training and temperament, Elizabeth felt an instinctive mistrust for these contentious and unruly citizens. Her system required a uniformity of belief; and she had heard that, in one diocese alone, there were six preachers 'which do preach six sundry ways', and that London merchants held nightly conventicles where the Holy Scriptures were boldly expounded and discussed. Such individualism, applied to problems of faith, might lead to dangerous thought on other questions; men 'so curious in searching matters above their capacity' might soon be turning their attention towards affairs of government. Session by session, her 'loyal Commons', who included a large body of Puritan sympathizers, became more obstinate and restive.

That restiveness originated in a sense of power[1]—Parliament's power to grant or to withhold the large financial subsidies their sovereign needed. Elizabeth was a shrewd economist; but her royal revenues, although during her later life she sold off some of her jewels and portions of the crown lands, were quite inadequate to the expense of equipping fleets and sending armies overseas; and she was obliged to fall back on further direct taxation, which could be levied only with the consent of her assembled legislators. Already the financial crisis was under way that would bedevil two succeeding reigns, as Parliament, through its control of taxation, sought to achieve a greater share in the management of public policy. More imposing, more sensitive and persuasive, than either James I or Charles I, Elizabeth, while she lived, was able to avoid an open rupture. She often expressed her warm affection for the Commons; and the Commons would return the compliment, protesting their

[1] See Joel Hurstfield: *Elizabeth I and the Unity of England*, 1960.

unbounded loyalty: not long before her death, a member exclaimed that a message the House had just received should be recorded in characters of pure gold. But the 'Golden Speech' with which she followed it—probably the last she ever delivered—on November 30th, 1601, was designed to placate an ill-disposed parliament, then up in arms against the most unpopular of her various makeshift money-making schemes, the sale of monopolies that gave private entrepreneurs an exclusive hold over certain important forms of commerce.[1] Elizabeth's 'fluent eloquence and princely boldness'— both qualities she had always excelled in—at once disarmed her angry critics. But the upshot was a decisive victory for the Commons. She promised immediate relief. That her grants should be made grievances to her people was something, she declared, that her royal dignity could not suffer: 'when I heard it, I could give no rest unto my thoughts until I had reformed it . . .'

Yet everywhere doubts and suspicions lurked. The Queen was now an old woman who refused doggedly to name her heir; and, while she continued to dally and temporize, politicians' nerves remained on edge. The most hopeful claimant, after his mother's execution, which Elizabeth preferred to describe as an unfortunate mishap, was James VI of Scotland, son of her arch-adversary Mary Queen of Scots. But the Infanta of Spain, a descendant of John of Gaunt, was also sometimes put forward; and the merest mention of the Infanta, and of the secret understanding alleged to exist between the Spanish government and members of the Cecil group, was enough to alarm the Puritans and excite their numerous influential allies. All the great politicians of the day were anxiously considering their own future, and took the precaution of paying their respects to the Scottish King beyond the Tweed: Robert Cecil himself kept up a correspondence with James which he felt it advisable to transact by stealth, since he feared that his mistress' age, 'joined to the jealousy of her sex', might possibly overcloud her judgment. And then, a new generation was springing up around the sovereign, a generation that detested the 'old gang', the two Cecils and their con-

---

[1] Private individuals had recently acquired the sole rights to manufacture salt and starch; the starch monopoly was particularly valuable now that both men and women affected elaborate ruffs.

federates, on whom the Queen still put her trust—ambitious young men with a taste for adventure; whereas their bureaucratic opponents weighed the real value, and counted the exact cost, of every military or naval enterprise. Nor was this restless mood limited to the Court: it pervaded the entire kingdom. The Queen might be sure of her subjects' loyalty; but by 1595 her triumphant reign had already lasted thirty-seven years; and 'things of long continuance, though never so good' (noted an acute observer) must inevitably become tedious. Gratitude and loyalty count for little beside the deep-rooted human love of change.

Shakespeare, in fact, discovered and developed his genius against a somewhat gloomy background, during a period, not of progressive national growth but of disillusionment and anti-climax. His own sympathies, no doubt, were with the young; and his chosen patron was closely allied to a brilliant and belligerent leader who personified the attitude, and voiced the claims, of the rebellious younger generation. Yet outwardly the Elizabethan kingdom provided a splendid and impressive show. Elizabeth's court was the most magnificent in Europe; and, although the Queen was otherwise parsimonious and usually grudged any expense not calculated to produce a quick return, as a royal householder she left nothing undone that could reflect her glory or increase her state. From her attendants she demanded a high degree both of elegance and of sophistication. Herself a proficient linguist, who conversed easily, not only in modern languages, but also in Greek and well-turned Latin, she expected that her servants should display an equal fluency; and when, towards the close of her reign, the Duke of Bracciano visited the Queen at Whitehall, where he apparently attended the first performance of a pleasing comedy named *Twelfth Night*,[1] he noticed that her courtiers —'all dressed in white, as was the whole Court that day', but decked with a dazzling profusion of gold and jewels—spoke most of them Italian, and many of them French, while some, at least, had mastered Spanish. According to the pre-Copernican view of the universe, heaven and earth were linked together by a mysterious chain of correspondences: all earthly phenomena had some heavenly counterpart; and Elizabeth, being queen of her sphere, maintained, like the

[1] J. Leslie Hotson: *The First Night of Twelfth Night*, 1954.

planets above, her regular ceremonial course. Now, accompanied by gigantic baggage-trains, she travelled to and fro among her numerous palaces, of which her favourite was Nonsuch; now she left London on one of her yearly progresses, to gratify and alarm her noblemen and gentlemen, or test her wits against the erudition of the learned inhabitants of Oxford and Cambridge. At home in Whitehall, apartments were arranged *en suite:* from the Great Chamber one moved to the Presence Chamber, from the Presence to the Privy Chamber; and beyond the threshold of the Privy Chamber lay the smaller rooms in which she slept and studied. As often as she quitted her private apartments—for instance, on her way to chapel—a host of attentive courtiers lined her path, eagerly awaiting a look or a friendly word.

Lord Herbert of Cherbury, whose story of his early life[1] includes many revealing details of an Elizabethan education, describes how, as a very young man, he had knelt to watch the royal luminary pass: 'I was . . . upon my knees in the presence-chamber, when she passed by to the chapel'. As soon as she saw him—he was uncommonly handsome and elegant—she paused and, swearing her usual oath, 'God's death!' she exclaimed, 'Who is this?' Nobody could inform her: 'until Sir James Croft, a pensioner,[2] finding the Queen stayed, returned back and told who I was, and that I had married Sir William Herbert of St Julian's daughter. The Queen . . . looked attentively upon me, and swearing again her ordinary oath, said it is a pity he was married so young, and thereupon gave her hand to kiss twice, both times gently clapping me on the cheek.' But none of the familiarities she dispensed—and at times she could be surprisingly familiar—detracted from her air of majesty. Impossible to forget she was the scion of kings, though it was her grandfather who had founded the Tudor line, or that, if she saw her subjects as her children, she also regarded them as personal servants. Let Endymion beware of offending Cynthia! Elizabeth had always been a jealous mistress; and perhaps because she was herself frustrated, and the various amatory relationships she had engaged in had never reached

---

[1] *The Autobiography of Edward, Lord Herbert of Cherbury*, edited by Sidney L. Lee, 1886.

[2] The Gentlemen Pensioners were the Queen's private bodyguard, recruited from good-looking, well-born youths.

their proper end, she kept a sternly vigilant eye upon the behaviour of her private household. She was no puritan; but she punished licentious conduct, just as she reproved unlicensed thought; and the favourite who married without her leave, or seduced an attractive maid of honour, was at once dismissed from her presence and sometimes, like Ralegh and Southampton in their day, committed to a prison cell.

Nothing escaped her, contemporaries said; nor was her omniscience confined to her own court. And this peculiar insight, together with her courage and wisdom and the gift she showed, if the occasion demanded it, for diplomatic double-dealing, marked her out among her fellow sovereigns as the type of accomplished modern ruler—a princess worthy to stand beside Machiavelli's famous Prince. Even the Pope had ruefully acknowledged her qualities: she was 'certainly a great Queen,' remarked Sixtus V soon after he had ascended the pontifical chair; 'and, were she only a Catholic, she would be our dearly beloved.' A mere woman; yet look how well she governed, monarch of half an island, but feared and respected by the whole of Europe! . . . Foreign envoys who visited her kingdom reported back in equally admiring strains. Beneath the great reddish-coloured wig, her face was 'long and thin and very aged'; but it was 'not possible,' wrote one diplomatist, 'to see a woman of so fine and vigorous a disposition.' '*Par Dieu*,' ejaculated a Spanish agent, '*cette Reine est extrêmement sage, et a des yeux terribles. Oh, che grandezza!*' Just as remarkable as her appetite for business were the Queen's gaiety and feminine vanity and her passionate devotion to every kind of entertainment. She loved music, played 'exceedingly well' on the virginals, danced 'high and disposedly'—in 1589, when she was fifty-six, she would dance six or seven galliards[1] between leaving her bed and sitting down to dinner—enjoyed a game of chess—which reminded her, she observed, of the game of international politics—liked hunting and hawking, riding out to meet her loyal subjects and gracing the elaborate festivities they had prepared, or, if she could not quit her palace, walking energetically around the Privy Garden. Whatever she did, she did with youthful gusto, and with the energy and distinction of a woman born to rule.

[1] A particularly gay and energetic dance, with five steps to a phrase.

She did not underestimate either her natural gifts or the astonishing breadth of her accomplishments. 'I thank God,' she announced, 'I am endued with such qualities that if I were turned out of the realm in my petticoat, I were able to live in any place in Christendom.' And, on another occasion: 'I am supposed to have many studies, but, most, philosophical. I must yield this to be true, that I suppose few that be no professors have read more.' Yet her exalted sense of her personal and royal dignity did not preclude her from ordinary human contacts. She had the art, if she chose to exercise it, of meeting her simplest subjects on their own level; and, just as the court lady who had lost a son would receive a charming and tenderly sympathetic letter, so the country parson, whose embarrassment she had noticed while he stumbled through a Latin speech, would be uplifted by her prompt assurance that his was the best speech she had ever heard. Again if she were in the right mood, she was easily amused and pleased. Her constant journeyings were frequently held up by some capricious last-minute change of plan; and one day, when the Court was leaving Windsor, a carter in the yard below, having been told for the third time that the Queen had decided that she would not move, slapped his thigh with the infuriated exclamation: 'Now I see that the Queen is a woman as well as my wife!' His angry voice reached Elizabeth's ears: she was standing at her open window. 'What a villain is this!' she cried appreciatively, and sent him down a present of three angels.[1]

Yet it was rash to presume on her good nature. Her mind might appear to be ruled by a puzzling combination of design and impulse —and her impulses, though occasionally mischievous, were very often wise and kindly; but in the last resort they were always held in check by her native caution and her shrewd political flair. No doubt she was capable of love; but her feelings seldom overcast her judgment; and she never lost the habit she had contracted as a girl of probing suspiciously into human motives, of seeking the face behind the mask and the real intention that underlay the words. 'The Queen did fish for men's souls . . .' recorded Hatton in his old age. 'When she smiled, it was pure sunshine,' wrote her engaging godson Sir John Harington, 'that everyone did choose to bask in if they

---

[1] The angel is thought to have been worth about 6s. 8d. in modern money.

could; but anon came a storm . . . and the thunder fell in wondrous manner . . .' Yet the sunshine, so long as it lasted, had an intoxicating effect on those who felt its warmth, causing them to open their 'most inward thoughts to her; when . . . she would ponder in private on what had passed, write down all their opinions, draw them out as occasion required, and sometimes disprove to their faces what had been delivered a month before . . .' Many aspiring advisers were thus betrayed and put to shame; and, indeed, there was none of her counsellors or favourites who had escaped his time of trial. Her rage was volcanic—in that, as in so much else, she resembled her terrible father King Henry: it roared around her ministers' ears and drove her trembling courtiers from her presence. Foreign ambassadors bowed beneath its onrush, as did the presumptuous Polish envoy who had dared to begin his mission by delivering a message from his master that almost amounted to a reprimand; at which Elizabeth's reply, couched in extempore Latin, blasted the impertinent diplomatist where he stood. Such explosive displays of energy delighted and reassured her subjects: to them she was not only a mortal sovereign, with numerous feminine failings that they often permitted themselves to criticize, but the divine Cynthia, idol of a nationwide cult and personification of her people's fortunes.

In her immediate circle, no Christian ruler has been more nearly deified. Real devotion and personal opportunism sometimes speak the same language; but, when we have allowed for the element of self-interest and discounted the Elizabethan use of flattery, we must still admit that the feelings she aroused went deeper than mere politic reverence. From a twentieth-century point of view, few features of the age are quite so difficult to understand. Thus, we find Ralegh, disgraced after the exposure of his secret marriage with Elizabeth Throckmorton, composing the eleventh book of a long series of poems entitled *The Ocean's Love to Cynthia*, in which the unkind goddess he apostrophizes is both Elizabeth herself and the radiant incarnation of a philosophic principle.[1] If, on one plane, he loved Elizabeth Throckmorton, on another he certainly adored the Queen. His passion had a deep emotional origin; and during his imprisonment, when Cynthia in her royal barge glided down the Thames

[1] M. C. Bradbrook: *The School of Night*, 1936.

beneath his windows, he fell, as contemporary lovers were always apt to do, into a wild frenzy of amorous despair, and attacked his gaoler with a knife before he could be restrained and disarmed. The Queen's favourites were not merely successful courtiers, but the dedicated guardians of her royal sanctuary. They competed fiercely for the privilege of serving her; and this daily competition excited them to put forth every virtue they possessed. Court rivalry, writes a modern historian, had helped to kindle 'the intense spirit of the age;[1] and that rivalry, which towards the close of her reign often degenerated into dangerous faction, Elizabeth was at constant pains to keep alive. By pitting man against man she persuaded each to make a double effort; the resultant trial of strength gratified her self-esteem, but also advanced the interests of the whole kingdom.

The feelings that Elizabeth aroused in her servants were matched by her conception of her own powers. Sovereignty was a god-given attribute; even in the animal kingdom there were natural followers and natural leaders; and the human ruler was the apex of a system that corresponded with systems both above and below, all of them divinely ordered and administered by divine authority. To lay impious hands on a sovereign was to shake the harmonious fabric of creation. 'Those who touch the sceptres of princes deserve no pity,' cried the Queen, hearing of a palace conspiracy against the French monarch, Henri of Navarre, whom latterly she had had little reason to respect. Towards her hated antagonist Mary Queen of Scots her attitude, throughout their long relationship, remained curiously ambivalent; for, although the 'Daughter of Debate' was an acknowledged enemy, she had none the less been crowned a Queen; and, year after year, Elizabeth shrank from the dreadful responsibility of countenancing her execution. She had hinted that Mary might perhaps be poisoned, or otherwise quietly and discreetly put away; but Mary's custodian, Sir Amias Paulet, had answered with a bold refusal —'God forbid,' he replied to Walsingham, who had been instructed to sound him, 'that I should make so foul a shipwreck of my conscience'; and it was therefore his mistress's conscience that had to suffer for her kingdom's safety. She signed the death warrant, but, once her rival was dead, experienced a revulsion of feeling that

[1] J. E. Neale: *Queen Elizabeth I*, 1934.

reduced her to the verge of breakdown. Her grief was violent; she would not eat or sleep; and just as violent were the recriminations through which she attempted to shed the burden of her guilt. She declared that her emissary had exceeded his orders; and he was incarcerated in the Tower and condemned to pay a heavy fine.

Such views on the nature of kingship were not, of course, peculiar to the Queen. They were shared by most contemporary Englishmen, and as part of the general climate of opinion found their way into Shakespearian drama, which often depicts the tremendous consequences that spring from the death of a sovereign or the usurpation of a crown. Though his real opinions are difficult to determine, the popular historical playwright always adopted the attitude of a romantic royalist; but certainly, towards the end of the reign, he seems to have undergone a secret change of heart. A sharp collision then occurred between his public and his private loyalties; and, when the Queen died and his fellow poets set to work composing mournful verses, Shakespeare shocked a respectable acquaintance by omitting to shed a single literary tear. Meanwhile, in the background of his life, that impressive figure must have loomed large. The theatrical company to which he belonged frequently played before Elizabeth, either at one of her palaces or in the house of some distinguished subject; and again and again, he must have beheld her enthroned at the centre of a crowded audience, remote and resplendent among her courtiers and guard of handsome Gentlemen Pensioners, the jewels winking on her aged bosom or caught like fireflies in her russet wig, her lean, long-toothed, thickly painted face encircled with a shimmering hoop of lawn. Luckily, she enjoyed plays, as she enjoyed every kind of stately show; and her interest did something to protect the stage against its numerous influential critics. Had she been a melancholy *dévote* of the same stamp as her half-sister Mary, the puritanical magistrates who governed the City might perhaps have been allowed to do their worst; and once the players had been driven from London, and the theatres closed or torn down, the inspiration of the Elizabethan drama might well have flickered out before it reached maturity.

Equally, had it been confined to court circles, it might have achieved a less robust flowering. Both aristocratic support and popular patronage were required to make it what it was—a hybrid growth that combined many different strains in the late-sixteenth-century national character and, since its origins were so strangely diverse, appealed to just as many tastes. Great noblemen safeguarded the players' existence by allowing them to wear their liveries, filled the more comfortable seats in the playhouses and even, like Derby and Oxford, tried their hands at writing plays; but actors and dramatists also depended upon the teeming population of the City, its merchants, tradesmen and artisans, and the cheerful, disorderly crowd of young apprentices, whose chosen playgrounds were London's streets and the suburban fields in which the new theatres stood. A great distance separated the Court from the City—yet each contributed to the development of Shakespeare's genius. If the English Court dazzled foreign visitors, London itself, as the largest metropolis in Northern Europe, commanded universal praise. The Elizabethan merchant class, who had not yet begun to ally themselves with the territorial aristocracy—not until 1592 did the son of a rich alderman marry the daughter of an impoverished peer, and until 1599 no English peer had married the daughter of a London merchant[1]—formed their own aristocracy behind the City's walls, and carried on their absorbing affairs with exemplary success and self-assurance.[2] In their 'fair and large-builded' houses they kept an almost princely state; at home they lent money—often to their social superiors— and accumulated tracts of landed property; while abroad their maritime ventures were pushed out across the oceans of the world, towards the Americas and the East Indies, India, the African coastline and the countries of the Far East. Thomas Whythorne, musician and autobiographer, who flourished in the 1560s,[3] records that a mercantile patron of his had 'doings for merchandise and ventures' simultaneously on foot in Muscovy, Tartary, Persia, Guinea, 'Macrogumba', Nova Spania and Florida. Whythorne's employer, it so happened, was a cultivated and sympathetic man; but his master's

[1] 'The Peer and the Alderman's Daughter', by Lawrence Stone, *History Today*, January, 1961.

[2] The merchant was distinguished from fashionable persons by his soberly conservative wardrobe. Thus the merchant Kitely, in Jonson's *Every Man in his Humour*, complains that his wife's friends 'mock me all over, from my flat cap unto my shining shoes'.

[3] Thomas Whythorne, *op. cit.*

associates, Whythorne complained, talked incessantly of 'gain and loss . . . such merchandise as it was best for them to transport into this country and that country, and likewise of the commodities . . . to be brought hither wherein gain was to be gotten. And then for the exchange of money—how that went from time to time . . . There was no other talk among these aforesaid but of gain and riches.'

Every social system is acquisitive; but the Elizabethans' lust for gain was as uninhibited as their general appetite for life. The Queen's servants might plunder the Spaniards; in her turn, she was herself plundered; and, when the 'Great Carrack' was brought into Dartmouth, officers and men had already looted a large proportion of her precious cargo. Though Robert Cecil was sent down to the West Country, followed by Ralegh who, for that purpose, had been provisionally released from his imprisonment in the Tower, nothing could deter the thieves; they streamed towards London, laden with the booty they had gathered; and Cecil, as he passed them, declared that he could almost smell them out; for their baggage contained, in addition to pearls and damask, quantities of the musk and ambergris that the *Madre de Dios* had been carrying home. The Elizabethan explorer was also a freebooter and a keen commercialist.[1] Yet the emotion that inspired his voyages seems to have transcended their immediate aim. Thus Ralegh's lifelong search for gold became inextricably connected with a very different set of motives. The Eldorado he sought was not merely the gold-rich kingdom that promised its conquerors unlimited power and wealth, but Arcadia, the Earthly Paradise, an Eldorado of the spirit. For a brief period, in 1595, as his oarsmen ferried him up the Orinoco, he thought he had discovered it: 'On both sides of the river we passed the most beautiful country that ever mine eyes beheld . . .' The huge river, 'winding into divers branches', rolled to the ocean between banks of smooth green turf, with here and there graceful clumps of trees that might have been disposed by human skill, 'the deer crossing in every path, the birds towards evening singing in every tree . . . cranes and herons of white, crimson and carnation'; while over this majestic, unviolated landscape a gentle easterly wind blew.[2] Yet Ralegh

[1] '. . . They are good sailors, and better pirates, cunning, treacherous and thievish'. Paul Hentzner. *op. cit.*

[2] *The Discovery of the Large, Rich and Beautiful Country of Guiana,* 1596.

remained a practical explorer; and, as a modern critic has pointed out,[1] besides exulting in the beauty of the landscape, he noted its commercial possibilities and its military advantages: 'every stone that we stooped to take up promised either gold or silver', and the 'ground or hard sand' would make marching easy 'either for horse or foot'.

In such a fusion of romantic and practical interests, there was nothing at all surprising from the Elizabethan point of view. As an adventurer, Ralegh's objects were various—

> To seek new worlds, for gold, for praise, for glory,
> To try desire, to try love severed far

—and the love that he professed, though it was strengthened by ambition and an insatiable thirst for self-enrichment, burned in his heart like a flame that constantly demanded fresh fuel. That passion is the basic theme of the lyrics he addressed to Cynthia:

> Love is a durable fire
> In the mind ever burning:
> Never sick, never old, never dead,
> From itself never turning

Here the symbolism that the poet employs has a peculiarly Elizabethan cast; for his contemporaries regarded fire as an emblem of the human spirit. 'As the fire,' wrote Ralegh in his *Treatise of the Soul*, 'mounteth of itself upward and is carried round with the heavens, so the soul of man is led upward . . . by the senses, and doth many things in and out of the body without them . . . Is it not a manifest argument that it cometh from God, seeing in all things it resteth not till it come to God? The mind, in searching causes, is never quiet till it come to God . . .' There is a close parallel, remarks an authority on Ralegh and the coterie of which he was the centre,[2] between this passage and the famous declamations uttered by Marlowe's Tamburlaine and Dr Faustus:

> Nature, that fram'd us of four elements . . .
> Doth teach us all to have aspiring minds:

[1] Helen Morris: *Elizabethan Literature*, 1958.
[2] M. C. Bradbrook, *op. cit.*

> Our souls, whose faculties can comprehend
> The wondrous architecture of the world,
> And measure every wandering planet's course,
> Still climbing after knowledge infinite,
> And always moving as the restless spheres,
> Will us to wear ourselves, and never rest . . .[1]

True, it is towards universal monarchy, 'the sweet fruition of an earthly crown', that Tamburlaine directs his efforts, whereas Faustus, the fated scholar, hopes to control his surroundings by satanic science; but each is a restless soul, in passionate revolt against his limitations, and each reflects the mood of the dramatist's own aspiring age.

Aspiration, indeed, lawful or lawless, was one of the ruling characteristics of the Elizabethan temperament. Courtiers, lovers and poets felt that they burned with the same upward-leaping blaze; and the exquisite miniaturist Nicholas Hilliard, in a particularly fine portrait, gives an unknown lover, who has evidently lost his love, a golden background composed of tongues of flame wreathing and flickering behind his head. The pursuit of worldly advantage was scarcely distinguishable from the pursuit of virtue: they provoked the same determination to excel, and were often expressed with the help of the same vehement poetic imagery. To be inactive was to be thwarted in body and mind; and Edmund Spenser when he depicted the malaise caused by a sense of unexploited powers—

> The noble heart that harbours virtuous thought
> And is with child of glorious great intent,
> Can never rest until it forth have brought
> The eternal brood of glory excellent[2]

—spoke for a society whose greatest triumph was the creation of the Elizabethan drama. But, despite its brilliance, it was not a mature society. Though the soaring spirit of the age found the release that it needed in varying types of literary art—magnificent verse and vigorous idiosyncratic prose—it could show very few achievements either in painting or in sculpture. The Italian Renaissance had already

[1] *Tamburlaine the Great, Part I* Act II Scene vii.
[2] *The Faerie Queene* I. V.

F

come and gone: England had not yet completely thrown off the restrictive influence of the Middle Ages. Even the popular vision of the universe still conformed to the mediaeval pattern. Copernicus' great book *De Revolutionibus Orbium Coelestium*, which displaced the earth from the centre of the cosmic system, had been published as long ago as 1543; and the Copernican theory had been adopted in England by two or three eminent 'natural philosophers', including the celebrated Dr Dee, mathematician, astrologer and occultist, renowned for his 'Theoricall Speculations and most cunning Calculations', and Dee's pupil, the ingenious Thomas Digges, whose *Perfit Description of the Celestiall Orbes* appeared in 1576. But for the ordinary Englishman, even at Oxford and Cambridge, the cosmos preserved its geocentric pattern. His feet were still planted upon a central and unmoving earth, around which swung the crystalline spheres, as they turned one above the other discoursing strains of heavenly music.

It was a vision that, to judge from his plays, notably from *The Merchant of Venice*, Shakespeare must himself have harboured. There can be no doubt that it was a highly poetic vision—the mighty assemblage of revolving spheres, translucent, adamantine, polished and perfected by the creative hand of God, with the visiting moon and the ever-wandering planets and the innumerable company of stars scattered here and there across their concave surface. Everything below the moon belonged to the elementary region, where the four warring elements, Earth, Air, Fire and Water, engaged in a perpetual strife; and Shakespeare uses the word 'sublunary' to distinguish the realm of discord and change from the harmonious ethereal order. The eighth sphere, entitled the Firmament, was the starry vault we admire above our heads; but beyond it extended the *Primum Mobile*, which controlled the motions of the celestial system; and beyond that again stretched the Empyrean, also known as the Abode of Fire, home of the Creator and his pure spirits. Each link in this chain of existence was perfectly fashioned and adroitly joined; it represented not only a physical organization but a moral hierarchy.

Higher than the moon nothing was at fault; all was peace and dazzling radiance:

Far far above these heavens, which here we see,
Be others far exceeding these in light,
Not bounded, not corrupt, as these same be,
But infinite in largeness and in height,
Unmoving, uncorrupt, and spotless bright . . .[1]

Each detail had been planned by God; and each had some super-natural or symbolic import. Although the earth itself was the scene of discord, it bore witness to divine sagacity: everything it contained, every sentient creature—from the lions and eagles, which ruled the animal kingdom, to the lowly oysters which headed their own class, higher, of course, than the plants, yet lower than the animals—had attributes that illustrated its purpose and betokened its peculiar virtue; 'as every herb, plant, fruit and flower . . . hath the like. For . . . these were not created to beautify the earth alone and shadow her dusty face but otherwise for the use of man and beast to feed them and cure them.[2] Besides accepting the pre-Copernican view of the earth's position in the universe, Shakespeare also accepted the medieval theory of 'degree', by which the whole creation formed a majestic hierarchy that extended upwards until it reached Heaven, where 'angel is set over angel, rank upon rank' beneath the throne of God. This doctrine was the chief support of conservative Eliza-bethan thinkers, who insisted that human society must preserve the same hierarchical design, since, if the laws of degree were once broken, mankind would plunge into self-destructive chaos.[3] It is the belief that Ulysses would presently expound in *Troilus and Cressida*:

Oh, when degree is shaked,
Which is the ladder of all high designs,
The enterprise is sick! How could communities,
Degrees in schools, and brotherhoods in cities . . .
Prerogative of age, crowns, sceptres, laurels,
But by degree, stand in authentic place?
Take but degree away, untune that string,
And hark what discord follows.

[1] Spenser: *Hymn of Heavenly Beauty*, 1596.
[2] Ralegh: *History of the World*, 1614.
[3] See E. M. W. Tillyard: *The Elizabethan World Picture*, 1943.

Shakespeare's conservatism, which seems to have prejudiced him against the scientific speculations of his age, extended, so far as we can judge, to political organization and the art of government.

Here he reflected the prevailing mood: despite its rebels and its adventurers, Elizabethan society was, in the main, conservative, eager for new discoveries yet always tenacious of established rules. Protocol hedged its existence around, even for its greatest poets; and many literary images that we admire today as brilliant flights of individual fancy have a conventional symbolic basis that escapes the uninstructed modern reader. When the Elizabethan dramatist speaks of a lion, an eagle or a dolphin, he is not concerned merely to produce an impression of pride and strength and unfettered natural grace, but remembers—and is reminding his audience—that these magnificent beasts were among the lords of creation, who governed and exploited the lesser animals by means of the 'sovereignty' they had received from Nature.[1] Similarly, inherited tradition often determined a man's private conduct. The melancholy lover—and any lover was apt to run melancholy mad should he be denied the loved one's smiles—fell into the attitude that custom dictated and immediately advertised his wretched plight. He would fold his arms,[2] lower his eyes, pull his head-covering down across his brows:

> Deep in a dump John Forde was alone got
> With folded arms and melancholy hat

—writes a Jacobean, describing the author of *The Lover's Melancholy*, *'Tis Pity She's a Whore* and *The Broken Heart*, most haunted and pessimistic of all the post-Shakespearian playwrights. Just as certain attitudes signified states of feeling, so, we learn, did certain colours.[3] Thus Malvolio is directed to express his emotions by assuming a pair of yellow stockings; and, in real life, Thomas Whythorne tells how he had wooed his employer, a rich and somewhat frivolous person—he himself was a Malvolio of a very much more amiable kind—by appearing before her clad in russet, 'which colour signifieth the wearer to have hope', and exhibiting a garland of hops, again a

[1] E. M. W. Tillyard: *Elizabethan World Picture*, 1943.
[2] 'This senior-junior giant dwarf, Don Cupid, Regent of love-rhymes, Lord of folded arms . . .' *Love's Labour's Lost* Act III Scene i.
[3] 'Green, indeed, is the colour of lovers . . .' *Love's Labour's Lost* Act I Scene ii.

symbol of hope, wreathed about his hat-brim.[1] His mistress promptly caught his drift, and made it evident that she did not share his interest. 'If you have any hope in me,' she exclaimed, '*The suds of soap shall wash your hope*,' thereupon sharply dismissing him to flounder on through fresh disasters.

In few respects could one of Shakespeare's contemporaries, whether the position he occupied were mean or exalted, regard himself as an entirely free agent. Among his fellows controlled by the laws of degree, he was also governed by the 'secret influence' of the stars, which reproduced far above his head the social hierarchy that obtained below. His own physical organism was compounded of the four elements; and each element corresponded to a bodily humour—Earth to melancholy, Water to phlegm, Fire to choler, Air to blood—a man's psychology being finally determined by the proportions in which they circulated through his body, from the liver, where they had their origin, towards the kingly heart where his dominant emotions reigned. The 'humorous' character was therefore an unbalanced man whose constitution included too large a share of some single elementary trait, and who afforded a tragic or comic instance of how that quality might endanger reason. Only reason, Heaven's gift to Man, could enable him to maintain the balance that he needed—an excess of air and fire, though much nobler, was almost as dangerous and delusive as an excess of watery and earthy humours; and reason was constantly at war with the ungovernable force of passion, which transforms man into the semblance of 'that beast to whose sensuality he principally declines'.[2] Man, the Proteus of creation, was alone endowed with free will, unlike the beasts who preserved their 'natural dignity' because, in the chain of existence, they always kept their proper place. But it is evident that, although Man was free to choose, as an individual his freedom was limited by a host of predetermined factors.

Within this framework of somewhat primitive beliefs the Shakespearian drama grew up and flourished, until old terms had at length been incorporated in the vocabulary of a new poetic language.

[1] Thomas Wythorne, *op. cit.*
[2] *David's Tears* by Sir John Hayward, 1623, quoted by E. M. W. Tillyard in *The Elizabethan World Picture.*

Meanwhile, during his period of apprenticeship, Shakespeare's talents seem to have been greedily assimilative rather than acutely critical: he took the good and the bad, the inherited superstitions of his day as readily as the ideas he received from the humanist literature of Renaissance Europe. Here he resembled his countrymen, whose acquisitive and assimilative habits astonished every foreign visitor, and who imitated and created with equal energy and lack of false shame. It is difficult to determine when Renaissance influences first reached the English literary world; Wyatt and Surrey were bold poetic reformers, but their reforms had no immediate sequel; and between the death of Wyatt and the publication of Spenser's *Shepheardes Calender* there was a lapse of nearly four decades. While poetry burst into sudden flower, the other arts had lagged behind. Inigo Jones had not yet emerged as the first great English classical architect; and the immense edifices raised by the Elizabethan ruling class upon the ruins of the monasteries were frequently embellished by architects and craftsmen employing foreign 'pattern books'. Some of the 'prodigy houses' they produced were splendidly original buildings—Hardwick, for instance, where a huge expanse of glass is contained by narrow stone ribs, so that the whole facade appears to consist of one gigantic window. Others, though majestic in conception, in detail are often ponderous and crude.

For Elizabethan taste was always erratic, particularly in questions of applied ornament; and sixteenth-century carving is sometimes difficult to distinguish from a clever nineteenth-century pastiche. A *parvenu* taste, typical of an aristocracy that included many 'new men', it favoured size and solidity and grandeur. Nor did the Elizabethans display much sense of style in their expensive and elaborate clothing. Again the effect was apt to be heavy and clumsy; and the farthingale was certainly one of the ugliest fashions ever imposed upon the human frame. Elizabeth and her assembled ladies must have recalled a range of glorious puppets, their arms concealed from shoulder to wrist in unbecoming 'cannon' sleeves, the upper part of the body sheathed in a cylindrical bodice finished with a pointed stomacher, the legs entirely invisible beneath their pleated wheel-top skirts, their hair raised over pads, and their faces and bosoms thickly painted. Male fashions were almost equally concerned to change and distort the outlines of the body. True, the lower limbs were freely displayed—trunk-hose now barely covered the hips, and the rest of the leg, whether young or old, elegant and muscular or lean and shrivelled, was clad in thin, tight-fitting 'nether stocks'; but the shape of the torso was frequently deformed by a 'peascod-bellied' doublet that gave even the slenderest courtier a kind of narrow artificial paunch,[1] with a row of buttons bisecting it and running upwards to where his ruff began. In many portraits, those buttons are pearls; for pearl-fisheries were still exploited at the mouths of various English rivers; and a picture of the youthful Essex shows him wearing over his cuirass a thickly pearl-embroidered outer-garment; while in another canvas, which represents Ralegh, besides the big orient pearl that dangles from his left ear, we notice broad bands of small close-set pearls striping the whole length of his fur-lined cloak.

The Elizabethans were enamoured of luxury and sometimes astonished by their own extravagance. What improvements they had made in comfort and splendour and in the general art of living, since their rustic ancestors had eaten and drunk from horn, earthenware or wooden vessels—instead of the silver or pewter plates and fragile 'Venice glasses' that were used today[2]—and, retiring to rest, had laid their heads, not upon plump swan-stuffed pillows, but uncomplainingly upon 'a good round log'![3] Yet domestic furniture remained comparatively sparse; at Whitehall itself, grumbled a courtier, the stools were intolerably small and hard; and, though Leicester had employed them to soften his floors, carpets were more often employed to cover tables or to mask windows, and the floorboards were usually strewn with sweet-scented rushes.[4] The Queen's numerous residences were not palaces, in the modern meaning of the word, so much as royal caravanserais, between which she moved as her inclination might prompt, followed by a heavily laden waggon-train

[1] This fashion is preserved in Mr Punch's traditional costume.
[2] Falstaff: glasses, glasses is the only drinking . . . *Henry IV, Part II* Act II Scene i.
[3] 'Their beds are covered with tapestry, even those of farmers. . .' Paul Hentzner, *op. cit.*
[4] Oddly enough, the Elizabethans seem not only to have walked on rushes, but also to have danced upon them. Thus Romeo, at the Capulets' ball, mentions that the floor is rush-covered:

. . . Let wantons light of heart
Tickle the senseless rushes with their heels . . . *Romeo and Juliet*
Act I Scene iv.

carrying all the household stuff she needed. She alone enjoyed some measure of privacy; the average Elizabethan shared a bed and lived in public. Even the great house was essentially a public place, crowded with the nobleman's family and friends and servants; and to the central hall and the attached withdrawing-rooms was added an extensive gallery, where, beneath a fretted plaster ceiling, he could walk and talk in foul weather. The Elizabethan constitution demanded regular and vigorous exercise, if the 'vital spirits' were to be kept on the move and the shadows of melancholy held at bay. Activity was the secret of happiness; for most Elizabethans, as for the ancient Athenians, the public existence was the good existence.

Naturally, their active and gregarious trend had a considerable influence on their artistic tastes. The arts they particularly appreciated were usually those which had a social value: poetry, which they could recite or sing; music and the dance, which united a whole company; the drama, which included both poetry and music, and created a world of imagination that every member of the audience could share. To music they had always been deeply sensitive; and the Elizabethan Age was an age of celebrated composers. John Dowland, William Byrd, Orlando Gibbons and John Bull all of them outlived Shakespeare; excepting Dowland, each received the Queen's bounty as a member of the Chapel Royal, where Byrd served for many years, though a pious Catholic and an obstinate recusant; and Bull—another Catholic—travelled widely abroad and achieved a European reputation. 'The chief glory of the Elizabethan musical age (writes a transatlantic historian) was its secular music for voices. This consisted of madrigals for several voices unaccompanied, and ayres for solo voice accompanied by a lute.' From a handbook to *Practicall Musicke*, published by Byrd's pupil Thomas Morley, 'we learn that a well-educated Elizabethan was expected to be able to sing at sight. In the imaginary conversation that forms the framework of the book, one of them confesses that while spending the previous evening at a friend's house, music books were passed about and he had to confess his inability . . .' His friends were incredulous, 'and finally "every one began to wonder, yea some whispered to others, demanding how I was brought up".[1] No such whisperings

[1] Morrison Comegys Boyd: *Elizabethan Music and Musical Criticism*, 1940.

can have been directed at Shakespeare, for whom, as for most of his contemporaries, music was the soul of feeling, the expression of moods and emotions that otherwise might never find utterance, and who refers to music more often and more evocatively than to any of its sister arts.

With a love of music went a passion for the dance, which, according to a gifted minor poet, Sir John Davies, whose long but lively *Orchestra, or A Poem of Dancing* was written about 1594 and published in 1596, sprang from the primeval cosmic dance that had once reconciled the warring elements:

> Dancing, bright lady, then began to be
> When the first seeds whereof the world did spring,
> The fire, air, earth and water did agree
> By Love's persuasion, nature's mighty king,
> To leave their first disorder'd combating . . .

The planets dance; the stars dance; the sun and moon are rhythmic revellers; and their movements were suitably reproduced in the favourite pastimes of the Elizabethan court: the Galliard, 'a swift and wandering dance . . . with passages uncertain, to and fro'; the sliding measures of the Coranto, 'that on a triple dactyl foot do run'; and the impetuous Lavolta—[1]

> A lofty jumping, or a leaping round,
> When arm in arm two dancers are entwin'd,
> And whirl themselves with strict embracements bound,
> And still their feet an anapest do sound . . .

For Davies, the idea of a woman's beauty is linked with the idea of rhythm:

> Love in the twinkling of your eyelids danceth,
> Love danceth in your pulses and your veins . . .

Even her fingers, as they manage her needle-point, cause it to dance as it pierces silk or canvas.

More prosaically considered, dancing helped to mould the body. Actors were taught to 'move in music'; and, besides fencing and

---

[1] Said originally to have been imported from Italy to France by 'night-dancing witches'. Reginald Scot: *The Discoverie of Witchcraft*, 1584.

'riding the great horse', Lord Herbert of Cherbury recommends that his descendants should early enlist the services of an 'accurate' French dancing-master; since that exercise 'gives one a good presence and address to all companies' and 'disposeth the limbs to a kind of *souplesse* (as the Frenchmen call it) . . . insomuch as they seem to have the use of their legs, arms, and bodies, more than any others, who, standing stiff and stark in their postures, seem as if they were taken in their joints . . .' The graces that an Elizabethan gentleman sought to exhibit—they included a knowledge of how to enter and leave a room, 'make courtesies handsomely' and 'how to put off and hold his hat'—were undoubtedly mimicked on the Elizabethan stage; and could we now join a contemporary audience, watching the first performance of a sixteenth-century drama, we should be impressed by the stylised gestures of the cast, by the length and importance of the musical interludes, and by the bouts of expert sword-play—very different from the clumsy rattle-and-clash with which modern actors wield their swords. The whole effect would be far more artificial, far more solemn-sounding and elegantly mannered—except, of course, for the noisy outrageous clowns—than any revival we have yet seen.

Meanwhile, among the writers and composers, a single out-standing painter had emerged. Born in 1547, the son of a prosperous Exeter goldsmith, Nicholas Hilliard reached London at the age of fifteen, was himself apprenticed to the goldsmith's trade—an honoured and extremely profitable branch of Elizabethan craftman-ship—married his employer's daughter and soon afterwards turned his attention from manufacturing cups and jewelled ornaments to producing miniature portraits on card or vellum. His first portrait of the Queen was painted in 1572; and, about 1576, he and his wife Alice paid a long visit to the French capital, where he made the acquaintance of Pierre de Ronsard and became attached to the court of the youthful duc d'Alençon, Elizabeth's pertinacious suitor, whom, despite his pock-marked, bottle-nosed visage, she found an attractive companion and nicknamed tenderly her 'little Frog'. Perhaps it was his stay in France that quickened the development of Hilliard's genius. To his goldsmith's feeling for intricacy and delicacy he added a sureness of touch and a poetic sense of style seldom found among Elizabethan artists; and these qualities were themselves accompanied by his curious insight into human nature. Just as Holbein had immortalized the grim society of early Tudor England, so Hilliard preserved the lineaments of the Elizabethan ruling-class. But how unlike their predecessors—that race of cold-eyed, reptilian *arrivistes*—Hilliard's courtly subjects are! The aristocratic world he represented had begun to temper wealth with elegance; his men and women, for all their spreading finery, wear very often a remote and pensive look; and now and then he inserts an enigmatic symbol that seems to hint at some concealed sorrow.

Again and again, scrutinizing Hilliard's sitters, we recall the dramatis personæ of Shakespeare's comedies. It is always dangerous to attempt to draw a parallel between two completely different arts; but the painter as revealed in his self-portrait, executed at the age of thirty, which shows a dark, alert, gallantly moustachioed face, a velvet cap pushed on the back of the head to disclose a wiry tuft of curls, would have made an admirable Berowne or perhaps a fine Petruchio; and the beautiful Alice Hilliard, whose delicate heart-shaped features, encircled and supported by her fashionable ruff, suggest a flower inside a paper frill, is the perfect image of an accomplished Shakespearian heroine, after she has concluded her wanderings and put aside her boyish travesty. No less suited to a Shakespearian setting are some of Hilliard's unknown characters: the languid youth in long white stockings who leans against a tree-trunk amid a bush of tangled roses; the disconsolate lover (mentioned elsewhere) whose plight is symbolized by a curtain of ascending flames; and the bearded man, no doubt an unhappy widower, who, with an air of mysterious resolution, clasps a feminine hand descending from a cloud. In later life, Hilliard composed an essay, entitled *A Treatise on the Arte of Limninge*,[1] which tells us much about his aims and methods. Painting is a calling 'fittest for gentlemen'; and the gentlemanly painter should avoid strenuous bodily exercise and all undue excitement. Silk should be his only wear; his utensils should be scrupulously clean; and he should pay careful attention to every change in his sitter's private mood, when he seeks to catch the 'lovely graces, witty smilings and . . . stolen glances' that suddenly

---

[1] Hilliard did not sign his manuscript. It has been attributed to him, however, on what appears to be good evidence. See Erna Auerbach: *Nicholas Hilliard*, 1961.

flit across the human countenance as summer lightning flashes across the sky. The limner, he insists, should be a shrewd psychologist, and study both the outward likeness and the secret movement of the mind and soul.

Hilliard, however, had no immediate English rivals: Isaac Oliver, an almost equally gifted miniaturist, was a Norman Frenchman who had settled down in London. Otherwise Elizabethan painting remained a craft rather than an imaginative art; and very little that could properly be described as sculpture was produced throughout the whole reign. The sumptuous elaboration of English court-life— the antique ceremonial that surrounded the Queen's person, her rich attire and fantastic jewellery, the massy gold plate that loaded her table—often dazzled foreign eyes; but, should the visitor have come from Rome or Florence, the Venetian Republic or one of the ducal courts of Northern Italy, he may have reflected that, compared with an Italian palace, Whitehall, Greenwich, Nonsuch, Oatlands, though large, complex and pretentious buildings, made a somewhat poor display. No great painters had been called in to decorate their walls and roofs; their cabinets enclosed no precious bronzes; none of their fountains upheld a Cupid, a Mercury or a group of naked graces, created by a Donatello, a Verrocchio, even a Benvenuto Cellini. Huge heraldic beasts, decorative sundials and lavishly jewelled clocks advertised the royal owner's wealth and state; and most of the palaces among which the Queen moved had been inherited from her extravagant father, who had imported Italian and French craftsmen to build Nonsuch in a Gothic-Renaissance style that seems nowadays to have combined the special faults of both periods. The entire facade was smothered with ornament, either in plasterwork or in carved slate, representing 'kings, Caesars, sciences, gods'; and 'the invincible King Henry' faced the main gatehouse, seated upon a curule throne, 'treading underfoot a maned lion . . .'[1]

For over five hundred years, the oddities and anomalies of the English world have bewildered Continental critics; and the idea that the English were a race apart had its origins in the Elizabethan Age. Then the Englishman seems first to have emerged as a strange, distinctive type, the inhabitant of 'half an island' that had challenged

---

[1] Henry VIII's chief architectural employee was an Italian exile, Nicholas da Modena. See 'Nonsuch Palace', by Martin Biddle, *History Today*, March, 1961.

the united power of Catholic Europe, absurdly vain, inordinately rich, devoted to his outlandish conceits and customs. Particularly remarkable was his insular arrogance. The highest praise that an Englishman could bestow on a foreigner, noted a Venetian envoy, consisted of the grudging admission that he might almost have been English-born. Yet these bigoted, bellicose islanders were eagerly appreciative of Continental modes; they liked to adopt French and Italian fashions—a weakness their own poets ridiculed[1]—usually with rather bad results; and, according to an old saying, the Italian-ate Englishman became a fiend in human guise. But, for all their rough, unruly habits, they did not undervalue the minor graces of life; they kept large, luxurious households; and they 'excelled', we are informed, 'in music and dancing', whereas their neighbours were specially versed in fencing and the management of horses. More-over, they were a peculiarly effusive race; and Erasmus had already recorded, when he visited England during the reign of Henry VIII, that his hosts had a disconcerting way of showering kisses on him in and out of season, young and pretty girls just as unselfconsciously as sober matrons and respectable men of letters.

If the Elizabethan surprised his foreign contemporaries, he also surprises his twentieth-century offspring. Between the modern Englishman and his emotional, garrulous, music-loving ancestors is there any real link? National characters change; and, since the con-clusion of the sixteenth century, the Anglo-Saxon temperament would appear to have changed beyond all recognition. As a people, we are no longer devoted to music and, unlike the Elizabethans, now attach an exaggerated importance to our domestic privacy. For the pleasure of talking and hearing others talk, we have ceased to congregate in public places, as did Elizabethan Londoners, who caused the nave of medieval St Paul's to reverberate with their incessant buzz:[2] Mercutio, though given an Italian background, was

[1] Report of fashions in proud Italy,
Whose manners still our tardy apish nation
Limps after in base imitation
King Richard II Act II Scene i.

[2] The Elizabethans, according to foreign observers, like modern Italians loved noise for its own sake. As Hentzner noted, they were 'vastly fond of great noises that fill the ear, such as the firing of cannon, drums, and the ringing of bells, so that it is common for a number of them, that have got a glass in their heads, to go up into some belfry and ring the bells for hours together for the sake of exercise.' Paul Hentzner, *op. cit.*

plainly based upon some London wit, perhaps a denizen of one of the Inns of Court or a member of the Essex-Southampton circle. But what puzzles us most about the Elizabethan character is its blend of contradictory qualities, and the ease with which these qualities were reconciled in the lives of individual human beings. Evidently it was a grasping, acquisitive age, and, at least among members of the Established Church, seldom visited by other-worldly passions. Elizabeth's bishops were sound administrators and capable disciplinarians rather than men of strong religious feeling; and not until the seventeenth century did England produce a series of inspired devotional poets, the splendid line that begins with John Donne and comes to an end with Henry Vaughan. Yet Ralegh himself, nominally a Protestant but denounced by his opponents as a devilish atheist, during his later years proclaimed his belief in the existence of a transcendental God, towards whom all human reason strives, just as all the streams and rivers of the globe hurry towards the great ocean; while from Man's possession of certain redeeming 'faculties'—hope, faith, love and joy—which he can never fully realize on earth, since they 'acquiesce only in the perfect, eternal, and infinite', Herbert of Cherbury deduced that they must be intended by the Creator for use upon the supernatural plane. 'I appeal to everybody,' he wrote, 'whether any worldly felicity did so satisfy their hope here, that they did not wish and hope for something more excellent . . . whether they could place their love on any earthly beauty, that it did not fade and wither, if not frustrate or deceive them, or whether their joy was so consummate . . . that they did not wish much more than it . . . The proper object of these faculties therefore . . . is God only . . .'[1] Both Ralegh and Herbert of Cherbury seem at heart to have been philosophic deists—ambitious courtier-poets who loved and admired the world, but whose restless appetite for life had provoked a deeper restlessness that no sublunary reward could ever quite appease.

[1] Herbert of Cherbury, *op. cit.*

CHAPTER IV

Early Poems

A TYPICAL ACHIEVEMENT of its period is the Elizabethan great house. Often built to resemble a giant E, sometimes topped by a file of huge three-dimensional stone letters, which as they march around the parapet spell out a punning Latin motto, its massive and complex fabric is almost always rich in symbolism. Just as charged with literary meaning are many details of the vast interior. From the lofty chimney-pieces, the carved screen that completes the hall and the ribbon of plaster bas-reliefs that surround the state apartments, look down a fantastic parade of allegorical or mythological beings—divinities and demi-divinities, muses, satyrs, fauns and nymphs, among homelier hybrid figures, half classical and half contemporary. In their English surroundings, they rarely seem quite at home: they appear embarrassed by their own naked flesh; their limbs are squat and heavily muscled; and their broad-cheeked, big-eyed faces are apt to wear a slightly doltish smile. Since they left their native southern landscape, they have travelled far and suffered much; but, although they have kept little of their antique elegance, they retain a faint aura of their distant Grecian past and suggest how deeply that past had stirred the Elizabethan mind. The intrepid navigators of the New World were also re-discovering Rome and Hellas; and the chief guide who led the Elizabethans back into the miraculous territories of Graeco-Roman legend, where the Graces danced, the fatal Sirens sang, and the god, pursuing a nymph, clasped a swathe of reeds or embraced a branch of fragrant laurel, was the Augustan erotic poet Publius Ovidius Naso, now recognized as the prince of lyricists and the main source of ancient lore and fancy.

When the Elizabethans learned to enjoy his verse, he had held that position for several hundred years. The grim interregnum of the [Dark Ages had temporarily obscured his fame—it had been over-shadowed by the legend of the renowned magician Virgil; but towards the beginning of the twelfth century Ovid had returned in triumph, as the favourite poet of the Goliards, or medieval wander-ing scholars, who carried his reputation from court to court, and filled their lubricious canticles with Ovidian tags and references. Thus began the *aetas Ovidiana*, during which a French doctor was burned to death because, amid other heretical precepts, he had asserted that God had spoken through Ovid no less than through Augustine. Simultaneously, the *Metamorphoses* became a recommended school-book; Christian artists adopted him, and scenes he had described were sculptured round the doors of Chartres Cathedral. Chaucer celebrates 'Venus clerke, Ovyde', and assigns him a statue in his *House of Fame*; while both Boccaccio and Petrarch, the latter the acknowledged master of Surrey and Wyatt, were his impassioned votaries. In 1560, his story of Narcissus was first translated into English verse; and it was followed by Arthur Golding's translation of the *Metamorphoses* between 1565 and 1567. Thenceforward the dissipated Roman dandy, with his 'well-bred, well-natured, amorous and libertine' nature, his 'wonderful facility and clearness',[1] his deep knowledge of the human passions and his gift of depicting the passions in vivid, sensuous, dramatic images, achieved the final conquest of every educated Elizabethan reader. Not only did scholars discuss him, poets study and copy him, and schoolboys construe and obediently memorize his lines;[2] but pastry-cooks produced mythological centre-pieces, illustrating Ovidian episodes —Daphne and Apollo, Pan and Syrinx—for their cultured employers' dinner-tables.

Sweetness was a quality the Elizabethans valued; and Ovid was pre-eminently sweet. Nor were they averse from his over-sweetness and the touches of baroque elaboration with which he loaded his poetic pictures. He liberated the imagination of the age, taught

---

[1] See Dryden's comparison of Ovid and Chaucer.

[2] As early as 1530, boys at Winchester were expected to learn a dozen lines a week. For this, and for many other interesting details, see L. P. Wilkinson: *Ovid Recalled*, 1935.

the senses to understand their freedom, showed his admirers glimpses of a world in which pleasure was untouched by a conviction of sin. Here beauty was not a badge of virtue, but its own justification and its own reward. Ovid fostered the growing aestheticism of the Elizabethan temperament, which had not yet quite succeeded in shaking off the restrictive effects of its medieval education. What Machiavelli did on the plane of political thought, Ovid helped to do upon the plane of literature; and each of these rebellious spirits was welcomed and cherished by Christopher Marlowe, who, besides studying *The Prince*, translated the *Amores*. More important, about 1593—he had been granted a bachelor's degree in 1584—he composed his *Hero and Leander*,[1] the most successful of English Ovidian poems. Musaeus[2] provided the groundwork; but Ovid supplied the general colouring; and the result was the lavishly decorative work that George Chapman concluded after Marlowe's death, adding four new sestiads—compared with his friends' verse, ponderous and sententious stuff—in which he rounded off the lovers' story.

Shakespeare seems to have read the manuscript and fallen immediately beneath its spell[3]—he was always appreciative of other men's gifts, and quick to grasp the possibilities of any new poetic form; and during the same year he published his own ambitious counterpart, *Venus and Adonis*, a quarto volume, 'imprinted by Richard Field . . . to be sold at the sign of the White Greyhound in Paul's Churchyard'. Presumably he was following Marlowe's lead; but he handled his Ovidian subject matter in a very different and much less practised style; for, whereas Marlowe appears to be perfectly at his ease in the baroque pseudo-classical scenes his imagination conjured up—in Hero's rose-strewn chamber above the Hellespont and the fabulous sanctuary where she serves as priestess—

So fair a church as this had Venus none:
The walls were of discolour'd jasper-stone,

[1] It remained unpublished until 1598.
[2] This Greek author of the fourth or fifth century AD was identified by the Elizabethans with the pupil of Orpheus, 'whose verses had the authority of oracles'.
[3] Shakespeare's reference to Marlowe as the 'dead shepherd', followed by a one-line quotation from *Hero and Leander*, was made in *As You Like It* after the publication of the poem; but there are also references in *Love's Labour's Lost*, probably written before 1594.

G

> Wherein was Proteus carv'd; and over-head
> A lively vine of green sea-agate spread . . .

—Shakespeare never grows quite acclimatized to the landscape
through which Adonis flees from his greedy Cytherean persecutor;
and he is at his happiest when the background of the poem most
clearly recalls some familiar English prospect. If we knew nothing
else of Shakespeare's achievement, what are the inferences we
should draw about the poet's life and tastes? That he had studied
Ovid, of course, either in the original or in the current English
rendering; but that the experience, though no doubt enjoyable, had
not yet penetrated the deeper layers of his poetic consciousness. That
he was more interested in the everyday modern world, than in the
exotic flora and fauna of classical mythology; and that he was a
country-bred Englishman, devoted to country sports and rustic
sights and sounds, who understood the points of a good horse—or
had friends who were fond of discussing the horses they bred—and
had sometimes risen early to follow a pack of harriers on foot across
his native fields. To these images he often returns, apparently with
some relief, when he is a little tired of the amorous goddess and her
unaccountably reluctant victim; and such passages have a poetic
strength for which we look in vain among surrounding stanzas. Even
the observations he had gathered in the stable-yard are put to
admirable literary use:

> Look when a painter would surpass the life
> In limning out a well proportioned steed,
> His art with nature's workmanship at strife,
> As if the dead the living should exceed;
> So did this horse excel a common one
> In shape, in courage, colour, pace, and bone.

> Round-hoof'd, short-jointed, fetlocks shag and long,
> Broad breast, full eye, small head and nostril wide,
> High crest, short ears, straight legs and passing strong,
> Thin mane, thick tail, broad buttock, tender hide;
> Look, what a horse should have he did not lack,
> Save a proud rider on so proud a back.

The expert, however, is also a man of feeling, who has the poetic gift of identifying his own emotions with the life of the creature that he contemplates. He loves the proud stallion for its strength and valour and beauty, its hide burnished by sun and air, its shining wind-blown mane and tail—

> Through his mane and tail the high wind sings,
> Fanning the hairs, who wave like feath'red wings

—and he sympathises with the beast when its pride is humbled, and the restive mare it has been courting spurns at its love and scorns its heat—

> Then, like a melancholy malcontent,
> He vails his tail, that, like a falling plume,
> Cool shadow to his melting buttock lent;
> He stamps, and bites the poor flies in his fume.

Just as sympathetic and expertly detailed is the celebrated description of the hunted hare, doubling and turning and feinting as it flits ahead of men and hounds:

> And when thou hast on foot the purblind hare,
> Mark the poor wretch, to overshoot his troubles,
> How he outruns the wind, and with what care
> He cranks and crosses with a thousand doubles . . .
> By this, poor Wat, far off upon a hill,
> Stands on his hinder legs with list'ning ear,
> To hearken if his foes pursue him still;
> Anon their loud alarums he doth hear;
> And now his grief may be compared well
> To one sore sick that hears the passing-bell.

But the sportsman, who follows the hare to its death, had his contemplative and sedentary moods. Now and then, his face close to the earth, he has teased a snail upon a blade of grass—

> As the snail, whose tender horns being hit,
> Shrinks backward in his shelly cave with pain,
> And there, all smoth'red up, in shade doth sit,
> Long after fearing to creep forth again . . .

—and from the banks of a shallow English river has watched the timid, elusive little grebe[1]—

> Like a dive-dapper peering through a wave,
> Who, being look'd on, ducks as quickly in . . .

Another deduction the reader might possibly make is that this practical, countrified, sport-loving poet felt comparatively little interest in the romantic commerce of the sexes. *Venus and Adonis*, based on a story taken from the tenth book of Ovid's *Metamorphoses*, of which Richard Field had printed a handsome edition only four years earlier, is designed as an erotic poem, dealing with the struggle between love and chastity, between Venus the Queen of Love and the obstinate youth whom her passion cannot subdue. Yet its erotic content is remarkably slight; it has a minimal effect upon the modern reader's senses, and, at least in so far as its subject is love or lust, seldom touches his imagination. Shakespeare's Venus is an awkward divinity, better at delivering long euphuistic speeches than at exerting her seductive powers. The attack she launches against the young man's virtue soon develops into an extended rhetorical debate; and when, his ears afire, he presently breaks away—

> Mine ears that to your wanton talk attended
> Do burn themselves for having so offended—

he leaves Venus lying lumpishly on her back like a discontented country girl:

> With this, he breaketh from the sweet embrace
> Of those fair arms which bound him to her breast,
> And homeward through the dark laund runs apace;
> Leaves Love upon her back, deeply distress'd.

Very different is the effect of *Hero and Leander*, one of the most whole-hearted tributes to the force and beauty of desire yet produced by any English poet.[2] Hero's movements are swift and spontaneous as those of Venus are conventional and clumsy:

[1] Otherwise known as the dabchick, according to Carew 'so named of his diving and littleness'. To dap is defined by the O.E.D. as 'to dip lightly or suddenly into water'.

[2] By contemporaries, nevertheless, the two poems were thought to have an equally erotic effect; and they are described in a play as 'two luscious marrow-bone pies for a young married wife'. Marrow bones were regarded as an aphrodisiac.

Where both deliberate, the love is slight:
Who ever lov'd, that lov'd not at first sight?
He kneel'd; but unto her devoutly pray'd:
Chaste Hero to herself thus softly said,
'Were I the saint he worships, I would hear him' . . .

Later, when Leander revisits her room, she flies towards him on a sudden gust of joy:

She stay'd not for her robes, but straight arose,
And, drunk with gladness, to the door she goes . . .

Then, after all the decorative discursions that ornament Marlowe's earlier passages—the elaborate picture of 'Venus' church', and of the 'sapphire-visag'd god' who emerges to delay Leander's progress—we reach the 'right true end of love' and the poignant climax of a beautiful, unedifying tale:

Even as a bird, which in our hands we wring,
Forth plungeth, and often flutters with her wing,
She trembling strove: this strife of hers, like that
Which made the world, another world begat
Of unknown joy. Treason was in her thought,
And cunningly to yield herself she sought . . .
Leander now, like Theban Hercules,
Enter'd the orchard of th'Hesperides;
Whose fruit none rightly can describe, but he
That pulls or shakes it from the golden tree.
Wherein Leander, on her quivering breast,
Breathless spoke something, and sigh'd out the rest . . .

There is nothing as direct, moving or realistic as this in the whole extent of *Venus and Adonis*, which reminds us of the mythological motifs employed by Elizabethan architects, or of a piece of contemporary needlework, a heavily embroidered valance, that illustrates the same legend and shows Venus and her attendant nymphs wearing ruffs and farthingales.[1] Perhaps his theme was uncongenial to the poet. Looking back across a period of eleven years, towards the summer of 1582, he may have remembered how he himself had once unhappily played Adonis, with an older woman in the part of Venus;

[1] Now in the Victoria & Albert Museum.

and that experience and its inconvenient results may have prejudiced Anne Shakespeare's husband against the greedy Female
Principle. Alternatively, he may perhaps have been influenced by the
private situation, involving a beloved youth and a desired, detested
woman, that he was soon to outline when he came to write his
sonnets. Certainly, *Venus and Adonis* is an immature poem, a calculated piece of literary invention. Yet it enjoyed a lasting popular
success; and from the moment when copies of the quarto volume
were first put on sale under the sign of the White Greyhound in
St Paul's Churchyard, the author's fame began to grow, particularly at the Universities and the Inns of Court, where before long
ardent young men would sleep with *Venus and Adonis* beneath their
pillows, hang his picture on their study walls, and acclaim 'sweet
Mr Shakespeare' as the modern Ovid, the victorious rival of Chaucer
and Spenser. Like Swinburne's *Poems and Ballads*, it had an agree-
ably disturbing effect upon the imaginations of the 'younger sort';
and it continued to charm them, Gabriel Harvey tells us, at a time
when the older and 'wiser sort' preferred to read its immediate
successor or the poet's adult plays.

A young man's poem, though the product of a poet who, by
Elizabethan standards, had now reached the threshold of middle age,
Venus and Adonis—which Shakespeare entitles 'the first heir of my
invention', thus formally distinguishing it from all his previous
literary efforts—was dedicated 'to the Right Honourable Henry
Wriothesley, Earl of Southampton, and Baron of Titchfield', the
handsome twenty-year-old courtier who had recently made his mark
in the innermost circle of the Queen's attendants. Complimentary
yet not unduly effusive, Shakespeare's dedication would appear to
suggest that his patron, if not yet a friend, was at least a supporter he
already trusted:

RIGHT HONOURABLE

I know not how I shall offend in dedicating my unpolished lines
to your Lordship, nor how the world will censure me for choosing

---

[1] Gabriel Harvey (1545?-1630), poet, miscellaneous writer and controversialist,
Spenser's 'Hobbinol', arch-enemy of Greene and Nashe, inscribed his tribute on the
fly-leaf of a copy of Chaucer: 'The younger sort takes much delight in Shakespeare's
Venus and Adonis; but his *Lucrece*, and his Tragedy of *Hamlet, Prince of Denmark*, have
it in them to please the wiser sort.'

so strong a prop to support so weak a burthen, only if your
Honour seem but pleased, I account myself highly praised, and
vow to take advantage of all idle hours, till I have honoured you
with some graver labour. But if the first heir of my invention
prove deformed, I shall be sorry it had so noble a godfather: and
never after ear so barren a land, for fear it yield me still so bad a
harvest . . .

Your Honour's in all duty,

WILLIAM SHAKESPEARE

Evidently, Southampton was pleased with the poem—and, perhaps, in the way of aristocratic patrons, even more pleased with the
credit he derived from having sponsored so popular and fashionable
a book; for, a year later, he received a second dedication, this time
attached to *The Rape of Lucrece*, another quarto volume, again
'printed by Richard Field . . . to be sold at the sign of the White
Greyhound'. But between the dedications there is a significant
contrast: the author of *Lucrece* is no longer modest and tentative,
and adopts the tone of a devoted friend:

The love I dedicate to your Lordship is without end: whereof
this Pamphlet without beginning is but a superfluous Moiety. The
warrant I have of your Honourable disposition, not the worth of
my untutored Lines makes it assured of acceptance. What I have
done is yours, what I have to do is yours, being part in all I have,
devoted yours. Were my worth greater, my duty would show
greater; meantime, as it is, it is bound to your Lordship; to whom
I wish long life still lengthened with all happiness.

Yet, oddly enough, despite the experience he had gained, *Lucrece*
itself does not compare very well with its triumphant predecessor.
But once more it proved extremely successful among the cultivated
'younger sort'; during the year of its publication, an elegist who
signed himself W. Har,[1] accords 'you that have writ of chaste
Lucretia' a place among our greater poets; while, during 1595, 'All
praiseworthy. Lucrecia sweet Shakespeare', observed William Cowell
in a note printed on the margin of his *Polimanteia*. For the apprecia-

---

[1] Among the claimants are William Harvey, Southampton's future step-father, and a
curious minor poet named William Harbert.

tive Elizabethan critic, this frigid production was full of warmth and life; and he found in it not only voluptuous appeal but a sound lesson in conventional morality. Today we sympathize with the judgement of William Hazlitt, who likened both *Venus and Adonis* and *The Rape of Lucrece* to 'a couple of ice-houses . . . as hard, as glittering, and as cold'. Shakespeare, he wrote, was apparently 'all the time thinking of his verses, and not of his subject—not of what his characters would feel, but of what he shall say . . . The whole is laboured uphill work . . . Sentiment is built upon plays of words; the hero or heroine feels, not from the impulse of passion, but from the force of dialectics. There is besides a strange attempt to substitute the language of painting for that of poetry . . .' Although the theme of the story is one of lust and lawless violence—an outburst of violent passion, followed by wild remorse and guilty fear—the cumulative effect that it produces is pictorial rather than emotional, and we read it much as we examine the story that runs around the tapestried walls of an Elizabethan bed-chamber.

Shakespeare himself may presently have learned to smile at the naïve extravagances of his early method. Elizabethan poets were fond of apostrophizing Night, parent of evil and cloak of sin; and Lucretia, having been briefly ravished, rails lengthily upon the satanic power of Darkness:

> O comfort-killing Night, image of hell!
> Dim register and notary of shame!
> Black stage for tragedies and murders fell!
> Vast sin-concealing chaos! nurse of blame!
> Blind muffled bawd! dark harbour for defame! . . .
>
> O hateful, vaporous and foggy night!
> Since thou art guilty of my cureless crime,
> Muster thy mists to meet the eastern light,
> Make war against proportion'd course of time . . .

Later, when he was writing *A Midsummer Night's Dream*, and parodying contemporary poetic jargon in the mouths of Bottom and his stage-struck cronies, the poet recollected that aggrieved apostrophe and gave it an endearing comic twist:

8 An Elizabethan court beauty: Mary Fitton. She wears a wheel-top farthingale and the fashionable 'cannon sleeves'. Her necklace is of pearls and rubies

10 Robert Devereux, Earl of Essex. Essex is shown in later life, wearing the beard that he grew during his victorious expedition to Cadiz

9 (*left*) An Elizabethan great house: Hardwick Hall, Derbyshire, the east front

11 William Cecil, 1st Lord Burghley, Elizabeth's trusted minister and Essex's most dangerous opponent

12 Robert Cecil, 1st Earl of Salisbury. Like his father, an expert bureaucrat, 'trained to manage the secret machinery of government'

O grim-looked night! O night with hue so black!
O night, which ever art when day is not:
O night, O night, alack, alack, alack,
I fear my Thisby's promise is forgot.

Every educated Elizabethan reader had received a thorough
training in the art of rhetoric; and just as masterly, from a sixteenth-
century standpoint, as Shakespeare's long descriptive passages—
Lucrece, an exquisite piece of human confectionery, her golden
locks, her blue-veined skin, and her hand, bedewed with pearly
beads of sweat, daisy-white upon the green quilt; Tarquin, that 'foul
night-waking' tom, at whose ominous apparition the 'wandering
weasels' shriek in fear—were the cunningly antithetical stanzas by
which these pictures are supported and enclosed:

But she hath lost a dearer thing than life,
And he hath won what he would lose again.
This forced league doth force a further strife,
This momentary joy breeds months of pain,
This hot desire converts to cold disdain;
Pure Chastity is rifled of her store,
And Lust, the thief, far poorer than before.

With the publication of *Venus and Adonis* and *The Rape of
Lucrece*, Shakespeare had at length completed the first stage of his
poetic journey. The unknown literary artisan had become—or was
now well on the way to becoming—a fashionable and widely-read
poet; and he appears to have owed his success partly to the fact that
he had been cut off for many months from his usual source of
revenue. At the beginning of the year 1593, the plague had again
attacked London; and towards the end of January so many deaths
were reported that the Council, besides ordering that all infected
households should be locked in and kept under constant watch,
prohibited every kind of public assembly and ordered the theatres to
shut their doors. The actors were either thrown out of work or
obliged to tour provincial districts; and Shakespeare, with time
on his hands and still a family to maintain at Stratford, may have
looked around him for some new employment that would occupy

him until the epidemic ceased. Luckily—he was always a fortunate man—at about the same moment he evidently met his young patron. How the meeting occurred, we cannot tell; but Southampton loved poets and poetry, and is known to have been an enthusiastic playgoer; and no doubt he had already explored the lively world behind the scenes. Hitherto it had circumscribed the poet: Southampton appeared as an emissary from the larger world of power and privilege. He was also an exceedingly attractive youth, with the disarming self-assurance of a born seducer.

At this, as at every stage of his existence, the great majority of statements that we make about Shakespeare's character and private life must be made in a conditional form. If, however—to follow the customary practice—he had a genuine regard for the aristocratic young man who accepted the dedication of his early poems, and if, between 1593 and 1594, from having been a literary client the poet became a devoted personal friend, he must very soon have encountered Southampton's closest ally, the even more magnificent Earl of Essex. If, again, he was peculiarly susceptible to the charm of gallant, handsome young patricians, he would almost certainly have been drawn towards this dominant and splendid figure. It may be argued that an aspiring actor-poet was unlikely to associate on familiar terms with one of the highest noblemen of the Elizabethan Court. But then, Essex, we are told, was proud of 'living popularly'; enemies and friends alike were impressed by his democratic manners; and Shakespeare himself, in Richard II's account of his seductive rival Bollingbroke, appears to have left us a detailed description of how he solicited the approval of the London crowds:

> Ourself and Bushy
> Observed his courtship of the common people,
> How he did seem to dive into their hearts,
> With humble and familiar courtesy . . .
> Off goes his bonnet to an oyster-wench,
> A brace of draymen bid God speed him well,
> And had the tribute of his supple knee,
> With 'Thanks, my countrymen, my loving friends'
> As were our England in reversion his,

And he our subjects' next degree in hope.[1]

Shakespeare, I believe, presently experienced the attraction not only of Southampton but of Essex, and both in his prime, when he was writing his historical plays and his romantic comedies, and in his later life—the 'Dark Period'—after he had turned to deeply tragic themes, they had jointly an important influence upon the formation of his poetic gifts. When he wrote the dedication of *Venus and Adonis*, Essex was in his twenty-seventh year. Related to the sovereign by blood through his mother, the fiery and irrepressible Lettice Knollys,[2] he had been conspicuous among her attendants since the age of seventeen; for it was in 1584, as the stepson of Leicester, the once-powerful royal favourite whose hold over Elizabeth was now declining, that the tall, distinguished, fair-haired youth had first made his bow at Whitehall, where his 'goodly person, and a kind of urbanity and innate courtesy', soon aroused the Queen's interest. By the end of the decade, he was beginning to occupy the post that Leicester had so long held. During her expeditions, wrote a court-gossip, Anthony Bagot, in May 1587, nobody approached the sovereign 'but my L. of Essex; and, at night, my Lord is at cards, or at one game or another with her, that he cometh not to his own lodging till the birds sing in the morning'. He would never entirely lose his power; the Queen's affection would never wholly vanish, though it was qualified, as time went on, by growing suspicion and resentment; but, having conquered his mistress' heart, he dreamed of achieving a unique authority. These visions, noble enough in their way, ultimately led him to complete disaster.

Meanwhile his position at Court was not maintained without intense effort. Of his many foes, none was more dangerous and more persuasive than his arch-opponent Walter Ralegh, whom latter-day admirers have often represented as the very soul of Elizabethan

[1] *Richard II* Act I Scene iv. A similar, but more hostile, account is provided by a contemporary satirist, Guilpin, in his *Skialetheia*, 1598:

> For when great *Felix*, passing through the street,
> Vaileth his cap to each one he doth meet,
> And when no broom-man that will pray for him,
> Shall have less truage than his bonnet's brim;
> Who would not think him perfect courtesy?
> Or the honeysuckle of humility?

[2] His grandmother, wife of Sir Francis Knollys, had been the sister of Queen Anne Boleyn.

virtue, but whom many of his contemporaries regarded as the type of modern Machiavel, arrogant, unscrupulous, cruel-hearted, probably a philosophic atheist and, through the commercial monopolies he exploited, allegedly a ruthless 'skinner of the poor'. Like Essex, in the siege he laid to the Queen, he made use both of his physical charm and of his fascinating literary gifts; the struggle of personalities was also a conflict of eloquence; and, whereas Essex preferred to attack in prose, employing the boldest and best-turned hyperboles that his imagination could conceive, Ralegh generally assaulted in verse, in a lengthy series of fervent love-poems, expressing his passionate attachment to the Queen's person or bewailing an inexplicable loss of favour.

Nearly as dangerous, from Essex's point of view, was the opposition of the Cecils—William, first Lord Burghley, the shrewd, resolute middle-class statesman who spent four decades in the management of the Queen's affairs, and his younger son Robert, afterwards first Earl of Salisbury, who had inherited his cunning and patience and devotedly industrious nature, and who, as Secretary of State, became Elizabeth's premier civil servant. Throughout his adult existence, Essex was engaged in a perpetual strife against these two opposing groups—the Cecils, prosaic bureaucrats, trained to manage the secret machinery of government, and the Ralegh clique, who shared his interests and ambitions, and, whether at Whitehall or abroad in the wars, were determined to defeat him on his own ground. The chances of the struggle constantly varied; sometimes Ralegh and Essex pretended to forget their quarrel and agreed to swear a firm friendship; sometimes the Cecils, overawed by Essex's martial renown, sought to placate him with conciliatory advances—the Earl's 'matchless merit', reported Anthony Bacon in 1596, 'hath made the Old Fox to crouch and whine, and to insinuate himself by a very submissive letter . . .' But at no stage could Essex claim that he had yet scored a single lasting triumph; and, as the years elapsed, his anxieties and hatreds acquired the strength of a corroding passion. He was rarely at peace; he could not sufficiently excel; he must go on feverishly pursuing power and wealth and popular applause— always conscious that whatever advantage he gained his opponents, crafty and watchful, would do their best to snatch away.

Nor was he happy in his relations with the Queen, the central source from whom all power flowed. She loved him; but she did not trust him, as, for instance, she had learned to trust Cecil. He revered her and affected to worship her, a divinity among mortal women on whose smiles his worthless life depended; but his inborn impatience and irritability quite unfitted him for the difficult role he played, and he was constantly revolting against the state of domestic servitude to which Elizabeth had chosen to reduce her court. Physically speaking, he may not have been her lover, despite those extended conferences in her private apartments, from which he emerged as dawn was breaking above the palace roofs and the earliest birds began to sing —when Essex was twenty, Elizabeth was fifty-four; and, although she had experienced some strong physical attractions, her attitude towards the commerce of the sexes had always been ambiguous. But their relationship was plainly lover-like, since it gave birth to passionate storms of jealousy; and beneath their affection lay a fund of antagonism that sometimes exploded into ugly public scenes. If she was willing enough that he should do himself credit, she was also unwilling to allow him to leave her sight; and no sooner had he bidden her farewell, and hurried off in pursuit of martial glory, than she would cancel her previous orders and proceed at once to call him back. Evidently, she needed his presence; but, not without reason, she had grown to suspect his character. She knew him for a rash, unruly spirit; and she understood that such a spirit as his might one day threaten her autocratic rule. She believed, nevertheless, that, because she loved him, she might yet succeed in taming him, in 'breaking him of his will' and 'pulling down his great heart'; and for many years she continued alternately to raise his hopes and circumvent his plans. She was his inspiration, a cherished royal mistress; at the same time, a sternly suspicious guardian, slow to acknowledge his devoted services, quick to castigate the smallest failure.

By 1594, the year that saw the publication of *The Rape of Lucrece*, Essex had already made his name as a dashing and courageous commander in the field. Four years earlier, his clandestine marriage to the widow of Sir Philip Sidney—daughter of Sir Francis Walsingham, 'Mr Secretary' before Robert Cecil—had cost him several months of disgrace, since any favourite rash enough to wed invariably felt the Queen's displeasure. But in 1591, after he had pleaded with her on his knees and his entreaties had been thrice refused, she permitted him to leave England, to join the armies of the Protestant King of France, the mercurial Henri of Navarre, then battling with his Catholic subjects. If Essex and his contingent brought little real help, undoubtedly they added to the external splendour of the campaign and enlivened the dreary story of sieges and skirmishes with a gleam of high chivalric daring. On Essex's first campaign, in the Low Countries, when he was eighteen years old, Sir Philip Sidney, about to die of his wounds, had bequeathed his 'best sword' to his 'beloved and much honoured' friend; and, besides marrying Sir Philip's relict, Essex had accepted this symbolic heritage. Yet, although he displayed both courage and energy, his weakness was that he treated warfare as a game. He had a propensity for issuing personal challenges; and, during the siege of Rouen, he dared the governor of the town to meet him in an individual trial of strength, when (he proclaimed) 'I will maintain that the King's quarrel is juster than the League's, and that my mistress is fairer than yours'. That same year, having decided to visit the French king, from whom the English forces were at the moment cut off, he had executed a headlong dash through thirty miles of Catholic territory; and, when he reached Henri's outposts with no baggage and but a single clean shirt, he had not only conducted military discussions but had feasted and danced and joined the cheerful French court in an al fresco leaping match, where, being young and athletic, the English visitor 'did over-leap them all'. Such escapades failed to amuse his sovereign, who censured his ridiculous lack of caution and referred sharply to time and money wasted.

Early in 1592, he had been ordered home: '*ce seigneur* [noted the French envoy], *en s'embarquant pour l'Angleterre, tira son épée, et en baisa la lame.*' But, when the summons originally caught him up, he had exploded in a furious burst of temper, and his chest had swelled with impatience and indignation, so that 'all the buttons of his doublet brake away as though they had been cut with a knife'. The story of his rage and despair, which, no doubt, was widely reported, may perhaps have lingered on in Shakespeare's memory;

for, later, portraying a very different, but equally rash and desperate, hero, he makes a companion describe how Antony had broken the buckles of his Roman corselet:

> . . . His captain's heart,
> Which in the scuffles of great fights hath burst
> The buckles on his breast . . .

Recalled home, obedient but restive, Essex devoted himself to politics with the same intemperate energy he had brought to war; and, between 1592 and 1596, he laboured to build up his political strength. The older generation of the Queen's counsellors were rapidly disappearing from the stage. True, Burghley still clung to life; but he was an infirm and aged man; and Robert Cecil was a delicate hunchback who might not long survive his father. Into the promised political vacuum Essex now prepared to move. He had many diplomatic advisers, among whom was a writer and thinker of genius—Francis Bacon, nephew to Burghley, son of Sir Nicholas Bacon, Elizabeth's Keeper of the Great Seal, a young lawyer with his way to make in the world, but aggrieved by what he considered his cautious uncle's lack of family feeling. During his youth, Bacon had announced that he had 'taken all knowledge to be my province'. As an aspiring politician, however, he was not averse from worldy compromise. 'We are much beholden to Machiavel and others [he remarked with a brave display of candour] that wrote what men do, and not what they ought to do. For it is not possible to join serpentine wisdom with the columbine simplicity, except men know all the conditions of the serpent.' Bacon's serpentine voice was often heard in Essex's counsels. Let him seek that 'domestical greatness' which had once belonged to Leicester! His puissant stepfather had set him a high example, a favourite who had not only served but ruled; and Essex, being a kinsman of the Queen, was doubly qualified to fill his place. Yet, while he advanced his own designs, Bacon liked to assure himself that the welfare of the kingdom was his chief interest; and afterwards, when he was concerned to justify his behaviour, he explained that he had at that time—mistakenly, he agreed—held 'my Lord to be the fittest instrument to do good to the State, and therefore I applied myself to him in a manner which I think happeneth rarely among men'.

Francis Bacon had an able lieutenant in his elder brother Anthony. He, too, had hoped that his powerful uncle would help him on his path through life; he, too, had been quickly disillusioned and had sought the protection of the rising star. In the 'shadow cabinet' of personal advisers that Essex began to assemble as soon as he returned from France, the younger Bacon was his diligent Prime Minister, Anthony his brilliant Foreign Secretary. Anthony had already travelled much and had worked for Walsingham's far-flung secret service; he now established his agents in every European city, and collected a regular supply of news which he at once relayed to Essex House. Thus Essex gained the reputation of being, not only brave and energetic, but singularly well-informed. The handsome favourite was becoming a weighty and judicious statesman; and he might presently have achieved the 'domestical greatness' he coveted —Ralegh, who during the summer of 1592 married one of Eliza-beth's ill-behaved maids of honour, fell temporarily into deep dis-grace—had it not been for the suspicions he aroused in the Queen and the persistent opposition of the two Cecils. These were aggra-vated by the natural defects of his character. With his romantic charm went a strain of romantic instability; in a successful action courageous and resolute, once he had encountered a reverse he was apt to sink beneath the blow. Then his resolution would suddenly collapse; some inexplicable malady would strike him down. Often he believed—and his physicians announced—that he had not many hours to live; and at such crises he would turn to religion and would call in the various Puritan chaplains whom he employed to bring him ghostly comfort. While other advisers encouraged his pride and ambition, they ministered to his secret fears.

Essex kept a populous household—at the time of his death he had 160 servants in his pay. It revolved around a tall and dignified man, with a long attractive face, keen, intelligent eyes, but a somewhat weakly shaped mouth, who, although every courtier must aspire to fashion, was unusually careless about the details of his clothes, and, although the Queen had a life-long love of dancing, is said himself to have been a poor performer. He walked stoopingly, his head thrust forward; at dinner, he ate little and often fell into a profound reflec-tive silence. From the time he woke, he was surrounded by friends, with whom he talked as his attendants dressed him and he glanced through the letters and petitions he had received. Generally, his expression was abstracted and remote; and, if on shipboard or the battlefield he suggested the impulsive man of action, in his private existence he recalled a writer or a scholar.[1] Essex House contained a large library; and its owner occasionally protested that he would have preferred the calm enjoyment of his books to the dangers and anxieties of public life. Yet, despite his piety and his annihilating bouts of melancholy, by temperament he was extremely amorous. Lady Essex retained his devotion; but he proved a markedly unfaithful husband, and scored many easy triumphs among impressionable ladies of the court. He may have resembled Hamlet in his fits of gloom; but, like Hamlet, he sometimes revealed a certain touch of moral levity.

His advisers' old mother, Lady Bacon, who shared their interest in his prospects, was among the friends who felt obliged to warn him against the heinous sins of adultery and concupiscence; and, humbly enough, Essex replied, assuring her that, for some time now, he had been 'free from taxation of incontinency with any woman that lives', and claimed that he was by no means the hardened profligate his envious detractors represented. Yet Essex House, for all its political background, had no doubt a fashionable, bohemian side. His sister, Lady Rich, who often lodged there, was a beautiful and wilful woman of the world, who had deserted her unsympathetic consort to live openly with a young and gallant lover, Charles Blount, Lord Mountjoy. Penelope Rich had been adored by Philip Sidney—she was the radiant 'Stella' of his famous sonnet sequence; and Essex thus sheltered beneath his roof, not only Sidney's widow, but the mistress he would have preferred to marry. Still dazzling in early middle age, with her brilliant dark eyes, Penelope was a typical Elizabethan heroine, compact of vigour and ebullience. During her life, she bore twelve children, seven presumably by Lord Rich, five admittedly by Charles Blount, whose legitimate partner, after her divorce, she at length became in 1605.

[1] '. . . For my affection: in nature it was indifferently to books and arms, and was more inflamed with the love of knowledge than the love of fame: witness . . . my contemplative retirement in Wales, and my bookishness from my childhood . . .' Essex to Anthony Bacon, 1598.

H

As befitted Sidney's Egeria, Lady Rich was the patroness of literary men;[1] and her brother, though he did not share his friend Southampton's reputation as a 'dear lover and cherisher of poets', had a cultivated taste in English prose: either he employed a gifted literary secretary—is it possible that Southampton recommended some likely writer of his own acquaintance?—or himself manipulated the language with uncommon grace and skill. All his surviving letters are clearly and forcefully written; but in the letters he addressed to the Queen he performed his boldest feats of eloquence. Here in prose, as Ralegh did in verse, he employed the vocabulary of fervent love. Sexual attraction and concealed self-interest are often difficult to tell apart; and in Essex's letters the designing courtier is almost indistinguishable from a genuinely passionate lover. Thus, even when he writes to Robert Cecil in a businesslike official message, he concludes with the request that the Secretary will 'let my dear Sovereign know I do spiritually kiss her fair royal hands, and think of them as a man should think of so fair flesh'. Addressing the Queen in her proper person, he adopts a correspondingly exalted tone, voices his soul's 'humble, infinite, and perfect' gratitude for some parting tokens she has given him, or declares that, as a man, he has been 'more subject to your natural beauty, than as a subject to the power of a king . . .' Passion and jealousy are themes that constantly recur; and now and then—for example, in 1591, when he was campaigning with the French monarch—he weaves his desires and fancies into an elaborate symbolic pattern. Though he loves action, he longs to return to her presence; and, once he has returned, 'I will humbly beseech your Majesty that no cause but a great action of your own may draw me out of your sight, for the two windows of your privy chamber shall be the poles of my sphere, where, as long as your Majesty will please to have me, I am fixed and unmoveable. When your Majesty thinks that Heaven too good for me, I will not fall like a star, but be consumed like a vapour by the same sun that drew me up to such a height. While your Majesty gives me leave to say I love you, my fortune is my affection . . .' The penultimate

---

[1] The co-dedicatee of Florio's *Montaigne*, she received similar tributes from Richard Barnfield, Gervase Markham, John Ford, B. Yong, the translator of Montemayor's *Diana* and other poets and dramatists, and was addressed in congratulatory sonnets by Henry Constable and John Davies of Hereford.

sentence of this poetic tirade has a curiously Shakespearian ring; and
we remember Wolsey's celebrated lament on the mutability of a
royal favourite's life:

> I have touched the highest point of all my greatness,
> And, from that full meridian of my glory,
> I haste now to my setting. I shall fall
> Like a bright exhalation in the evening,
> And no man see me more[1]

At Essex House, therefore, and in the wider circle of Southampton's friends, Shakespeare may well have found the personal stimulus
his expanding talents needed. But we must assume that he was
chiefly attracted towards the brilliant young man who had received
the dedication of his poems; and, luckily, we know enough of
Southampton to be able to reconstruct a fairly vivid likeness. It is not
quite so engaging as that of Essex; and, although similar in temperament, tastes and ambitions, the friends differed considerably in one
important detail. Whereas, through the Devereux, Essex was
descended from the medieval aristocracy, Southampton's paternal
grandfather had sprung from the new world of the Tudor ruling
class, a former employee and client of Thomas Cromwell, whose
grim philosophy he had absorbed. Having first ingratiated himself at
Court by his 'labour in the King's great business'—the annulment of
Henry's marriage to Katharine of Aragon—after the Reformation
Thomas Wriothesley became a notorious despoiler of the Church,
his chief prize being Hyde Abbey near Winchester, which he pulled
down with 'amazing rapidity' to cart off and sell its rich materials.
Few politicians of the day were more widely or more deservedly
loathed. His son, however, the second Earl, swung back again
towards the old religion, and was involved in a perilous intrigue to
marry the Queen of Scots to the Catholic Duke of Norfolk. As often
happens with the son of a self-made man, he had a high opinion of
his aristocratic dignity; and Gervase Markham, in a posthumous
panegyric, draws a comparison between the noble state he maintained and the meagre and tawdry fashions of the present day: 'his
muster roll never consisted of four lackeys and a coachman, but of

[1] *Henry VIII* Act III Scene ii.

a whole troop of at least a hundred well-mounted gentlemen and yeomen. He was not known in the streets by guarded liveries, but by gold chains, not by painted butterflies ever running as if some monster pursued them, but by tall goodly fellows that kept a constant pace . . .'

During his lifetime, he quarrelled bitterly with his wife, from whom he was said to have been alienated by an unworthy member of his household. But he died in 1581 while he was still comparatively young; and his son, Henry Wriothesley, third Earl of Southampton, succeeded to the title just before his eighth birthday. Like Essex, five years earlier, the boy was made a royal ward and entrusted to the guardianship of Burghley, Master of the Court of Wards. At the age of twelve, he went up to Cambridge, which he left when he was sixteen; and it was about this time that, with singular intelligence, he took into his 'pay and patronage' John Florio, the famous Anglo-Italian scholar and translator, who in 1598 was to dedicate to his patron his notable Italian-English dictionary *A World of Words*. Nor was Florio his only protégé: in 1591, Barnabe Barnes inscribed a sonnet to the young man's honour, and Gervase Markham, who had written so appreciatively of his father's way of life, dedicated to Southampton his patriotic poem on the exploits of Sir Richard Grenville; in 1594 he accepted the dedication of Nashe's picaresque novel *The Unfortunate Traveller*, where he is described as a nobleman who had always loved and cherished poets. Simultaneously, he was acquiring distinction at Court and had entered the coterie of the Queen's favourites. About 1590, when he was seventeen years old, he had been presented to his nearly sexagenarian sovereign; and by 1592, having accompanied Elizabeth on a ceremonial visit she paid to the University of Oxford, he took his place among her courtiers as one of the most accomplished and elegant of all her gifted young men. Like Essex, he seemed to reflect the virtues of an earlier, less prosaic age. Thus, in 1595, after he had performed with conspicuous grace and valour at the jousts held to celebrate the thirty-seventh anniversary of the Queen's accession, George Peele, chronicling the festivities, compared him to the famous English paladin Bevis of Southampton. Loving and beloved by women, he was also loved and flattered by his own sex.

Such, in his more superficial aspect, was the golden youth whom Shakespeare followed. It is clear that he possessed unusual charm. But then, charm is a very dangerous attribute; and Southampton was evidently well aware both of his juvenile good looks and of the fascination that they exercised. He made a habit of having his portrait painted; and fifteen of these portraits still survive. One of the earliest, and probably the best known, displays him in the hey-day of his youth and vigour, with his plumed tilting helmet on a velvet-covered table, against which he negligently rests his arm, and a fine damascened cuirass standing beside him on the marble floor. His clothes are in the height of contemporary fashion—a white satin doublet above slashed and padded trunk hose and, beneath his trunks, a secondary pair of breeches of the kind entitled 'canions'. A red leather gorget shields his breast, and a wide lace collar—a 'falling band'—replaces the customary Elizabethan ruff. Gorget, breeches and sword-belt are enriched with gold and silver thread; and he wears purple embroidered garters to secure his white silk stockings. From this resplendent carapace emerges a head that appears strangely small in relation to the body—a long pointed, sharp-nosed face, fledged by faint moustaches and a fringe of beard. The eyes are remarkable, bright and protrusive—during middle age, they were to become glassy and perhaps a little watery; and Southampton, we know, was always proud of his hair, which once involved him in a humiliating scene at Court. Brushed back from his lofty forehead, his thick reddish-gold love-locks ripple down across his left shoulder, falling half way to his narrow waist. His beautifully gloved hand rests on his padded hip; and he fixes the painter with a steady, arrogant regard.

Other, and somewhat unpleasing, traits were to develop in Southampton's character; but at this period the worst faults imputed to him were those of incontinence and youthful vanity. Like Essex, he made many victims among the ladies whom he met at White-hall, particularly among the maids of honour; but, like Lord Oxford (to whom some enthusiasts have attributed the authorship of the whole Shakespearian canon) he was also credited, in malicious contemporary gossip, with undisguised homosexual leanings. Thus, during February 1601, Robert Cecil received a letter from a certain

William Reynolds, who wished to inform against a treasonable personage named Pearse Edmunds, 'the Earl of Essex' man, born in Strand near me . . . His villainy [writes the informer] I have often heard complained of; he . . . was corporal general of the horse in Ireland under the Earl of Southampton. He ate and drank at his table and lay in his tent. The Earl of Southampton would cole[1] and hug him in his arms and play wantonly with him.' Thanks to this favouritism, Edmonds had reaped 'many preferments'; and he had approached Reynolds, offering me 'great courtesy, telling me what pay and gifts the Earls bestowed upon him . . .' But Reynolds adds that he had virtuously abstained from seeking the personal notice of either errant nobleman.

Cecil's self-righteous informer is, of course, a highly suspect witness; but there is no doubt that Southampton's conduct as a young man disappointed and disturbed his family. He showed, for example, an obstinate reluctance to settle down in Christian marriage. When he was seventeen, Burghley, according to contemporary reports, had offered him his own grand-daughter Lady Elizabeth Vere, daughter of the Earl of Oxford. Yet Southampton had brusquely refused the match, although it promised him a solid position in the world; and, five years later, he besieged and seduced one of his sovereign's prettiest maids of honour, the round-faced, golden-haired Elizabeth Vernon, who adored him to distraction and thought her innocence well lost—a hazardous step, since the Queen guarded her maids almost as carefully and jealously as she watched over her masculine favourites themselves. At the same time, he was much addicted to gambling, and lost more money at 'primero' and other fashionable games than he could yet afford to throw away.[2] Altogether, he was of a slightly rakish turn, attractive, endearing, open-handed, but impulsive, vain and quarrelsome. Just such a difficult young man—a masterpiece of grace and charm, impaired, if not disfigured, by inconstancy and 'sensual faults'—is depicted in the series of sonnets that Shakespeare began to compose probably about 1594. Here adoration is mingled with reprobation, the recital

---

[1] A form of the obsolete verb 'cull': 'to fondle in the arms, hug', as in 'cull-me-to-you' rural name of the pansy. See O.E.D.

[2] He was to celebrate the birth of his eldest child by losing eighteen hundred crowns at a Parisian tennis-match.

of a lover's woes and grievances with the delivery of moral maxims. But the poet would also appear to be acting as the spokesman of his hero's family and friends: seventeen sonnets enforce a single argument—that he should marry and beget issue.

CHAPTER V

'His Sugared Sonnets'

NOTHING WE KNOW about Shakespeare would suggest that he
was a shadowy, secretive or retiring personage; his natural 'civility'
and uprightness are among the qualities that Chettle praises; and he
appears to have played his worldly part without pretension and without concealment. It is especially ironic, then, that an impenetrable
cloud-covering should obscure so many aspects of his life and work,
and that, where he comes closest to deliberate self-portrayal, the
effect that he produces should nowadays seem most mysterious.
Hundreds of patient and learned enquirers have already attacked the
problem of the *Sonnets*—a problem once compared to a haunted
cavern, with countless footprints scattered around its entrance, 'none
of them pointing in the outward direction';[1] but the great majority
of questions we ask still await a satisfactory answer. At what period
were the *Sonnets* written? By whom were they inspired? Who were
the subsidiary characters depicted? Can we assume that the poet's
intention was to compose a coherent autobiographical narrative?
Every age has tended to credit Shakespeare with its own peculiar
virtues and vices; and the Romantic era, being an age of introspec-
tion, welcomed the theory that the *Sonnets* were a painstaking essay
in detailed self-analysis: that the sonnet-form was the small poetic
key with which, as Wordsworth imagined, he chose to unlock the
secrets of his heart.

The Elizabethans had a very different attitude towards the purpose
and the scope of literature; 'originality [we are reminded] was not

[1] Sir Walter Ralegh, quoted by Logan Pearsall Smith: *On Reading Shakespeare*, 1933.

the glory, not the aim of the Elizabethan poet';[1] he was customarily interested in the development of general themes, which his personal experience of life helped him to refresh and re-adorn, rather than in studying and describing the adventures of an individual spirit. Although Shakespeare may have used the sonnet as a key, was that his primary reason for turning sonneteer? Above all else, he was an extraordinarily practical man, seldom averse from adapting his gifts to some prevailing literary mode; and, during the last decade of the sixteenth century, sonnet-writing had become a highly fashionable pursuit. Sonnet-sequences were widely read and admired; and, since the fashion had been launched by Sir Philip Sidney, whose sonnets were addressed to Essex's sister, it had no doubt a particularly strong hold upon members of the Essex household. True, much earlier, Wyatt and Surrey—according to George Puttenham,[2] 'the first reformers of our English metre and style'—had both of them elected to write sonnets, 'imitating very naturally and studiously their master Francis Petrarcha'; but it was Sidney's *Astrophel and Stella*, the account of his passion for Penelope Rich, published in 1591, five years after his heroic death at Zutphen, that introduced the possibilities of this new and graceful form to most Elizabethan readers. Sidney's book was followed in 1592 by Samuel Daniel's *Delia*; in 1593, by Thomas Watson's *Tears of Fancy* and Barnabe Barnes's *Parthenophil and Parthenope*; in 1594, by Henry Constable's *Diana* and Michael Drayton's *Idea's Mirror*; in 1595, by Edmund Spenser's *Amoretti*—to name only a few of the various collections issued; until, in 1598, the Elizabethan affection for the sonnet showed a sudden falling-off. Meanwhile Shakespeare had entered the field—exactly when we cannot say; but, as he usually exploited the demand created by contemporary taste, and, as his sonnets include certain echoes from the work of Michael Drayton, he must have embarked upon their composition about 1594 or 1595. They can scarcely have been written earlier—though a distinguished authority wishes us to believe that some of them at least were composed as early as 1589,[3] at a time when that obviously juvenile pro-

---

[1] *Daniel's Delia and Drayton's Idea*: Introduction by Arundell Esdaile, 1908.
[2] *The Arte of English poesie*, 1589.
[3] J. Leslie Hotson: *Shakespeare's Sonnets Dated*, 1949.

duction *Venus and Adonis* had not yet been given to the public—for, despite their occasional shortcomings, they are the work of a fully developed poet; and a number of sonnets cannot have been produced later than 1598, when Francis Meres referred to Shakespeare's 'sugared sonnets' as already well known among his 'private friends', or 1599, when two poems were printed, presumably without the author's leave, in a volume entitled *The Passionate Pilgrim*.

The problem of dating, however, seems comparatively insignificant beside the problem of the dedication. Written to be handed around a friendly circle—which, if the circle comprehended Southampton, Essex and their coterie, would have been as pleasant and profitable a method of making them known as publication through a London printer—the *Sonnets* remained in manuscript until May or June 1609. But, during that year, on May 20th, Thomas Thorpe registered his intention of publishing 'a book called Shakespeare's sonnets', and entrusted its sale to a bookseller 'John Wright . . . at Christ Church Gate'. Shakespeare himself probably was not consulted; clearly he did not correct the proofs; and almost certainly he had no share in framing the curious dedicatory formula. That was the enterprising publisher's contribution; and Thomas Thorpe was an industrious businessman, who earned a livelihood by picking up manuscripts—there was then nothing that resembled a law of copyright to protect the unlucky author's claims—and either selling them to members of the book-trade or issuing them beneath his own imprint.[1] Having acquired a copy of Shakespeare's famous sonnet sequence, he sat down to design a prefatory flourish. The terms he employed were conventional: when a noble patron could not be invoked, the publisher often dedicated a book to some respected personal acquaintance, using the dedicatee's initials and wishing him prosperity and happiness. But, whether intentionally or inadvertently, Thorpe managed to give his dedication a strangely provocative and elusive cast:

> TO . THE . ONLIE . BEGETTER . OF .
> THESE . INSUING . SONNETS .
> MR. W. H. ALL . HAPPINESSE .

[1] Thorpe's earliest coup had been the acquisition in 1600 of the first book of Marlowe's English rendering of Lucan.

AND . THAT . ETERNITIE .

PROMISED .

BY .

OVR . EVER–LIVING . POET .

WISHETH .

THE . WELL–WISHING .

ADVENTURER . IN .

SETTING .

FORTH .

T. T.

No other piece of English type-setting has provided posterity with a darker puzzle, or during the last century-and-a-half has unloosed a more prodigious flood of words.

The first response of Shakespearian critics, when the *Sonnets* began to attract their interest as a separate subject of enquiry, was to assume that 'the only begetter' must necessarily have been the beloved youth who had inspired their composition; and, while some identified 'MR. W. H.' with William Herbert, Earl of Pembroke— one of the 'incomparable pair of brethren' to whom, in 1623, Heminge and Condell would dedicate the earliest edition of the dead dramatist's collected plays, reminding the brothers that they had been pleased to befriend and encourage the 'author living'—a rival group sponsored Henry Wriothesley, for many reasons an even likelier choice; though it was difficult to see why Thorpe should have printed Southampton's initials in the wrong order. But then, both Herbert and Southampton were rich and powerful noblemen; and 'Mr' was not a style of address that Thorpe would have presumed to apply to any wearer of an earl's coronet—Southampton had borne his title since boyhood; Pembroke, who succeeded his father in 1601, had previously been known as Lord Herbert. Faced with these difficulties, Shakespeare's foremost Victorian biographer devised an entirely new hypothesis:[1] 'MR. W. H.' was Thorpe's friend in the trade, a stationer's assistant named William Hall, him-self a literary Autolycus, whose initials had already appeared upon the title page of Robert Southwell's poems. He was the 'begetter' of

[1] Sidney Lee: *A Life of William Shakespeare*, 1908. Appendix V 'The True History of Thomas Thorpe and "MR. W. H".'

the *Sonnets*, not, of course, because he had inspired them, but because he had procured them or obtained them—a possible Elizabethan usage, according to the ingenious theorist's view. He had given the manuscript life by delivering it into a publisher's clutches.

There remains a fourth suggestion, which has some advantages over all the others. Like most rich Elizabethan widows, Southampton's mother, the Dowager Countess, had found it convenient to re-marry. In 1594, she had chosen Sir Thomas Heneage, Elizabeth's Vice-Chamberlain, as her second husband. But Sir Thomas did not long survive the marriage; and in May 1598 she wedded a comparatively young man—Sir William Hervey 'of Armada fame',[1] who had also served gallantly at Cadiz and on the Islands Voyage, where he must have come into close touch both with Southampton and with Essex. Hervey's interest in their domestic affairs may have begun at an even earlier period—possibly it was his love of Southampton that, by a gradual process of emotional transference, directed him towards his friend's mother; and, some time before he made her his wife, he may have become an *ami de la maison*, to whom she unfolded all her doubts and anxieties about her son's unruly conduct. Southampton was rash, extravagant, fickle. Worse still, he refused to marry . . . In the circumstances, Hervey may well have promised to exert such personal pressure as he could, and have enlisted the help of Southampton's favourite poet to lend his appeals an attractive literary colouring. Thus Shakespeare's sequence, although it was soon to develop along completely different lines, opens with a series of seventeen sonnets, begging a noble, intemperate young man to marry and reproduce his image. His beauty itself imposes an obligation:

> From fairest creatures we desire increase,
> That thereby beauty's rose might never die . . .

He has inherited that legacy, moreover, through a once-beautiful, adoring parent:

[1] The date of Hervey's birth is uncertain; but he did not die until 1642, and must therefore have been comparatively young at the time of the defeat of the Armada, when he boarded a Spanish galleon and slew its commander single-handed. He received a baronetcy from James I in 1609, and was created Lord Hervey of Kidbrooke in 1627. Attention is drawn to William Hervey's claims by Charlotte Carmichael Stopes: *The Life of Henry 3rd Earl of Southampton, Shakespeare's Patron*, 1922.

Thou art thy mother's glass, and she in thee
Calls back the lovely April of her prime . . .

—a legacy that the 'beauteous niggard' should transmit to future
ages. And, at the same time, he must reflect on the consolation that
he will presently derive from seeing his lovely children gathered
round him:

When forty winters shall besiege thy brow,
And dip deep trenches in thy beauty's field,
Thy youth's proud livery, so gaz'd on now,
Will be a totter'd[1] weed of small worth held.
Then being ask'd where all thy beauty lies,
Where all the treasure of thy lusty days,
To say within thine own deep-sunken eyes
Were an all-eating shame, and thriftless praise.
How much more praise deserv'd thy beauty's use,
If thou could'st answer 'This fair child of mine
Shall sum my count, and make my old excuse'
Proving his beauty by succession thine.

Shakespeare's poetic campaign did not immediatelv achieve
its object: for several years Southampton delayed marrying, and
then surrendered his liberty somewhat against his will, a few months
after Lady Heneage had accepted the hand of Sir William Hervey.
The likeliest instigator of this campaign seems to have been Southampton's future step-father—styled by Thorpe 'MR. W. H.',
though Hervey had received a knighthood during the victorious
Cadiz expedition. But, at that time, even a knight's wife would
address him now as 'Sir' and now as 'Mr'; and for the purposes of a
publisher's dedication he may have decided not to use his title.
William Hervey was the 'begetter' of the *Sonnets* since he had encouraged or commissioned the production of the opening series,
and perhaps eventually handed Thorpe his copy of the manuscript;
while he was entitled to a share of 'that eternity promised by our
ever-loving poet' in as much as the conception of the work at the
outset had been partly his. Shakespeare was well-used to re-shaping

[1] tattered.

other men's verses; and Hervey may have suggested that, here and there, he had provided a rough draft.

Let us assume, then, that Shakespeare set to work on the first sonnets in 1594 or 1595, and that during the next few years he continued to enlarge and enrich his original scheme. The so-called 'dating sonnet', for example, appears to have been written in 1596, despite assertions that the great public event described was either the defeat of the Armada in 1588 or the death of the old Queen and the peaceful accession of King James I in the Spring of 1603:

> Not mine own fears, nor the prophetic soul
> Of the wide world dreaming on things to come,
> Can yet the lease of my true love control,
> Suppos'd as forfeit to a confin'd doom.
> The mortal moon hath her eclipse endur'd,
> And the sad augurs mock their own presage;
> Incertainties now crown themselves assur'd,
> And peace proclaims olives of endless age.
> Now with the drops of this most balmy time
> My love looks fresh, and Death to me subscribes,
> Since spite of him I'll live in this poor rhyme
> While he insults o'er dull and speechless tribes.

Much turns on the meaning of the word 'endur'd'. The 'mortal Moon' being Elizabeth herself—again and again, by Ralegh and others, she was deified as Cynthia the moon-goddess—the phrase must surely indicate, not that her radiance had been at length eclipsed, but that she had passed through some crisis in her life and triumphantly emerged from it. Now 1596 was the year of the sovereign's 'grand climacteric'. Every seven years, according to the Elizabethans, marked a dangerous crisis in the individual's life-span; and during 1596 the years of the Queen's life numbered sixty-three, or seven multiplied by nine, both mystic and portentous digits. Among her loyal subjects alarm was widespread; and the Bishop of St David's—one of the 'sad augurs' whose gloomy prophecies were afterwards proved false—preached at Court a lugubrious sermon on the significance of mystical numbers and on the perils the ageing Queen ran, a discourse that considerably annoyed Elizabeth, since she did not care to think of death and found the bishop's pious solicitude equally offensive and unwarrantable. As it happened, the year 1596 was glorified by the English victory at Cadiz; Spain had been checked and humiliated; the period of national conflict seemed to be drawing to a close. Home from his foreign exploits under Essex's standard, Shakespeare's gallant friend may well have looked particularly fresh and cheerful.

His beloved image dominates the whole sequence. But a reader, who wishes to examine the poems' personal and autobiographical structure, should bear in mind that they also embody many purely derivative and traditional elements. Numerous themes can be traced back to Latin, Italian and French verse[1]—as when Shakespeare, like Ovid, Petrarch and Ronsard, boasts of the immortality that his poems will confer and challenges the devouring power of Time—and not only to the works of the past, but to other productions of the Elizabethan age. Evidently, Shakespeare had been interested and stimulated both by Samuel Daniel's *Delia* and by Michael Drayton's *Idea's Mirror*. Drayton was the better poet; but Daniel's contribution was the more direct; and there is an obvious link between his Sonnet IV:

> Let others sing of knights and paladins
> In aged accents and untimely words,
> Paint shadows in imaginary lines
> Which well the reach of their high wits records.
> But I must sing of thee, and those fair eyes
> Authentic shall my verse in time to come,
> When yet the unborn shall say, 'Lo, where she lies,
> Whose beauty made him speak that else was dumb.'

and Shakespeare's Sonnet CVI:

> When in the chronicle of wasted time,
> I see descriptions of the fairest wights,
> And beauty making beautiful old rhyme,
> In praise of ladies dead, and lovely knights,
> Then in the blazon of sweet beauty's best,

[1] J. B. Leishman: *Themes and Variations in Shakespeare's Sonnets,* 1961.

> Of hand, of foot, of lip, of eye, of brow,
> I see their antique pen would have express'd,
> Even such a beauty as you master now.[1]

Poets are as often inspired by a fellow poet's work as excited by their own experience; and *Idea's Mirror*, if Shakespeare began to write the *Sonnets* in 1594 or 1595, was still an extremely recent publication. But, whereas Drayton's poetic heroine is a distant and elusive shape—she is supposed to have been a Lady Rainsford, daughter of Sir Henry Goodere, at whose house, Polesworth Hall, the writer had been brought up—Shakespeare's idol is portrayed with all the emphasis of passionate personal feeling. Not that the story told is a very complex one: the adventures related are few and simple, and usually spring from the contrasted positions of the poet and the difficult but enchanting youth he loves. The poet feels that he is growing old—Shakespeare was in his early thirties, at a time when the expectation of human life was considerably shorter than it is today. He follows a somewhat ignominious calling; and, without undue modesty or any lack of dignity, he refers to his 'branded name' and to 'the public means which public manners breeds', imposed upon him by his unkind fortune:

> Alas, 'tis true I have gone here and there
> And made myself a motley to the view,
> Gor'd mine own thoughts, sold cheap what is most dear,
> Made old offences of affections new.

He is steeped, he admits, in the atmosphere of the stage, in its vulgarity and intellectual falsity—

> And almost thence my nature is subdu'd
> To what it works in, like the dyer's hand.

Yet, at his worst, he is consoled and uplifted by thoughts of the friend, who understands, but does not share, his plight:

[1] There is an even closer parallel between Drayton's 'An evil spirit your beauty haunts me still . . .' and Shakespeare's 'Two loves I have of comfort and despair'. But Drayton's sonnet was not included in the edition of 1594; and, by the time later editions were published, he would have had an opportunity of reading Shakespeare's sequence.

When in disgrace with Fortune and men's eyes,
I all alone beweep my outcast state,
And trouble deaf heaven with my bootless cries,
And look upon myself, and curse my fate,
Wishing me like to one more rich in hope,
Featur'd like him, like him with friends possess'd,
Desiring this man's art, and that man's scope,
With what I most enjoy contented least;
Yet in these thoughts myself almost despising,
Haply I think on thee, and then my state,
Like to the lark at break of day arising
From sullen earth, sings hymns at heaven's gate . . .

Their relationship, however, is constantly impeded by differences of wealth and rank:

I may not evermore acknowledge thee,
Lest my bewailed guilt should do thee shame,
Nor thou with public kindness honour me,
Unless thou take that honour from thy name . . .

And then, the poet's despised profession dooms him to travel up and down the country. He is often absent on some long theatrical tour: once at least a whole spring and summer find him wandering through a rich and placid landscape that he observes and admires but cannot enjoy, since he misses the supreme stimulus of the beloved's presence. There are coldnesses and reconciliations. The poet apologizes for having given away a set of 'tables', or pocket notebooks, that had been a friend's gift; he resents the influence of a rival poet, customarily identified with George Chapman, and makes lively fun of that poet's pretensions to write under the control of disembodied spirits.

Finally, between older and younger man slides the shadow of a dark and sensual woman—the poet's mistress who seduces his friend, and whose treachery he accepts in a mood of masochistic resolution, only begging that, although he himself remains enslaved, she will not deprive him of his second self:

I

So now I have confess'd that he is thine,
And I myself am mortgag'd to thy will,
Myself I'll forfeit, so that other mine
Thou wilt restore to be my comfort still.
But thou wilt not, nor he will not be free,
For thou are covetous, and he is kind;
He learn'd but surety-like to write for me
Under that bond that him as fast doth bind

The identity of the 'Dark Lady'—so-called not by the poet but by his more romantic commentators—is among the most vexed, but at the same time the most popular, of all subsidiary Shakespearian problems. But, before we plunge into imaginative guesswork, one point should be firmly underlined. The notorious Sonnet CXXX—

My mistress' eyes are nothing like the sun;
Coral is far more red than her lips' red;
If snow be white, why then her breasts are dun;
If hairs be wires, black wires grow on her head.
I have seen roses damask'd, red and white,
But no such roses see I in her cheeks;
And in some perfume is there more delight,
Than in the breath that from my mistress reeks[1]

—rather than a serious poem appears to be a cynical *jeu d'esprit*, in which the writer amuses himself by turning inside out the conventional terms of amatory compliment; it may, indeed, be a deliberate parody of Drayton's Sonnet LXXI, where such similes are profusely scattered:

Who list to praise the day's delicious light,
Let him compare it to her heavenly eye,
The sunbeams to the lustre of her sight;
So may the learned like the simile,
The morning's crimson to her lips alike,
The sweet of Eden to her breath's perfume,
The fair Elysium to her fairer cheek,
Unto her veins the only Phoenix' plume . . .

[1] Compare Baudelaire's juvenile poem to his squinting maîtresse 'Louchette', which begins with a disclaimer of the same kind: '*Je n'ai pas pour maîtresse une lionne illustre . . .*

In Shakespeare's poem, the emphasis falls heavily upon the first possessive pronoun:

My mistress' eyes are nothing like the sun . . .

Let happier poets indulge in wild hyperbole! *He* does not claim that the object of his love has superlative beauty or conspicuous merit. And this flippant approach accords with the suggestion, made by a modern editor of the *Sonnets*, that the 'Dark Lady' was not a lady of the Court—certainly not the Queen's Maid of Honour, the unfortunate Mary Fitton, as Bernard Shaw's old acquaintance spent a lifetime vainly attempting to prove[1]—not even a bohemian member of the London middle class, but a well-known courtesan nicknamed 'Lucy Negro', celebrated for her dark complexion.[2] On the other hand, Shakespeare tells us that, besides deceiving him and ensnaring his friend, she has been unfaithful to her 'bed-vow'; from which we might perhaps infer that she was the wife of some rich City merchant, one of the 'beauties of the Cheap and the wives of Lombard Street' whose vanity, promiscuity and taste for fashion often scandalized Elizabethan critics.

Whoever she may have been, she provoked in Shakespeare's heart a double conflict—between his affection for his friend, 'a man right fair', and the detested attraction that inevitably drew him towards 'a woman colour'd ill'; between the obsessive strength of lust and the feelings of fatigue and remorse and moral nausea that completed enjoyment left behind. Further than that it is difficult to go: in the *Sonnets*, 'the Dark Lady' is an evil spirit, an occasion of offence, but scarcely takes shape as a human personage, though we learn that she was fond of music and skilled at playing on the virginals, and that the poet, as he watched her play, would sometimes envy the privilege of the nimble jacks, which leapt from the wooden keyboard to kiss the 'tender inward' of her moving fingers. Nevertheless, Shakespearian enthusiasts have traced her path throughout his whole life—from the composition of *Love's Labour's Lost*, where Berowne abuses his 'whitely wanton', and *Romeo and Juliet*, which tells us of Romeo's early love for dark, disastrous Rosaline, to his

[1] *The Dark Lady of the Sonnets: Preface.*
[2] *The Sonnets, and A Lover's Complaint*, edited by G. B. Harrison, 1938. Notes.

full-length presentation, in *Antony and Cleopatra*, of a swart, seductive gipsy. The type of face and body that excited the poet has been reconstructed down to the smallest details—'mourning' eyes, a lofty 'velvet' brow, a delicate foot, skin unusually fine and smooth, 'laced with blue of heaven's own tinct'.[1] It is clear that, both in men and in women, Shakespeare was now exquisitely sensitive to the *minutiae* of physical beauty; but it seems equally clear that, so far as the *Sonnets* are concerned, sexual enjoyment and emotional admiration were divided by a deep gulf; that every emotion he accounted praiseworthy was reserved for his cult of the 'man right fair', while the dark woman, despite her compulsive charm, received at best a sensual residue.

The Sonnets, in fact, may be described as a monument to homosexual love raised by an otherwise heterosexual poet. This is a view of the problem, however, that would have offended and disgusted most Victorian critics, who hastened to observe that an Elizabethan writer invoking his patron, like a contemporary courtier addressing his sovereign, often employed, apparently with good effect, the language of romantic adoration, and that Southampton was not the only Maecenas whom a grateful writer styled 'lovely'.[2] Shakespeare's praises could therefore be written off as 'celebrations of a patron's favour in the terminology . . . invariably consecrated to such a purpose by a current literary convention'; though it 'was likely enough [his biographer admitted] that beneath all the conventional adulation bestowed by Shakespeare on Southampton there lay a genuine affection . . .'[3] The poet, we are asked to assume, was both sincere and insincere—disinterested in his expressions of friendship, which, rather unfortunately, he chose to call 'love', but interested wherever his panegyrics seem to offend against the rigid standards of nineteenth-century good taste. A modern reader finds it much more

[1] Ivor Brown: *Shakespeare*, 1949.

[2] Sir Philip Sidney, for example, received the following tribute:
> His personage seemed most divine,
> A thousand graces one might count
> Upon his lovely cheerful eyne.

Nor was Shakespeare the only poet to celebrate Southampton's charm. Nash addresses him in a dedicatory epistle as
> . . . Sweet flower of matchless poetry
> And fairest bud the red rose ever bare . . .

[3] Sidney Lee, *op. cit.*

difficult to explain away the amatory burden of the *Sonnets*. Either the whole collection is a stupendous literary fraud, composed with the deliberate intention of flattering a vain, attractive youth—and intellectual dishonesty seldom makes for true poetry—or the poet must mean what he says: that the feelings his friend has aroused in him exceed the bounds of ordinary masculine friendship; that he is as jealous, possessive and demanding as if the beautiful youth had been a beautiful woman. Yet his love, in its way, was innocent—Shakespeare himself has patiently made this clear: the emotional cult that he professes does not ask for any physical return. Any hint of practising 'perversion' is contradicted in *Sonnet XX*, which first describes the hero's feminine graces:

> A woman's face with Nature's own hand painted,
> Hast thou, the Master Mistress of my passion;
> A woman's gentle heart, but not acquainted
> With shifting change, as is false woman's fashion . . .

—then goes on to deny that the attachment is sensual, inserting a salacious *double entendre* of the kind that delighted Elizabethan readers:[1]

> . . . For a woman wert thou first created;
> Till Nature, as she wrought thee, fell a-doting,
> And by addition me of thee defeated
> By adding one thing to my purpose nothing.
> But since she prick'd thee out for women's pleasure,
> Mine be thy love, and thy love's use their treasure.

Yet the *Sonnets* are still a series of love poems; and, notwithstanding the traditional elements we detect in some passages, the dogged obscurity that disfigures others, and Shakespeare's habit, as shown in Sonnet CXXXIV, quoted above, of lapsing into legal jargon, they appear to form a connected personal message and to include references to a disastrous private story—references that only the beloved recipient perhaps could ever fully understand. The devotion they express was neither literary nor conventional: it was violent, spontaneous, uncontrolled, and presumably all the more

[1] For a further *double entendre* of this kind, see *Sonnet CLI*.

devastating because it denied itself a physical outlet. Maybe Southampton, if he was indeed the hero, had a deeper knowledge of the passion he aroused than the almost middle-aged poet who felt and suffered—Southampton, as we have seen, was once accused of homosexual tendencies; and the older man may have fallen a victim to the rakish and experienced youth. But then, the poetic value of the *Sonnets* does not depend upon the tale they tell—or the tale they so nearly tell in a series of bewildering fragments. Their real subject, which gives them their lasting interest, is the transience of youth and beauty, the fallibility of love, the terrifying strength of lust, the 'continual oscillation' in a lover's mind 'between doubt at the heart of assurance and assurance at the heart of doubt . . .'[1] Shakespeare's contemporaries and Caroline successors evidently shared this point of view: they appreciated his 'sugared sonnets' not so much because they felt they were entering the secret places of the poet's heart, as because they admired the superlative wit and eloquence with which he adapted and enlarged familiar poetic situations. Thus, in 1640, when John Benson issued an abridged version entitled *Poems: written by Wil. Shakespeare, Gent.*—the first to be printed since 1609—he attached a prefatory advertisement, announcing that the reader would find them '*serene*, clear and elegantly plain, such gentle strains as shall recreate and not perplex your brain, no intricate or cloudy stuff to puzzle intellect, but perfect eloquence; such as will raise your admiration to his praise . . .' The author's 'excellent and sweetly composed poems' had not, the publisher agrees, 'had due accommodation of proportionable glory, with the rest of his ever-living works'. But that was due to their 'infancy' at the time of the poet's death, rather than to anything in the least mysterious about their style and subject-matter.

By the end of the eighteenth century, the literary world had changed its climate; and George Stevens, in 1793, prefaces his new collected edition of the plays with the remark that he has not re-printed the *Sonnets*, 'because the strongest act of parliament that could be framed would fail to compel readers into their service . . . Had Shakespeare produced no other works than those, his name would have reached us with as little celebrity as time has conferred

[1] J. B. Leishman, *op. cit.*

on that of Thomas Watson, an older and much more elegant sonnet-teer'. Shakespeare's lack of Augustan elegance and clarity did not, of course, disturb Romantic writers; and Keats informs Reynolds, in November 1817, that he has never before 'found so many beauties in the sonnets—they seem to be full of fine things said unintention-ally—in the intensity of working out conceits'. But, even then, it was no longer possible to pretend that the *Sonnets* were serene, clear and elegantly plain. A modern critic is obliged to agree that they are often dark and turbulent, that 'the sequence is radically uneven, and so is the average sonnet within the series'.[1] The heavenly music of the opening passage is seldom maintained throughout the whole poem; elsewhere (according to the same critic) they 'die as poetry at the couplet; or cease somewhat less suddenly at the close of a quatrain . . . as if Shakespeare had recognized that once his burden had been discharged the remainder of the journey could be made by a substitute'. But who was the substitute? Are we to believe that certain parts of the series were struck off in a friendly duel of wits, Shakespeare supplying a couplet or quatrain, which contained the poetic essence of the theme, and which he challenged his ambitious rival to seize upon and carry further? It seems more probable that the close-knit sonnet, with its restrictive rhyming scheme and tradi-tionally prescribed length, did not afford him the latitude he needed or, except in brilliant momentary flashes, bring out all his latent powers. As certain tragedies and comedies remind us, he was apt to grow tired of his own works. Enthusiasm would diminish; fatigue would set in; he would hurry impatiently towards an abrupt con-clusion; and his sonnets often reveal a similar slackening of vital energy. On such occasions, the development of a sonnet betrays the splendid promise of its introductory lines; dawn breaks magni-ficently, but soon dwindles into glimmering dusk.

Yet how memorable those luminous preludes are; and how rapidly and triumphantly their illumination sometimes spreads! Shake-speare's imagery not only fixes and defines, but tends always to enlarge its subject, causes it to expand beneath the reader's eye, invests it with a wider range of meaning. In the *Sonnets*, the images

---

[1] Mark Van Doren: *Shakespear*, 1939, quoted by F. E. Halliday: *Shakespeare and his Critics*, 1958.

he employs are particularly bold and spacious. The beloved himself seems to acquire an almost supernatural dignity, so complex is the host of associations he suggests to an imaginative lover:

> What is your substance, whereof are you made,
> That millions of strange shadows on you tend?

The poet's mind resembles a royal audience chamber, whither his memories are summoned to hold senatorial conclave:

> When to the sessions of sweet silent thought
> I summon up remembrance of things past . . .

Passion is an uncharted wilderness:

> Th'expense of spirit in a waste of shame
> Is lust in action . . .

Time creeps on like the sea, advancing wave by wave against a shingly beach:

> Like as the waves make towards the pebbled shore,
> So do our minutes hasten to their end . . .

Visions of events unborn haunt the slumbers of the dormant earth:

> Not mine own fears, nor the prophetic soul
> Of the wide world dreaming on things to come . . .

From the heavens, the stars look down and comment on our trivial destiny:

> When I consider every thing that grows
> Holds in perfection but a little moment,
> That this huge stage presenteth nought but shows
> Whereon the stars in secret influence comment;
> When I perceive that men as plants increase
> Cheered and check'd even by the self-same sky,
> Vaunt in their youthful sap, at height decrease,
> And wear their brave state out of memory . . .

Yet the *Sonnets* are also replete with homely and familiar details: we read of the man who, deluded by the warmth of a sunny morning, decides foolishly to leave his cloak behind; the tired poet, on a tired horse, jogging gloomily away from London; the 'careful house-wife' who runs to catch her chickens, while her 'neglected child' follows her crying across the garden or the yard; the actor who forgets his lines; the 'decrepit father' who admires his vigorous son; the dyer's indelibly stained hand; the windy night that forecasts a rainy morrow. These poems may tell us comparatively little about the circumstances of the poet's life; but they tell us much about the character of his mind as it had developed during early middle age. Some degree of disillusionment appears already to have crept in; he is half disgusted with the calling he practises, and often mistrustful of his own gifts. He suffers from spells of profound lassitude, both physical and intellectual; and at such times he is troubled by sleeplessness and finds it hard to control his racing thoughts:

> Weary with toil, I haste me to my bed,
> The dear repose for limbs with travel tired,
> But then begins a journey in my head
> To work my mind when body's work's expired

Yet, beneath the exhaustion and disillusionment, he preserves, though it does not always comfort him, a sense of undiminished power; and his proud claim that his verses will bestow immortality upon their beloved subject seems to be something more than a traditional literary trope. Better still, his appetite for experience remains extraordinarily fresh and keen. He is a man of the world, to whom the human microcosm affords a perpetually engrossing spectacle; but towards the mysteries of the divine macrocosm—the ruling stars and their 'secret influences'—he very seldom lifts his eyes. He is aware of the over-arching heavens; but they fail to distract him from the richly various earth. He has none of Marlowe's fierce resentment against the limitations of ordinary human knowledge.

The Sonnets were private poems, designed originally for a small friendly circle; and meanwhile, as he continued to work on the series, his public reputation was growing year by year. When Chettle defended him, in December 1592, he had not mentioned the injured poet's name; but towards the end of 1594 an extremely curious work was registered and published under the title *Willobie*

His Avisa, including a set of commendatory verses, signed *Vigilantius: Dormitanus*, which, for the first time in literary history, link his name with one of his most popular productions: 'And Shakespeare paints poor Lucrece' rape' wrote the two young Oxonian scribblers, whose punning pseudonyms are said to denote Roger Wakeman and Edward or Edmund Napper of Balliol College. According to the editor, also pseudonymous, the author of the volume, which consists of a clumsy poetic dialogue sprawling through eighty-four cantos, was his 'very good friend and chamber fellow M. Henry Willobie, a young man and a scholar of very good hope', believed to have been Henry Willoughby of West Knoyle, Wiltshire, who in 1591 matriculated from St John's College, Oxford, at the age of sixteen, and who was a friend of Sir Thomas Russell, afterwards an overseer of Shakespeare's testament. Clearly, these ill-turned verses, and the prose narrative attached to them, are an elaborate piece of youthful humour; but for the Elizabethan public they must have possessed some topical, and probably scandalous, significance. The book, at least, enjoyed a considerable sale, and was re-printed on five occasions between 1594 and 1609. Today, its literary charm has evaporated, and its hidden satirical meaning defies discovery; but it has been immortalized by its passing reference to Shakespeare, and by some vague subsequent allusions that may possibly illuminate a secluded corner of his private life.

The heroine of *Willobie His Avisa* is an innkeeper's wife in the West Country, so beautiful that she draws to the inn a crowd of greedily importunate gallants, so virtuous that, whatever their rank and wealth, she makes haste to drive them all away, even threatening to murder a certain nobleman rather than permit him to besmirch her honour. The latest victim is 'H. W.', who (the prose commentary explains) 'being suddenly infected with the contagion of a fantastical fit at the first sight of A., pineth a while in secret grief; at length . . . bewrayeth the secrecy of his disease unto his familiar friend W. S., who not long before had tried the courtesy of the like passion, and was now newly recovered of the like infection. Yet, finding his friend let blood in the same vein, he took pleasure for a time to see him bleed; and instead of stopping the issue, he enlargeth the wound with the sharp razor of a willing conceit, per-

suading him he thought it a matter very easy to be compassed, and
no doubt with pain, diligence, and some cost in time to be obtained
. . . In viewing afar off the course of this loving comedy, he determined to see whether it would sort to a happier end for this new
actor than it did for the old player. But at length this comedy was
like to have grown to a tragedy, by the weak and feeble estate that
H. W. was brought unto . . . In all which discourse is lively represented the unruly rage of unbridled fancy . . . with the divers and
sundry changes of affections and temptations, which Will, set loose
from Reason, can devise.'

The dialogue itself is a singularly awkward production. To
'H. W.', deep in amorous melancholy, enters his familiar friend:

> W. S. Well met, friend Harry, what's the cause
> You look so pale with Lented cheeks?
> Your wanny face and sharpened nose
> Show plain your mind something mislikes . . .

> Well, say no more; I know thy grief,
> And face from whence these flames arise,
> It is not hard to find relief
> If thou wilt follow good advice.
> She is no saint, she is no nun:
> I think in time she may be won.

The last couplet seems to recall two lines of that immensely popular
Shakespearian melodrama *Titus Andronicus*:

> She is a woman, therefore may be wooed;
> She is a woman, therefore may be won . . .

More suggestive are the initials 'W. S.', and the fact that they belong
to an 'old player'; though possibly he may be styled a player merely
because he has played his part in the tragi-comedy of frustrated
passion. But modern critics are inclined to think that he was indeed
the author of the *Sonnets*, which he probably began just about the
time that *Willobie His Avisa* reached the public; and there is no
doubt that the narrative was a *roman-à-clef*, and owed its popularity
to its topical appeal, rather than to the picture it draws of the pangs of

disappointed love. Elizabethan society was small and gossip-ridden; Shakespeare had already made his name there, at least among cultured young men who attended the Universities and the Inns of Court, and among the poets, dramatists, journalists and booksellers who earned a livelihood around St Paul's Churchyard. Most readers who knew his name would also know something of his personal existence—enough to recognize the old player and appreciate his Machiavellian strategy as, 'with the sharp razor of a willing conceit', he enlarged and deepened his friend's secret wound. True, Shakespeare was often applauded for his natural kindliness and gentleness; while 'W. S.' takes a detached interest in the spectacle of human misery. But few writers, even when their victim is a friend, can always resist the temptation of using the expert surgeon's probe and knife.

CHAPTER VI

Romeo and Juliet

THE OUTBREAK OF PLAGUE that, early in 1593, had closed the playhouses and dispersed the players, was among the severest that had yet attacked London. Month by month, the toll of deaths increased. At the beginning of June, the Court left for Windsor, whence Londoners and citizens of other infected places were commanded to absent themselves; in July, the holding of Bartholomew Fair was temporarily prohibited; and, on August 14th, it was reported that, during the course of a single week, between seventeen and eighteen hundred persons had died within the walls of the City alone. Until autumn came, there was no relief from the sickness. Meanwhile Shakespeare was travelling; or maybe he had returned to Stratford. He had used his leisure to write *Venus and Adonis*; and, at the same time, he appears to have composed a new comedy, *Love's Labour's Lost*, which many scholars believe was specially written for a private audience. That audience may have been Southampton's party, assembled like the narrators of the *Decameron* in his country house at Titchfield. It is an odd and interesting play; and what distinguishes it from earlier and later comedies is not its construction but its general tone. It seems to have been designed less to please the groundlings than to amuse a small sophisticated group, who would appreciate all the esoteric jokes with which the text is thickly strewn. It suggests a fashionable pantomime, full of snip-snap repartee;[1] and the points made in its dialogue are

---

[1] Armado: 'Now by the salt wave of the Mediterranean, a sweet touch, a quick venue of wit, snip snap, quick and home, it rejoiceth my intellect . . .' *Love's Labour's Lost* Act V Scene i.

sometimes so elusive that they continue to baffle enquiring modern critics. As for the dramatis personae, two of the chief characters are called after the supporters of King Henri of Navarre—for Shakespeare's purposes, Ferdinand of Navarre—Berowne after the maréchal de Biron, Longaville after the duc de Longueville.[1] Essex had been campaigning alongside Henri of Navarre, and had cut a gallant figure amid his courtiers, in 1591 and 1592; and these references would therefore appeal to a gathering that included some of his most devoted friends.

First published in 1598, *Love's Labour's Lost* was described at that time, on the title page of the Quarto edition, as 'newly corrected and augmented' by the author; and Shakespeare may then have inserted some of the finest, least immature speeches. But, considered as a whole, it is not an adult work; and, judging by its contemporary allusions, it must have been produced about 1593. Later, Shakespeare might possibly have hesitated to make his heroes courtly Frenchmen; for Henri, whom Elizabeth herself would presently style 'the Antichrist of ingratitude', had soon fallen out of English favour, whereas in 1593 he was still a gallant and romantic ally, champion of the Protestant cause against the strength of Papist Europe. But, besides its reference to Essex's former associates, the play includes some satirical strokes aimed apparently at his most dangerous foe. Here is the origin of the celebrated phrase that has since become attached to Walter Ralegh's circle—'the School of Night'; which not only recalls George Chapman and that poet's strange preoccupation with tenebrous nocturnal imagery,[2] but also hints at the dark and devilish doctrines said to be propagated by other members of the group. Shakespeare ridicules their scientific studies, their efforts, for example, to map the starry firmament:

> These earthly godfathers of heaven's lights,
> That give a name to every fixed star,
> Have no more profit of their shining nights
> Than those that walk and wot not what they are.

Armado, entitled Braggart in the Quarto text, has often been

[1] Dumain, on the other hand, is named after one of Henri's chief adversaries, the duc du Mayne.

[2] Chapman's *The Shadow of Night* was published in 1594.

identified with the proud and mettlesome Ralegh; but the pedant Holofernes is rather more difficult to place. He can scarcely be a portrait of John Florio, as modern critics have now and then suggested; for Florio was befriended by Southampton, who had recently taken him into his 'pay and patronage'; unless, of course, the scholar's longwinded utterances made him a recognized butt among his patron's company.

The dramatist's central theme, however, is the unending battle between Man and Woman. Ferdinand, King of Navarre, and his courtiers, Berowne, Dumain and Longaville, have determined to form 'a little Academe' from which feminine society shall be excluded, but are pursued and besieged by the Princess of France, whose aides-de-camp are her three ladies, Rosaline, Maria, Katharine. Excepting Berowne, Rosaline's reluctant victim, none of these decorative personages can be said to possess a third dimension. Ferdinand, it is true, reveals a fine poetic gift, as when he describes the dangerous 'affections' that he and his confederates have resolved to hold at bay—'the huge army of the world's desires', encamped in force around their citadel. But Berowne is both a literary misogynist and an impassioned individualist, apt to regard love not as a generalized threat but as the arch-opponent of his own integrity. His complaints anticipate the burden of some of Shakespeare's most embittered sonnets: they express the same attraction, the same exasperated revulsion and—although here on a tragi-comic plane—the same lingering sense of moral nausea.

Such an attitude towards love, and toward Woman as the agent of love, was fairly common in the Elizabethan Age. Perhaps, like other literary phenomena, poetic misogyny had a social origin. England, according to a continental proverb, was 'the Hell of horses, the Purgatory of servants and the Paradise of Women'.[1] An Englishman was still the master of his household; but there are constant suggestions that, at least among the upper and upper-middle classes, the domestic authority he wielded was becoming more and more precarious. As the national wealth increased, so did feminine extravagance and greed; until, early in the next century, we find Lady Compton, the daughter of a rich London merchant, whose large

[1] Fynes Moryson: *Itinerary*, 1617.

fortune her courtier husband had not long ago inherited, demanding peremptorily that her lord should grant her a yearly allowance of over £2,000, and provide two gentlewomen, six or eight gentlemen, 'two coaches, one lined with velvet to myself, with four very fair horses, and a coach for my women', a bevy of chambermaids and laundresses, and a wardrobe of twenty gowns, 'six of them excellent good ones, eight of them for the country, and six of them very excellent good ones', as well as £2,000 'to put in my purse', £6,000 to purchase jewels and £400 'to buy me a pearl chain'.[1] But, if Elizabethan women had a taste for splendour, they shared their sovereign's appetite for knowledge. Often they were highly educated, speaking several modern languages, and versed in the Greek and Roman classics; and, under a female ruler, it was natural enough that they should show a proud and self-assertive tendency. No less natural was the masculine counter-revolt that, during the latter years of Elizabeth's reign, inspired a lengthy succession of dramatists, satirists and religious moralists.

In Berowne's predicament, a complicating factor is the sixteenth-century Cult of Love, a legacy from Europe's medieval past, which had reduced the disorderly commerce of the sexes to a kind of expert courtly game, with its own language, its own prescribed responses, its own system of rewards and penalties. This was the game that Essex and Ralegh played during their ceaseless competition for the Queen's favour; and its vocabulary was borrowed and improved on by innumerable Elizabethan poets, who, in their attachment to the idea of love, often lose sight of their passion's human object, deifying their mistress as 'Delia' and 'Celia', and raising sexual attraction to the height of a sublime infatuation. But Berowne is a modern man, a cynical philosopher, an embittered realist; and the whole adored and pampered sex arouses his resentful fury. His description of a woman's natural shortcomings may be compared with that of George Chapman, who reminds us that women are creatures of the Moon, subject to her demoralizing monthly sway:

> . . . Women, that (of all things made of nothing)
> Are the most perfect idols of the moon,

[1] G. Goodman: *The Court of James I*, 1839, quoted by Lawrence Stone, *op. cit.*

(Or still-unwean'd sweet moon-calves with white faces)
Not only are patterns of change to men,
But, as the tender moonshine of their beauties
Clears or is cloudy, make men glad or sad.[1]

More prosaically, Berowne likens the female organism to an ill-
functioning piece of household clockwork:

> What I! I love! I sue! I seek a wife!
> A woman that is like a German clock,[2]
> Still a-repairing, ever out of frame,
> And never going aright . . .
> And among three to love the worst of all—
> A whitely wanton with a velvet brow,
> With two pitch-balls stuck in her face for eyes,
> Ay and, by heaven, one that will do the deed,
> Though Argus were her eunuch and her guard!
> And I to sigh for her, to watch for her,
> To pray for her, go to: it is a plague
> That Cupid will impose for my neglect
> Of his almighty dreadful little might.

Significant is his allusion to 'the deed'—elsewhere in Elizabethan
drama often called 'the deed of darkness'—which evokes the
mingled feelings of attraction and repulsion stirred by memories of
the sexual act. Critics have already pointed out a link between
Berowne's picture of his 'whitely wanton' and the sallow black-eyed
heroine of the *Sonnets*; and between this Rosaline and her fascinating namesake, who, before he encounters Juliet, has engendered
a 'loving hate' in Romeo's soul. Romeo, too, remarks that Job's
comforter Mercutio, has been 'stabb'd with a white wench's black
eye'. Berowne, however, for the purposes of the comedy, has at
length to make his peace. He does so under singularly harsh conditions, having agreed not only to curb his intelligence and weed the
wormwood from his 'fruitful brain', but to spend twelve months
among 'the speechless sick', where—

[1] *Bussy d'Ambois* (1612), Act IV Scene i.
[2] The comparison was a proverbial one.

K

> your task shall be,
> With all the fierce endeavour of your wit,
> To enforce the pained impotent to smile.

Meanwhile, he has recognized the authority of love and nobly
acknowledged its omnipresent influence:

> . . . Love, first learned in a lady's eyes,
> Lives not alone immured in the brain;
> But with the motion of all elements,
> Courses as swift as thought in every power . . .
> It adds a precious seeing to the eye;
> A lover's eyes will gaze an eagle blind;
> A lover's ear will hear the lowest sound . . .
> Love's feeling is more soft and sensible
> Than are the tender horns of cockled snails . . .
> For valour, is not Love a Hercules,
> Still climbing trees in the Hesperides?
> Subtle as Sphinx, as sweet and musical
> As bright Apollo's lute, strung with his hair;
> And, when Love speaks, the voice of all the gods
> Make heaven drowsy with the harmony.

Here, as in almost everything that Shakespeare produced, are
reminiscences of his past, and anticipations of his future, work.
Reading the mention of the snail, we look back to *Venus and Adonis*;
at the same time, the speech transcribed above suggests both the
poetic style and the emotional tenor of *Romeo and Juliet*. Shakespeare's plays and poems form an extraordinarily homogeneous
body, which seems to have developed, stage after stage, at a steady,
unforced but unrelaxing pace. Each step, as we review his development, appears a prolongation of the step before it. In *Romeo and
Juliet*, the stylized passions of *Love's Labour's Lost* re-emerge upon a
different level; and, having introduced an exquisitely appropriate
song into *The Two Gentlemen of Verona*, the author rounds off *Love's
Labour's Lost* with one of his most enchanting lyrics, a pastoral ditty
that embraces an entire landscape, now warm and placid and flower-
beset, haunted by the refrain of the provoking cuckoo; now snow-

bound and gaunt and dark-hedged, milk frozen in the pails, servants carrying home logs, and a country congregation huddled coughing beneath the parson's pulpit:

> When icicles hang by the wall,
> And Dick the shepherd blows his nail:
> And Tom bears logs into the hall,
> And milk comes frozen home in pail . . .
>
> When all aloud the wind doth blow,
> And coughing drowns the parson's saw:
> And birds sit brooding in the snow,
> And Marian's nose looks red and raw:
> When roasted crabs hiss in the bowl,
> Then nightly sings the staring owl,
> Tu-whit to-who.
>   A merry note,
>   While greasy Joan doth keel the pot.

Shakespeare's professional progress was no less regular and smooth. Until 1592 an industrious apprentice, in 1593 and 1594 he steps forth as a rising master, attached to an influential young grandee and, through Southampton, allied to the important political faction headed by the Earl of Essex. He is a conservative, even a reactionary, an opponent of Ralegh's school and their subversive doctrines, a man whose lively intelligence does not seek to challenge the established order. The themes that excite his imagination are drawn from private, rather than from public, life; and, although the current demand for historical plays often obliges him to deal with large issues, he is apt to give his public personages, the monarchs, statesmen and steel-clad nobles, a somewhat blank and formal air. Meanwhile the English theatre had been undergoing an extensive transformation. Once the plague slackened, the players' companies, which it had driven out of London, began to take the homeward road; and, during the summer of 1594, Edward Alleyn, having failed to form a successful alliance between the Lord Admiral's and the Lord Chamberlain's men (previously known as Lord Strange's men), founded a new Lord Admiral's Company, which he managed at the Rose playhouse. That autumn, a new Lord Chamberlain's Company, which included Shakespeare, William Kempe, the celebrated clown, and Richard Burbage, the ambitious young tragedian, moved to the Shoreditch Theatre, which Burbage's father James, himself a veteran player, had built in 1576. Shakespeare, we learn, was now a 'sharer'—entitled, that is to say, to receive a proportion of the profits. Among his fellow players, he held a prominent position; and the royal Chamber Accounts, covering the Christmas festivities of 1594 and 1595, record a payment, 'for two several comedies or interludes showed . . . before her Majesty in Christmas time last past . . . £13.6s.8d, and by way of her Majesty's reward £6.13s.4d', made, upon the Council warrant, 'to William Kempe, William Shakespeare, and Richard Burbage, servants to the Lord Chamberlain . . .' Those three evidently controlled the company: the diligent man-of-all-work had risen to the front rank.

About Shakespeare's histrionic gifts we know unfortunately very little, except that he frequently acted both in his own and in other dramatists' plays, and that, according to Nicholas Rowe, who had gathered together many old theatrical traditions, 'the top of his performance' was the Ghost in *Hamlet*. Since he was allotted this comparatively small part, his acting may have been competent and dignified rather than particularly inspired. Kempe and Burbage, however, were highly original and distinguished artists: Kempe, after Richard Tarlton's death the greatest comedian of the day, whose broad and bawdy humour was set off by his songs and jigs, with which, being a popular favourite, he was inclined to monopolize the whole scene; Burbage, who, in 1594, had not yet reached his twenty-seventh year but was fast developing a tragic style that promised to eclipse Alleyn's, a style lighter and quicker and easier, yet, as his portrayal of Richard III had demonstrated, equally capable of rendering intense emotion. Such were Shakespeare's chief professional associates, his colleagues, advisers and daily companions while he produced his early master-works. The life they shared was a bohemian one; it involved much travelling, many changes of background and numerous exhausting last-minute efforts to suit their material to a new audience. A play that did well at the Theatre might not entertain the Queen's entourage or win the approval of the literary Inns of Court. Shakespeare's company was in constant demand. Thus, towards the end of December, 1594, we hear of their visiting Greenwich Palace where they successfully amused the Queen; but on December 28th they were back again in London, enacting *The Comedy of Errors* before the gentlemen of Gray's Inn, who had invited their friends of the Middle Temple to attend an elaborate Christmas pageant. The occasion was a conspicuous social failure; a vast crowd had packed the hall; many of the Gray's Inn men became exuberantly drunk; a disorderly multitude embarrassed the stage; and the visitors from the Inner Temple had left in a tantrum before the platform could be disencumbered and Shakespeare's comedy allowed a decent hearing. Next morning, the ill-conducted hosts felt properly ashamed of themselves; and afterwards that disgraceful evening was always referred to as 'The Night of Errors'. Shakespeare and his fellow comedians must have got home late and tired.

Luckily, his genius did not demand solitude, which, even though he had needed and yearned for it, would have been hard to come by in sixteenth-century London; and the second period of his creative growth, extending from 1594 to the end of the decade, was yet busier and more prolific than the first. Among his earliest achievements was *Romeo and Juliet*, based on Arthur Brooke's versified rendering of a popular Italian novel.[1] To convey the spirit of youth is frequently the privilege of those who are themselves no longer very young, but still occupy a midway position between the Spring of life and early middle age. Shakespeare was now about thirty years old. In *Venus and Adonis*, which may perhaps have been written some time before it found a publisher, he had shown a slightly dubious attitude towards the whole subject of romantic love: the young are often too easily hurt to understand all the advantages they enjoy. But in his new tragedy he could afford to look back on youth with affection and compassion and regret, and unfold the story of 'a pair of star-cross'd lovers', and 'the fearful passage of their death-mark'd love', from the imaginative standpoint of an almost middle-aged man. As usual, he was not ashamed to borrow: Brooke's verses

---

[1] Brooke's poem, founded on Luigi da Porto's *Historia novellamente retrovata di duo nobili amanti*, had been published in 1562; and an English novel by William Painter, on the same subject, in 1565.

provided one or two hints; and, since Brooke tells us that he had witnessed 'the same argument lately set forth on stage', Shakespeare may also have been following the outlines of an old drama. If such a drama existed, it has now completely disappeared. Shakespeare's tragedy is Shakespearian throughout; to any plumes he appropriated he gave a fresh and dazzling lustre.

The play shines—that is its distinguishing quality—now with a solar, now with a lunar, brilliance. In *Romeo and Juliet*, remarks an acute analyst of Shakespeare's symbolism,[1] 'the dominating image is *light*, every form and manifestation of it'. The tapers and torches that burn for Capulet's ball are put to shame by the flood of moonlight that lies beneath his daughter's window, and 'tips with silver all these fruit-tree tops'; Juliet appears in a brightly-lit casement—

> As glorious to this night, being o'er my head,
> As is a winged messenger of heaven
> Unto the white-upturned wondering eyes
> Of mortals that fall back to gaze on him
> When he bestrides the lazy-passing clouds . . .

She compares the shock of Romeo's sudden wild declaration to the effect of a glimmering sheet of summer lightning:

> . . . Although I joy in thee,
> I have no joy of this contract tonight:
> It is too rash, too unadvised, too sudden,
> Too like the lightning, which doth cease to be
> Ere one can say 'It lightens' . . .

The lovers' moment of happiness ends with the dawn, as 'envious streaks' begin to lace the East, and 'Night's candles' slowly pale and die; and the beauty and brevity of love itself—that 'brief light', doomed to quick extinction, celebrated in Catullus' famous lyric—are set off by the 'perpetual darkness' of ancient Capulets' sepulchral vault.

Yet Shakespeare's play has its sensuous undertones, and is alive with worldly bustling characters. His wit is seen at its boldest and bawdiest. The opening passage, where Sampson and Gregory,

[1] Caroline F. E. Spurgeon: *Shakespeare's Imagery*, 1935.

servants of the Capulets, decide to pick a quarrel with the retainers of the Montagues, is already rich in sexual jokes; and Mercutio is a fount of genial obscenities, including one reference so abstrusely phrased that it escapes the average modern reader.[1] Shakespeare's bawdy has often puzzled his critics. Robert Bridges believed that it was imposed on him by his disreputable contemporary audience, 'those wretched beings who can never be forgiven their share in preventing the greatest poet and dramatist of the world from being the best artist'; while Bernard Shaw suggested that his 'incorrigible addiction to smutty jokes' was fostered by his snobbish anxiety to resemble a member of the upper classes, the aristocrat, according to Shaw, being always particularly lewd in speech. Shakespeare, however, was representative of his period; and, although the Elizabethans' attitude towards love was not uncomplicated by neurotic feelings—with a pagan delight in the flesh went disgust, remorse and guilty fear—they understood that the Heavenly and the Earthly Venus are twin manifestations of the same divinity, and that, if one is to be properly served, the other must be duly honoured. Quite apart from its popular appeal, bawdy wit is a release and a corrective; and in Shakespeare's presentation of romantic love it fulfils a very useful end, reminding us that Romeo's passion has a basis of desire, which Juliet welcomes and acknowledges, and that, when he speaks of ascending her balcony and gaining 'the high top-gallant' of his joy, his thoughts, despite their lyrical utterance, are set on giving and receiving pleasure.

Yet Romeo's passion transcends his immediate object, like the passions of Faustus and Tamburlaine and, indeed, the dreams of Walter Ralegh. So long as he loves Rosaline, he is recognizably human, Mercutio's love-lorn but amusing friend; but, once he has encountered Juliet, both he and his thirteen-year-old mistress become a pair of disembodied voices, engaged in an unending beautiful debate that lifts them far above 'the realm of discord'. The effect might be over-rarified, were not Mercutio and Juliet's Nurse at hand to provide a secondary form of music—the background music of human experience, against which the lovers' voices rise and fall. The old woman and the fashionable wordling keep the drama firmly

[1] Act II Scene i, lines 34-36.

grounded; and each of these talkative personages seem to have fascinated and enthralled their author. 'Shakespeare,' wrote Dryden, 'showed the best of his skill in his Mercutio, and he said himself, that he was forced to kill him in the Third Act, to prevent being killed by him.'[1] Mercutio, we assume, as Shakespeare developed his character, threatened to acquire an independent and refractory life; he refused to be confined and held down; and his strain of wild eloquence, so strangely intermixed with his flow of exuberant social chatter, began to exceed its allotted function and dominate the whole play. At the outset, Mercutio may perhaps have been drawn from some contemporary London model, possibly from a garrulous member of the Inns of Court, who frequented the 'gentlemen's rooms' at the theatre, and whom Shakespeare met behind the stage; no doubt his puns and his quibbling pleasantries reproduce a current conversational style. But Shakespeare's characters were always apt to grow as they passed through his imagination; and Mercutio grew to so inordinate a size that a moment came when he must be killed off. Shakespeare, however, kills him off in style: Mercutio retains his splendid natural panache, and expires not gloomily or fearfully, but with a spirited curse pronounced on the rival clans and their foolish self-destructive feud. His indignant cry, 'A plague o' both your houses!', thrice furiously repeated in tones of mounting rage and anguish, is among the most poignant and dramatic of all Shakespearian last words.

As for the Nurse, she illustrates the comprehensive sympathy that Shakespeare extended to his favourite subjects. We have the impression that he is depicting a life-long acquaintance; that what he tells us, for the purposes of his story, is but a fragment of what he *could* tell; and that a part of his creation, like the basis of an iceberg, remains undisclosed beneath the surface. Here it is worth noting that, in many of his later plays, he adopted much the same method, giving his characters not only a present but a past, and associating their present-day personalities with the experiences they have already lived through. From the wonderful monologues of Juliet's Nurse— she is a proud, obstinate old woman, whom, once she has embarked

[1] *Essay on the Dramatique Poetry of the Last Age.* 'But, for my part,' Dryden adds, 'I cannot find he was so dangerous a person . . . He might have lived to the end of the play, and died in his bed, without offence to any man.'

13 Sir Walter Ralegh and his son, 1602. Described by his contemporaries as 'damnable proud', he was also popularly regarded as a 'Machiavel' and 'atheist'

14 (*left*) An important member of the Essex circle, Charles Blount, Lord Mountjoy

15 (*right*) Henry Wriothesley, 3rd Earl of Southampton; painted in his youth with his tilting-helmet beside him on a velvet-covered table. Fifteen portraits of Southampton have survived

16 (*below*) Southampton with his favourite cat, during his imprisonment in the Tower, when he was much troubled by the 'continuance of his quartern ague' and a swelling of his legs

17 Southampton as a middle-aged courtier

on a stream of memories, it is very difficult to call to order—we gain vivid, though discontinuous, glimpses of her former years and lost affections. There was her husband, 'a merry man', inclined to treat Juliet as a child with somewhat unbecoming levity, who, when the little girl fell and hurt her forehead, had picked her up in his arms and cracked an improper joke:

> 'Yea,' quoth he, 'dost thou fall upon thy face?
> Thou wilt fall backward when thou hast more wit;
> Wilt thou not, Jule?' And, by my holidame,
> The pretty wretch left crying, and said 'Ay'.

The Nurse's own daughter had died in childhood, as she remembers briefly yet tenderly, during her prolonged attempt to establish Juliet's right age:

> Even or odd, of all days in the year,
> Come Lammas-Eve at night shall she be fourteen.
> Susan and she—God rest all Christian souls—
> Were of an age. Well, Susan is with God;
> She was too good for me. But, as I said,
> On Lammas-Eve at night shall she be fourteen:
> That shall she, marry; I remember it well.
> 'Tis since the earthquake now eleven years,
> And she was weaned—I never shall forget it—
> Of all the days of the year, upon that day:
> For I had then laid wormwood to my dug,
> Sitting in the sun under the dove-house wall.
> My lord and you were than at Mantua . . .
> 'Shake,' quoth the dove-house: 'twas no need, I trow,
> To bid me trudge.

This mastery of the rhythms of common speech foreshadows Shakespeare's most mature achievements. But *Romeo and Juliet* is still a play that includes some immature and clumsy writing: the interminable passage in which Friar Lawrence, like the Messenger of an old-fashioned Senecan tragedy, recapitulates the last scenes, and—no doubt a sop to contemporary taste—Juliet's lengthy evocation of the horrors of the charnel-vault.

On the modern stage, *Romeo and Juliet* demands extremely skilful handling. Romeo must leap an orchard-wall, descend from a balcony and break open a sepulchral monument; and no one can explain just how such accessories were constructed in an Elizabethan playhouse. Although the Henslowe papers include an indenture drawn up, at the beginning of the next century, between Philip Henslowe, his associate Edward Alleyn and a carpenter named Peter Street, which contains exact specifications for the building of a new theatre, it deals only with the house's permanent fabric and leaves many subsidiary details unexplained. To the indenture we can add the copy of a sketch of the Swan Theatre, made about 1596 by a Dutch traveller Johannes de Wit. Here we see an extensive quadrangular stage, labelled *proscaenium*, jutting far out into a central yard, from beneath a lofty roof, or 'shade', supported on two massive pillars. The stage itself is raised above the yard by what appear to be solid props, with a cavernous open space beneath. At the rear of the proscenium, below the roof, is a wall, pierced by two doors, which de Witt has marked as 'the players' house' or *mimorum aedes*; while covered galleries curve round to the left and right, enclosing Shakespeare's famous 'wooden O'. While the Fortune, which Henslowe commissioned Street to build, was square, other theatres were octagonal or round; and it is obvious that the Elizabethan actor did not, as in a modern theatre, invariably face his audience, who must have looked up at him from the yard or looked down on him, if they sat in the more expensive galleries, from several different points of view. De Witt's sketch, indeed, illustrates a crowded gallery right above 'the players' house', though the actors, occupying the front of the stage, have their backs turned towards this group of patrons. Were Elizabethan dramas meant to be played 'in the round'? A particularly adventurous and disturbing theory was advanced not long ago[1]— that, until the unfortunate introduction of the seventeenth-century Italian 'picture stage', every type of Elizabethan play was still organized upon a circular principle within a ring formed by the spectators' benches; and that, instead of entering through the doors at the rear—which we had previously imagined led into the 'tiring house' or dressing-room—the players climbed up from a win-

[1] J. Leslie Hotson: *Shakespeare's Wooden O*, 1959.

dowed apartment situated directly underneath the boards, and awaited their cue in a series of 'houses', or curtained, easily removable booths, representing mansions, monuments, city-walls, the show being equally complete and effective whichever way the encircling audience looked.

This suggestion is an interesting one; but it raises various awkward problems. We may assume that, when the players performed in a palace or a college hall, they employed the temporary 'houses' that their isolated positions required amid a circular array of seats; but it does not necessarily follow that they adopted the same methods when they had the use of a playhouse and its fixed stage. After all, they were experienced improvisers; perhaps, if they needed a balcony, they sometimes borrowed the public gallery behind. And then, whereas some Shakespearian scenes might well be presented in an amphitheatre, others surely would be almost impossible to produce upon a house-encumbered scenic island? The busy artists who developed stagecraft have left no helpful written records. But Henslowe has bequeathed us a fund of less exciting information, about the structure of the theatre itself and how it was partitioned off to hold his clients. The Fortune, which, he specified, should reproduce many of the features of the Globe, in its turn presumably modelled on the Theatre and the Curtain, was to include 'a Stage and Tiring-house . . . with a shadow or cover over the stage'. The said stage must 'contain in length forty and three foot of lawful assize, and in breadth . . . extend to the middle of the yard . . . the same stage to be paled in below with good strong and sufficient new oaken boards' and 'be in all proportions contrived and fashioned like unto the stage of the said playhouse called the Globe; with convenient windows and lights glazed to the said tiring house'.[1] The galleries should incorporate 'four convenient divisions for gentlemen's rooms', and elsewhere 'divisions for twopenny rooms, with necessary seats to be placed and set as well in these rooms as throughout all the rest of the galleries'; and the gentlemen's rooms and the twopenny rooms were to be sealed 'with lath, lime and hair; and all

---

[1] Dr Hotson's theory that the tiring-house was constructed beneath the stage is difficult to support against Henslowe's evidence—that the stage was 'paled in below' and the tiring-house provided with 'convenient windows and lights'. Dr Hotson, however, argues that what, in de Witt's drawing, we had taken to be props upholding the stage are actually intended to represent a pair of casements.

the floors of the said galleries, storeys and stage to be boarded with good and sufficient new deal boards of the whole thickness, where need shall be'.

Surmounting the yard and the forty-foot stage was a massive edifice three storeys high. Below the uppermost storey projected the 'shade', upborne by monumental posts; and under this roof the actors could withdraw, when a rainstorm drenched the yard beyond. In the back wall were the doors already mentioned; and between them, according to the usual theory, opened alcove-like an inner stage,[1] screened off, when it was not required, with a curtain or a piece of arras, where Othello would have strangled Desdemona, Polonius have hidden to spy on Hamlet, and Ferdinand and Miranda been discovered at their game of chess. But, considering the space allowed to the players, the playhouse as a whole was not extensive, less than sixty feet wide by sixty feet long, with a broad-built stage that reached the centre of the yard. Into this claustrophobic receptacle Shakespeare and his fellows packed their audience, which is thought to have numbered, at the Globe, about five hundred and fifty on an average afternoon.[2] Its composition was remarkably various; 'the place,' noted Dekker,[3] 'is so free in entertainment, allowing a stool as well to the farmer's son as to your Templar: that your stinkard has the self-same liberty to be there in his tobacco-fumes which your sweet courtier hath: and that your carman and tinker claim as strong a voice in their suffrage, and sit to give judgement on the play's life and death, as well as the proudest Momus among the tribe of critic.' But the groundlings, or 'penny-knaves', were not the illiterate mob sometimes represented by nineteenth-century historians. The trade guilds of the day often insisted that a prospective apprentice should have learned to read and write; cheap reading primers were widely distributed;[4] and the crowd that filled

---

[1] For an expert discussion of this and other points, see C. Walter Hodges: *The Globe Restored*, 1953.

[2] T. W. Baldwin, quoted by Alfred Harbage: *Shakespeare's Audience*, 1941.

[3] *The Gull's Handbook*, 1609.

[4] 'In view of the profusion of schools, of the tendency of trade guilds to make literacy a qualification even for entrance into apprenticeship, and of the manifest interest in self-instruction, we must revise any impression we may have had that London workmen were "nine-tenths illiterate". In a period of eight months during the year 1585, the publishers disposed of ten thousand copies of their reading primer, *The ABC and Little Catechism*.' Alfred Harbage: *op. cit.*

the theatres came in search not only of entertainment but of the instruction that the stage provided. The theatre was their window on the world; and 'many poor pinched, needy creatures', we are told, 'that live of alms, and that have scarce neither cloth to their back nor food for the belly, yet will make hard shift but they will see a play . . .'[1]

For the City magistrates, however, the London playhouses were a constant source of anxiety and trouble. In 1592, 1594, 1595 and 1597, the Lord Mayor addressed a similarly worded petition to the Queen's government at Whitehall, protesting that the plays acted there showed 'nothing but profane fables, lascivious matters, cozening devices and scurrilous behaviours . . . so set forth as they move wholly to imitation and not to avoiding of those faults and vices which they represent'. The magistrates dreaded the disorderly crowds that collected, the riots that frequently occurred and the opportunities such gatherings offered for hatching seditious plots against the realm. Certain tradesmen, too, besides announcing that stage plays encouraged young men to an 'impudent familiarity with their betters', so that 'often times great contempt of masters, parents and magistrates followeth thereof', were convinced that play-going tended to damage their commerce; for the vintners, alewives and victuallers, as Nashe pointed out, supposed that, 'if there were no plays, they should have all the company that resort to them lie boozing and beer-bathing in their houses every afternoon'. As to the Puritans, they saw the modern playhouse as a general nursery of sloth and sin. Its 'common haunters,' declared Henry Crosse during the period of Shakespeare's greatest triumphs, 'are for the most part the lewdest persons in the land, apt for pilfery, perjury, forgery or any rogueries, the very scum, rascality and baggage of the people . . . A play is like a sink in a town, whereunto all the filth doth run; or a bile in a body that draweth all the ill humours unto it.' At the playhouse, the sinner increased his knowledge of sin, and also learned a new vocabulary. 'They that are evil-disposed,' a Puritan critic had already lamented in the year 1580, 'no sooner hear anything spoken that may serve their turn, but they apply it unto themselves.' Such was the 'wiliness and craft of the stage' that tags from

[1] *Virtue's commonwealth*, 1603.

the current tragedies and comedies found their way, with demoralizing effect, into ordinary conversation. 'Every punk and her squire',
said Dekker, could 'rant out by heart' some favourite lines.

As in the Roman theatres that Ovid had attended, the crowded
galleries were a focus of amorous intrigue. Designing youths, complained the Puritans, would first walk round the yard below and cast
a glance along the seats; 'then like unto ravens, where they spy the
carrion thither they fly and press as near to the fairest as they can'.
Stephen Gosson, whose *School of Abuse* had been published in 1579,
describes the keen young ravens settling down to prey:

> In Rome, when plays or pageants are shown, Ovid chargeth his
> pilgrims to creep close to the saints whom they serve, and show
> their double diligence . . . In our assemblies at plays in London,
> you shall see such heaving and shoving, such itching and shoulder-
> ing, to sit by women: such care for their garments, that they be not
> trod on: such eyes to their laps, that no chips light in them: such
> pillows to their backs that they take no hurt: such masking in their
> ears, I know not what: such giving them pippins to pass the time:
> such playing at foot saunt without cards: such ticking, such toying,
> such smiling, such winking, and such manning them home when
> the sports are ended, that it is a right comedy . . . Not that any
> filthiness in deed is committed within the compass of that ground,
> as was done in Rome, but that every wanton and his paramour,
> every man and his mistress, even John and his Joan, every knave
> and his quean, are there first acquainted and cheapen the merchan-
> dise in that place, which they pay for elsewhere as they can agree.

Much more exasperating to the players themselves was the
insolent behaviour of 'capricious gallants', so imbued with a 'habit
of dislike in all things that they will approve nothing, be it never so
conceited and elaborate, but sit dispersed, making faces and spitting,
wagging their upright ears',[1] and uttering loud abusive comments.
Some of these gallants filled the 'gentlemen's rooms'—

> . . . Base detractors and illiterate apes
> That fill up rooms in fair and final shapes[2]

[1] Ben Jonson: *The Case is Altered*, 1609.
[2] Ben Jonson: *Poetaster*, 1602.

but other 'fastidious impertinents' looked down from the 'lords' room', which may probably be identified with the gallery above the tiring-house, or occupied stools upon the stage, having entered through the tiring-house door. Meanwhile the public in the yard who had paid a penny, whereas a cushioned gallery-seat would have cost them threepence, smoked tobacco-pipes, noisily cracked nuts, munched apples and drank bottled ale. A visit to the theatre was a less expensive form of entertainment than a visit to the London stews. Idle citizens, we are told, would spend their afternoons either in 'gaming, following of harlots, drinking or seeing a play'; and no doubt both the chaste and the frugally-minded preferred the cheap and innocent pleasures of theatre-going, which need not cost them more than twopence, to 'sixpenny whoredom' or 'sixpenny damnation' at one of the notorious Bankside brothels. Elizabethan Englishmen did not dislike a crowd; and the galleries of the playhouse must have been comfortable enough. But the groundlings were tightly packed in, and stood 'glued together' throughout the entire play; 'when they came forth', these penny-patrons 'looked as if they had been parboiled'.[1]

Their consolation, as they sweltered or shivered, was not only the dramatic excitement of the plays they saw enacted but the general splendour of the whole performance. According to Johannes de Witt, the London playhouses were all distinguished by their 'notable beauty', the Rose and the Swan being yet 'more magnificent' than the Theatre and the Curtain. The stage itself seems to have been richly furnished; for Henslowe's accounts in 1598 contain a list of sumptuous properties—a rock, a cage, three separate tombs, 'a pair of stairs for Phaeton', 'the City of Rome', 'one tree of golden apples', 'Tantalus' tree', 'Bellendon stable', 'two moss banks' and 'one cauldron for the Jew', with such additional equipment as a golden fleece, 'old Mahomet's head', Phaeton's chariot, Mercury's wings, Tasso's picture, 'the cloth of the Sun and Moon', 'Neptune's fork and garland', Iris' rainbow, 'one ghost's crown', bridles, sceptres, a gilded spear, lions' heads, timbrels and the skins of wild beasts.[2]

[1] Thomas Dekker: *Seven Deadly Sins of London*, 1606.
[2] Henslowe: *op. cit.* These properties belonged to the Admiral's Men; and Henslowe's list includes various items, such as 'the cauldron for the Jew', evidently used in the production of Marlowe's plays.

Nor were the players' costumes meagre makeshift affairs; it is no longer believed that the Elizabethan actor donned contemporary clothing. In 1595, on a manuscript copy of *Titus Andronicus* now preserved at Longleat, Henry Peacham made a pen-and-ink drawing, to illustrate Tamora pleading for her son, which shows the Emperor wearing classical dress, as recreated by an Elizabethan artist, Tamora, a loosely flowing robe, and the black-visaged Aaron, buskins and a Roman kilt; though the two pike-trailing figures behind the sovereign exhibit sixteenth-century trunk-hose.

In this world of magnificent illusions, the successful Elizabethan actor was soon inclined to change his social status. The wardrobe he acquired was far too splendid for his rank or the wandering bohemian life he led; and Puritans, who attacked the evils of the stage, also thundered against his bad example: '. . . In a commonweal, if private men be suffered to forsake their calling because they desire to walk gentleman-like in silk and velvet . . . proportion is so broken, unity dissolved, harmony confounded, that the whole body must be dismembered.'[1] Among the 'glorious vagabonds'[2], rapidly enriching themselves about the year 1595, was Shakespeare, the prosperous 'sharer' and playwright, colleague of William Kempe and Richard Burbage, who during the course of the following year would secure for John Shakespeare his coveted grant of arms. But, before he had achieved that object, and had seen his father raised to gentlemanly rank, the poet lost his only son. On August 11th, 1596, the eleven-year-old Hamnet Shakespeare died and was buried in Stratford parish church. Evidently, once he had begun to make a name, Shakespeare had formed the habit of paying regular visits to the town; he was accustomed, Aubrey tells us, to return to his native country every twelve months. We do not know whether he was able to attend the funeral, or in what circumstances Hamnet died. Stratford had a rather unhealthy site; Elizabethan children, if they survived the nursing period, were always apt to drop off early; and

---

[1] Stephen Gosson: *Plays Confuted in Five Actions*, 1582.
[2] England affords these glorious vagabonds,
　　That carried earst their fardels on their backs,
　　Coursers to ride on through the gazing streets,
　　Swooping it in their glaring satin suits.
　　The Return from Parnassus, 1598.

more prolific parents usually accepted their loss in a mood of Christian resignation. But, to judge from the inferences we may permissibly draw from his work, Shakespeare's sense of loss went very deep. His interest in childhood and the tenderness he felt for children has been mentioned on an earlier page. Even the stern Prospero has a tender recollection of his daughter's unprotected infancy:

> ... i' th' dead of darkness
> The ministers for th' purpose hurried thence
> Me—and thy crying self

And Leontes in *The Winter's Tale*, gnawed by the earliest pangs of sexual jealousy as he watches his Queen and his former play-fellow Polixenes 'paddling palms and pinching fingers', turns for relief towards his son Mamillius:

> Art thou my boy?
> Mamillius: Ay, my good lord.
> Leontes: I'fecks!
>   Why, that's my bawcock. What, hast smutch'd thy
>   nose?
>   They say it is a copy out of mine. Come, captain,
>   We must be neat; not neat, but cleanly, captain: ...
>   ... How now, you wanton calf?
>   Art thou my calf?
> Mamillius: Yes, if you will, my lord.

Still more poignant are the references that crept into his latest play. Shakespeare's *King John*, listed by Francis Meres among Shakespeare's tragedies in 1598, is generally dated about 1595; and there Constance, bereft of her son Arthur, refuses the specious consolation offered by the Papal legate:

> There was not such a gracious creature born:
> But now will canker-sorrow eat my bud ...
> And he will look as hollow as a ghost,
> As dim and meagre as an ague's fit,
> And so he'll die; and, rising so again,

L

> When I shall meet him in the court of heaven
> I shall not know him . . .

Pandulph: You hold too heinous a respect of grief.
Constance: He talks to me that never had a son.
King Philip: You are as fond of grief as of your child.
Constance: Grief fills the room up of my absent child:
> Lies in his bed, walks up and down with me,
> Puts on his pretty looks, repeats his words . . .
> Stuffs out his vacant garments with his form;
> Then have I reason to be fond of grief!

Disease is doubly terrible when, before it kills, it disfigures and diminishes; and perhaps Hamnet Shakespeare, attacked by one of the paludal fevers that often ravaged damp, low-lying Stratford, as the sickness changed him and wore him down was reduced to a mere plaintive shadow. It seems obvious that Hamnet's death provoked some kind of moral crisis; for *King John* contains the opening version of a theme that runs through many of his later tragedies:

> Life is as tedious as a twice-told tale
> Vexing the dull ear of a drowsy man . . .

The human condition is both cruel and meaningless, and, because it lacks any discernible meaning, not only dark and tragic but wearisome and insignificant.

Typical of Shakespeare's genius, however, is the balance he maintained between his contradictory attributes, between a strain of deep, instinctive pessimism, and the no less instinctive love of life that drew him back towards the 'sweet world'. He had his father's robust and sanguine temperament; and he was soon busying himself about his ordinary affairs. There were plays to be written, productions to be staged and rewards to be accumulated; and, on October 28th, 1596, John Shakespeare, who, acting presumably through William, had renewed the application that he had been obliged to relinquish in 1575, was granted by the Garter Principal King of Arms[1] 'this shield or coat of arms, viz: Gold, on a bend

---

[1] The Garter Principal King of Arms' grant was presently challenged, though without effect, by his disputatious colleague the York Herald, who announced that John Shakespeare was one of the base persons whose claims he had chosen to favour.

sables, a spear of the first, steeled argent. And, for his crest or cognizance, a falcon, his wings displayed, argent . . . supporting a spear gold steeled as aforesaid, set upon a helmet with mantels and tassels as hath been accustomed . . .' The grant was justified by a mention of the 'faithful and valiant services' that John Shakespeare's 'late grandfather' was alleged to have rendered to 'the most prudent prince, King Henry the Seventh', and of his own marriage to 'the daughter and one of the heirs of Robert Arden of Wilmcote . . .' Shakespeare was not alone in aspiring to the rank of gentleman; seven members of his company eventually became armigerous;[1] and many satirists, including Ben Jonson, ridiculed this absurd contemporary craze. Gentlemen, had written Sir Thomas Smith, thirteen years earlier, 'be made cheap in England'; while 'I can write myself gentleman now,' boasted Jonson's Sogliardo, in *Every Man Out of his Humour*, whose motto 'Not without mustard' recalls Shakespeare's 'Non sans Droict'; 'here's my patent; it cost me thirty pounds . . .' Such aspirations are characteristic of a social system still rapidly changing and developing, in which the gentry were gaining power at the expense of the nobility, and at the same time attracting numerous recruits from the honest yeoman class, the solid sub-stratum of the system to which Shakespeare and his friends belonged.[2]

In 1597, Shakespeare further consolidated his position by acquir-ing an important piece of property—New Place, once the Cloptons' home and, despite its recent decay, among the noblest of all Stratfordian houses. Its absentee landlord William Underhill, son of a successful London lawyer, had put up the vacant house for sale; and on May 4th Shakespeare completed the bargain, paying a sum of sixty pounds and purchasing, besides the house itself, 'two barns, and two gardens and the appurtenances', situated near the school

---

[1] With mouthing words that better wits have framed
    They purchase lands and now esquires are named
                                  The Return from Parnassus.
[2] 'The facts reveal a society in which there is not only an increasing degree of mobility but in which social classes are changing their relations. In it the nobility are becoming less important than the gentry as a whole—even though the decline of the nobility has been exaggerated; the gentry are going from strength to strength, recruiting considerable elements from the yeomanry . . . the most dynamic class in Tudor society'; while 'the smaller folk and the poor. . become poorer.' A. L. Rowse: *op. cit.*

and the Guild Chapel in the very heart of Stratford. The playwright was now a substantial householder; he had founded a modest private fortune, realized John Shakespeare's disappointed hopes and raised the yeoman Shakespeares to a rank where they stood on an equal footing with his mother's family. All this thanks to his practice of a profession that most decent-minded citizens despised! In Stratford he might be liked and respected; but in London he and his company were still regarded by their Puritan opponents as a set of dangerous vagabonds. Towards the end of 1596, the City magistrates had revived their long campaign against the London players; and, with the permission of the new Lord Chamberlain—Lord Cobham, a foe of the stage, who briefly held that office between the two Lords Hunsdon[1]—they were excluded from the City Inns, where, during the winter months, they found it easier to collect an audience. At the same time, a speculative goldsmith named Francis Langley, who had bought Paris Garden among the fields of the Bankside, began to raise his own theatre. This playhouse, which Langley christened the Swan, 'built of a concrete of flints . . . supported by wooden columns so painted that they would deceive the most acute observer into thinking they were marble', was the stately edifice that Johannes de Witt admired. Langley's project enraged the City Fathers. Yet, although the Lord Mayor addressed yet another petition to the Council couched in the customary opprobrious terms, protesting that the Swan would not only provoke an assemblage of 'thieves, horse-stealers, whoremongers, cozeners, coney-catching persons, practisers of treason and such other like', but distract the populace from 'their resort unto sermons' and similar religious duties, his objections failed to move the Queen's government. Still to be reckoned with, however, was a local Surrey magistrate William Gardiner, who, under Cobham's less tolerant régime, made his authority felt along the Bankside. He and Langley were soon involved in noisy public disputation and Langley adopted the current legal device of 'craving sureties of the peace' against Gardiner and Gardiner's step-son William Wayte, declaring that his life was threatened. He himself had already styled the justice a 'false, foresworn and perjured knave'.

[1] The Hunsdons were related by blood to the Queen, and therefore, from the players' point of view, particularly valuable allies.

Shakespeare was presently drawn into the squabble. At Michael-mas Langley had 'craved sureties'; and, on November 29th, 1596, William Wayte, who would appear to have been Gardiner's creature and business agent, in his turn craved 'sureties of the peace against William Shakespeare, Francis Langley, Dorothy Soer, and Anne Lee, for fear of death, and so forth'.[1] The whole episode remains mysterious. Who were Dorothy Soer and Anne Lee? Here is 'gentle' Shakespeare caught up in a fracas that seemed likely to have a fatal end, possibly because the offensive Wayte, who acted on Gardiner's behalf, was interfering with his means of livelihood. But then, the average Elizabethan was often as violent and blood-thirsty as he was litigious; and we remember how, at the Theatre in 1590, Richard Burbage and his father James had fought a pitched battle with a Mistress Brayne, the widow of James' one-time partner, and the friends who championed her right to a fair share of the box-office re-ceipts; and how Richard's parents, looking out of a window had called them whores and murderous ruffians, while Richard laid about him with a broom and, catching hold of an antagonist's nose, handled it 'scornfully and disdainfully'. Such a contretemps may have occurred in the precincts of the Swan; and Shakespeare, Langley and the two unknown women who assisted them presumably came off victorious. The Swan continued to stand on the Bankside, though Langley soon ran into some further troubles; and Shakespeare, who had previously inhabited the parish of St Helen's, Bishopsgate, at length decided to move across the river, leaving behind him, we learn from official records, an unpaid due of five shillings.

[1] J. Leslie Hotson: *Shakespeare versus Shallow*, 1931.

CHAPTER VII

Romantic Comedies

ALTHOUGH 'NOT WITHOUT RIGHT' was the motto attached to John Shakespeare's brave new coat of arms, the successful dramatist could certainly have claimed that he was the industrious architect of his own fortunes. But, while he was still founding them, he may have received some help; and Rowe announces that 'he had the honour to meet with many great and uncommon marks of favour and friendship from the Earl of Southampton', including a display of aristocratic munificence 'so singular . . . that if I had not been assured that the story was handed down by Sir William Davenant, who was probably very well acquainted with his affairs', as a cautious biographer he would have preferred to disregard it: namely, that 'my Lord Southampton, at one time, gave him a thousand pounds, to enable him to go through with a purchase which he heard he had a mind to'. This bounty, adds Rowe, was 'very great, and very rare' at any period, being 'almost equal to that profuse generosity the present age has shown to French dancers and Italian eunuchs'. Large enough in the year 1709, the sum was extravagant by Elizabethan standards—after all, Shakespeare paid only £60 to become the master of New Place, with barns, gardens and appurtenances; and, should we remove a zero and reduce the amount to a hundred, it remains an uncommonly lavish gift. Yet, since the story was derived from Shakespeare's godson, it may have had some solid basis; and Shakespeare may have employed the money either to purchase a share in the Chamberlain's Company during the latter months of 1594, or—which appears less probable: by that stage he was already fairly affluent—to complete the transaction that brought him New Place.

Southampton was known as a 'cherisher' of poets; and this tale suggests that in his treatment of Shakespeare he proved a generous and far-sighted friend. But, assuming that he is the hero of the *Sonnets*, his admirer's debt was even more extensive; for the whole sequence, despite its sorrowful refrain, records an undiminished sense of gratitude—the artist's gratitude to any fellow human being who has strongly affected his imagination. And then, under Southampton's guidance, he may have generally enlarged his knowledge of the world, through the glimpses that his supporter provided into the life of high politics and high fashion. Shakespeare's interest in aristocratic company has again and again been pointed out, and how easily and confidently he describes the existence of the Elizabethan ruling classes. True, the fact that a man of genius depicts an unfamiliar milieu need not always mean that he is personally acquainted with it: like Balzac, Stendhal and Proust, Shakespeare was a middle-class writer who possessed an extraordinarily assimilative mind, and any indirect hints he gained from the Southampton circle he would have quickly snapped up. On the other hand, the cycle of romantic comedies that he composed between 1594 and 1600 seem to possess a very special colouring. The tone is 'young-mannish' observes a modern commentator; and the poet's male protagonists are inclined to 'hunt in threes';[1] they are fond of discussing love; they talk of poetry and philosophy, and share a quibbling 'coterie-speech'; but they are careful to avoid an undue display of seriousness, and give their conversation a lightly cynical turn, particularly when they are confronted and challenged by one of Shakespeare's boyish heroines. Was this the tone of Southampton's acquaintance? Well, whether Shakespeare invented this ideal aristocracy or it is a reflection of a life he knew, the comedies he produced in his middle period have an unmistakably aristocratic bias. The characters he treats affectionately are without exception young and nobly born; ridicule is usually reserved for the unlettered, course and ill-bred.

Hence the discomfort that the comedies have sometimes inspired

[1] '. . . So persistent is the triangle that it is hard to resist a suspicion that the same triangle existed among the "divers of worship" for whose eyes and ears they were primarily intended.' John Dover Wilson: *The Essential Shakespeare*, 1932.

among our sterner twentieth-century critics. For the average play-goer, everything that is lyrical in Shakespeare's genius is epitomized in *As You Like It, Much Ado About Nothing* or *A Midsummer Night's Dream*; yet now and then a detractor arises who takes the lyrical dramatist solemnly to task, attacks his snobbish prejudices, derides his comic machinery and emphasises the deplorable flimsiness of his dramatic workmanship. The comedies, we learn, were not written so much as loosely thrown together: 'the plots are engineered . . . with only the most off-hand concern for pantomime probability'; and both *As You Like It* and *Twelfth Night* 'show Shakespeare the provincial social climber at his most unsympathetic, ingratiating himself with the court set at the expense of his own social equals'. Into his 'arrogantly patrician comedies' Shakespeare mixed 'some popular ingredients—dirty jokes, pretty songs, great thoughts, titillating sex confusions, slapstick and class propaganda'—and topped off the result with a coating of 'creamy poetry'.[1] This is an extreme expression of the frankly hostile point of view; but almost as disturbing are the efforts of critical admirers who, when they attempt a detailed analysis of the plays, attribute to them a kind of intellectual solidity and moral muscularity that the poet's innocent text can scarcely claim. Shakespeare's romantic comedies are neither serious criticisms of life nor direct 'evaluations of experience'. Whatever a great artist produces must have some bearing on his attitude towards the world. But, so far as intention goes, the comedies are slight enough; Shakespeare set out to devise an entertainment, a dramatic fantasy or a poetic *capriccio*. His comedies have as little, and as much reference to the 'real world' as a picture of a courtly gathering painted by Watteau or a *fête champêtre* by Fragonard.

They belong in spirit to an imaginary universe, comic and idyllic, through which tragic personages—Shylock and Malvolio—sometimes make their unexpected way. All were probably composed to suit a festive occasion. Thus *A Midsummer Night's Dream* appears to have been written for a fashionable wedding, possibly that of William Earl of Derby and Elizabeth Vere, which took place at Greenwich on January 26th, 1595, and was attended by the Queen herself, to whom the dramatist inserted a flattering, but strangely

[1] Alan Brien: *Sunday Telegraph*, January 21st, 1962.

enigmatic, reference. As Titania reminds her angry lord, the previous summer had been wet and miserable;[1] and, although the summer seasons of 1595 and 1596 ran an almost equally unpleasant course, after a second and third calamity the subject of bad weather and poor harvests must surely have become a little stale. But, whenever it was composed, *A Midsummer Night's Dream* seems not to have been intended for an ordinary London playhouse; it requires the less prosaic background of a spacious and high-raftered hall, where torches and a galaxy of wax tapers would have thrown an inconstant light across the stage and suggested the mysterious labyrinths of a haunted 'wood near Athens'. Essential to the play is its atmosphere of dream-like illusion; and rather surprisingly, since it was composed for a marriage, its theme is the illusory nature of romantic love. 'Here,' wrote Benedetto Croce, 'the quick ardours, the inconstancies, the caprices, the illusions, the delusions, every sort of love folly, become embodied and weave a world of their own[2] . . .' Shakespeare's drama embraces a whole series of worlds, separate but superimposed, each occupying a different plane; and apart from the world of Theseus and Hippolyta, who sit enthroned to watch the spectacle, on each of these superimposed planes discord and confusion flourish. Love is represented as a form of madness that sends its human victims groping blindly through the wood, and drives the ethereal Queen of the Fairies into the clumsy arms of an astonished mortal.

Among the source-books that Shakespeare obviously employed was Reginald Scot's massive volume, *The Discoverie of Witchcraft*, first published in 1584. Scot, who had earlier produced an important agricultural treatise which he called *A Perfect Platform of a Hop Garden*, was a realist concerned with the superstitions of the time only to expose their falsity, and to defend foolish, crack-brained old women against 'the tyrannical cruelty of witchmongers and inquisitors'. He does not presume to question the real existence of devils, demons and supernatural entities; but he ridicules the elaborate hierarchy of Satanic princes and dukes drawn up by contemporary demonologists, remarking that 'he that can be persuaded that these

[1] Act II Scene i.
[2] *Ariosto, Shakespeare, and Corneille*, translated by Douglas Ainslie, 1920.

things are true . . . may soon be brought to believe that the moon is made of green cheese'. In the process, however, Scot had managed to collect a vast quantity of illuminating information, both on the subject of witches and witchcraft, and on the popular beliefs of Elizabethan England as they were dinned into a child's ears:

> . . . In our childhood, our mothers' maids have so terrified us with an ugly devil having horns on his head, fire in his mouth, and a tail in his breech . . . and they have so frayed us with bull-beggars, spirits, witches, urchins, elves, hags, fairies, satyrs, pans, fauns, sylens, kit-with-the-canstick, tritons, centaurs, dwarfs, giants, imps, calcars, conjurors, nymphs, changelings, *Incubus*, Robin Good-Fellow, the sporne, the mare, the man-in-the-oak, the hell wain, the firedrake, the puckle, Tom Thumb, hobgoblin, Tom Tumbler, Boneless, and such other bugs, that we are afraid of our own shadows . . .

Belief in the fairy kingdom, and in the powers exercised by a large company of domestic sprites, including Puck or Robin Good-Fellow, was particularly prevalent among Elizabethan country people. These 'jocund and facetious spirits are said to sport themselves in the night by tumbling and fooling with servants and shepherds in country houses, pinching them black and blue, and leaving bread, butter and cheese sometimes with them, which if they refuse to eat some mischief shall undoubtedly befall them . . . And many such have been taken away by the said spirits, for a fortnight or a month together, being carried with them in chariots through the air, over hills and dales, rocks and precipices, till at last they have been found lying in some meadow or mountain, bereaved of their senses, and commonly of one of their members to boot'. Allied to the 'innumerable troops' of fairies, 'there are also nymphs of the woods, mountains, groves and fountains . . . said to be altogether of the feminine kind, sporting and dancing and feasting amongst the trees in the woods', and bathing in fresh and limpid waters. About the exact organization of the fairy realm, Scot is excusably a little vague; but he writes of Madam Sibylia, 'gentle virgin of fairies', who resembles a beautiful woman in glistening white raiment; 'three sisters of fairies', who confer 'the ring of invisibility'; a fairy king and 'the Lady of the fairies', known as Sibylla, Minerva, or Diana, who is closely associated with witches and, in their company, 'delicately banquets with the Devil' and sees them off on their nocturnal jaunts. 'Friar Bartholomaeus saith that the witches themselves, before they anoint themselves, do hear in the night time a great noise of minstrels, which fly over them with the Lady of the fairies. But then I marvel again [Scot cautiously remarks] that nobody else heareth nor seeth this troops of minstrels, especially riding in a moonlight night. It is marvel that they think this to be but a dream.'

Brought up in rural Warwickshire, not far from a village that, even during the twentieth century, is still sometimes reputed to be a centre of the witch-cult, Shakespeare must have acquired a solid groundwork of current supernatural lore. But Scot's book clearly attracted him; and, among other points, he noted the story, which he would have encountered under another guise in Apuleius' picaresque novel,[1] of how a certain English seaman, 'a sturdy young fellow', whose ship was visiting a Mediterranean port, 'went to a woman's house . . . not far from the seaside, to see whether she had any eggs to sell', and was there, by the woman's magical arts, transformed into the semblance of an ass. But Shakespeare also borrowed from Chaucer's 'Knight's Tale', which furnished him with Theseus, Hippolyta and some hints for the disputatious lovers; while from Ovid he derived the name 'Titania', attached by the Roman poet to the huntress Diana, and from Lord Berners' early-sixteenth-century version of *Huon of Bordeaux* the name he allotted to her royal consort. His childhood memories of the splendid Kenilworth pageants may have supplied some supplementary details, and the sovereign's presence have inspired Oberon's famous description of the 'fair vestal', the 'imperial votaress' still fancy-free, against whom Cupid, 'flying between the cold moon and the earth', had once loosed his ill-directed arrow.[2] All these elements are assembled and fused

[1] William Adlington's translation of *The Golden Ass* was first published in 1566, and thrice reprinted during the next thirty years.

[2] Act II Scene i. If Essex was present at the wedding, the reference would have had a double edge; since, among her subjects, it was Essex's stepfather Leicester who had made the deepest impression on the Queen's heart, though he had failed ultimately to capture it. Can the 'little western flower', on whom Cupid's shaft fell, have been his susceptible mother Lettice, disgraced after her marriage with Leicester, who then retired to an estate in the West Country? True, Lettice's real character seems to have been anything but flower-like.

together to form the substance of a waking vision, a long frieze of diverse poetic imagery like the pictured ribbons of dissolving dream-stuff that Hans Andersen, in his story, *The Snow Queen*, describes, as they sweep through the palace, wreathing and unrolling above little Gerda's head.[1] Such a vision is necessarily evanescent; and, to convey the brilliance and the brevity of love, Shakespeare uses the image he had already employed in *Romeo and Juliet*, that of a tremulous sheet of lighting which quivers suddenly across a darkened sky:

> Ay me! for aught that I could ever read . . .
> The course of true love never did run smooth;
> But, either it was different in blood . . .
> Or else misgraffed in respect of years . . .
> Or else it stood upon the choice of friends . . .
> Or, if there were a sympathy in choice,
> War, death, or sickness did lay siege to it—
> Making it momentary as a sound,
> Swift as a shadow, short as any dream,
> Brief as the lightning in the collied night,
> That, in a spleen, unfolds both heaven and earth;
> And ere a man hath power to say 'Behold!'
> The jaws of darkness do devour it up:
> So quick bright things come to confusion.

La Vida es sueño—life is a dream—to use the title of Calderon's play, written some fifty years later—or, more exactly, a succession of dreams, different yet, for the purposes of Shakespeare's comedy, interwoven in a single pattern. Each dreamer has his self-centred vision of existence; each is enclosed within his separate past; and again Shakespeare summons up snatches of the past to heighten our appreciation of the present day. Thus, Hippolyta recollects the pleasures of a royal hunt—

> I was with Hercules and Cadmus once,
> When in a wood of Crete they bayed the bear
> With hounds of Sparta: never did I hear

[1] '. . . There was a rushing sound as of something passing; strange-looking shadows flitted rapidly along the wall; horses with long, slender legs and fluttering manes; huntsmen, knights, and ladies. "These are only Dreams!" said the Raven; "they come to amuse the great personages here at night . . ." '

Such gallant chiding, for besides the groves,
The skies, the fountains, every region near
Seem'd all one mutual cry. I never heard
So musical a discord, such sweet thunder.

—and Oberon and Titania exchange hurtfully vivid memories of one
another's former whims:

Oberon: Ill met by moonlight, proud Titania.
Titania: What, jealous Oberon! Fairies, skip hence—
    I have forsworn his bed and company.
Oberon: Tarry, rash wanton. Am not I thy lord?
Titania: Then I must be thy lady: but I know
    When thou hast stol'n away from fairy land,
    And in the shape of Corin sat all day,
    Playing on pipes of corn, and versing love,
    To amorous Phyllida. Why art thou here . . .
    But that, forsooth, the bouncing Amazon,
    Your buskin'd mistress and your warrior love,
    To Theseus must be wedded . . .
Oberon: How canst thou thus for shame, Titania,
    Glance at my credit with Hippolyta,
    Knowing I know thy love to Theseus?
    Didst thou not lead him through the glimmering night
    From Perigenia, whom he ravished?

Whereas the distracted lovers lost in the wood are mere decorative
literary puppets, both Oberon and Titania, dream-figures though we
know them to be, are charged with life and fiery feeling; and it is
their shrill vivacity that serves to distinguish them from their unruffled fellow sovereigns, King Theseus and Queen Hippolyta, who
reflect the modern magnificence of Elizabeth and her court seated
opposite the stage. Each group is set off by Bottom and his friends,
including Snug the Joiner, possibly modelled on the Kenilworth
Arion, honest Harry Goldingham. Towards these 'rude mechanicals'
and their ridiculous play, Shakespeare and Theseus alike adopt a
roughly patronizing air; but Bottom at least eludes such patronage
and asserts his individual dignity, when, stretched out upon

Titania's bed, he, too, enjoys his royal dream, issuing his commands and extending his princely favour with a benign aplomb that would do Theseus credit. The weaver is introduced as a low and foolish person—'the shallowest thick-skin of that barren sort'—born to bandy broad jokes, misuse the language and afford mild amusement to his social betters. Shakespeare echoes their well-bred derision; but, whatever his purpose may have been, he cannot wholly countenance it. There are few 'common men' in his tragedies and comedies, unless they form part of an indistinguishable mob. Any character who receives his close attention, on whom the beam of his poetic insight falls, almost at once begins to display some absorbing native singularities.

Compared with the lavish, romantic, flower-wreathed *Dream*, *The Merchant of Venice*, probably written about the same date, seems a somewhat frigid and unattractive work. But it reveals the complete mastery of English blank verse that Shakespeare had achieved since he set to work on *Romeo and Juliet* only two or three years earlier; and, even more strikingly perhaps than the *Dream*, it illustrates the curiously eclectic method by which he gathered and absorbed his raw material. In the first place, he was indebted to an old play, or possibly to several old plays; for, as early as 1579, Stephen Gosson, during the course of his violent attack on poets, players and 'such like caterpillars of a commonwealth', applauds certain contemporary dramas that convey a salutary moral lesson, among them a play entitled *The Jew*, which exposes 'the greediness of worldly choosers' and the 'bloody minds of usurers'. The story of Shylock's bond and the casket episode were both derived from published sources; and the dramatist was clearly stimulated by the popular success of Marlowe's *Jew of Malta*. At the same time, his imagination was stirred by a lurid piece of modern history—the dreadful fate that, early in the summer of 1594, had befallen the Queen's physician Dr Lopez, a learned Portuguese Jew, who had also attended Leicester and Sir Francis Walsingham, but who, despite his learning and his powerful political friends, had paid the ghastly penalty reserved for traitors.

It had been a horrible and deeply mysterious affair. Lopez had already spent seventeen untroubled years in England, when Esteban

Ferreira, one of the adherents of Don Antonio, the impoverished pretender to the Portuguese throne who held his shabby court at Windsor, was arrested on suspicion of having conspiratorial dealings with the Spanish government. Under duress, Ferreira incriminated Lopez; and the royal physician proceeded to behave in an extremely evasive and compromising fashion, and presently acknowledged that he had received a diamond-and-ruby ring from a messenger of the Spanish sovereign himself. Evidently he had something to hide: he may well have been a double agent; and Walsingham, chief architect of the English secret service, who might conceivably have saved him, had been dead since 1590. William and Robert Cecil supported this trusted servant; but Essex seized on the issue and determined to make it a political trial of strength. Lopez therefore was removed to Essex House, where the favourite conducted his own enquiry and soon elicited the right evidence: 'I have discovered,' he assured Anthony Bacon, his lieutenant, 'a most dangerous and desperate treason. The point of conspiracy was her Majesty's death. The executioner should have been Dr. Lopez; the manner, poison.' Although Elizabeth took the Cecils' side and, in one of her frequent outbursts against Essex, denounced him as a 'rash and temerarious youth', Lopez, confused and terrified, was slowly involved in his accusers' toils, until at last they had broken him down and wrung out of him the admissions that they needed. He was then convicted of high treason with his alleged accomplices, and dragged on a hurdle from the King's Bench, through the streets of London, towards Tyburn in the open country. Beneath the gallows, he declared his innocence and protested that he loved the Queen as dearly as he loved Jesus Christ—a speech that, as he had been born a Jew, moved the assembly to loud, derisive laughter.

Thus in 1594, and during the years that followed, any representation of a villainous Jew was likely to attract an audience;[1] and it would have particularly appealed to Essex, Dr Lopez' self-appointed judge, who could claim that, with patriotic diligence, he had unravelled and laid bare the whole conspiracy. The Doctor's name was often spelt Lopus; and Gratiano exclaims that the spirit of a wolf, gibbeted for killing a man, must have passed into the womb of

---

[1] Marlowe's old-fashioned *Jew of Malta* was revived at the time of the Lopez trial.

Shylock's mother. So far Shakespeare's intention seems plain enough—he would draw the portrait of a blood-thirsty Jewish miscreant; but, as he wrote, the imaginative artist assumed control of the commercial playwright, and Shylock began to address the audience, no longer furiously for himself alone, but passionately and eloquently on behalf of an entire persecuted race whose sufferings comprehended his:

> I am a Jew. Hath not a Jew eyes? hath not a Jew hands, organs, dimensions, senses, affections, passions? fed with the same food, hurt with the same weapons, subject to the same diseases, healed by the same means, warmed and cooled by the same winter and summer, as a Christian is? If you prick us, do we not bleed? if you tickle us, do we not laugh? if you poison us, do we not die? and if you wrong us, shall we not revenge? if we are like you in the rest, we will resemble you in that . . . The villainy you teach me I execute, and it shall go hard but I will better the instruction.

He was bound to think, remarked Nicholas Rowe, that 'the incomparable character of Shylock . . . was designed tragically by the author'. Burbage, who no doubt played the Jew as a conventional melodramatic villain, scored yet another triumph in the part, wearing a red wig and a long red beard; but, at least since the opening of the nineteenth century, when Edmund Kean revived Burbage's role, the spiritual disproportion between Shylock and his persecutors has fascinated European critics. 'That he has but one idea,' wrote Hazlitt, 'is not true; he has more ideas than any other person in the piece; and if he is intense and inveterate in pursuit of his purpose, he shews the utmost elasticity, vigour and presence of mind, in the means of attaining it.' Shylock is a determined hater:

> So can I give no reason, nor I will not,
> More than a lodged hate and a certain loathing
> I bear Antonio . . .

Yet somehow the sheer compression of his feelings commands our respect, and even extorts a kind of sympathy: because his opponents have so much less capacity for feeling, their grievances carry far less weight. Shylock has been misjudged and maltreated—that is the suspicion that slowly steals across a modern audience. Kean drove the suspicion home; and Heine describes seeing a performance of the play at Drury Lane, during his visit to the British capital, when 'a beautiful pale-faced Englishwoman', who stood behind him in the box, 'wept profusely at the end of the fourth act, and called out repeatedly: "The poor man is wronged". Her face was of the noblest Greek cast . . . I have never been able to forget those big dark eyes weeping for Shylock.'[1] Perhaps Shakespeare, considered the German-Jewish writer, 'had in mind to create . . . a trained werewolf, a loathsome fabulous monster thirsting for blood, and thereby losing his daughter and his ducats . . . But the genius of the poet, the universal spirit which inspires him, is always above his individual will'. And certainly, in the Jew's antagonists—'the bankrupt Antonio . . . a weakling without energy . . . a dull worm's heart', Bassanio 'a true fortune-hunter', and Lorenzo, the accomplice of 'an infamous burglary'—Shakespeare has produced a sufficiently unattractive group of characters, whose smug self-congratulations strike a false and petty note.

Like so many of the dramatist's largest personages, Shylock is a lonely being; and his solitude gives him a bulk and majesty denied to his talkative, gregarious foes. He faces the terrible reality of his position: they exist in an atmosphere of gay poetic make-believe. Not that Shakespeare is inclined to discount their charm; he understood both modes of living. He could visualize the plight of Lopez questioned by Essex in his book-lined study, confronted with the prospect of entering the Tower and suffering on its well-used rack, and yet appreciate the delightful, carefree existence that went on elsewhere in the same house, among the Antonios, Bassanios and Lorenzos who enjoyed the great man's generous friendship. Lorenzo, writes Heine, is 'not only the receiver of stolen ducats and jewels, but also receptive to beauty, to moonlit landscapes and music'; and he and Jessica celebrate their deliverance in some of the loveliest verses that Shakespeare ever wrote. All poetry is said to aspire to the condition of music; and the idea is seldom more intelligible, or comes closer to perfect fulfilment, than in the first scene of the fifth act. Shylock has rushed out, doomed to ignominious baptism and followed by

---

[1] *Shakespeare's Women and Girls*, 1839.

M

Gratiano's savagely expressed regret that he has not received a far less lenient sentence; and Portia has despatched the deed that her fallen adversary must willy-nilly sign. Then the scene shifts to the moonlit gardens of Belmont:

> Lorenzo: The moon shines bright. In such a night as this,
> When the sweet wind did gently kiss the trees,
> And they did make no noise, in such a night
> Troilus methinks mounted the Troyan walls,
> And sighed his soul toward the Grecian tents,
> Where Cressid lay that night.
>
> Jessica: In such a night
> Did Thisbe fearfully o'ertrip the dew,
> And saw the lion's shadow ere himself,
> And ran dismayed away.
>
> Lorenzo: In such a night
> Stood Dido with a willow in her hand
> Upon the wild sea banks, and waft her love
> To come again to Carthage.
>
> Jessica: In such a night
> Medea gathered the enchanted herbs
> That did renew old Aeson.
>
> Lorenzo: In such a night
> Did Jessica steal from the wealthy Jew,
> And with an unthrift love did run from Venice
> As far as Belmont.
>
> Jessica: In such a night
> Did young Lorenzo swear he loved her well,
> Stealing her soul with many vows of faith,
> And ne'er a true one.[1]

This exquisite antiphonal melody must surely owe something to Shakespeare's recollections of an Elizabethan part-song. It is interrupted by 'the footing of a man'—Stephano heralding his mistress Portia, and Launcelot, another cheerfully discordant presence, who comes hallooing through the dusk. Their interruptions supply the

---

[1] It has been suggested that, while writing this passage, Shakespeare may have referred to Chaucer's *Legend of Good Women*, where Troilus, Thisbe, Dido and Medea pass in quick succession.

necessary pause; after which Lorenzo, for the occasion a great poet, can introduce a second lyric theme:

> How sweet the moonlight sleeps upon this bank!
> Here will we sit, and let the sounds of music
> Creep in our ears—soft stillness and the night
> Become the touches of sweet harmony.
> Sit, Jessica. Look how the floor of heaven
> Is thick inlaid with patens of bright gold,
> There's not the smallest orb which thou behold'st
> But in his motion like an angel sings,
> Still quiring to the young-eyed cherubins;
> Such harmony is in immortal souls!
> But whilst this muddy vesture of decay
> Doth grossly close it in, we cannot hear it.

Lorenzo's speech has the 'life-enhancing' quality that Berensonian critics distinguish in the noblest works of visual art; and our immediate response, as we read, is a glorious sense of amplitude and freedom. There is nothing contrived about the movement of the verse; nothing obstructs its steadily expanding flow; it spreads through the imagination like an advancing tide; the effect it produces is so subtly natural that we are apt to forget that it has achieved its effect by strenuously artificial means. Shakespeare's blank verse, remarks Hazlitt—he has attempted a comparison of Shakespeare and Milton—'is not stately and uniformly swelling . . . but varied and broken', and owes its enchanting variety to 'the inequalities of the ground it has to pass over in its uncertain course . . .'[1] In earlier plays, Shakespeare builds up his speeches with the help of the rhyming couplet or the single line, each a self-contained unit; but here the unit he employs is the sentence or the verse paragraph, each forming a separate source of melody, and providing an ingenious contrast to the music of the lines that follow. No less easy and masterful is his treatment of his subject matter. If we study a Shakespearian comedy or tragedy after examining the productions of a contemporary dramatic poet—those of George Chapman, for example, his ambitious but laborious rival—we notice that, whereas his contemporaries

Lectures on English Poets, 1818.

seem to be hard at work, struggling to give the subject they have chosen an appropriate literary shape, hammering their meaning into words and then refining on the words themselves, Shakespeare's use of language resembles an alchemic process that lends the subject with which he happens at the time to be engaged a completely fresh and unexpected value, as association adds to association, and from one evocative image springs another. In the passage I have transcribed above, his subject is a vision of the starry sky, the pre-Copernican picture of the heavens revolving round a central earth. This theory scientists were beginning to discard; but, since it was still rooted in the mind of the ordinary man, Shakespeare gladly takes it up. It affords him the point of departure he needs; and, revived by him, it acquires a new validity. Under his direction, the crystalline translucent spheres still revolve in heavenly concert, and the eternal hymn of the planets and stars is raised towards the Empyrean.

The remaining comedies of Shakespeare's middle period are thought to have been written during its last few years—*Much Ado About Nothing* in 1598 or 1599, *As You Like It* in 1599 or 1600; while *Twelfth Night* may have been presented at Whitehall on Twelfth Night in January 1601, just before the downfall of Essex had cast a gloom across the Court, when Elizabeth entertained a visiting Italian nobleman, Don Virginio Orsino, Duke of Bracciano.[1] As usual, the dramatist was content to borrow his plots—those of *Much Ado* and *Twelfth Night* from translations or adaptations of Italian stories by Bandello, and the outline of *As You Like It* from Lodge's *Rosalynde*, itself derived from a medieval romance. In such popular tales, with their elaborate deceptions and disguises and complex amatory mishaps, Shakespeare found the material that he needed for his boy-actors. Little is recorded of these gifted adolescents—how they were engaged and trained or the kind of personal lives they led; but some of them are known to us by name; and one, Nathan Field, who, having begun his career at the age of thirteen, grew up to be an adult actor, had his portrait painted as a young man, the picture of a dark-eyed, sensitive, melancholy face, which still retains considerable traces of the subject's boyish good looks.

[1] See J. Leslie Hotson: *The First Night of Twelfth Night*, 1954

Presumably both looks and talent were required; boy-actors must fit naturally into the parts of pretty well-bred girls, have waists that would suit a stomacher, and sufficient agility and grace to manage the cumbrous skirts of an Elizabethan farthingale. In Shakespeare's company, there was a somewhat diminutive boy and another of unusual height; and, while he was writing *A Midsummer Night's Dream*, it was for the smaller of the two that he designed the part of Hermia, who speaks scornfully of her rival's 'tall personage' and compares Helena to a 'painted maypole'[1] The boy actor, too, must cut a fashionable figure in doublet, cloak and trunk-hose; girls travestied as boys were always immensely popular with an Elizabethan audience; and Shakespeare not only allowed his comic heroines frequent excuses to put on masculine apparel, but gave their mentality and speech a slightly ambiguous, hermaphroditic cast. With their strange mixture of innocence and experience, romantic feeling and sharp-spoken candour, masculine bravado and feminine nervosity, they tread a delicate line between the sexes. None of them is a completely mature woman; they belong to a period of human existence when the mildest girl is sometimes tomboyish, and even the most energetic boy may now and then shed girlish tears.

None is afraid of a *double entendre* or shrinks before a bawdy joke. They are impetuous, high-spirited, headstrong, naturally provocative and at times aggressive; and in *Much Ado About Nothing* Shakespeare reverted to the desperate battle of the sexes with which he had already dealt in *The Taming of the Shrew* and *Love's Labour's Lost*. Here his chosen adversaries, Beatrice and Benedick, though designed as subsidiary characters, soon monopolize the whole play; beside them, the virtuous Hero, the jealous Claudio and the melancholy, vicious Don John—he is another of Shakespeare's self-centred solitaries—make at their best a remarkably vague impression. These personages merely carry on the plot, a rather foolish story of deception and intrigue; but meanwhile, between the brilliant antagonists,

Now I perceive that she hath made compare
Between our statures, she hath urged her height,
And with her personage, her tall personage,
Her height, forsooth, she hath prevailed with him . . .
How low am I, thou painted maypole? speak . . .
                                        Act III Scene ii.

springs up a blaze of loving-hatred, as the 'kind of merry war'
that inspires their first exchanges develops into a fierce involuntary
struggle, and the stirrings of an unacknowledged attraction sharpen
their resentment and enhance their fury. Beatrice, when she rages
against Benedick, is also raging against her own nature; Benedick,
despite his pride and stubbornness, admits now and then, that
he is exhausted and bewildered almost to the point of stupefac-
tion:

> O, she misused me past the endurance of a block: an oak but with
> one green leaf on it would have answered her . . .

And neither will admit that only a submission to instinct can provide
the solution they are both seeking, until Benedick grasps his beloved
enemy in his arms and 'stops her mouth' with a sudden, violent kiss.

Since every comedy must have its clowns, Shakespeare added the
rustic humours of Dogberry and his fellow watchmen. According to
an old tradition reported by John Aubrey, the dramatist had encountered a similar constable at Grendon in Buckinghamshire on a
journey between London and Stratford. Like Bottom, the verbose,
officious underling—the part was apparently composed for Kempe,
while Richard Cowley, another important member of Shakespeare's
company, took the part of Verges—seems to have been intended to
raise a cultured laugh: he represents the Elizabethan lower-classes,
with their awkward interest in self-improvement. But he, too, once
Shakespeare has had time to examine him and, so to speak, has
walked around him, acquires a certain native dignity; and, when he
hears Conrade flout his age and office and roundly 'write him down
an ass', he is not so much indignant—though indignation heightens
his inward turmoil—as gravely astounded and magnificently
incredulous:

> I am a wise fellow, and which is more an officer, and which is
> more—a householder, and which is more—as pretty a piece of
> flesh as any is in Messina, and one that knows the law, go to, and
> a rich fellow enough, go to, and a fellow that hath had losses, and
> one that hath two gowns, and everything handsome about him.
> Bring him away. O that I had been writ down an ass!

For Sicilian Messina, we may, of course, substitute any English town or village. Shakespeare's Mediterranean backgrounds are always enlivened by English country references; and especially English is the setting of *As You Like It*, where the Warwickshire Forest of Arden, the domesticated woodland region north-east of Stratford, is re-peopled with romantic outlaws. Among the comedies of the poet's middle period, it is probably the most enjoyed; and some commentators would have us assume that it includes an edifying moral framework, being 'centred on the vision of the happiness available in this world through personally satisfying, humanely poised and socially accepted love'. The forest glades, we are further informed, provide 'a space temporarily free from the operation of vice', in which 'the central figures, Rosalind, Celia and Orlando, can face the reality of vice and yet escape contamination, can face the deviations of folly and yet, through self-knowledge and self-discipline, dismiss them with an effortless superiority'.[1] Such an encomium might have pleased, but would undoubtedly have puzzled, Shakespeare; and it is arguable that, although our study of an artist involves continuous re-interpretation, and although what, in fact, he did sometimes bears very little resemblance to what we may imagine was his original purpose, we should refrain from employing terms that reflect the theories and prejudices of a completely different social era. I cannot believe that Rosalind sets out on her pilgrimage seeking, with the help of self-knowledge and self-discipline, to achieve the happiness that accompanies humanely poised, socially accepted passion. She is pursuing love as the reward of a courtly game, in which considerations of vice and virtue, except for their obvious dramatic appeal, play a very small part. Even Jaques, the gloomy spectator of the action, is not an independent moralist. His moralizings are a symptom of his state, rather than expression of deeply felt views; for he is a 'humorous' character—a person, that is to say, whose temperament is governed and deformed by the excess of a single bodily humour; which, in the constitution of Jaques, is the 'melancholic humour', otherwise the black bile. Incidentally, his speech on the Ages of Man comes straight from the Elizabethan classroom; Jaques, clearly a student of rhetoric, combines Aristotle's

[1] G. K. Hunter: *William Shakespeare: The Late Comedies*, 1962.

description of the Three Ages with many later passages of much the same type.[1] His theory that 'All the world's a stage' was already current as 'an old proverb'.[2]

Despite Jaques' atrabilious interventions, *As You Like It* is not a moral comedy. Than Rosalind, its gallant boyish heroine, no one could be more at home in the world in which she finds herself, or less concerned to fit her experience of life into a predetermined moral pattern. She and her friends are only distinguished from the 'country copulatives', Touchstone and Audrey, by their wit and good breeding. Her view of love and marriage appears to be lightly cynical: 'Love is merely a madness; and, I tell you, deserves as well a dark house and a whip as madmen do.' She ridicules the amatory superstitions of the day: ' . . . These are all lies: men have died from time to time and worms have eaten them, but not for love'. Compared with Orlando, she is a blithe dispassionate realist, who has a proper appreciation of physical desires:

> . . . There was never any thing so sudden but the fight of two rams . . . Your brother and my sister no sooner met but they looked; no sooner looked but they loved; no sooner loved but they sighed; no sooner sighed but they asked one another the reason; no sooner knew the reason but they sought the remedy: and in these degrees they have made a pair of stairs to marriage, which they will climb incontinent, or else be incontinent before marriage: they are in the very wrath of love, and they will together; clubs cannot part them.
> Orlando:
> They shall be married tomorrow . . . But, O, how bitter a thing it is to look into happiness through another man's eyes!

Of Shakespeare's Rosalind, Bernard Shaw, who claimed that he knew *As You Like It* 'almost as well as I know Beethoven's Pastoral Symphony', once wrote that she was 'to the actress what Hamlet is to the actor—a part in which, reasonable presentability being granted, failure is hardly possible'. But Rosalind, he added, 'is not a complete human being: she is simply an extension into five acts of the most

---

[1] Many references to the Seven Ages of Man are to be found in fifteenth-century literature and painting.
[2] See p. 53.

affectionate, fortunate, delightful five minutes in the life of a charming woman. And all the other figures in the play are cognate impostures. Orlando, Adam, Jaques, Touchstone, the banished Duke, and the rest each play the same tune all through.' It was in *As You Like It*, Shaw continues, 'that the sententious William first began to openly exploit the fondness of the British Public for sham moralizing and stage "philosophy" '.[1] But Shaw's attitude towards Shakespeare was compounded of many different feelings: although he ridiculed Victorian 'bardolatry' and despised what he thought to be Shakespeare's cynicism, facile romanticism and lack of any real 'ideas', periodically he succumbed to deep unwilling admiration, and would then agree that the poet's 'enormous command of word music' often prevailed against one's better judgement, and that Shakespeare's method of portraying character, which owed its effect to the magical beauty of the line, let us into the secret of the 'utterer's mood, not by its commonplace meaning, but by some subtle exaltation, or stultification, or slyness, or delicacy, or hesitancy ... in the sound of it'. Rosalind, whom Shakespeare makes no attempt to portray with psychological or social accuracy, is not a character so much as the characterization of a mood, an exquisite poetic 'essence'. We cannot tell which of his boy-actors he chose to represent his heroine; but he himself is thought to have played Adam; and an ancient Stratfordian neighbour, asked for his recollections of the poet, remembered that he had seen him 'brought on the stage, upon another man's back . . .'[2]

If *As You Like It* is an amoral comedy, still less edifying is the effect of *Twelfth Night*, which shows us Virtue—at least a well-meaning simulacrum of virtue—overthrown by Idleness and Folly. I have suggested elsewhere that Malvolio deserves to rank among the dramatist's tragic characters; for his predicament is unquestionably tragic, though here portrayed with comic licence. Like Shylock, he

---

[1] *Shaw on Shakespeare*, edited by Edwin Wilson, 1961.
Much of Shaw's resentment seems to have been based on the fact that Shakespeare appeared not to have grasped the tremendous didactic possibilities of the drama, and that he was neither an early Ibsen nor a prototype of Shaw himself. Yet Shaw concedes that 'a "Doll's House" will be as flat as ditch water when "A Midsummer Night's Dream" will still be as fresh as paint. . . . Ibsen's play, however, will have done more work in the world; and that is enough for the highest genius, which is always intensely utilitarian.'
[2] Edward Capell: *Commentary*, 1774.

is a lonely man, who, since he cannot escape from his inward solitude is mocked and abused by his gregarious fellows; and, strangely enough, there is even a distinguishable link between Malvolio, 'sick of self-love', and Richard III, who, as death approaches and his enemies close around him, perceives how obstinately he loves himself. Richard is reduced to admiring his shadow; and Olivia's steward, at the peak of his self-esteem, when he imagines that he has snared her fancy, is detected by her woman Maria rehearsing deportment in the garden: '. . . He has been yonder i' the sun practising behaviour to his own shadow this half hour . . .' Yet, except for his strain of complacent egotism, Malvolio exhibits few discreditable traits. 'He is not essentially ludicrous,' Charles Lamb observes, '. . . but dignified, consistent, and . . . rather of an over-stretched morality . . . His quality is at the best unlovely, but neither buffoon nor contemptible. His bearing is lofty, a little above his station, but probably not much above his deserts. We see no reason why he should not have been brave, honourable, accomplished . . . His dialect on all occasions is that of a gentleman and a man of education.'[1] The steward's chief offence is that he should have attempted to introduce some kind of order and decorum into his mistress' sadly ill-run household; the two gentlemanly parasites, Sir Toby and Sir Andrew, resent his pompous but meritorious efforts, and aided by Olivia's meddlesome waiting woman, bring out the frailty that undermines his character. He is relegated to a domestic cell 'as dark as ignorance', thrown on to a miserable bed of straw and branded as a raving lunatic; but from that 'hideous darkness' he addresses his persecutors in the voice of desperately patient reason.

Malvolio is at last released, to meditate revenge and nurse his injured pride. 'He hath been most notoriously abused', concludes Olivia; and the Duke sends after him a messenger of peace. Marriages are planned:

> A solemn combination shall be made
> Of our dear souls

Then *Exeunt all, except Clown*, left on the empty stage to dismiss the audience and sing his beautiful, doleful nonsense-poem:

[1] *On Some Old Actors.*

When that I was and a little tiny boy,
With hey, ho, the wind and the rain:
A foolish thing was but a toy,
For the rain it raineth every day.

But when I came to man's estate,
With hey, ho, the wind and the rain:
'Gainst knaves and thieves men shut their gate,
For the rain it raineth every day.

But when I came alas to wive,
With hey, ho, the wind and the rain:
By swaggering could I never thrive,
For the rain it raineth every day . . .'

The singer, no doubt, was Robert Armin; for about 1598 the celebrated William Kempe, 'that most comical and conceited cavalier Monsieur du Kempe, jestmonger and viceregent general to the ghost of Dick Tarlton', who had inherited Tarlton's tradition of broad and ribald slapstick clowning, sold his share in the Chamberlain's company and literally danced away from London. As good a dancer as he was a droll, Kempe embarked on a marathon morris dance that took him half across the country; and he was replaced by Armin, the son of an East Anglian tailor, once apprenticed to the goldsmith's trade, a sensitive and intelligent mime, possessed himself of a certain literary talent. Beside Kempe, he was a highly civilized comedian; and perhaps he bore some resemblance to the famous nineteenth-century French artist, Charles Deburau, with his pale haunted face and elegantly limp gestures, who at the Parisian *Funambules* created the romantic Pierrot. Deburau was apparelled all in white. How Elizabethan clowns were dressed is a problem that has puzzled modern scholars; probably it was not in mediaeval cap-and-bells, but in a long 'fool's-coat' made of parti-coloured stuff—the sort of material known as 'motley'—such as was also worn by 'naturals' or half-witted persons.[1] Thus Armin would have had a woebegone, wistful look, perfectly suited to the song he sings. His ditty reflects the sad wisdom of the changeling or neglected demi-

[1] J. Leslie Hotson: *Shakespeare's Motley*, 1952.

idiot, inhabitant of a twilit world upon the frontiers of ordinary human knowledge.

Twelfth Night, which is thought to have been produced at Court, was later played before the students of the Middle Temple; and John Manningham notes in his diary,[1] against February 2nd, 1602, that 'at our feast we had a play called "Twelve Night, or What You Will", much like the Comedy of Errors, or Menechmi in Plautus, but most like and near to that in Italian called *Inganni*. A good practice in it to make the steward believe his lady widow was in love with him . . .' By the time Shakespeare wrote this comedy, however, a new form of comic entertainment, sponsored by a new and ambitious artist, had already entered the dramatic field. Generous and good-natured as ever, the older and more experienced dramatist seems to have lent a helping hand; Rowe tells us that it was Shakespeare who first noticed and recommended Ben Jonson; and, when the Chamberlain's Men acquired the manuscript of *Every Man in his Humour* during the autumn months of 1598, among the 'principle comedians' who performed it at the Curtain were 'Will Shakespeare, Ric. Burbage', John Heminge and Henry Condell. Here was a fresh approach to the art of comic writing based on the pseudo-scientific theory then widely held and eagerly discussed by fashionable young men. An individual was alleged to be the victim of his 'humours', and the word 'humour' gained the same unfortunate vogue as 'complex' at a later period.[2] It was employed, with similar frequency and vagueness, to explain any type of human failing; and it had already inspired both dramatists and satirists to exhibit wildly 'humorous' characters; George Chapman wrote *An Humorous Day's Mirth*, and Joseph Hall and John Marston produced volumes of satirical invective. Next came Jonson, still an almost unknown hireling, the impoverished poet to whom, in July 1597, Henslowe lent £4 and, in December, £1 on the security of a yet unfinished 'book', of which the poet had 'showed the plot unto the company', and which he promised they should have by Christmas. Jonson had previously worked for Pembroke's Men, a short-lived and unimportant company; and, in 1597, he had collaborated with Nashe upon

---

[1] Edited by J. Bruce, 1868.
[2] G. B. Harrison: *Elizabethan Plays and Players*, 1940.

a daring topical production called *The Isle of Dogs*—'a lewd play', decided the Council, 'containing very seditious and slanderous matter'; whereupon Nashe absconded, and Jonson and the actors Gabriel Spencer and Robert Shaw were thrown into a London gaol. But *Every Man in his Humour* was Jonson's first undoubted triumph.

Its text has reached us under two different guises—the version that Shakespeare's company performed, of which a quarto edition was published in the year 1601, and the corrected and considerably re-written version that appeared in the folio of 1616. The second is much the more interesting; for, whereas the scene of the earlier play is an imaginary Italian city and the dramatis personae bear Italian names, the revised text has a London background and is populated by a swarm of English characters. And then, Jonson added an extensive *Prologue*, which, as it ridicules some of the theatrical devices they used, would scarcely have appealed to Shakespeare and his friends, but which sets forth, in a bold, even arrogant, style, the author's own dramatic concepts. Moral realism was the aim he set himself; he was also determined that he would preserve the unities of place and time. No infant should be carried on to the stage, and allowed to grow up as the play proceeded; nor would he allow the players to indulge in endless mimic battles and

> with three rusty swords,
> And help of some few foot-and-half-foot words,
> Fight over *York* and *Lancaster's* long jars:
> And in the tiring-house bring wounds to scars.
> He rather prays you will be pleased to see
> One such, today, as other plays should be.
> Where neither *Chorus* wafts you o'er the seas;
> Nor creaking throne comes down, the boys to please;
> Nor nimble squib is seen, to make afear'd
> The gentlewomen; nor rolled bullet heard
> To say, it thunders; nor tempestuous drum
> Rumbles, to tell you when the storm doth come;
> But deeds and language, such as men do use:
> And persons, such as *Comedy* would choose,

When she would show an image of the times,
And sport with human follies, not with crimes.

This was the dramatist's design as he afterwards remembered it—
to present a modern comedy, framed in everyday terms, on a stage
stripped of all superfluous devices, and to display a lively 'image of
the times' rather than parade the heroic figures of the past. Jonson's
ambition, however, exceeded his skill; *Every Man in his Humour* has
a somewhat awkward and pedestrian plot, concerned with the
elaborate subterfuges by which Brain-Worm (or Musco), a scheming
servant attached to Kno'well (otherwise Lorenzo), a worthy old
gentleman plagued by his poetic son, discovers the fears and suspicions of his self-deluded fellow characters and, having shown up
their 'humorous' extravagances, obliges them to admit the folly of
their ways. But the dialogue, couched in 'language such as men do
use', vigorous, eloquent, idiomatic, is admirable throughout the
whole comedy; here is the conversation, faithfully reported, of the
Elizabethan street and counting house, of the rich merchant's break-
fast table, perfumed with rose-water by his fastidious wife, of the
epicurean magistrate's parlour and the needy soldier's squalid
lodgings. Captain Bobadill, braggart and duellist, a 'Paul's-man', one
of those 'stale knights and captains out of service' who, with their
tarnished finery and long rapiers, used to pace up and down the
cathedral nave, is a splendidly convincing portrait; and just as
persuasive are his hostess Tib and Tib's husband, the honest water-
carrier Cob, spokesman of the plain unlettered, unfashionable, and
consequently unhumorous, public: ' . . . What is that humour?' he
demands, 'some rare thing, I warrant'; and 'I'll tell thee, Cob,'
replies a more knowing acquaintance, 'It is a gentleman-like monster,
bred in the special gallantry of our time, and fed by folly . . . Humour
is nothing, if it be not fed.' How a humour was nourished and sustained we observe in other episodes. A clever young man is encouraged by a companion to do his proud and melancholy nature
full justice: 'but hold up your head, so: and let the *Idea* of what you
are be portrayed in your face'; and the pupil readily agrees, promising
henceforward to be 'more proud, and melancholy, and gentleman-
like . . .' Melancholy is associated with good breeding, but also with

poetic genius: 'Oh, it's your only fine humour, sir; your true melancholy breeds your perfect fine wit, sir: I am melancholy myself divers times, sir; and then do I no more but take pen and paper presently, and overflow you half a score or a dozen of sonnets at a sitting.' Melancholy, we know, was a peculiarly Elizabethan weakness, and of all the humours that afflicted mankind was usually believed to make the deepest inroads.[1] 'You shall understand,' wrote Reginald Scot, 'that the force which melancholy hath, and the effects that it worketh in the body of a man . . . are almost incredible.' Not only was it rife among disappointed lovers, whom, temporarily or permanently, it might drive mad; but often it attacked a jealous husband, who, during the transports of a melancholy fit, like Jonson's Kitely, the suspicious London merchant, would imagine that 'the air rained horns'. Finally, it troubled the contemplative intelligence, the mind of a Jaques or a Hamlet, overtaxed with thought and study. Thus 'humour', though frequently an affectation, sometimes sprang from a profound involuntary crisis, and, in either form, revealed a lack of moral harmony that offended Jonson's classic common sense.

For Jonson was above all a classicist, a learned, widely read poet. Not for him were the convenient short-cuts by which Shakespeare had climbed the foothills of Parnassus. Son of a minister, who, he liked it to be known, was the offspring of an ancient Northern family, but now the stepson of a London master bricklayer, he had received his education at Westminster School, where he had been taught by the famous antiquary William Camden, afterwards his close friend. Later, he had been apprenticed to the bricklaying trade, an avocation 'he could not endure', had joined the English armies campaigning in the Low Countries, and, during his service, he told Drummond of Hawthornden,[2] had fought a single-handed battle between the English and the enemy camps, killed his foe and carried off the spoils. Having laid down pike or musket, 'soon he betook himself to his wonted studies'. Poverty had obliged him to enter Henslowe's stable; but now, at the age of twenty-six, he emerged as an inde-

[1] See Lawrence Babb: *The Elizabethan Malady: A Study of Melancholia in English Literature from 1580 to 1642*, 1951.

[2] *Ben Jonson's Conversations with Drummond of Hawthorn*, edited by R. F. Patterson, 1923.

pendent dramatist. His way of life, however, remained adventurous; and, that same autumn, Henslowe, writing to Edward Alleyn, then in the provinces, communicated 'hard and heavy' news. 'Since you were last with me,' he lamented, 'I have lost one of my company, which hurteth me greatly; that is Gabriel Spencer, for he is slain in Hoxton Fields by the hands of Benjamin Jonson, bricklayer.'[1] Jonson's victim was the actor Gabriel Spencer, a quarrelsome personage who had already accounted for an adversary in a London barber's shop. Though Spencer had shared Jonson's imprisonment following the suppression of the notorious *Isle of Dogs*, evidently they had fallen out when Jonson deserted to the Chamberlain's Men; and Spencer may have been yet more deeply annoyed by the triumphant reception of the new play. It was produced on September 16th; on the 22nd, swords were drawn—Spencer's, his enemy announced, had considerably the longer blade—and Jonson, a Middlesex jury decided, 'feloniously and wilfully beat and struck the same Gabriel, giving then and there to the same Gabriel Spencer . . . a mortal wound of the depth of six inches and the breadth of one inch, in and upon the right side . . . of which mortal blow the same Gabriel Spencer . . . then and there died instantly.' Jonson was imprisoned and arraigned, but escaped the gallows by pleading 'benefit of clergy'—that is to say, he read aloud in court and thus gave proof that he was an educated citizen.[2] Nevertheless, his goods were declared forfeit and, as a mark of ignominy, his thumb was branded.

To house that bellicose, much-enduring spirit, nature had provided Jonson with a massive frame. In his latter years, he weighed nearly twenty stone; and his 'mountain belly' and his 'rocky face'— his clear, fair skin had become enflamed and scorbutic, and one eye was larger and lower than its fellow—were as alarming, he feared, to the beautiful women he courted as his poetic blandishments, he hoped, were pleasing.[3] Like another English writer who bore a

---

[1] *Henslowe Papers, op. cit.*

[2] Established after the death of Thomas Becket in 1170, this privilege freed 'clerks', or clerics, from the jurisdiction of the royal courts, and was gradually extended, with modifications, to other educated first offenders. Since 1547, however, it had not protected murderers, highwaymen and housebreakers. Jonson's offence was that of manslaughter. 'Benefit of clergy' was eventually abolished in 1827.

[3] 'My Picture Left in Scotland', verses that commemorate Jonson's northern walking-tour during the year 1618.

variant of his name, he was both an omnivorous student and an inveterate sloven. 'I have heard Mr. Lacy, the player, say,' reports John Aubrey, 'that he was wont to wear a coat like a coachman's coat, with slits under the armpits. He would many times exceed in drink (Canary was his beloved liquor): then he would tumble home to bed, and, when he had thoroughly perspired, then to study. I have seen his studying chair which was of straw, such as old women used . . .' We also hear of the wife he married—'a shrew yet honest'; of a son who died very young and to whom he dedicated some simple verses:

> Rest in soft peace; and, ask'd, say here doth lie,
> Ben Jonson his best piece of poetry

—of his amatory exploits, which were numerous and varied; of his visions and his misadventures in drink, as when Sir Walter Ralegh's son, to whom he was acting as bear-leader, loaded him dead drunk on to a hand-cart and had him dragged around the streets of Paris; and how he had 'consumed a whole night in lying looking to his great toe, about which he hath seen Tartars and Turks, Romans and Carthaginians, fight in his imagination'. None of his literary contemporaries has left behind such ample records. Jonson was interested in the judgement of the future: he diligently edited and revised his own works. And then—which again distinguishes him from Shakespeare, who, besides treating his manuscripts with contemptuous carelessness, showed no inclination to found a clique or school—Jonson was naturally qualified to teach and lead. Over 'the tribe of Ben', supporters of his old age, he extended a benign and majestic influence; and, for one of his disciples, the young Lord Falkland, just as impressive as his power to instruct was the modesty he displayed in seeking knowledge:

> He had an infant's innocence and truth,
> The judgement of grey hairs, the wit of youth,
> Not a young rashness, not an ag'd despair,
> The courage of the one, the other's care;
> And both of them might wonder to discern
> His ableness to teach, his skill to learn.[1]

[1] Lucius Cary, 2nd Viscount Falkland (1610?-1643), statesman, soldier, poet, fought with Charles I at Edgehill and the siege of Gloucester, killed at the Battle of Newbury.

N

It is an indication of the strength of both characters, at many points so strangely different, that a friendship should have sprung up between Shakespeare and Jonson, which they maintained successfully until the elder poet's death. Yet they were rivals, by tradition and instinct: Jonson, scholar and poetic doctrinaire, whose gifts were harnessed to a predetermined theory; Shakespeare, who had developed through improvization, and whose literary temperament, endlessly versatile and elastic, responded anew to each new set of difficulties, deriving rules from his solution of the problems he encountered rather than imposing them ready-made upon his subject. When Jonson announced that Shakespeare had 'wanted art',[1] he meant, not that he had wanted genius, but that his genius was of the Dionysiac, as opposed to the Apollonian, type, and that he lacked the ability to revise and correct and improve that, in his own conception of art, was an essential adjunct of the artist's calling. Although Drummond found him a rash and intemperate critic—'a great lover and praiser of himself, a contemner and scorner of others . . . jealous of every word and action of those about him (especially after drink, which is one of the elements in which he liveth) . . . passionately kind and angry, careless either to gain or keep'—his criticism of Shakespeare's achievement is almost always just and generous, given the beliefs he held and the examples that he had sought to follow. True, his judgement was coloured by personal affection. He had 'loved the man', he wrote in *Timber*,[2] a posthumous selection from his notebooks, 'and do honour his memory (on this side idolatry) as much as any. He was, indeed, honest, and of an open and free nature: had an excellent Fancy, brave notions and gentle expressions: wherein he flowed with that facility that sometimes it was necessary he should be stopped.' Shakespeare's defect was that he did not govern his wit, and was thereby occasionally led into palpable extravagances. The players, he recollected, had 'often mentioned it as an honour to Shakespeare that in his writing (whatsoever he penned) he never blotted out line. My answer hath been, would he had blotted a thousand, which they thought a malevolent speech.' Yet, Jonson concludes, 'he redeemed his vices with his

---

[1] Drummond of Hawthornden, *op. cit.*

[2] *Timber; or Discoveries; Made upon Men and Matter*, 1641.

virtues. There was ever more in him to be praised that to be pardoned.'

At times, however, the obvious vices would rankle; among his
private acquaintances Jonson frequently reproached the dead poet
'with the want of learning and ignorance of the Ancients'; and even
the stately panegyric that he composed to grace the First Folio
dwells in passing on his meagre scholarship. Yet, despite his 'small
Latin and less Greek', the modern poet—from Jonson a significant
admission—could afford to hold up his hand against the greatest
writers of the antique world. Every artist, when he discusses a famous
contemporary, shows some touches of ambivalent feeling. But,
although Jonson would now and then laugh at his friend, deplore his
extravagant comic inventions—'Tales, Tempests and suchlike
drolleries'—and, descending to more private foibles, deride his
brand-new coat of arms, he noted and admired the superabundant
vitality that excused a lack of formal artifice. In *Poetaster*, produced
during Shakespeare's lifetime, he presents Horace paying an
eloquent tribute to the master-poet Virgil:

> His learning labours not the school-like gloss,
> That most consists in echoing words and terms . . .
> But a direct and analytic sum
> Of all the worth and first effects of arts.
> And for his poesy, 'tis so rammed with life,
> That it shall gather strength of life, with being,
> And live hereafter, more admired than now.

The identification of Virgil with Shakespeare has been questioned by
well-known Shakespearian authorities;[1] but Horace's description
echoes the panegyric that Jonson published in the Folio; and
Shakespeare's dramas are certainly 'rammed with life', a life so
ebullient and intense that it threatens to overflow its structural
framework, a fiery compound of thought and emotion where the
emotion is indistinguishable from the thought.

[1] See E. K. Chambers, *op. cit.*

CHAPTER VIII

Historical Drama

WHEN SHAKESPEARE WAS composing his five exuberant comedies, he was simultaneously engaged on a much weightier dramatic cycle; and, just as the finest of his comic productions appear to have been written to please a courtly audience, so the historical plays were evidently calculated to interest Essex and Southampton and their friends, all self-proclaimed patriots, leaders of the English war-party and opponents of the cautious, diplomatic Cecils, whom the no less cautious Queen upheld. His scope was extensive—from the reign of King John, at the beginning of the thirteenth century, until the accession of the Queen's father, early in the sixteenth, and the joyful public celebrations that had marked her own birth. With *Henry VIII*, a stately pageant play, he was to complete the cycle towards the very end of his career. Meanwhile, having already disposed of Kings Henry VI and Richard III, he produced *Richard II* about 1595, *King John* in 1596, the two parts of *Henry IV* in 1597 and 1598, and *Henry V* between the spring and autumn months of 1599.[1] Thus he built a dramatic bridge that linked the troublous period of medieval kingship to the triumphant foundation of the present monarchy. Its structure was diverse. In *King John*, for example, he was merely re-handling a popular play, *The Troublesome Reign of John, King of England*, originally published only five years earlier; but Shakespeare compressed the action, revised and recast almost every line, made the sixteen year-old Arthur a helpless child—which allowed him to give an additionally pathetic turn to the circumstances of

---

[1] As elsewhere, I follow the chronological system laid down by E. K. Chambers, *op. cit.*

Arthur's imprisonment and death—and built up the commanding
role of Philip Faulconbridge, the royal bastard obsessed by his
bastardy, yet dominated by his faith in his royal blood, who becomes
the mouthpiece of the famous patriotic tirade—

> This England never did, nor never shall,
> Lie at the proud foot of a conqueror,
> But when it first did help to wound itself . . .
> Come the three corners of the world in arms,
> And we shall shock them

—with which Shakespeare exorcizes the spirit of civil discord and
brings the drama to a solemn close.

Far subtler in its effect, and more complex in its characterization,
is *The Tragedy of King Richard II*. John has betrayed his sacred
office; and in his agony he descends, like Richard Crookback, into
a hell of unshared suffering:

> I do not ask you much,
> I beg cold comfort; and you are so strait
> And so ingrateful, you deny me that.
> Prince Henry: O, that there were some virtue in my tears,
> That might relieve you!
> King John: The salt in them is hot.

Richard, on the other hand, is a portrait of a half-attractive failure,
bad unquestionably as an anointed sovereign, as an individual
neither bad nor good. Among Shakespeare's personages, remarked
André Gide, we note the existence of two great human families, '*les
gens d'action et les irrésolus*'. Again and again, he shows these families
in conflict; often the irresolute man is the hero of the play, which
exhibits his progressive deterioration as he withdraws before his
natural foe, who is better qualified than himself to execute the
ordinary tasks of living.[1] Shakespeare's unhappy ruler is one of the
irresolute; and, if he required any historical support, apart from the
evidence supplied by Raphael Holinshed, whose *Chronicles* provided
the framework of the drama, he might have found it by leaving his
desk and wandering through Westminster Abbey. There, on a royal

[1] André Gide: *Journal* 1942-1949.

sepulchre, lies the gilt-copper effigy that Nicholas Broker and Godfrey Prest, coppersmiths of London, created during Richard's lifetime. A large forehead and a lengthy pointed nose dwarf an indecisive mouth and chin; the face, with its small forked beard, recalls pictures of the young Swinburne, sensitive but febrile and neurotic, beneath a cap of waving curls. A doomed face; and the agents of Richard's doom are his mischievous and grasping favourites; while Bolingbroke, the resolute man of action, organizes and presents the last scene. The abdication of an anointed sovereign, however, was at the time an extremely dangerous subject; and, for the Elizabethans, the fall of Richard II always held a very special meaning. As we shall learn, it haunted the Queen's mind. That his servants should arise and dethrone a monarch was an outrageous offence against the laws of proportion and degree, one that shook the harmonious fabric of existence and might call down retribution from above. Yet there were some, including Essex at a later period and certain talkative Puritan divines, who dared to suggest that royal authority could and should be circumscribed, the Puritans troubled by doctrinal doubts, Essex disturbed by secret ambitions and his dearly-bought private acquaintance with an intransigent royal character. Such suggestions had the charm of the forbidden; and Shakespeare, when he wrote his tragedy, was venturing on to difficult ground. It grew all the more perilous after the issue, in 1596, of a Papal Bull, encouraging the enslaved English Catholics to take up arms against their perjured mistress; and, when the first Quarto edition of the tragedy was printed in 1597, over a hundred-and-fifty lines—the whole of the abdication scene—were omitted by the careful publisher.

That scene is the story's key-point. Nothing becomes Richard so well as the dignity with which he casts aside his kingdom. The King is a self-pitying Narcissus, who comments at length upon his own ruin; but he is also a word-master who finds in the beauty of language an exquisite substitute for thought and action. But, here and elsewhere, Richard's poetic style shows the powerful influence of Marlowe; and the play, as it stands, could scarcely have been written had *Edward II* never reached the author's hands. The King is a distinctly Marlovian personage, who accompanies and underlines

each gesture with some sonorous poetic trope. Thus, when he prepares
to descend from the ramparts of Flint Castle—in an Elizabethan
playhouse, from the gallery or upper stage—he begins by announcing
what he means to do:

> Down, down I come, like glist'ring Phaethon:
> Wanting the manage of unruly jades.
> In the base court? Base court, where kings grow base,
> To come at traitors' calls and do them grace.
> In the base court? Come down? Down court! down king!

Earlier, he has heard his majesty compared to the sun emerging from
a bank of cloud:

> See, see, King Richard doth himself appear,
> As doth the blushing discontented sun
> From out the fiery portal of the east . . .

The effect is to enhance our view of the monarch as a remote and
semi-deified being, majestic even in his errors and imperfections,
perpetually surrounded by the awful trappings of his state. This
was not a view that the contemporary audience, accustomed to Queen
Elizabeth's performance of her role, would have found at all
mysterious. The sovereign dwelt on an inaccessible height; if he lost
his footing, he would fall proportionately low.

As for the usurper, he had incurred the wrath of Heaven; Bolingbroke's guilt is an inescapable penalty, that embitters his whole reign
and darkens the shadows round his death-bed:

> God knows, my son,
> By what by-paths and indirect crookt ways
> I met this crown . . .

—and he is condemned to expiate it both through civil strife and
through the anxieties and disappointments inflicted by his wild,
unruly son. Preparing the two parts of *King Henry IV*, Shakespeare
again had recourse to the printed version of an old play. Hall, Stow
and Holinshed furnished the basic framework of the plot; Edward
Hall's work, *The Union of the Noble and Illustre Families of Lancaster
and York*, usually called his *Chronicle*, had appeared in 1542; Stow's

Chronicles of England, in 1580; but it was from *The Famous Victories of Henry V*, probably written about 1586,[1] that he drew the raw material of his comic, and some of his heroic, episodes. The Achillean victor of Agincourt had been traditionally a debauched young man; and legend connected the tale of his pranks and follies with a disreputable middle-aged boon-companion, whom the earlier dramatist entitled Sir John Oldcastle and who also bore the nickname 'Jockey'. *The Famous Victories* is an extremely inferior production, dismissed by Shakespearian critics as 'contemptible', 'worthless', 'a miserable performance', 'a crude piece', 'a medley of nonsense and ribaldry'. Crude and ribald it undoubtedly is; but here are the primitive origins of some of Shakespeare's best-known scenes and characters—the ambush on Gadshill, the tavern in Eastcheap, hints for the part of the Eastcheap hostess and a preliminary sketch of the dissolute Sir John. Shakespeare's fat knight has yet to emerge from chaos; and most of the comedy is provided by Derick, 'a poor carrier', whom the Thief, Cuthbert Cutter, alias 'Gad's Hill', a desperado in the Prince's service, has robbed upon the London road, and who particularly regrets the loss of a 'great raze of ginger that Bouncing Bess with the jolly buttocks should have had'. Derick's treatment of his landlady, John Cobbler's wife, recalls Falstaff's attitude towards the hostess; but everywhere Shakespeare has assimilated and transformed, enlarging and emphasizing and adding fresh relief and colour. Thus, the King's celebrated farewell speech is based on a brief pedestrian passage:

> God give thee joy, my son. God bless thee . . . and send thee a prosperous reign! For God knows, my son, how hardly I came by it, and how hardly I have maintained it.

—and his successor's renunciation of his unworthy associates is derived from a flat, perfunctory exchange:

> King: I prithee, Ned, mend thy manners, and be more modester in thy terms; for my unfeigned grief is not to be ruled by thy flattering and dissembling talk. Thou

[1] See Seymour M. Pitcher: *The Case of Shakespeare's Authorship of 'The Famous Victories'*, 1962. Dr Pitcher sets out to prove that *The Famous Victories* was an early play—perhaps his first—written by Shakespeare at the age of twenty-two; but his case must be regarded as definitely not proven.

sayst I am changed; so I am, indeed; and so must thou be, and that quickly, or else I must cause thee to be changed.

Jockey: God's wounds, how like you this? Zounds! 'tis not so sweet as music.

From such meagre beginnings, Shakespeare proceeded to develop an extraordinarily rich and various play. None of his English historical dramas is more densely 'rammed with life'; but that abundant life is unevenly distributed; and the incomparable vitality of the richest and liveliest scenes shows up the comparative poverty of others. Again we ask ourselves what the dramatist *really* thought of public personages and the game of high politics. Though some commentators pretend to distinguish in his works a deep political intelligence, there are far stronger reasons for regarding him as, above all else, a private man, whose chief concern, when he could afford to display it, was with purely private subjects—the nature of friendship and love; the difficulty of any form of genuine communication between individual human beings; the sense of solitude to which we are born, and the desperate solitude in which we die. Action is often an escape from thought; and Shakespeare's men of action are most vividly portrayed when they happen to be least active, and he is describing, not a boldly consistent record, but the secret inconsistency of their ideas and feelings. Thus Hotspur attracts him, less as a valiant rebel, who leads a revolt against Henry IV and dies upon the field of Shrewsbury, than as a restive, irritable, impatient spirit, whose professed aversion from the intellect goes with an obstinately searching mind, who lives like a loud-mouthed soldier, yet dies a poet and a philosophic sage. Elsewhere, Shakespeare's historical figures are apt to resemble animated suits of armour, clanking heavily across the boards, uttering sonorous challenges and defiantly enunciating one another's titles. This was the view of history that the chroniclers encouraged, and an Elizabethan audience admired, as they watched the events of a long and bloody campaign compressed into half a dozen bouts of exciting modern sword-play. Shakespeare satisfied his popular patrons with his usual brisk, perfunctory skill. Two rebellions emerge and are crushed; he whirls us through the court and camp, and provides the customary allowance of weighty and sententious speeches, couched in the involved, allusive and frequently obscure style then considered appropriate to grave discussion among public characters.

The quality of the verse is unequal; and a foreign reader who knew nothing of his circumstances, or of the conditions of the Elizabethan stage, might be astonished to learn that the same dramatist had produced the scene in the inn-yard, the magnificent interview between the dynamic Hotspur and his outlandish ally, Owen Glendower, a vague, lymphatic Welsh magician, and the two uninteresting scenes where the rebels, under Mowbray, Hastings and the Archbishop of York, allow themselves to be disarmed by John of Lancaster's promises, and, as soon as their army has broken up, are handed over to the King's exemplary justice. Then, into a sound conventional speech, that may or may not have been altogether his, but was certainly within the reach of many of his gifted fellow poets, Shakespeare slips one of those incomparable images which diffuse their light throughout the whole drama. We read of the 'buzzing night-flies' that surround the poor man's pillow but fail to disturb his dog-tired sleep; of the 'wet sea-boy' alone at the mast-head, while the ocean surges roll beneath him and the 'slippery clouds' stream overhead; of the tidal stream, viewed perhaps from the arches of London Bridge, momentarily at a turbulent standstill, neither advancing nor retiring; of the stranded leviathan, on an English beach, exhausted by its own gigantic efforts.

Time, in *Henry IV*, is an obsessive preoccupation with Shakespeare's soldierly and royal personages. To Hotspur it provides a constant challenge:

> O gentlemen, the time of life is short!
> To spend that shortness basely were too long,
> If life did ride upon a dial's point,
> Still ending at the arrival of an hour.

—and he defies it in the moment of his death:

> But thought's the slave of life, and life time's fool;
> And time that takes survey of all the world
> Must have a stop.

As for the guilt-laden King, he is dominated by terrifying glimpses of futurity:

> O God! that one might read the book of fate,
> And see the revolution of the times
> Make mountains level . . .
>   how chance's mocks
> And changes fill the cup of alteration
> With divers liquors! O, if this were seen,
> The happiest youth, viewing his progress through,
> What perils past, what crosses to ensue,
> Would shut the book, and sit him down and die

—while Warwick, foreshadowing the Neapolitan philosopher Vico,[1] believes that the vicissitudes of the future are already implicit in the memorials of the past:

> There is a history in all men's lives,
> Figuring the natures of the times deceased:
> The which observed, a man may prophesy,
> With a near aim, of the main chance of things
> As yet come to life, which in their seeds
> And weak beginnings lie intreasured:
> Such things become the hatch and brood of time . . .

But to these 'great ones', with their lofty concerns and heroic view of human action, Shakespeare added a character who, as he gradually took shape, was destined to outgrow and overtop them all. They are haunted by their dreams of the past and the future; Falstaff exists for the present day, which circumscribes and comfortably encloses him, sustains his hardihood and nourishes his pride. Immune from anxiety and guilt, he is the antithesis of public and domestic virtue. Yet, if the achievement of inward harmony be the object of existence, wherever we find it and however we accomplish it, John Falstaff, unlike his exalted companions, understands the art of living.

[1] Giovanni Batista Vico, 1688-1744. The first edition of his book, *Scienza Nuova*, developing the cyclical theory of historical events, which profoundly influenced the work of James Joyce, appeared in 1725.

In almost every great Shakespearian play, there is one recalcitrant unbeliever, who rejects the audience's moral assumptions and opposes the whole tendency of what, at a preliminary glance, the drama might seem to be 'about'. Boldest of such antibodies is the incorrigible Falstaff, compounded by Shakespeare from the three disreputable, spendthrift knights, Ned, Tom and Sir John Oldcastle, or Jockey, sketched in *The Famous Victories of Henry V*, and from Derick, the blustering carrier, who victimizes his friends and preys on his good-natured hostess. Shakespeare's chief comic character was originally named Sir John Oldcastle; but the real Oldcastle had been a gallant and distinguished soldier who, having joined the Lollard sect, sacrificed his life to his religious views; and the current Lord Cobham, an influential figure at Court and a member of the same family, made a strong protest against the use of his name, which obliged Shakespeare to substitute 'Falstaff', evidently a reminiscence of the Sir John Fastolfe already portrayed as coward and poltroon in Part I of *Henry VI*.[1] Falstaff, then, is a literary hybrid; he was 'not properly one humour', wrote Dryden, 'but a miscellany of humours or images, drawn from so many several men . . .' An odd judgement for a critic of Dryden's percipience. Falstaff's origins were certainly various; but, as soon as Shakespeare had taken hold of the character, he began to develop and enlarge it, blending all his borrowed material into a single homogeneous scheme. A mere 'miscellany' would never command affection; and the friendly feelings he has aroused through the years are a proof of Falstaff's individual strength. Even so stern a moralist as Samuel Johnson pays a measured tribute to his private qualities:

> Percy is a rugged soldier . . . and has only the soldier's virtues . . . But Falstaff, unimitated, inimitable Falstaff, how shall I describe thee! thou compound of sense and vice; of sense which may be admired, but not esteemed; of vice which may be despised, but hardly detested. Falstaff is a character loaded with faults, and with those faults which naturally produce contempt. He is a thief and a glutton, a coward and a boaster . . . At once obsequious and

[1] He omitted, however, to remove a reference to Falstaff as 'my old lad of the castle'. His treatment of Sir John Fastolfe was equally unmerited and, among Fastolfe's Elizabethan descendants, caused no less indignation.

malignant, he satirizes in their absence those whom he lives by
flattering . . . Yet the man thus corrupt, thus despicable, makes
himself necessary to the prince that despises him, by the most
pleasing of all qualities, perpetual gaiety, by an unfailing power of
exciting laughter, which is the more freely indulged, as his wit is
not of the splendid or ambitious kind, but consists in easy scapes
and sallies of levity, which make sport, but raise no envy.

Falstaff is a man at his ease in the world; which Johnson, much as
he appreciated the spectacle of life, and gay and exuberant though he
often was, at no time could have claimed to be; and another uneasy
personage, William Hazlitt, found Falstaff's firm control of his
existence correspondingly admirable and attractive. 'His body,' he
wrote, 'is like a good estate to his mind, from which he receives rents
and revenues of profit and pleasure . . . Wit is often a meagre substitute for pleasurable sensation . . . Falstaff's wit is an emanation of a
fine constitution . . .' His sensuality does not deaden his faculties;
but 'his imagination keeps up the ball after his senses have done with
it'. He is gifted, too, with 'a masterly presence of mind, an absolute
self-possession, which nothing can disturb. His repartees are involuntary suggestions of his self-love; instinctive evasions of everything that threatens to interrupt the career of his triumphant jollity
and self-complacency.' Falstaff, then, is the *homme moyen sensuel*,
blown up to an immense size, surrounded by men who, through
accident or design, are endeavouring to play a more than human
part. Falstaff alone accepts his limitations, happy just as he is,
content to enjoy the simple fact of living; and the stubborn energy
that he shows in pursuing and achieving his aims marks him out as
that very rare phenomenon—a man who has successfully taken his
own measure and knows exactly what he seeks. By contrast, he
exposes the vanity and absurdity of the obstreperous 'iron men', his
fellow characters.

While it is their proud belief that they are 'making history', often
a destructive and self-destructive business, Falstaff represents a
substratum of our race that historical changes leave almost undis-
turbed. 'Dost thou think,' demands Sir Toby of Malvolio, 'because
thou art virtuous, there shall be no more cakes and ale?' Falstaff, in

his own way, poses a similar question: have his noble acquaintances the effrontery to imagine, because they themselves are gallant, ambitious, vigorous, concerned with large and grandiose issues, that the basic human interests he so strongly supports will lose the smallest fraction of their power? Thus, in one aspect, he is the Devil's Advocate: Falstaff, it has been pointed out, bears some resemblance to the Vice, or scurrilous Tempter, of the old morality plays. Amid his Christian surroundings, he is the spirit of unbelief, paganism incarnate, sensual egotism personified. Imprisoned in a huge, misshapen body, he knows the loneliness of utter self-absorption: 'I have a whole school of tongues in this belly of mine, and not a tongue of them all speaks any other word but my name.' Yet Falstaff is far more than a symbol; he is most deeply impressive and persuasive as an individual human being; and in that capacity he rolls through the play like some gigantic monster of the deep, breaking the moralist's hooks and nets, and spouting defiance at the starry heavens. Only twice do the heavens retaliate. First, when, having proclaimed his eternal youth in the harangue he addresses to the Lord Chief Justice—'You that are old consider not the capacity of us that are young'—suddenly, with Doll on his knee, he feels the icy touch of age and impotence:

Falstaff: Thou dost give me flattering busses.
Doll: By my troth, I kiss thee with a most constant heart.
Falstaff: I am old, I am old.
Doll: I love thee better than I love e'er a scurvy young boy of them all.
Falstaff: What stuff wilt have a kirtle of? I shall receive money o' Thursday . . . A merry song, come! grows late, we'll to bed. Thou'a't forget me when I am gone.

Again, when he is renounced by the ungrateful Prince, and the illusion of youth, which he has always clung to and cherished, at last for ever disappears.

Meanwhile he imagines that the Prince loves him, and knows that he is loved and admired by the raffish frequenters of the Boar's Head. They esteem his endearing personal qualities; they also look up to his social rank. Falstaff, among many other things, is the comic portrait of the English Gentleman, far from 'gentlemanly' in the Victorian sense of the term, yet unquestionably armigerous, who assumes that the current social system has been evolved for his especial benefit, and who has the inherited strength of mind to transfer that re-assuring assumption to his ill-bred hangers-on. Compare Doll Tear-sheet's attitude towards Falstaff with her scornful treatment of the Cockney braggart. Pistol pretends that he is an officer; but he is clearly not a gentleman. Nor is he a man of taste, though he is an ardent playgoer and has the deplorable habit of quoting scraps of modern poetry. Doll sees through him, and roughly demolishes his pretensions: 'You a captain! you slave, for what? for tearing a poor whore's ruff in a bawdy-house? He a captain! hang him, rogue! he lives upon mouldy stewed prunes[1] and dried cakes.' The hostess Mistress Quickly herself, whom Falstaff has 'eaten out of house and home', and persuaded to lend him thirty shillings, a debt he now proposes to increase by a further loan of £10, cannot long resist the aristocratic panache with which he conducts his predatory opera-tions. He has engaged to marry her; he swears a gentlemanly oath; he grandly waves away all talk of losses:

Falstaff: As I am a gentleman. Come, no more words of it.
Hostess: By this heavenly ground I tread on, I must be fain to pawn both my plate and the tapestry of my dining-chambers.
Falstaff: Glasses, glasses, is the only drinking—and for thy walls, a pretty slight drollery or the story of the Prodigal or the German hunting, in waterwork,[2] is worth a thousand of these bed-hangers and these fly-bitten tapestries. Let it be ten pound, if thou canst. Come, an 'twere not for thy humours, there's not a better wench in England. Go, wash thy face, and draw the action.

Just as masterfully adroit is Falstaff's treatment of his Gloucester-shire acquaintance Justice Shallow. His behaviour is a trifle patroniz-ing, but not unduly condescending—he is a Londoner and a courtier; the justice, a mere country magnate; and he is glad to humour

[1] Stewed prunes, that innocent nursery dish, were then reputed to have aphrodisiac qualities and were often served at London brothels.
[2] Painted cloths were a popular substitute for the heavier, more expensive tapestry.

Shallow's inclination to wander back into their joint past. It is a memorable journey the old men make together, around Clement's Inn and 'the windmill in Saint George's field', reviving memories of Jane Nightwork, a celebrated 'bona-roba' of the time; and Falstaff concludes it with one of those Shakespearian phrases which leave behind them an eternal echo:

> Shallow: Ha, cousin Silence, that thou hadst seen that that this knight and I have seen! Ha, Sir John, said I well?
> Falstaff: We have heard the chimes at midnight, Master Shallow.

Shakespeare's mastery of the rhythms of common speech, displayed now in verse and now in prose, enables him not only to suggest a voice and convey its characteristic tone, but simultaneously to evoke a face, the expressions that underline the words, even the typical movements of the speaker's body. As we hear, we find we are also seeing—Falstaff, immense and dignified, who wears a half-tolerant, half-amused smile, pleased to be flattered and entertained, impatient, however, to get down to business; Shallow, self-important and awkward, carried away by his delightful memories, yet well aware of the effect he produces upon his vacant, tongue-tied cousin Silence. Later, in Shallow's orchard, Silence breaks through his habitual modesty. Flushed with the wine he has drunk at supper, he displays a shy man's sudden courage; and, when Falstaff gravely congratulates him—'I did not think Master Silence had been a man of this mettle'—makes a bold, almost a truculent, rejoinder: 'Who, I? I have been merry twice and once ere now'—a remark that, like certain remarks in the novels of Jane Austen, appears to sum up an entire character and life; after which, he presently collapses and Falstaff, as always commanding the situation, directs that he shall be carried off to bed.

So much for the hereditary ruler of men; Falstaff at the same time is a lord of language. The mythomaniac is a hugely gifted artist, who lives among words and images, from which he draws his vital energy. The first edition of *Les grandes et inestimables cronicques du grand et énorme géant Gargantua* had been published at Lyons in 1532; Shakespeare must surely have studied Rabelais; and Falstaff, though reduced to more human dimensions, is a member of the same

tectum

porticus

sedilia

orchestra

ingressus

mimorum aedes.

proscaenium.

planities siue arena.

Ex obseruationibus Londinensibus Johannis de witt

18 A contemporary copy of a drawing made about 1596 by a Dutch traveller, Johannes de Witt, showing a performance at the Swan Theatre and the general arrangement of the Elizabethan stage

19 A reconstruction of a playhouse, *c.* 1595

20 Seventeenth-century swordsmanship. Such displays were an important part of Elizabethan and Jacobean drama

gigantic brood. His accustomed style has a Rabelaisian gusto; and it preserves its gusto throughout his whole career. 'That trunk of humours, that bolting-hutch[1] of beastliness, that swollen parcel of dropsies, that huge bombard[2] of sack, that stuffed cloak-bag of guts, that roasted Manningtree ox with the pudding in his belly', remains an unselfconscious poet, capable of lending an air of epic magnificence to every theme that his imagination touches. Scholars are inclined to distrust the pleasant story that Elizabeth herself requested Shakespeare 'to write a play of Sir John Falstaff in love', and that, after a fortnight's toil, he completed *The Merry Wives of Windsor*. But evidently he was writing to satisfy his public, who refused to let the old knight die; and by the time Falstaff had been resurrected— at the beginning of the next century, between 1600 and 1601—he had lost something of his original stature and become an established comic personage. Nevertheless he has preserved his literary skill; and his account of his sufferings in the buck-basket, raises knock-about comedy to the level of tragedy:

> . . . Away went I for foul clothes: but mark the sequel, Master Brook. I suffered the pangs of three several deaths: first, an intolerable fright . . . : next, to be compassed, like a good bilbo,[3] in the circumference of a peck, hilt to point, heel to head; and then, to be stopped in, like a strong distillation, with stinking clothes that fretted in their own grease; think of that—a man of my kidney; think of that—that am as subject to heat, as butter; a man of continual dissolution and thaw; it was a miracle to 'scape suffocation. And in the height of this bath, when I was more than half stewed in grease, like a Dutch dish, to be thrown into the Thames, and cooled, glowing-hot (in that surge!) like a horse-shoe; think of that—hissing hot; think of that, Master Brook!

His plight is an emblem of the human condition. Falstaff suffocating beneath a load of dirty clothes is Falstaff sweltering beneath the burden of his flesh.[4]

---

[1] a meal bin.   [2] a large leather vessel.

[3] A bilbo was a sword of the type made by the swordsmiths of Bilboa. Since the material was latten, a comparatively soft metal, it had a particularly elastic blade.

[4] Modern psychologists, no doubt, would call Falstaff a 'compulsive eater'. He claims to have been slim and graceful in his youth: '. . . When I was about thy years, Hal, I was not an eagle's talon in the waist, I could have crept into any alderman's thumb-ring. . . .' *Henry IV, Part I* Act II Scene iv.

O

Among those who have had their say on Falstaff are the myth-interpreters and anthropologists. For them, Henry IV is the Old King, whose age and guilt threaten to destroy the realm, and whom his successor must ritually put to death that the soil may bear again and the spring-time crops may rise. 'By a displacement common enough in the evolution of ritual', the Prince, we are told, refrains from slaying his father, but kills instead a father-substitute.[1] Falstaff provides the vicarious sacrifice; already his relationship with the Prince is that of a wicked father and a scapegrace son; and, in the party at the Boar's Head, he parodies the King's role, the Prince kneeling before him on the tavern-floor to receive his admonitions and reproofs. A highly ingenious theory; but, alas, the symbolic sacrifice of Falstaff takes place *after* the Old King's death; and it seems more likely that the tragic rejection scene may have been inspired by some poignant personal experience. Later, in *Coriolanus*, Shakespeare returned to the theme: the Roman general coldly dismisses Menenius Agrippa, the elderly senator he had once loved and trusted. Shakespeare, we know from the *Sonnets*, sometimes felt that he was prematurely aged and decrepit; compared with the youth he adored, he saw himself as a vulgar professional comedian. Was the poet occasionally treated by his friend as the soldier-aristocrat of the drama elects to treat his ageing crony? Or may Shakespeare have suspected that a disastrous end to their friendship was implicit in its fair beginnings; that, if it had not yet come, it must eventually come; and that he, too, devoted and over-confident, would at last be set aside? Falstaff accepts his loss with appropriate dignity. King Hal, whom he claims as his 'sweet boy', delivers the callous, pompous *coup de grace*:

> I know thee not, old man. Fall to thy prayers.
> How ill white hairs become a fool and jester!
> I have long dreamed of such a kind of man,
> So surfeit-swelled, so old, and so profane;
> But, being awakened, I do despise my dream.

—But, although Falstaff has spoken from the heart, he does not show his heart is broken.[2] Humiliated in the presence of his admirer

[1] J. I. M. Stewart: *Character and Motive in Shakespeare*, 1949.
[2] Hostess: 'The King has killed his heart'. *Henry V*, Act II Scene i.

and creditor, he still makes a wry pretence of courage. The royal thunderstroke, we may imagine, is meant to be followed by a long and dreadful hush; from which out speaks the fallen favourite, decisive and authoritative even in the moment of calamity:

Master Shallow, I owe you a thousand pound

—whereupon, knowing that Shallow, who can always be coerced into throwing good money after bad, will undoubtedly foot the tavern bill, he invites the bewildered company to dinner.

Seen through modern eyes, *Henry V* is a disappointing and disturbing work. While Shakespeare's Danish biographer asserts that the poet was attracted towards Prince Hal by 'some of the most deep-rooted sympathies of his nature',[1] Hazlitt observes that Falstaff was undeniably 'the better man of the two. We think of him and quote him oftener'. Again, we notice a dramatic discrepancy between Shakespeare's intention and his execution. Like Mercutio and, indeed, like Shylock, John Falstaff is a runaway character; and, like Mercutio, if the stage were to be cleared and lightened, and the drama to preserve its original design, the Gargantuan hero needed killing off. For *Henry V* is the climax of a series of dramas, designed to please, though not actually addressed to, the champions of the English war-party, whose generalissimo was just then embarking on one of the greatest adventures of his military existence. During the same year, George Chapman dedicated his translation of the *Iliad* to that 'living instance of the Achillean virtues, eternalized by divine Homer, the Earl of Essex . . .' The Earl, he declared, was a 'true Achilles'; and Shakespeare, not to be left behind, had undertaken to compose the official portrait of an Achillean conqueror. But Henry's virtues were counterbalanced by a large proportion of the ancient warrior's vices; we remember the reputation that he and his armies earned among the helpless peasants of medieval France.[2] Shakespeare accepted his shortcomings as gladly and unconcernedly as he

---

[1] George Brandes: *William Shakespeare*, translated by William Archer, 1898.

[2] Even today, I am told, in some country districts, the word *'anglais'* has a strongly pejorative meaning; and, during the German occupation, an old peasant woman was heard to exclaim: *'Ils sont des vrais anglais, ces allemands!'* The belief that the English were devils with tails was inspired by the English infantryman's habit of wearing behind his buttocks a long dagger, which he used to finish off the enemy wounded.

described his merits. Thus Henry threatens the citizens of Harfleur, should they refuse to yield up their town, with the prospect not only of seeing it totally destroyed but of watching their daughters ravished and their infant children butchered:

> I will not leave the half-achieved Harfleur,
> Till in her ashes she lie buried.
> The gates of mercy shall be all shut up,
> And the fleshed soldier, rough and hard of heart,
> In liberty of bloody hand shall range
> With conscience wide as hell, mowing like grass
> Your fresh fair virgins and your flowering infants . . .
> What is't to me, when you yourselves are cause,
> If your pure maidens fall into the hand
> Of hot and forcing violation?

Later, incensed by the plundering of his camp—'Kill the poys and the luggage! 'tis expressly against the law of arms', exclaims Fluellen, whom Shakespeare is thought to have modelled on Sir Roger Williams, a valiant, explosive Welshman in the Queen's service[1]— Henry orders a general massacre of prisoners. 'O, 'tis a gallant king!', Gower echoes Fluellen; and there is no suggestion that Shakespeare himself, mindful always of his audience, found these details difficult to reconcile with his romantic picture of a patriot-monarch. But his verse suffers—or that is our modern impression. All his genius appears in the scene where the Hostess, Pistol, Nym and Bardolph— the last soon to be hung for robbing a church—discuss the news of Falstaff's death. But Henry, whom Hospur dubbed a 'vile politician' and a twentieth-century poet[2] has called 'the one commonplace man' in Shakespeare's eight historical plays, despite his fine rhetorical exhortations is a flat and uninspiring figure. True, he is eloquent; but we are always conscious of the poet to whom he owes his eloquence hovering behind the mailed puppet. No doubt Shakespeare had grown weary of the cycle; and, perhaps because he had imbibed Jonson's theories, he now apologizes for the primitive restrictions against which he is obliged to work:

---

[1] Williams had served under Essex in the Low Countries.
[2] John Masefield: *William Shakespeare*, 1911.

> . . . Pardon, gentles all,
> The flat unraised spirits that have dared
> On this unworthy scaffold to bring forth
> So great an object. Can this cockpit hold
> The vasty fields of France? or may we cram
> Within this wooden O the very casques
> That did affright the air at Agincourt?

His remedy is to provide a Chorus, who supplies the action with a spacious imaginative setting, unrolls a panorama of the English fleet as it plunges out towards the French coast, and, in a magnificent night-piece, evokes the mood of the armies restlessly waiting for tomorrow's battle:

> From camp to camp, through the foul womb of night
> The hum of either army stilly sounds;
> That the fixed sentinels almost receive
> The secret whispers of each other's watch.
> Fire answers fire, and through their paly flames
> Each battle sees the other's umbered face.
> Steed threatens steed, in high and boastful neighs
> Piercing the night's dull ear: and from the tents
> The armourers, accomplishing the knights,
> With busy hammers closing rivets up,
> Give dreadful note of preparation.
> The country cocks do crow, the clocks do toll,
> And the third hour of drowsy morning name.

If one were inclined to believe that the young Shakespeare, some years before he reached London, had seen active service under Leicester's flag, this passage might be produced as evidence. Many English armies, medieval and Elizabethan, must thus have watched among their camp fires, and observed the lights and listened to the noises of a nearby hostile camp; while home-sick countrymen marked the pleasant familiar sounds that welcomed in a new day.

Henry V scored a popular success: two quarto editions were soon published. But it was *Henry IV*, thanks to 'the humours of Sir John Falstaff and swaggering Pistol', that always drew the larger crowd;

and before long Falstaff, like some of Dickens' characters, began to detach himself from his creator and lead an almost independent life. Treated as personages of ordinary flesh and blood, he and his friends and hangers-on made their way into private talk and letters. During July 1599, for example, Lady Southampton, writing to her husband in Ireland, remarks that 'all the news I can send you that I think will make you merry is that I read in a letter from London that Sir John Falstaff is by his dame, Mistress Pintpot, made father of a goodly miller's thumb, a boy that's all head and very little body . . .'[1] Similarly, Sir Charles Percy, brother to the Earl of Northumberland and another member of the Essex group, writes from his Gloucester-shire manor-house in 1600, that he was 'so pestered with country business' that he could not leave the neighbourhood: 'if I stay here long, you will find me so dull, that I shall be taken as a . . . Justice Shallow . . .' That Shakespeare was now a widely celebrated writer, well-known in the English literary world, is shown by a number of additional references, which date from 1595 to 1600 or 1601. Three years after William Covell's enthusiastic note on 'sweet Shakespeare' and his 'Wanton Adonis', Richard Barnfield, author of *Poems in Divers Humours*, pays him an extended tribute:

> And Shakespeare thou, whose honey-flowing vein,
> Pleasing the world, thy praises doth obtain;
> Whose *Venus* and whose *Lucrece*, sweet and chaste,
> Thy name in fame's immortal book have placed,
> Live ever you . . .

In 1598, Marston satirizes the modern playgoer, from whose lips

> doth flow
> Naught but pure Juliet and Romeo

and Gabriel Harvey, on a copy of an edition of Chaucer brought out in 1598, refers to *Venus and Adonis* as a work that pleases the young, but allows more serious praise to *Hamlet*, and classes Shakespeare, with Spenser, Chapman, Daniel, among the most 'flourishing

---

[1] *Salisbury Papers*. It has been conjectured that Lady Southampton's 'Falstaff' was the Lord Cobham who had protested against Shakespeare's treatment of Sir John Oldcastle. Cobham had no legitimate children; but, according to this scrap of gossip, he must have kept a Mistress Quickly. A miller's thumb was a small fresh-water fish.

metricians' of the age. And then, there are John Weever, who, in 1599, addresses 'honey-tongued Shakespeare' in a clumsy epigram; an unknown admirer who scribbled 'William Shakespeare', amid many other notes and names, including that of 'Mr Francis Bacon', over a blank page of his manuscript book;[1] and the amateur playwright, apparently an undergraduate at St John's, Cambridge, whose *Pilgrimage to Parnassus* and *Return from Parnassus, Parts I and II*, present a couple of stage-struck youths, Gullio and Ingenioso, both devoted to 'sweet Mr. Shakespeare', at the expense of every earlier poet. 'No more!,' cries the indignant Gullio, ' . . . Let this duncified world esteem of Spenser and Chaucer: I'll worship sweet Mr. Shakespeare, and to honour him will lay his *Venus and Adonis* under my pillow, as we read of one—I do not well remember his name, but I am sure he was a king—slept with Homer under his bed's head.'

Most important, however, is a work by Francis Meres, *Palladis Tamia: Wit's Treasury*, published during the autumn months of 1598. Meres was an earnest young man, who afterwards moved to a Rutlandshire parish where he became a parson and a schoolmaster. But, at the time, he was still in London, busily cultivating literary men; and his 'comparative discourse of our English poets with the Greek, Latin and Italian poets' introduced Shakespeare's name on no less than nine occasions. Contemporary English poets, Meres set out to prove, could bear comparison with the noblest writers of the past:

> . . . The English tongue is mightily enriched, and gorgeously invested in rare ornaments and resplendent abiliments by Sir Philip Sidney, Spenser, Daniel, Drayton, Warner, Shakespeare, Marlowe and Chapman . . . As the soul of Euphorbus was thought to live in Pythagoras, so the sweet witty soul of Ovid lives in mellifluous and honey-tongued Shakespeare, witness his *Venus and Adonis*, his *Lucrece*, his sugared sonnets among his private friends, etc. As Plautus and Seneca are accounted the best for tragedy and comedy among the Latins, so Shakespeare among the English is the most excellent in both kinds for the stage; for comedy, witness his *Gentlemen of Verona*, his *Errors*, his *Love's*

---

[1] For a description and facsimile reproduction of this curious document, see E. K. Chambers, *op. cit.*

Labour's Lost, his *Love's Labour's Won*,[1] his *Midsummer Night's Dream* and his *Merchant of Venice*: for tragedy, his *Richard II*, *Richard III*, *Henry IV*, *King John*, *Titus Andronicus* and his *Romeo and Juliet*. As Epius Stolo said that the Muses would speak with Plautus' tongue, if they would speak Latin, so I say that the Muses would speak with Shakespeare's fine-filed phrase if they would speak English . . .

Shakespeare is also classed among our greatest lyric poets, who deserve to rank with Pindar, Anacreon, Callimachus, Catullus, Horace, and among those who are 'most passionate . . . to bewail and bemoan the perplexities of Love . . .'

Meres' 'comparative discourse' itself may be reckoned a piece of harmless pedantry—the awkward effort of an ambitious young man to set up as a learned critic; but it illustrates the dimensions of Shakespeare's fame, and shows how securely he was now established. His financial prospects, too, were steadily improving; and he was careful and judicious in the employment of his funds. Once an Elizabethan playwright had sold a manuscript, he could not depend on any regular return. No copyright system protected the poet. Sometimes the players sold the 'book' to a printer; sometimes the printer obtained a transcript from an unscrupulous member of the cast.[2] The result was a quarto edition of the work, usually imperfect and often grotesquely mangled. During Shakespeare's life, eighteen of his thirty-six plays were thus given to the reading public. The quartos have been divided into good or bad; and their quality varied, no doubt, according to the method by which the printer had procured his text. But, however publication was arranged, it can have added little to the author's profits; and Shakespeare, therefore, enlarged his revenues by investing in his native county. The London poet became a Warwickshire businessman, whom his friends

[1] This play has not yet been satisfactorily identified. Meres' subsequent mention of Lord Oxford as one of 'the best for comedy' is supposed to strengthen the Oxfordian case; though, if Shakespeare's presumed works were really composed by Oxford, it is difficult to understand why Meres should have mentioned them as entirely separate writers.

[2] The theory that the printer may have posted an agent in the theatre to take a short-hand copy has now been exploded. No Elizabethan shorthand system was sufficiently effective.

approached if they needed a loan or, to enable them to carry through
some deal, such as the acquisition of local tithes, the completion of
a lease or the bulk purchase of knitted stockings, required a trust-
worthy financial backer. Richard Quiney, father of Thomas Quiney,
Shakespeare's future son-in-law, was one of these industrious appli-
cants. He followed his countryman's operations with respect, and
never despaired of his advice and help. In January, 1598, for example,
he received a letter from the prosperous Stratfordian Abraham Sturley, informing him that his father, Adrian Quiney, had heard that 'Mr
Shakespeare is willing to disburse some money upon some odd yard-
land or other at Shottery or near about us'; and that this might
be a suitable occasion 'to move him to deal in the matter of our
tithes'. At that moment, Quiney was visiting London; but Shakespeare, when approached, would seem temporarily to have shelved
his friends' proposal. During the autumn, Quiney had better luck.
He was again in London, concerned with legal business; and, on
October 25th, he addressed his 'loving good friend and countryman'
from the Bell in Carter Lane:

> Loving countryman, I am bold of you as of a friend, craving your
> help with thirty pounds upon Mr. Bushell's and my security, or
> Mr. Mytton's with me. Mr. Rosswell is not come to London as
> yet, and I have especial cause. You shall friend me much in helping
> me out of all the debts I owe in London, I thank God, and much
> quiet my mind which would not be indebted. I am now towards the
> Court in hope of answer for the despatch of my business. You
> shall neither lose credit nor money by me, the Lord willing . . .
> My time bids me hasten to an end, and so I commit this to your
> care and hope of your help. I fear I shall not be back this night from
> the Court. Haste. The Lord be with you and with us all. Amen.[1]

Of the varied correspondence that passed through Shakespeare's
hands, this letter is the sole remaining specimen. Shakespeare agreed;
and, that night, as soon as he returned to the Bell, Quiney sent a
reassuring message home.

Shakespeare's links with Stratford had by no means weakened;

[1] Now among the Wheler MSS. The securities Quiney mentions were the son of a
Warwickshire country gentleman and a gentleman servitor attached to the household
of Sir Edward Greville, lord of the manor of Stratford. The Privy Council, which
Quiney attended on his legal affairs, was then with the Court at Richmond.

indeed, preparatory to his eventual retirement, he was strengthening them every year. But, as he prospered, his native town declined. Two serious fires had burned out many houses; between 1594 and 1597, three drenching summers had nearly destroyed the harvest; in 1597, there was an epidemic of the plague. Bad harvests produced a general shortage; throughout England, exports of grain were prohibited by the Queen's Council; and, since barley was required for bread-making, maltsters were ordered to restrict their trade. Meanwhile, both at Stratford and elsewhere, 'a number of wicked people, in conditions more like to wolves and cormorants than to natural men', among whom, wrote the Council, were 'men which are of good livelihood and in estimation of worship', looked forward to a rise in prices and obstinately hoarded stocks. They included Abraham Sturley and Richard Quiney, each reported to be a 'great corn-buyer'; and, in January 1598, Sturley warned his fellow hoarder that the populace was growing 'malcontent'. The maltsters were generally hated and abused; one local tradesman had declared that he expected 'within a week to lead some of the maltsters in a halter'; another, that, 'if God send my Lord of Essex down shortly', he hoped 'to see them hanged on gibbets at their own doors'. But, although an official enquiry revealed that Richard Quiney was holding forty-seven quarters of barley and thirty-two quarters of malt in open defiance of the Council's edicts, he was neither hanged nor prosecuted. Even Sir Thomas Lucy and the Stratford parish priest had gambled on the malt market; and, at the beginning of February 1598, a list prepared by the justices mentions 'Wm. Shackespere' as holding ten quarters—much less than the diligent Richard Quiney; but only a dozen of his fellow Stratfordians had more. Shrewd, conservative, far-sighted, he would appear always to have been a moderate man.

These glimpses of the poet's commercial activities—lending money, accumulating malt, adding acre to acre and, latterly, prosecuting petty lawsuits—have offended numerous sensitive admirers, and encouraged and excited anti-Stratfordian critics. They forget that Shakespeare was a product of his age, in his outward life, so far as we can judge, largely moulded by its social standards; and that at few periods have idealism and opportunism, magnanimous aspirations and inglorious actions, been more inextricably bound up together. Quite apart from the lure of the profit motive, business dealings, for the average middle-class Elizabethan, had all the interest of a complex game. He loved lending, borrowing, acquiring small pieces of property and almost immediately re-selling them;[1] and he liked to complicate the simplest transaction by every means within his power, often by taking out a mortgage on which the mortgagee would eventually foreclose. The problem was then transferred to the law-courts—the Elizabethan man of property was apt to be engaged in several law-suits at the same time; but not infrequently, mistrusting the law's delays, either the plaintiff or the defendant would lose patience and resort to violent and unlawful measures. During January 1599, a considerable disturbance took place in and around the antiquated Theatre, which, with the equally dilapidated Curtain, was now some twenty-two years old. Shakespeare's company was occupying the Theatre; but the ground-landlord, Giles Allen, had elected to make endless difficulties over renewing Cuthbert Burbage's lease; and the Burbages, who claimed that the building was theirs, organized a posse of armed men, headed by Peter Street the carpenter, and proceeded to tear down the fabric. 'In most forcible and riotous manner', they seized and carried away its valuable woodwork, ferried their booty across the Thames, dumped the timber on a site near the Rose and set about the construction of a new building. Allen's action for damages failed—£800 was the enormous sum demanded; and an impressive playhouse, which its builders christened the Globe, began to rise above the Bankside marshes. Richard and Cuthbert Burbage owned half the property; Shakespeare and his professional associates, John Heminge, Augustine Phillips, William Kempe and Thomas Pope, each received a tenth share.

When, early in 1600, Henslowe retaliated by constructing the Fortune, he employed the same carpenter and specified that it should closely resemble the Globe; but, whereas the Fortune was square, the Globe was a polygonal edifice and the galleries, we know, were roofed with thatch. Otherwise, it must have incorpo-

---

[1] Since there were no banks, the Elizabethan found it convenient to invest any sum he received at the earliest opportunity.

rated the same large jutting stage; there would have been a balcony behind the proscenium, above the players' tiring house, and two or three public galleries would have completed the circumference of the 'wooden O'. It was a splendid structure—the second Globe, which immediately replaced the first, was said to be the fairest playhouse 'that ever was in England'; yet the site it occupied, though convenient for the audience, was both disagreeable and insalubrious. The Bankside was a rowdy bohemian suburb, full of 'divers streets, ways and winding lanes all full of buildings inhabited'; and among the houses wound muddy channels, through which the rising Thames flooded. The new theatre—'flanked with a ditch, and forc'd out of a marsh', wrote Ben Jonson—had been raised, like London Bridge, on piles. Hollar's famous panoramic view,[1] executed during the 1640's, looks westward over the Bishop of Winchester's residence, where groups of his friends or retainers are seen perambulating his extensive courtyard, across a huddle of proletarian roofs to the open field in which the Globe lay. Not far off was the Bankside brothel-district; and between the Globe and the built-up margin of the river stood the equally imposing Bear Garden.[2]

Devoted to the pleasures of the 'Royal Game', which Philip Henslowe and Edward Alleyn had been jointly managing since 1594, it must, for the players at the Globe, have been a particularly discordant neighbour. At its entrance, two rows of huge bloodthirsty English mastiffs kept up an incessant din; and from the spacious arena itself would have drifted a ferocious hubbub—the baying of the dogs as they were loosed on their victims, the yelling of an impassioned audience and the roaring and bellowing of tormented beasts. But Shakespeare was well accustomed to the sound. After leaving Bishopsgate, he had taken lodgings near 'the Bear Garden in Southwark'; and this kind of sadistic blood-sport was a favourite Elizabethan pastime, which even the Queen and her attendants and the young gentlemen of the Inns of Court enjoyed. The barbarities of our own period always seem trivial beside the barbarities of any other age. Shakespeare certainly attended the Bear Garden; for not only, in *King Henry V*, does he recall the obstinate courage of the

---

[1] In Hollar's view, the Globe and the Bear Garden occupy one another's rightful places.

[2] See John Norden's Map of 1593, as revised in 1600.

mastiffs—'foolish curs, that run winking into the mouth of a Russian bear, and have their heads crushed like rotten apples'; but he makes Shallow, remembering the pride of his youth, describe how he had once leapt down from the gallery and joined the reckless crowd below:

> I have seen Sackerson loose—twenty times, and have taken him by the chain: but, I warrant you, the women have so cried and shrieked at it, that it passed . . .

Sackerson and Harry Hunks were both Russian bears whose courage and heroic sufferings had endeared them to the Elizabethan mob. Sometimes the animals were blinded or their teeth were broken. In 1598, Paul Hentzner records that he visited a 'place built in the form of a theatre, which serves for the baiting of bears and bulls . . . To this entertainment there often follows that of whipping a blinded bear, which is performed by five or six men . . . Although he cannot escape from them because of his chain, he nevertheless defends himself, vigorously throwing down all who come within his reach . . . and tearing the whips out of their hands . . . At these spectacles and everywhere else, the English are constantly smoking the Nicotian weed which in America is called *Tobaca*[1] . . .' The Puritans alone found the pastime revolting—and then, not so much because it involved the torture of animals as because it degraded man to the semblance of a beast. From the 'foul beasts' who attended such spectacles, the Chamberlain's Men drew many of their own supporters. Enthusiasts for bull-baiting were also addicted to the stage. Yet it was Shakespeare who would afterwards suggest that our fellow creatures may perhaps suffer almost as exquisitely as we do ourselves, and that, far below the level of human misery, there may still be incalculable hells of pain:

> And the poor beetle that we tread upon
> In corporal sufferance finds a pang as great
> As when a giant dies.[2]

He cannot have watched with an entirely unmoved spirit the protracted death-pangs of blind Harry Hunks.

[1] Paul Hentzner, *op. cit.*
[2] *Measure for Measure*, Act III Scene i.

CHAPTER IX

The Fall of Essex

IN 1599, SOME time between the end of March and the latter days
of September, Shakespeare paid the only direct compliment that he
was ever to address to one of the great political figures of his age. As
we might have expected, it was addressed to Essex, then Lord
Deputy, or military governor, of 'yonder cursed country' beyond the
Irish Sea, which, with Southampton and other friends beside him,
he had set to reconquer and pacify and bring back under the Queen's
rule. In his prologue to the fifth act of *Henry V*, Shakespeare
imagines the hero returning from Ireland as Henry had returned
from France:

> But now behold . . .
> How London doth pour forth her citizens—
> The mayor and all his brethren in best sort,
> Like to the senators of th'antique Rome,
> With the plebeians swarming at their heels,
> Go forth and fetch their conquering Cæsar in:
> As, by a lower but loving likelihood,
> Were now the general of our gracious empress,
> As in good time he may, from Ireland coming,
> Bringing rebellion broached on his sword,
> How many would the peaceful city quit,
> To welcome him!'

When he accepted the commission, Essex had been fully aware of
the dangers and difficulties that lay ahead; and he had shouldered it,

so he informed Fulke Greville, in a sternly sacrificial spirit. If he might (he declared) 'with my death . . . quench the great fire of rebellion . . . I should joy to be such a sacrifice. But how much soever her Majesty despiseth me, she shall know she hath lost him who for her sake would have thought danger a sport and death a feast . . .' The Queen did not despise him; or she would scarcely have entrusted him with so important and so onerous a charge. But, during the last few years, her distrust had certainly begun to undermine her love; for he had shown himself, as he grew older, an increasingly recalcitrant and ill-disposed subject. One adventure, above all else, had helped to raise his opinion of his own abilities. During the summer of 1596, in conjunction with the Lord High Admiral, Howard of Effingham, a little later created Earl of Nottingham, he had led a brilliantly successful attack on the port of Cadiz; four of the largest Spanish galleons had been either captured or destroyed; the town had been taken and plundered, and the castle had been forced to yield. Although there were some who questioned his generalship—notably Walter Ralegh, who had accompanied the expedition in command of the third and fourth squadrons—none could dispute the leader's courage. Once again he had found a role that elicited his noblest qualities; jubilantly flinging his hat into the sea, he had embarked on the action like a paladin entering the lists; and, when the place was taken, he had displayed chivalric forbearance in his treatment of the vanquished enemy. Such an *hidalgo*, admitted Philip of Spain, he had not seen before among the heretics!

Deep-laden with its enormous booty, the English fleet set sail for England. Yet Elizabeth, as always weighing the cost of the expedition against the actual dividend she drew—much of the profit had been diverted into the hands of her greedy captains and lieutenants, even of common seamen and the military rank-and-file—was more critical than appreciative, and gave the victors a somewhat frigid welcome. Nothing, however, could diminish Essex' renown; and, although his next venture, the raid on the Azores in 1597, failed to achieve its main object, he was still England's most popular hero, type of all the martial virtues. That, at least, was the public impression he made—a courageous, soldierly aristocrat, with affable, unassuming manners; the private face, seen by his friends, often wore a very different look; and Francis Bacon, a subtle analyst of men, soon noticed that his patron's character was changing—or, if not changing, that it was rapidly developing in a direction that promised little good. Twenty-nine years old, at the height of his energies, handsome as ever with the broad golden beard he had grown during the Cadiz expedition—'Cadiz beards' became a mode that was adopted by many of his young followers—he was now not only attractive and commanding but often insolent and overbearing. To no purpose did Bacon suggest that he should endeavour to cultivate a mild, conciliatory tone, and that he should be especially careful to avoid offence in his attitude towards their mettlesome sovereign. Elizabeth, he pointed out, must necessarily suspect her general—'a man of nature not to be ruled . . . of an estate not grounded to his greatness, of a popular reputation, of a military dependence: I demand whether there can be a more dangerous image than this represented to any monarch living, much more to a lady, and of her Majesty's apprehension?' Essex should remember that the Queen was a woman, and approach her, not formally and brusquely (as he was nowadays inclined to do), but affectionately and deferentially. He should seize every chance of putting forward a proposal, merely in order to be able to abandon it when he saw that it did not meet her wishes. Let him appear contemptuous of popular acclaim, and 'pretend to be as bookish and contemplative' as he had been in days gone by . . . But none of these counsels of serpentine wisdom could deflect Essex from his inevitable course.

Perhaps his worst error, besides the obstinate continuance of his long feud with the Cecils, was that he had ceased to take into account the Queen's feminine appetite for love and flattery, and that he frequently treated her as a monarch to be warned and advised rather than as a mistress to be courted and adored. The Queen was doubly sensitive to this kind of unintentional affront, now that the autumn of her life was at last declining towards winter. 'A lady surprised by Time', to use Walter Ralegh's curiously eloquent phrase, in the year of the Cadiz expedition she had celebrated her sixty-third birthday; and, during the year that followed, her appearance had both impressed and astonished Hérault de Maisse, the French envoy, who

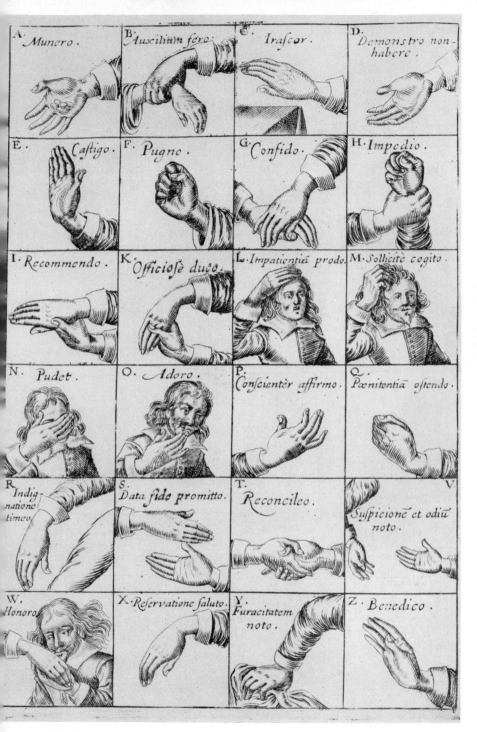

1 An alphabet of rhetorical gestures. Besides being taught to 'move in music', the Elizabethan actor must have adopted a system of elaborately stylised poses

22 King James I of England and VI of Scotland. Eight days after he had reached London, the new king confirmed Shakespeare and his company in their right to 'use and exercise the art and faculty of playing'

noted her dignity and grace and wit—'*une grande Princesse*,' he remarked, '*qui n'ignore rien*'—but commented on the somewhat eccentric splendour that distinguished all her personal trappings. She had received him 'strangely attired in a dress of silver cloth, white and crimson . . . This dress had slashed sleeves lined with red taffeta, and was girt about with other little sleeves that hung down to the ground, which she was for ever twisting and untwisting'. The collar was very high, 'the lining of the inner part . . . adorned with little pendants of rubies and pearls . . . She had also a chain of rubies and pearls about her neck. On her head she wore a garland of the same material and beneath it a great reddish-coloured wig, with a great number of spangles of gold and silver . . . On either side of her ears hung two great curls of hair . . . spangled as the top of her head'. Her bodice, unusually low-cut, disclosed a rather wrinkled breast; but farther down, so far as he could see, her flesh was 'exceedingly white and delicate'; and, while she talked with the envoy, she constantly pulled her dress open. As to her face, it struck him as 'very aged', long and emaciated, her teeth 'very yellow and unequal';[1] and her gestures were those of restless, irritable old age—she would 'rise from her chair, and appear to be very impatient with what I was saying', or would complain that the fire was oppressively hot and give orders that it should at once be put out. But her courtesy and dignity never failed; and the ancient, raddled mask still surmounted a tall and graceful figure. When the envoy took his leave, she summoned his attendant gentlemen; 'they made their reverence before her . . . and she embraced them all with great charm and smiling countenance'.

At the same time, Maisse had kept a watchful eye upon the Earl of Essex, 'a man who nowise contents himself with a petty fortune' but aspired to the highest position in the state. Essex, as it happened, was at that very moment bitterly contending against the Queen and Council over the honours recently conferred on Robert Cecil and his former colleague Nottingham. The squabble was at last composed, but not until Essex had succumbed to one of his familiar psychosomatic maladies, and had retired to his country house where he

---

[1] The discoloration of the Queen's teeth was attributed by foreign critics to the English love of eating sugar.

P

suffered a violent attack of ague, swaddled himself with heavy coverings and refused angrily to leave his room. The worst crisis in his relations with the Queen, however, occurred in 1598. On July 1st, at a meeting of the Council, when the problem of the Irish rebellion was again discussed and Essex's candidate for the post of Governor was peremptorily turned down by the Queen, he had given way to a petulant burst of rage, cast her a contemptuous glance and—unforgivable insult—roundly turned his back on her. Elizabeth's response was swift and decisive; bidding him go and be hanged, she incontinently boxed his ears; at which his hand flew to the hilt of his sword, and he might perhaps have drawn the blade, but for the intervention of the Lord Admiral, who checked the sacrilegious impulse. Swearing that he would not have accepted such an indignity even from the King her father, Essex stormed out of the Council and immediately left the palace.

That he should have been allowed to go his way suggests the strength of the position he still held. He was neither imprisoned nor degraded; but for the next month Essex remained aloof, darkly sulking in self-imposed exile and exchanging letters with the anxious well-wishers who begged him to reappear and make his peace. His refusals were far from conciliatory: 'There is no tempest [he wrote] comparable to the passionate indignation of a Prince; nor yet at any time is it so unreasonable as when it lighteth upon those who might expect a harvest of their careful and painful labours.' He had suffered a brutal insult; and he was provoked into boldly questioning, not only the Queen's recent conduct, but the very principle by which she exercised her power: ' . . . When the vilest of all indignities are done unto me, doth religion enforce me to sue? Doth God require it? Is it impiety not to do it? What, cannot Princes err? Cannot subjects receive wrong? Is an earthly power or authority infinite? . . . Let them acknowledge an infinite absoluteness on earth, that do not believe in an absolute infiniteness in heaven.' These vehement rhetorical questions have an ominous prophetic ring. Essex was closely allied to the Puritans, who entertained heterodox views as to rightful limits of the sovereign's power; and he had already shown an alarming disposition to appeal from constituted authority to the suffrage of his fellow subjects; earlier that year, he had composed an *Apology*, which Anthony Bacon, the recipient, had had copied out and circulated, defending his character and plans, and describing the machinations of his 'known enemies'. His latest appeal was addressed to Sir Thomas Egerton, the Lord Keeper, one of the highest officials of the kingdom; but presumably the writer did not expect that it would regarded as a confidential message.

For his friend Southampton, too, 1598 had proved a period of acute anxiety; and in January he had experienced a humiliating mis-adventure. One night, while the 'fantastical' young man, then 'full of discontentments', was playing primero in the Presence Chamber with Sir Walter Ralegh and a certain Mr Parker after the Queen had risen and retired to bed, her Squire for the Body, Ambrose Wil-loughby, against whom Southampton had a private grudge,[1] asked the gentlemen to end their game lest the noise they made should reach her Majesty. Since they lingered, he repeated his request, adding that, 'if they would not leave, he would call in the Guard to pull down the board; which Sir Walter Ralegh seeing, put up his money and went his ways. But my Lord Southampton took excep-tions at him, and told him he would remember it; and so, finding him between the tennis-court wall and the garden, struck him, and Willoughby pulled off some of his locks.'[2] Worse still, the Queen, hearing of the incident—there were few scandalous doings at Court of which she did not quickly learn—'gave Willoughby thanks for what he did . . . and told him he had done better, if he had sent him to the porter's lodge, to see who durst have fetched him out'. Com-manded to absent himself from Court, Southampton obtained leave to join Robert Cecil on a mission to the French King. He left behind him 'a very desolate gentlewoman', washing 'her fairest face with too many tears'; and, towards the end of August, he was summoned home by the news that Elizabeth Vernon was to bear his child. 'Mistress Vernon [announced a letter-writer] is from the Court and lies in Essex House. Some say that she hath taken a *venue*[3] under the girdle and swells upon it; yet she complains not of foul play but says

---

[1] 'I heard of some unkindness . . . between [Southampton] and his mistress, occasioned by some report of Mr. Ambrose Willoughby.' *Rowland Whyte to Sir Robert Sydney*, January 19th, 1598. *Sydney Papers*, Vol. II.

[2] *Rowland Whyte to Sir Robert Sydney*, January 21st. *Sydney Papers*.

[3] A fencing term for a successful pass.

the Earl will justify it.' The same correspondent also reported 'that he was lately here in great secret of purpose to marry her and effected it accordingly'. John Chamberlain had not been misinformed: Southampton—more chivalrous than the Earl of Pembroke who, in similar circumstance, refused to legitimize his affair with Mary Fitton, another reckless Maid of Honour—had posted home to London and contracted a clandestine marriage. Naturally, the story was repeated to the Queen, who ordered that both Southampton and his 'new-coined countess' should expiate their ingratitude in a London gaol.

Southampton was presently pardoned; but he found it inadvisable to return to Court and 'passed away the time merely in going to plays every day'. Meanwhile, by mid-September, Essex himself had reappeared at Whitehall. Again, he had developed a dangerous illness, and news of his sufferings had touched the Queen. She had sent him her private physician and a bevy of courtiers with friendly messages; and the injured favourite had at length despatched an appropriately submissive letter, declaring that her will was the law, and that she alone could save him from an early death. During his exile, the political prospect had changed: the Queen had lost her oldest counsellor—William Cecil, Lord Burghley, the devoted servant, long ago nicknamed her 'Spirit', who had ridden out all the storms of her rage, advised and encouraged her through all her perils, and whose personality, after forty years' service, seemed to be incorporated in the very fabric of her kingdom. The Queen had visited his sick-bed and even (the dying man informed his son) fed him like a 'careful nurse'; when she was told that the end had come, she dismissed her attendants and retired to weep in solitude. No doubt it was the disappearance of Burghley that enabled Essex to score his last triumph. Week by week, the position of the English government in Ireland grew more and more humiliating. Tyrone, the rebel chief, had captured Armagh; across the whole island, English soldiers and settlers were being driven out or massacred. The Queen and her Council, on which Essex had now resumed his place, were constantly debating the organization of some effective counter-stroke; and at their troubled meetings he eagerly advanced his claims as the properest leader of the royal forces. Despite her suspicions and her instinctive caution, these were claims that the Queen could not ignore. At the beginning of 1599, she allowed him to have his way—there were no other equally distinguished and persuasive candidates—and he received the title of Lord Deputy. Among those he enlisted to join his command were Southampton— he was expressly forbidden, however, to make Southampton his Master of the Horse—a second personal friend, the Earl of Rutland, and his young step-father, Sir Christopher Blount, a valiant, hot-headed Catholic gentleman, 'enterprising and prodigal of his own life', recently knighted for the courage he had shown during the attack on Cadiz.

Essex and his friends set out from London early in the afternoon of March 27th. They were escorted by an enormous cheering crowd —just such a crowd as Shakespeare would picture gathering to wel-come his victorious return; and 'when he and his company came forth . . . the sky was very calm and clear; but before he could get past Isledon[1] there arose a great black cloud in the N.E., and suddenly came thunder and lightning, with a great shower of hail and rain . . .' The Elizabethans were always firm believers in the meaning of natural signs and portents; and this dramatic darkening of the heavens was accounted by some 'an ominous prodigy'. Nor were soothsayers proved wrong: none of Shakespeare's hopes was realized. 'The Englishman's grave' according to a foreign ambass-ador, rebellious Ireland provided the tomb of the general's military reputation. Tyrone eluded him; the country defeated him; its 'moist, rotten' soil, peculiarly unkind to a man of rheumatic humour, slowly drained away his vital strength. In defiance of the Queen's instructions, he appointed Southampton Master of the Horse; and he did his best to keep up his friends' morale by liberally dispensing knighthoods. But, during his campaign against the Irish guerilla forces, no substantial gains were made. Back in Dublin after a sweep through Leinster and Munster, when he had been ordered to march into Ulster and defeat that 'base bush kern' Tyrone upon his own ancestral ground, he received angry letters from the Queen, speaking of funds squandered and orders disobeyed, and referring to the incompetence and inexperience of vainglorious young gentlemen

[1] Islington.

'that rather desire to do well than know how to perform it'. Reproaches were followed by reinforcements; but fresh reverses befell the English army; and in September he arranged to meet Tyrone and agreed to the conclusion of an ignominious truce. Essex had now reached a point at which he was ready for some desperate move. Knowing that he had failed, he could attribute his failure only to the machinations of his secret enemies; and with Southampton, who urged him on, and Christopher Blount, who recommended him to refrain from violence, he discussed the possibility of leaving Ireland and marching south to seize the Court.

It was typical of Essex that, if he were faced with two alternative lines of conduct, either of which, pursued to the end, might have had certain advantages, very often, at the moment of decision, he elected to take a third line, and that the line he took usually lacked the virtue of daring, on the one side, or of discretion on the other. Had he now remained in Ireland, he might perhaps have saved his credit; had he descended on London, supported by a powerful army, he might have thrust aside all opposition. But he did neither: he deserted his post, taking with him a mere handful of his friends, landed in England, hurried to Westminster, then rode at headlong speed to the Palace of Nonsuch, where, at ten o'clock on the morning of September 28th, 1599, he burst in unannounced. His face and his clothes were mud-bespattered; but he did not pause to wash or change. Down the long perspective of ceremonial rooms, past courtiers, servants, guards, he rushed straight into the Presence Chamber, and from the Presence into the Queen's bedchamber, the innermost sanctuary of the royal hive. The Queen had risen; but she was not yet dressed—he found her without wig or ruff or jewels; and around her unpainted cheeks hung strains of thin dishevelled hair. Such an attack on the sovereign's privacy was unprecedented in the annals of the Court; and Elizabeth, though naturally courageous, may have imagined that he had come to end her life. With a typical fusion of valour and shrewdness, she both disguised her alarm and hid her fury; and, when he knelt before her and kissed her hands and neck, she uttered some mild and non-committal phrases; so that he left her apartment happily reassured, remarking that, after tempests abroad, he had been welcomed at Nonsuch by 'a sweet calm'. That calm was of very brief duration; as soon as she had disarmed him and had had time to consider the crisis, she allowed herself to show her true feelings. Essex was summarily dismissed from the Court and driven to London under guard. Egerton, the Lord Keeper, was appointed his gaoler; and at York House, Egerton's Thames-side residence, he remained for several anxious months. In March, he was at length permitted to return to Essex House; but he was still in strict custody; and meanwhile he knew that the government was carefully deliberating on his prosecution.

Once more, he had fallen ill—so ill that his physicians prophesied his death; once more, he had relapsed into a deep religious melancholy, from which he emerged only to confer with his chaplains and write hortatory letters to his closest friends; and once more the Queen's affections were touched, and she sent him a posse of her own doctors. Londoners in general were deeply sympathetic; and his indignant associates, when they could reach him, began to offer good advice. They would rescue him; he must fly the kingdom. Mountjoy, Southampton, Sir Charles Danvers, all proposed their plans of action; but Essex obstinately shook his head, and appeared to sink deeper and deeper into a mood of self-destructive gloom. Simultaneously, his political opponents were making the most of the favourite's fall from grace; and, although Cecil's attitude was not vindictive—he had never been a man of blood—Ralegh hastened to advise him against any display of magnanimity. '. . . If you take it for a good counsel to relent towards this tyrant,' he wrote in about February 1600, 'you will repent it when it shall be too late. His malice is fixed and will not evaporate by any of your mild courses . . . Lose not your advantage. If you do, I read your destiny.' The 'tyrant's' existence was further imperilled by various ill-judged publications. Early in 1599, before he left England, a certain Dr John Hayward had published an historical survey of the deposition of King Richard II and the accession of King Henry IV, with a dedicatory epistle addressed to the Earl of Essex, whom he seemed to identify with the usurping monarch. The book, which was quickly suppressed, had troubled and alarmed the Council; and they were also vexed, during the year 1600, by the unauthorized printing of Essex's *Apology* and by the issue of a petition, defending her brother, that Penelope Rich had presumptuously handed to the Queen. Fearing that both supporters and adversaries had combined to produce his total ruin, Essex shook off his lethargy and himself apostrophized his angry mistress: '. . . I not only feel the weight of your indignation, and am subject to their malicious information that first envied me your favour . . . ; but, as if I were thrown into a corner like a dead carcase, I am gnawed on and torn by the basest creatures upon earth. The prating tavern-haunter speaks of me what he lists; they print me and make me speak to the world, and shortly they will play me upon the stage.'

In June, he was summoned before the Council, to hear the government unfold its case; and among his prosecutors, beside Coke, the ferocious Attorney General, he saw his serpentine adviser Francis Bacon, who, despairing of Essex's fortunes, had now transferred his allegiance to the opposite party. With damning effect, Bacon instanced the letter that Essex had once written to Sir Thomas Egerton, in which he had ventured to protest against the alleged infallibility of earthly rulers. 'Far be it from me,' he declared, 'to attribute divine qualities to mortal Princes; yet this I must truly say, that by the common law of England, a Prince can do no wrong.'[1] The case for the prosecution having been heard, the announcement of the Queen's pleasure was postponed until August 26th when the deserting general was released from custody but forbidden to return to Court; whereupon Essex announced that he would quit London, and seek the rustic peace he loved and needed. Perhaps he might have kept his promise, had he been spared a final crushing blow. He had never been a rich man, though he maintained a costly household; and hitherto he had depended largely upon the Queen's financial help—particularly upon 'the farm of sweet wines', the dues she had authorized him to collect as they were imported into England.[2] At the

---

[1] Characteristically, Bacon at once sought to justify himself in a private letter: 'I confess I love some things much better than I love your lordship, as the Queen's service . . . the good of my country and the like; yet I love few persons better than yourself, both for gratitude's sake, and for your own virtues . . .' Essex's reply was brief, dignified and cold.

[2] According to this system, the Crown sold to a favoured subject the right to collect customs' dues for a sum considerably less than their real value; and the subject then farmed out the customs to his own commercial agents, who collected the dues at English ports.

end of October, he learned that this source of revenue had been cut off, and that he confronted, in addition to political downfall, the ruin of his whole domestic economy.

The disaster shocked him back to life; and, with a sudden and characteristic change of mood, he reappeared in the guise of ambitious politician and vehement patriotic leader. He talked wildly, sometimes wantonly, shifting (observed Sir John Harington) 'from sorrow and repentance to rage and rebellion so suddenly, as well proveth him devoid of good reason or right mind'. During a transport of anger, he even inveighed against the Queen's person, exclaiming—a remark she soon heard—that she was now equally crooked in mind and body. All thoughts of rustic retirement abandoned, he again established himself at Essex House, his quadrangular battlemented mansion, opposite the Church of St Clement Danes on the present site of Essex Street, which overlooked an extensive garden and orchard running down to meet the Thames. There he gathered around him his friends and sympathizers—a strangely assorted body of adventurers, enthusiasts and malcontents: Puritan divines, members of a sect whom Elizabeth especially distrusted as 'dangerous to kingly rule', with their subversive opinions on the limits of royal authority and 'subtle scannings' of God's Holy Word; supporters of the old faith, like his step-father Blount; and 'all sorts of knights, captains, officers', who, 'to the great discontentment of her Majesty', had recently drifted back from Ireland. Essex had always felt a deep affection for his 'gentlemen adventurers': 'I love them [he wrote] for mine own sake . . . I find sweetness in their conversation, strong assistance in their employment, and happiness in their friendship. . . . They are England's best armour of defence and weapon of offence If we may have peace, they have purchased it; if we must have war, they must manage it.' To others, his military hangers-on seemed a somewhat reckless, raffish crew, 'green-headed youths, covered with gold and silver lace', needy younger sons, gamblers and rake-hells, proud to be regarded as gentlemen but condemned to exist upon the verge of poverty.

Such, in Shakespearian drama, is 'honest Iago'. The envious, rancorous outsider was a well-documented Elizabethan type, half serving-man attached to a noble household—a profession that must often have been humiliating, though, for a younger son, it involved no serious loss of caste—half independent companion of the lord or lady whom he followed. Essex himself had an Iago in his designing secretary Henry Cuffe,[1] a minor Machiavel perpetually egging him on and reproving him for any show of weakness. Just as deplorable were the activities of his bellicose steward Sir Gelly Merrick; and together they filled Essex House with a concourse of 'green-headed youths', whose noisy comings and goings aroused the suspicion of the vigilant Council. Meanwhile, as the year approached its close, Essex's private plans were still unsettled. Mountjoy was no longer a firm ally—despatched to Ireland to take Essex's place, he had proved himself an extremely efficient commander, and now advocated restraint and caution; but Southampton, Blount, Danvers were all for a revolutionary *coup de main*. Then, on January 9th, Lord Grey de Wilton, one of Ralegh's staunchest friends, happening to cross Southampton in a London street, fell upon him with his armed servants; and, although the Queen at once gave orders that Grey should be committed to the Fleet gaol, reports of the affray strengthened Essex's conviction that a desperate plot had been laid against his life. He was to be murdered: Ralegh and Cecil and their gang were determined to uphold the claim of the Spanish Infanta and exclude the King of Scots, the sovereign's rightful Protestant heir. A Catholic succession threatened. He must strike now both to preserve his own life and to ensure the kingdom's future safety.

On February 3rd, a plan was at length drawn up for surprising Whitehall and gaining access to the Queen. Conspirators would infiltrate the Palace, and occupy strategic positions in its various rooms. Blount would hold the principal entrance, while the halberds of the guards were seized; and Essex, as he had done at Nonsuch, would thrust his way into the Queen's chamber. Ralegh was to be arrested and parliament summoned; there would follow a public trial, at which the Earl's enemies would be arraigned and sentenced. But the conspirators also devised a plan for preparing the ground by enlisting popular sympathy; and here, if not Shakespeare himself, certainly the company with which he worked, became involved in the

---

[1] By Sir Henry Wotton, Cuffe is described as 'a man of secret ambitious ends of his own . . . smothered under the habit of a scholar and slubbered over with a certain rude and clownish fashion that had the semblence of integrity'.

execution of the scheme. On Friday, February 6th, Sir Charles and Sir Joscelyn Percy and other members of the Essex faction approached the Lord Chamberlain's Players 'to have the play of the deposing and killing of King Richard II' on Saturday. The prudent players objected that they 'thought it too old a play to fetch an audience, but Sir Charles Percy offered them 40s. beyond their profits, so they agreed to play it . . .' Next day, the actors kept their word; and Shakespeare's antiquated drama—of which memories had no doubt been revived by the publication of Hayward's book—was duly re-enacted at the *Globe* before an audience that included many distinguished persons who had crossed the Thames from Essex House. The downfall of an arrogant and ill-advised monarch was again presented to the groundlings; and the gentlemen in boxes and galleries emphasized its message with bursts of loud applause.

Naturally, the government had its spies abroad; and earlier that day, on Saturday morning, a royal message had summoned Essex to attend a meeting of the Council; but he had refused, replying that he was ill and could not leave his sick-bed. It may be his illness was genuine: unquestionably he was sick in heart and mind, and had succumbed to one of those bouts of prostration which were always apt to overcome him during periods of acute crisis. But the deepest conflict that disturbed his spirits arose from his attitude towards the Queen. For the Elizabethans, even the worst ruler wore a mantle of divine authority: for Essex, the sovereign was also a woman to whose affection he owed his whole career—a woman whom he had loved and resented and, because she was the stronger and more resolute of the two, he may perhaps at times have dreaded. The conspirators must respect her dignity—on that he seems to have insisted at all their secret meetings. His object, he believed, was merely to eliminate her evil counsellors and, once he had thrust them aside, to enter her presence as her faithful champion. But could it be done? The risks of such an attempt were obvious and terrifying. So Saturday went by; and the Essex party had not yet moved. While they delayed, the government prepared its measures, and the entrances of Whitehall were doubly guarded.

Now was the moment, the Council agreed, to force the conspirators to show their hand; and, early on Sunday morning, a large and imposing official cavalcade, headed by the Lord Keeper, the Lord Chief Justice, the Earl of Worcester and Sir William Knollys, dismounted on the threshold of Essex House. The gates were barred; but a wicket was opened; and, although their attendants were denied admission, the four officials bravely stepped through. Carrying the Great Seal that symbolized his high office, the Lord Keeper announced that he and his colleagues had come from her Majesty to enquire the import of this disorderly assemblage, and added that, if the gentlemen gathered had any private grievances, he could promise that they would receive a fair hearing. At which Essex exclaimed that a plot had been hatched to take his life; while his companions broke into an angry uproar, with shouts of 'Away, my lord', 'They abuse you', 'You lose time', and presently, as tempers rose, 'Kill them', 'Let us shop them up', 'Cast the Great Seal out of the window'. The deputation might well have been slaughtered, or at least severely manhandled, had not Essex hurried them away from the courtyard to his library, or 'book chamber', where he suggested that they should await his return until he had had time to visit the City and hold a consultation with the Mayor and Sheriffs. So saying, he locked the library door, posted sentinels to guard his hostages and hastened back to join the company.

Whether it was to be westwards against Whitehall or eastwards in the direction of the City, he must at length decide to march; and from the gates of Essex House he wheeled abruptly eastwards and led his mob of followers along the Strand—some two hundred gentlemen and their servants, on foot, armed most of them only with rapiers and daggers, unprotected by helmets or breastplates, but with their short, thick cloaks, which recall a modern bull-fighter's cape, wrapped around their left arms. Pouring down Fleet Street, they shouted to the citizens; and 'For the Queen! For the Queen! A plot is laid for my life', cried Essex, striding at their head. When they had entered the City through Ludgate,[1] astonished Londoners came running to their doors and hung from the casements of the wooden-framed houses that overlooked the narrow streets. But no one ventured forth to swell their ranks; and their shouts aroused no

---

[1] At an ordinary pace, the walk from Essex House to Ludgate would have taken them about seven or eight minutes.

answering clamour. Yet still Essex strode blindly on towards a sheriff's house near Fenchurch; for in Sheriff Smith, he had been told, he had a loyal supporter who would raise the City's trained bands. He was disappointed: the Sheriff immediately took fright and, having received his unwanted guests, slipped off by a back way and sought refuge with the Lord Mayor. Essex's dismay was obvious and pitiable: he spoke 'with a gast countenance . . . like a man forlorn'; and so heavily did he sweat that he was obliged to change his shirt. Amid the curious, unresponding crowd, his expostulations had an almost plaintive accent. 'Not for me, Pickering?' he implored, when an armourer he knew refused to open his shop and furnish a supply of pikes. Now that the crisis had arrived, he seemed to move in an unbroken hallucination.

> Between the acting of a dreadful thing
> And the first motion all the interim is
> Like a phantasma or a hideous dream . . .[1]

Powerless to stir the bystanders, he fell back on the sheriff's house. There he dined and, while his henchmen kicked their heels in the street, held a noisy, unrewarding conference.

Thus two or three hours went miserably past, before he heard that Lord Burghley, Cecil's half-brother, and a herald had ridden into the City and proclaimed the Earl of Essex and his confederates to be traitors and rebels against the Queen. At first, he affected to laugh. A herald, he said, would do anything for a shilling: 'Pish! the Queen knoweth not of it. That is Secretary Cecil.' And, in the meantime, a number of his followers, including a 'Captain or Lieutenant Orell . . . a most desperate rakehell . . . very quick and nimble . . . his silver-gilt rapier and dagger drawn', charged Burghley's posse and did some execution, with loud, hunting-field cries of 'Saw, saw, saw, saw, tray, tray!' Many of his partisans, however, were thinking better of the enterprise and began quietly to put up their swords. Essex, who had rushed from the table, his napkin still around his neck, soon noticed that his force was growing smaller and less bellicose; and reports reached him that Nottingham the Lord Admiral was now on the way with a strong detachment of

[1] *Julius Caesar*, Act II Scene i.

troops. The road to Whitehall was barricaded; the Queen herself, furious but calm and resolute—she had not failed to eat an excellent dinner—spoke of riding out in personal command. All that remained was to leave the ungrateful City and defend himself behind his own doors.

Essex and his friends were already doomed. But their adventure might have come to an end less abruptly and less ignominiously, had it not been for the appearance, that February afternoon, of a loyal and quick-witted gentleman, who happened to be riding from Blackfriars up the slope of Ludgate Hill. He was Sir John Leveson, a retired soldier; and as he passed, going towards St Paul's, beneath the massive arch of Ludgate, he encountered the Lord Bishop of London and the Earl of Cumberland, both on horseback among their armed followers, and both in a condition of deep perplexity. They seemed to recognize him, although he did not know them, and immediately appealed for his professional guidance. 'Having heretofore served her Majesty' as an officer in her wars abroad, would he not take charge of the pikemen and make the proper dispositions? Evidently a modest character, Leveson at first demurred. He was a stranger to them, he objected, 'and had no command over them, and he 'desired [as he recorded afterwards] the care thereof might be committed to some other'. But the agitated dignitaries proved insistent; and at last he agreed, 'bethinking myself that in times of such danger I could not take upon me any charge . . . that might turn to my disgrace, so as I might thereby give an assurance of my loyalty to my Sovereign . . .' He therefore resolved 'to do my endeavour'; and, his professional instincts now thoroughly aroused, seeing an onlooker with a halberd in his hand—'by his personage a tall man . . . one Waight who died of hurt received there'—he ordered him to bring up all the pikes he could find to the posts inside the gate and fetch the roundshot stored below the arch. Next, he posted a dozen halberdiers to block converging alleyways, and 'also moved the Lord of London to cause the chain to be drawn cross the street and to be fixed to the posts. This done, my Lord Bishop of London gave order to free the street of idle gazers, wherewith it was much pestered, and rode up and down encouraging the company . . . to stand to it like men'.

Behind the posts and the ponderous chain that had been linked across the empty street, the loyalists held their position for a little less than half an hour, until Essex and his supporters came hurrying out of St Paul's Churchyard. They halted at four pikes' length from the chain, and Essex, advancing ahead of the crowd, demanded that he should be allowed to pass. None could pass, he was told. Essex then made a personal appeal to Sir John Leveson whom he said he knew—perhaps Sir John had served in his army and they had campaigned together amid the Irish bogs; and, that appeal having failed, he despatched a series of persuasive envoys, each of whom protested that their leader merely wished to reach his own house, and that he undertook to 'pass peaceably without offering offence to any'. Nothing, however, could shake Sir John, now that he had decided where his duty lay, even though a messenger assured him that, should he persist, he might be responsible for 'the effusion of more blood of the nobility and gentry of England than any man born within my age, for, said he, there be earls, barons, knights, and the flower of the nobility and gentry . . . To this I answered that I was sorry for their being there, and that if there should be that effusion of blood he spoke of, the fault would prove theirs and not mine.'

'I tell you that my lord saith he will and must pass,' cried the exasperated messenger, 'and that he will pass by you as a true subject to her Majesty and a friend to the State, and that he only seeketh to suppress the tyranny of those who have sold and betrayed the State to the Spaniard.' But again Leveson had an answer ready, which he delivered with suitable military firmness: 'I answered that it was above my capacity to understand the designs of his lordship; and for his passage that way, I must and would deny it.' Faced by the barrier at Ludgate, with an unfriendly City in their rear, knowing that large forces of the Queen's troops would very soon be on the move, Essex's partisans grew more and more restive as they packed the narrow street. Their leader himself appears to have lost control. From the ranks a single voice suddenly vociferated 'Shoot! shoot!' and, at a range of 'within three quarters of a pike's length', pistols were discharged against the defenders of the gate, who, although their stock of ammunition was scanty, stood their ground and blazed back. Before either side had had time to re-load, Sir Christopher

Blount 'charged with his sword and target and came close to the chain and cut off the head of sundry of the pikes, and with him divers other of the Earl's company, of which some got between the post and the chain and let drive among our pikes and halberds'. It was a brief, confused, ridiculous affray; but blood was shed and several lives were lost. Despite his sword and his target, Sir Christopher Blount was promptly struck down, 'first by a thrust in the face, and then felled by a knock on the head', while Essex's page, 'young Mr. Tracey', received a shot or blow of which he died. Thereupon the defenders counter-attacked and drove their opponents up the street; and Essex called off his men and withdrew from Ludgate Hill to seek a fresh escape route.

Only the river remained; and they turned leftwards through the alleys that led downhill to the banks of the Thames. There were further alarums as they looked for oarsmen; but presently Essex and those of his company who had not yet slipped away were able to engage craft, which ferried them westwards to their original starting place. 'It was about four of the clock when the Earl came to Essex House'—he had left it, on his sleeveless errand, nearly six hours earlier; and there he learned that the hostages he had taken that morning had all escaped to Whitehall, released by an unfaithful associate, 'who, as it seemeth, in policy to save his own life, came with a feigned message . . . for the setting of them at liberty . . .' Nothing was left, except, of course, the always dubious consolation of making an heroic end; and in the meantime a 'little army' of troops had begun to ring the whole house, occupying the garden, which divided the house from the river, and massing in the Strand before its main entry. Lord Burghley, Colonel General of the Foot, directed the operation from the Strand, while Sir Robert Sidney and Nottingham, the Lord High Admiral, commanded on the garden side. The doors of Essex House had been barricaded; and its windows—a curious and interesting detail, which shows the dimensions of the owner's library—had been closed with piles of books. But Burghley's force soon broke down the main gate and poured into the central courtyard, where the defender's gunfire accounted for 'two common soldiers'; and, about nine o'clock, the Admiral despatched Sidney to bid Essex and his beleaguered companions yield. Essex himself had already appeared on the roof, accompanied by four or five of his partisans, waving his sword with a defiant theatrical flourish; and now Southampton stepped out across the leads and engaged his antagonist in a lengthy argument. Some of the speeches they exchanged—shouted down from the roof, or shouted up from the garden walks below, much as in a contemporary theatrical dialogue, when one actor speaks from the balcony and another from the centre of the stage—can still be read among reports of the episode made for the benefit of Robert Cecil. Certain passages deserve especial notice. Besides illustrating Southampton's character and the character of the fallen hero he supported, they suggest the strange complexity of emotions that had driven them to commit the act of *hybris*—the last presumptuous, irrevocable gesture that seals a tragic hero's ruin.

That he had intended sacrilegious violence against his anointed sovereign was an admission Essex could not yet face. The person of the Queen was sacrosanct: in his own mind he may never have been quite clear how he and his company could have seized Whitehall—or, according to their second plan, have raised the City against the Court and Council—without infringing the sacred dignity of the monarch round whom the Court revolved. During bursts of anger, Essex might have abused the Queen; on a different level of feeling, he liked to believe that he remained her loyal servant; and his friend's protestations from the roof were not entirely disingenuous. Nonetheless, Southampton endeavoured to temporize, quibbling and desperately playing for time. 'Dear Cousin Sidney,' he demanded, 'to whom would you have us yield—to our enemies?' 'No,' responded Sir Robert, 'you must yield yourselves to her Majesty.' That, said Southampton, they would willingly do, provided they were given hostages to secure their safe return to Essex House. They would then present themselves before her Majesty, 'to whom, God knows, we never intended the least harm, and whose royal disposition we know to be such that, if we might but freely declare our minds before her, she would pardon us, and blame them that are most blameworthy, those atheists and caterpillars, I mean, that laid plots to bereave us of our lives . . .'

Sidney checked him by administering a sharp reminder of the

Q

rightful relationship between monarch and subject. 'My lord,' he remarked shortly, 'You must not capitulate with your prince . . .' 'Good cousin,' complained Southampton somewhat pathetically, 'I do not capitulate with my prince: I do but expostulate with you . . . You cannot but know . . . that if we shall yield ourselves, we shall willingly put ourselves into the wolf's mouth . . . Then, good cousin Sidney, what would you if you were in our case?' 'Good my lord,' retorted Sidney, 'put no such questions. I hold you are best to yield; for you know this house is of no such force as it can long preserve you and my Lord Admiral hath already sent for powder and ordnance for battery; and, if that will not prevail, he is purposed to blow it up . . .' At this point, Southampton was joined by Essex, who delivered a similar tirade against 'those atheists my enemies' and announced that he 'would rather fling myself headlong from hence' than endanger his loving countrymen below; they were involuntary agents in an unsought quarrel, while his true foes 'keep aloof . . . and dare not once approach me'. He, too, refused to lay down his arms, no matter what the cost was. 'As for my life,' he told them, 'I hate it; I have loathed to live any time this twelvemonth and more.' An accent of passionate sincerity seems to be discernible in Essex's last words: ever since he had come hurrying back from Ireland—earlier perhaps, when, confronted with a problem he could not solve, his powers of clear thought and decisive action had suddenly, mysteriously broken down—no doubt he had begun to abhor an existence in which the gift of directing, inspiring and leading had always played so large a part.

For himself, Essex might now have welcomed death. But his threatened house sheltered a number of women, including his wife Elizabeth and his sister Penelope. The Lord Admiral agreed to let them go, and also agreed that the defenders should be allowed the space of two hours, in which to unfortify the door and then re-build the barricades. As they were at work, cannon arrived from the Tower; and, moved no doubt by the farewell pleas of the women, Essex and his confederates lost heart; 'they came forth again upon the leads, and the Earl told Sir Robert they would yield upon these conditions: first, that they might be used as honourable prisoners: secondly, that the Lord Admiral should make faithful relation to her

Majesty of what they should say for themselves in their own defence: thirdly, that they should have an honourable trial: and lastly, during their imprisonment, they should have divines to instruct them . . .' The Lord Admiral consented; whereupon they threw open the doors and 'each of them upon their knees delivered up his sword'. That night, the various London gaols had to accommodate a horde of prisoners. Essex and Southampton went directly to the Tower. But, before he left the house, Essex burned the contents of the little black leather bag that hung around his neck beneath his doublet, enclosing proof of his surreptitious correspondence with the King of Scotland.

Essex's trial and death are memorable both as the last act of a great contemporary drama, which exhibits a hero of the time in the period of his tragic decline and fall, and for the light they throw on the background of the age, and on the characters and motives of the men who helped to make it. His prosecutors included not only Coke —though a pillar of English jurisprudence, one of the savagest judges who have ever occupied the bench—but Francis Bacon, who during his wordly apprenticeship had flattered and encouraged Essex and had urged him to regain the 'domestical greatness' that in days past had been achieved by Leicester. Bacon had now convinced himself that his patron's subsequent conduct had absolved him from any last pretence of loyalty; and he devoted all his legal skill to preparing and developing the prosecution's case. Essex and Southampton appeared before their judges on February 19th, 1601; and, when they met at the bar in Westminster Hall, the two Earls 'kissed each other's hands, and embraced cheerfully'.[1] Essex's suit was entirely black, and he wore an expression of unruffled calm. He confronted a large assemblage of his fellow peers, some of whom he knew as his personal enemies; and, while Lord Grey was being sworn—the same Grey de Wilton who had attacked Southampton in the Strand—he 'laughed upon Southampton', we are told, and 'jogged him by the sleeve'. Similarly, while Ralegh was sworn in, 'What booteth it,' he demanded, 'to swear the fox?'—the supporters of his enemy's arms were a pair of foxes. Throughout the reading of the indictment, he had kept up a lively pantomime, making 'divers gestures with much smiling in countenance, and often whispering to

---

[1] Walter Bourchier Devereux: *Lives and Letters of the Devereux, Earls of Essex*, 1853.

his companion; acting also a vehement passion of admiration, with holding up his hands and shaking his head, blessing himself, as it were, at the strangeness of these accusations . . .'

Yet, at his most unperturbed, he can scarcely have doubted what the issue of his trial must be, though he was surprised to learn that several of his chief followers—among them Christopher Blount himself—had already provided full confessions in which they freely admitted that the object of their movements had been to seize Whitehall. After weighty speeches by Bacon, comparing Essex both to Peisistratus, the Athenian tyrant, and a famous contemporary rebel, the Duke of Guise, the prisoners were ordered to withdraw and their peers unanimously found them guilty of high treason. Essex's rejoinder, once he had heard the verdict, was admirable and characteristic. Since he had offended against the letter of the law, he declared that he would willingly die. But he disclaimed any treasonable purpose, and begged his judges to believe that he spoke the truth: 'Lying and counterfeiting my soul abhorreth; for I am not desperate nor devoid of grace, now to speak falsely. I do not speak to save my life, for that I see were vain; I owe God a death, which shall be welcome, how soon soever it pleaseth Her Majesty.' Southampton, on the other hand, when his turn to speak came, struck a less resounding note. 'The Earl of Southampton,' recorded an onlooker 'spake very well . . . and, as a man that would fain live, pleaded hard to acquit himself, but all in vain . . . whereupon he descended to entreaty, and moved great commiseration . . . Yet methought he was somewhat too low and submiss, and seemed loth to die before a proud enemy.'

Essex, however, remained calm and constant, even when he had listened to the hideous sentence traditionally pronounced for the crime of high treason: 'You must go back to the place from whence you came . . . from thence to be drawn on a hurdle through the streets of London, and so to the place of execution, where you shall be hanged, bowelled and quartered; your head and quarters to be disposed of at Her Majesty's pleasure . . .' He thought it fitting, he announced, that 'my poor quarters, that have done Her Majesty true service in divers parts of the world, should be sacrificed and disposed of' as his sovereign should direct; 'whereunto with all willingness of heart I do submit myself'. 'A man might easily perceive,' the same spectator noted, 'that, as he had lived popularly, so his chief care was to leave a good opinion in the people's minds now at parting.' In this spirit he returned to prison; but there, as had sometimes happened before, his resolution broke down. His courage dissolved; the bravado melted away; and, having received the ministrations of his Puritan chaplain, the 'base, fearful and mercenary' Ashton, he agreed to summon the hated Secretary and three other members of the Council. In their presence, he made an abject confession; first thanking them for having allowed him to hear the admonitions of 'this little man', his chaplain, then stigmatizing himself as 'the greatest, vilest and most ungrateful traitor . . .' Nor did he attack himself alone: he also implicated Mountjoy and spoke of Mountjoy's notorious love affair with his sister Lady Rich. The penitential mood persisted; and it was as a penitent that he made his last appearance— on the morning of February 25th, behind the ramparts of the Tower. Despite the sentence pronounced in Westminster Hall, he was spared the supreme degradation of quartering and disembowelling, and was conducted to the scaffold with all the ceremony due to a favoured victim of the State. Moreover, he was allowed to speak at length—a privilege that, being a true Elizabethan, and effusive even by contemporary standards, Essex no doubt greatly valued—during the night that preceded his execution to the guards beneath his window, afterwards on the scaffold itself, to the Lords and officers assembled there, always in the same pious, sententious and deeply penitential strain.

The clothes he had assumed for this his last appearance were rich and yet appropriately sober—a black gown of wrought velvet, a suit of black satin and a black felt hat, with 'a little ruff about his neck'; but, when he had addressed the gathering, prayed aloud and solemnly forgiven the executioner, who knelt down to receive his pardon, he was stripped of his gown and doublet and stood forth in a scarlet waistcoat. Then, 'laying flat along the board', he settled his head on the block with outstretched arms; and his head was 'severed . . . at three blows, the first deadly and absolutely depriving sense and motion'. Such were the details of 'A report of the Lord of Essex his death' delivered to Sir Robert Cecil. But soon other and more disquieting reports began to accumulate among the Secretary's papers. All over London, seditious ballad-sheets were being passed from hand to hand, in which the citizens, though during his hour of crisis they had deserted or cold-shouldered Essex, now claimed him as the people's champion, a fallen hero broken by his enemies at Court:

> Sweet England's pride is gone!
> *Welladay! Welladay!*
> Brave honour graced him still,
> *Gallantly, gallantly . . .*

Again, hearts were wrung by a lamentable ditty, entitled *Essex's Last Goodnight*:

> All you that cry O hone! O hone!
> Come now and sing O Lord! with me.
> For why? Our Jewel from us is gone,
> The valiant Knight of Chivalry.

Elsewhere, balladists gave a satirical account of the triumph of the hero's enemies, represented as now congratulating themselves on the courage or cunning with which they had brought him to a traitor's death—Machiavellian Cecil, brutal Burghley and that arch-atheist Sir Walter Ralegh:

> Little Cecil trips up and down,
> He rules both Court and Crown,
> With his Brother Burghley Clown,
> In his great fox-furred gown;
> With the long proclamation
> He swore he saved the Town.
> Is it not likely?

> Ralegh doth time bestride,
> He sits 'twixt wind and tide,
> Yet uphill he cannot ride,
> For all his bloody pride . . .

Ralegh was also denounced as a savage capitalist and a ruthless exploiter of the common people.

Yet, considering the gravity of the offence involved and the

Elizabethan attitude towards the crime of high treason, the penalties meted out to the conspirators do not seem to have been unduly savage. Including Essex and his step-father Blount, only six were executed.[1] The death sentence passed on Southampton was commuted to imprisonment for life; and fifty others were either fined and imprisoned, or forgiven upon payment of a large financial penalty. Robert Cecil himself may have intervened to save Southampton's life; he was a crafty, not a cruel, man; and his table was presently heaped with petitions written by despairing prisoners and their wives, in which they appealed for the Queen's mercy and her powerful Secretary's good offices. None of their appeals makes very pleasant reading; they showed a general tendency to abjure the lost leader or denounce him as an evil genius who, by his pernicious counsels, had contrived to lead his harmless friends astray. Even Southampton took this easy line. 'My reason,' he humbly assured the Council, 'was corrupted by affection to my friend (whom I thought honest) and I by that carried headlong to my ruin . . .' But then, Shakespeare's beloved patron was now experiencing many different ills. His rooms in the Tower were cold and damp; and he was troubled by 'the continuance of his quartern ague', and 'by a swelling of his legs and other parts', which sapped the strength of that lively and sanguine nature. But, although he moped in confinement, the physical vanity of his youth had not yet quite deserted him. At least, he summoned up resolution once again to have his portrait painted, the big black-and-white cat that consoled his solitude crouched near him on a comfortable ledge. He is dressed in black, with a broad white collar, and black gloves adorned with diminutive bows. His face is melancholy; the eyes are round and glazed—they bear a curious resemblance to those of the attendant cat. He had not yet cut off the celebrated love-locks, which fall profusely over both shoulders.

So long as the Queen existed, there was little likelihood he would regain his freedom. Meanwhile the aftermath of the conspiracy was being slowly liquidated. One by one, Southampton's fellow conspirators paid their fines[2]—£20,000 in the case of the Earl of

---

[1] See *The Salisbury Papers*, Historical Manuscripts Commission, Vol. II.

[2] Elizabethan fines, however, were not always paid in full. Once a proportion had been discharged, the offender was granted provisional liberty.

Rutland, £10,000 in that of the Earl of Bedford—and, more or less crippled by debt, emerged quietly and gratefully from goal. At the same time, Cecil had had to contend with the appeals of equally importunate suitors—those who had not taken part in the rising and proclaimed their well-known loyalty to the Queen, and who, now that the conspirators were broken and disgraced, begged to be allowed a modest proportion of the spoils. Thus, Lord Lincoln asked for a couple of stone shafts—'too fair to make pillars for a traitor's tomb'—originally brought from Cadiz by the late Sir Gelly Meyrick; another petitioner seized the opportunity of endeavouring to secure the lease of Drury House, vacated since the death of Sir Charles Danvers; a third was interested in a handsome gelding; a forth, the fashionable poet John Lyly, approached the Secretary with a euphuistic letter—as 'an humble suitor to her Majesty to have something out of the lands, leases, goods or fines, that shall fall into her Highness by the true fall of these false, desperate and disloyal traitors . . . that after thirteen years' service and suit for the revels, I may turn all my forces and friends to feed upon the rebels'. Seldom had the moral character of the age, always grimly acquisitive and fiercely competitive, been exhibited in so harsh a light.

With Essex's death at the age of thirty-four, a new mood—one of disillusionment and resigned dejection—appears to have descended upon the English court. It was felt by the Queen herself, who understood that many of her greatest subjects lived in eager expectation of her end; and, during the summer months of 1601, she held a curious private conference with the learned antiquary William Lambarde, who showed her his summary of a collection of historical manuscripts, some of them dating back to the reign of Richard II. It was the tragedy of Richard that Shakespeare's company had been commissioned to perform upon the eve of Essex's rising. Elizabeth remembered the occasion and immediately burst into speech: 'I am Richard II,' she exclaimed. 'Know ye not that?' Other observers, she suggested, had not missed the parallel: 'This tragedy was played forty times in open streets and houses.' From which her thoughts turned to the gloomy contrast between the hard, chivalric life of the Middle Ages and the political calculations of the present day: 'In those days force and arms did prevail; but now the wit of the fox is everywhere on foot, so as hardly a faithful or virtuous man may be found.' To that October belongs Sir John Harington's famous account of the old Queen in the winter of her life. Though her god-son and once a favourite attendant, Harington had lately offended his mistress by allowing Essex to dub him knight among other members of the Irish army; and, after the rising, when he was again at court, she had despatched Lord Buckhurst to him with a 'sharp message' that sent him hurrying out of London. 'Go tell that witty fellow, my godson,' she commanded, 'to get home; it is no season now to fool it here'—a message, says Harington, that he liked 'as little as she doth my knighthood, so took to my boots and returned to the plough in bad weather'. Meanwhile, she was 'quite disfavoured and unattired, and these troubles waste her much. She disregardeth every costly cover . . . and taketh little but manchet and succory pottage.[1] Every new message from the City doth disturb her, and she frowns on all the ladies . . . She walks much in her privy chamber, and stamps with her feet at ill news, and thrusts her rusty sword at times into the arras in great rage . . . The dangers are over, and yet she always keeps a sword by her table.'

Finally, on March 24th, 1603, the Mortal Moon experienced her last eclipse. It was not that Elizabeth's courage had failed her—once she had recovered from the shock of Essex's death, she rode, danced, walked in her garden, received the Venetian envoy wearing a constel-lation of jewels and a gay light-coloured wig, and seemed 'never so gallant many years, nor so set upon jollity'; yet a cloud of languor and spiritual depression slowly overcame her spirit. In March, she grew feverish and sleepless; and thereafter the decline was rapid, as she lay, defiantly awaiting the end, her finger between her lips, propped up against a heap of cushions. Although statesmen and politicians had long expected it, and had laid secret plans to safe-guard their own future, the news that her extinction was imminent had a temporarily stupefying effect on Court and City. From his cell beneath the leads of the Beauchamp Tower, within the precincts of the Tower of London, an imprisoned Jesuit priest, William Weston, who had been kept there in solitary confinement since December 1598, was looking down over the yard and ramparts and the house-

---

[1] Fine wheaten bread and pottage made of wild chicory, or endive.

tops that crowded round the walls. Already he had listened to the hubbub beneath his window when reports of the Essex revolt first reached the Tower, and had watched 'pikes . . . mail-jackets and muskets' being carried out of the main armoury; just as, later, he had heard the preparations for putting the rebel Earl to death. Now he was aware of an unaccustomed hush; 'there was nothing I could learn apart from what my warder chose to tell me. But this I did witness. During those few days in which she lay dying beyond all hope of recovery, a strange silence descended on the whole city, as if it were under interdict and divine worship suspended. Not a bell rang out. Not a bugle sounded—though ordinarily they were often heard.'[1]

In the chorus of panegyrics that accompanied the Queen's funeral, Shakespeare failed to raise his voice; and the omission was sufficiently conspicuous to disturb his former champion, Henry Chettle, who, in a volume of verse, entitled *England's Mourning Garment*, begged that 'Melicert' would remember his poetic and patriotic obligations and

> Drop from his honeyed muse one sable tear,
> To mourn her death that graced his desert
> And to his lays opened her royal ear.

The Queen had opened her ear to Shakespeare and his fellow actors as recently as the beginning of the previous February, when they had entertained the Court at Richmond Palace; their chance involvement in the Essex rising had been quickly pardoned and they had continued to enjoy their sovereign's patronage. But Shakespeare had been Southampton's man and, through Southampton, presumably, had entered Essex's charmed circle; and, while Southampton was still the Queen's prisoner—not to be released until the advent of King James—Essex, the 'flower of chivalry', had been cut off by the Queen's justice. The fall of Southampton alone might have embittered and unnerved his friend. The tragedy of Essex, however, aroused a far more complex set of feelings; not only was the hero betrayed, but during the course of the tragedy he had betrayed him-

---

[1] *William Weston: The Autobiography of an Elizabethan*, translated from the Latin by Philip Caraman, 1955.

self—by his irresolution, his display of moral cowardice, the final exhibition of abject repentance with which he had bowed the knee before his enemies.

Just as disturbing and unedifying had been the behaviour of acquisitive loyalists, equally eager to share in the spoils and to advertise their own devotion. Among the Elizabethans, an appetite for gain always kept pace with the love of glory. Greed was a peculiarly Elizabethan vice. Many of the richest aristocratic houses had been established on the plunder of the Church; the gallant piratical voyages, carried out by Drake, Hawkins and their followers, had added huge sums to the national revenue; and Timon's diatribes against his fellow Athenians bear evidently some direct reference to the moral climate of contemporary English life:

> Do villainy, do, since you profess to do't,
> Like workmen. I'll example you with thievery:
> The sun's a thief, and with his great attraction
> Robs the vast sea; the moon's an arrant thief,
> And her pale fire she snatches from the sun;
> The sea's a thief, whose liquid surge, resolves
> The moon into salt tears; the earth's a thief,
> That feeds and breeds by a composture stol'n
> From gen'ral excrement—each thing's a thief . . .
> All that you meet are thieves; to Athens go,
> Break open shops; nothing you can steal,
> But thieves do lose it . . .

Essex, 'the valiant knight', had seemed a personification of less ignoble standards. ' . . . Now [Shakespeare might have echoed his sovereign] the wit of the fox is everywhere on foot.'

CHAPTER X

A New Reign

ON APRIL 6TH, 1603, the new sovereign, James I of England and VI of Scotland, crossed the River Tweed at Berwick. Then, 'banqueting and feasting by the way', receiving the ready homage of noblemen and gentlemen, and acknowledging the enthusiastic applause of an 'obsequious and submissive' people, he led his courtiers slowly south. On May 3rd, he drew up at Theobalds, Sir Robert Cecil's splendid country residence, which Lord Burghley had begun to build in 1564 and his son had completed in 1585; and there the Privy Council welcomed him, Mr Secretary at their head, and he was conducted around the house and gardens. That England's premier civil servant, out of his own personal fortune, should have been able to build himself so rich and fantastic a setting sufficiently illustrated the kingdom's power and wealth. The roof of one hall, for example, represented the movements of the stellar system; stars shone forth as soon as dusk descended, and, driven by an ingenious clockwork device, the sun regularly revolved between the symbols of the zodiac. Up the walls climbed a procession of oak-trees, their trunks and branches clad in natural bark, blossoming into a wealth of leaves and flowers, with heraldic shields hanging from the boughs and birds' nests lodged among the foliage. Other apartments showed the march of English history and a huge map of the entire realm, which included 'the armorial bearings and domains of every esquire, lord, knight and noble who possesses lands and retainers to whatever extent'. There was also a polychrome fountain, and a gigantic chimney-piece topped by bronze statues.

In the gardens, the king was escorted through 'meanders compact of bays, rosemary' and similar sweet-scented herbs and shrubs, but was recalled to stand at a window and look down upon the cheering crowd beneath. Compared with his predecessor's formidable majesty, he cut an odd and unimpressive figure. His legs were weak—he always preferred to ride—and 'that weakness made him ever leaning on other men's shoulders; his walk was ever circular, his fingers ever in that walk fiddling about his codpiece'. Not very tall, he seemed much stouter then he was, since, fearful of assassins, he wore a thickly padded undergarment. When he sat down to table, he gobbled and guzzled at his cup, 'as if eating his drink', which, together with his dull eyes, loosely hanging lower lip and thick Scottish brogue, gave him a somewhat coarse and rustic air. Yet he was shrewd and resourceful and erudite—the wily product of a difficult and dangerous childhood—and so thoroughly a royal personage that, at least in his own estimation, he could afford to disregard his personal dignity. Early sufferings had left an indelible mark on his temperament. Because he had disliked, though he had scarcely known, his mother, he did not admire or love women; and, having been frequently terrorized and humiliated by his ferocious Scottish nobles, who again and again had made him feel his debility and insignificance, he had developed a romantic, half-homosexual adoration for simpler, stronger, more attractive men. His plain, sharp-tongued Danish consort accepted these tastes, which she would appear to have found neither embarrassing nor inconvenient. Both husband and wife were devoted to their private pleasures; and while the King was at his happiest in the hunting-field, or inspecting the large collections of exotic animals with which he stocked his menageries and parks, the Queen preferred dancing and theatrical displays and herself performed in masques and pageants.

There was no likelihood that they would banish the players. Once the King had gained Whitehall, he took steps to rearrange his household. Southampton, released from imprisonment, was soon playing a

---

[1] See 'Theobalds: A Lost Elizabethan Palace', by Sir John Summerson, *The Listener*, March, 1955. Theobalds is also described by Paul Hentzner, *op. cit.* James was so favourably impressed by the house that, in 1607, he persuaded Robert Cecil, then Lord Salisbury, to exchange it for the royal manor of Hatfield.

distinguished part at Court—to such good effect that, like Essex in his heyday, he received the farm of sweet wines; and, before the winter ended, Ralegh, accused of conspiring with the Spanish interest, had himself been relegated to the Tower, where he was to spend the next thirteen years, walking the battlements, considering the lessons of the past and framing his grandiose universal history. Many minor servants were immediately reappointed. James had reached London on May 11th; on the 19th, Shakespeare and his associates, Richard Burbage, Augustine Phillips, John Heminge, Henry Condell, Lawrence Fletcher, William Sly, Robert Armin, Richard Cowley, were licensed 'freely to use and exercise the art and faculty of playing'; and the Chamberlain's company became the King's Men. At the same time, they were appointed grooms of the chamber; and, having been granted four and a half yards of red cloth to provide them with liveries, they joined the coronation march. The old Queen's patronage had been generous; but the King's proved much more lavish. He greatly extended the period of Christmas revels; and, during the Christmas season of 1605, the King's Men gave eleven command performances. It is even said, though on somewhat slight authority, that the King wrote the dramatist an 'amicable letter'.

Around Whitehall, Shakespeare would have seen Southampton; but, if indeed they were able to meet and talk, probably the meeting did not revive their friendship. The fantastical youth was now thirty years old, a popular figure at Court—particularly popular with the Queen because he danced so well; and the ghost of his fallen leader had at last been laid. James referred to Essex as one of the martyrs of his cause; Ralegh, who had advised Cecil against any show of mercy towards the 'tyrant', had himself narrowly escaped a traitor's death. Vindicated heroes are often quickly forgotten—or, if they are still remembered, they lose their gift of arousing wrath or pity; yet Essex's spirit was destined to linger on, not in the minds of contemporary politicians, but in Shakespeare's greatest tragic dramas. At this point, however, we must look back. Before James I ascended his throne, Shakespeare had already written *Julius Caesar*, *Troilus and Cressida* and *Hamlet, Prince of Denmark*. The first may perhaps have been written as early as September 1599, when a German tourist,

Thomas Platter, enjoyed a play about 'the first Emperor, Julius Caesar', with 'at least fifteen characters' and a lively jig to wind up the performance, at a playhouse on the Bankside; but there were several old plays that treated the same theme, and the tragedy that he saw need not necessarily have been by Shakespeare. John Weever, on the other hand, quotes from Shakespeare's text in 1601.[1] *Julius Caesar*, therefore, must either have been written while Essex was still stationed abroad but planning an immediate return,[2] or during the year of his conspiracy and rising. The version of *Hamlet* that has come down to us seems also to have been produced in 1601; and each play suggests that the tremendous events of the time had stirred the dramatist's imagination. This does not mean that Shakespeare was directly concerned to depict the crucial drama of his own age: still less that, in *Julius Caesar*, with its talk 'of dark conspiracy and of noble idealism'[3] he hoped to warn Essex against the danger of drifting into armed revolt. Nor, I think, was *Troilus and Cressida*, believed to have been written about 1600,[4] a deliberate attack upon the military mind, intended to serve the dejected hero as a salutary moral lesson. Such hypotheses ignore the nature of genius, and the creative methods that men of genius employ. Every work of art is produced, not by a single decisive experience, but by the slow accumulation of ideas and feelings, to which some sudden experience acts as catalyst. Critics have argued that Shakespeare could not have been deeply affected by Essex because Essex, they have decided, was essentially a 'second-rate man'. Here they are adopting the historian's hindsight. For his contemporaries, the victor of Cadiz, whether they loved or detested him, was always a fascinating and imposing character. He had been regarded, rightly or wrongly, as a champion of social justice; and it is noteworthy that, when the Stratford tradespeople were infuriated by the activities of

---

[1] 'The many-headed multitude were drawn
   By Brutus' speech, that Caesar was ambitious.
   When eloquent Mark Antony had shown
   His virtues, who but Brutus then was vicious?' *Mirror of Martyrs.*
[2] Platter saw the play on September 21st, 1599: Essex reached Nonsuch Palace on the 28th.
[3] John Dover Wilson: *op. cit.*
[4] John Dover Wilson: *op. cit.* E. K. Chambers, on the other hand, thinks that it was composed in 1602, or even later.

the speculative malt-hoarders, they had prayed that 'my lord of Essex' might descend to hang the miscreants above their own thresholds.

Essex's tragedy, I believe, both during its preparatory stages and in its culmination was the crucial drama of Shakespeare's later life;[1] it had exhibited a noble mind brought low and a once-admirable friendship ruined and betrayed. The homosexual strain in Shakespeare's temperament may perhaps be over-emphasized; but there is no doubt that he was deeply sensitive to the emotional relations between man and man; and, although *Julius Caesar* is throughout a supremely moving and exciting play, surely its finest episode depicts the violent quarrel that blazes up to separate the doomed patriots, and the weary reconciliation that follows the quarrel and confronts them with their joint failure.[2] Each of them is exhausted beyond endurance; and Brutus, as he sits reading alone, while his attendants lie asleep on the ground and even Lucius his page nods drowsily above the lute he plucks—

> Gentle knave, good night;
> I will not do thee so much wrong to wake thee:
> If thou dost nod, thou break'st thy instrument;
> I'll take it from thee; and, good boy, good night

—imagines that he sees the ghost of the murdered dictator, phantom of his tired brain, but a messenger of imminent extinction, gliding through the tent door. Brutus and Cassius reach a unity in misfortune that they could never have achieved in triumph:

> Cassius: For ever and for ever farewell, Brutus!
> If we do meet again, we'll smile indeed;
> If not, 'tis true this parting was well made.
> Brutus: Why then, lead on. O, that a man might know
> The end of this day's business ere it come!
> But it sufficeth that the day will end,
> And then the end is known . . .

And it remains for Antony, an exuberant politician, practised mani-

[1] John Dover Wilson: *op. cit.*

[2] Of this scene, Coleridge wrote that he knew 'no part of Shakespeare that more impresses on me the belief of his genius being superhuman . . .'

pulator of the ready, effective phrase,[1] whose eloquence has already vanquished his adversaries and driven them headlong out of Rome, to pronounce a second funeral oration, far more perceptive and poetic than the first:

> This was the noblest Roman of them all:
> All the conspirators, save only he
> Did that they did in envy of great Cæsar;
> He only, in a general honest thought
> And common good to all, made one of them.
> His life was gentle, and the elements
> So mixed in him that Nature might stand up
> And say to all the world 'This was a man!'

Beside Antony's regard for the fallen Brutus—a human being who had realized the Elizabethan ideal of a character in which the various elemental attributes were justly blended to form a perfect whole—and the affection that, after their quarrel, springs up again between the two conspirators, the bond uniting Brutus to his wife seems slight and almost insignificant; and the resignation he displays when he learns of her death momentarily astounds Cassius:

> Brutus: Why, farewell, Portia. We must die, Messala:
> With meditating that she must die once
> I have the patience to endure it now.
> Messala: Even so great men great losses should endure.
> Cassius: I have as much of this in art as you,
> But yet my nature could not bear it so.

None of Shakespeare's other tragic achievements belongs quite so exclusively to the world of men. It is concerned with man's work and masculine emotions; and the images that wing its lines are appropriately large and powerful. Caesar's sheer magnitude has once enraged his enemies: 'like a Colossus' he bestrides Rome. Later, when the giant has been pulled down, Antony compares him to a

---

[1] 'Brutus' style is dry and noble, as from a book of law. It proceeds in the vein of reason and solicits the mind. Antony throws fire into the blood. He uses every licence of poetic form to throw the mob into a frenzy . . . Like all men to whom prose is the natural voice of public affairs, Brutus fails to recognise how much there is in politics of eloquent unreason'. George Steiner: *The Death of Tragedy*, 1961.

R

royal stag, remembering that the stag was among the monarchs of creation which exercised a natural sovereignty. Nor has his fate been ignoble; Caesar has had the antagonists he deserved:

> . . . Here wast thou bayed, brave hart;
> Here didst thou fall, and here thy hunters stand . . .
> How like a deer strucken by many princes
> Dost thou here lie!

—and those antagonists steadily increase their stature as they approach the tragic climax. Shakespeare's play presents no real villains; some degree of personal nobility is conferred on all the chief actors. Brutus is a disinterested legalist; and Cassius' advocacy of their 'honourable-dangerous' enterprise, despite certain touches of rankling private resentment, is inspired for the most part by unselfish motives. Since *Julius Caesar* is a tribute to humanity, to mankind's interest in truth and justice, *Troilus and Cressida*, which may have followed it a year, or two years, later, seems an especially surprising work. Again the story is connected with that of Essex; but now the militant leader, disgraced and stripped of his command, had begun to appear under a more depressing guise. Chapman had acclaimed him as modern Achilles. Well, at least he shared Achilles' habit of retiring from the battlefield and sulking in his own quarters! Brave men, Shakespeare reminds us, are very often stupid men; and, seizing on the Homeric legend as Chapman had translated it, he composes a ferocious parody, where 'the wit of the fox' invariably prevails against the lion's dignity and courage, and the lion, for all his inherited graces, is at best an arrogant and foolish creature. In *Julius Caesar*, Shakespeare's main source-book had been Sir Thomas North's *Plutarch*,[1] and he had followed the original text as closely as, while composing his English historical plays, he had often followed Holinshed and Hall. In *Troilus and Cressida*, he was indebted to Chapman's *Iliad*, Chaucer's *Troilus* and the collections of the 'histories of Troy' compiled by Caxton and John Lydgate; but he treated his antique material with much less regard for the style and spirit of the story. Shakespeare, unlike Jonson, was never an

---

[1] *The Lives of the Noble Grecians and Romans, compared together by that grave learned philosopher and historiographer Plutarke of Chaeronia, translated out of Greek into French by James Amyot . . . and now out of French into English by Thomas North*, 1579.

historical purist: Brutus hears a clock striking; from the roof-tops of Republican Rome bristles a forest of Elizabethan chimneys. The dramatist's Troy, on the other hand, is deliberately presented as a second London; his Trojans are neither noble nor ancient, but exemplify a multitude of fashionable vices.

If Shakespeare's early editors, anticipating Shaw, had divided his opus into 'pleasant' and 'unpleasant' plays, *Troilus and Cressida*, published as a quarto in 1609, when it was described as an entirely new production, 'never staled with the stage, never clapper-clawed with the palms of the vulgar', might have ranked among the most unpleasant of them all. Under the poet's eye, mankind disintegrates; its noblest qualities dissolve in chaos. Valour is reduced to idiocy; and Achilles, 'idol of idiot-worshippers', is displayed lolling at his ease, while Patroclus, his pederastic crony, amuses him with brilliantly spiteful imitations of his fellow Grecian leaders:

> The great Achilles, whom opinion crowns
> The sinew and the forehand of our host . . .
> Grows dainty of his worth, and in his tent
> Lies mocking our designs. With him, Patroclus,
> Upon a lazy bed, the livelong day
> Breaks scurril jests,
> And with ridiculous and awkward action,
> Which, slanderer, he imitation calls,
> He pageants us . . .
>   At this fusty stuff,
> The large Achilles, on his pressed bed lolling,
> From his deep chest laughs out a loud applause,
> Cries 'Excellent! 'tis Agamemnon right!
> Now play me Nestor; hem, and stroke thy beard . . .'

The speaker is Ulysses, the professional politician enraged by the coarse irreverence of the professional soldier, and not only by his ribald frivolity but by the contempt that he professes for sober diplomatic methods:

> They call this bed-work, mappery, closet-war;
> So that the ram that batters down the wall,

For the great swing and rudeness of his poise,
They place before his hand that made the engine . . .

Thus Cecil might have spoken of Essex, who had repeatedly 'taxed his policy and called it cowardice'; and, although no portraits, I assume, were intended—I hesitate to believe that Achilles and Patroclus represent Essex and Southampton—any spectator who had studied the General's moods, his neurotic collapses and sudden bursts of fury, would have been interested by the dialogue between Ulysses and Ajax when Achilles is pretending sickness:

Ulysses: We saw him at the opening of his tent:
He is not sick.
Ajax: Yes, lion-sick, sick of proud heart. You may call it melancholy, if you will favour the man; but, by my head, 'tis pride . . .

Since its publication in 1609, *Troilus and Cressida* has frequently been 'staled with the stage'; but this curious and haunting tragi-comedy has never pleased a very wide audience. It suggests too many doubts, raises too many problems: the impression it makes is too sharply astringent, yet, at the same time, somehow too elusive. Elsewhere the dramatist brings on a single character—a Mercutio or a Falstaff—who, whether intentionally or unintentionally, is cast in the role of Devil's Advocate; here almost every character is a rebel and, loudly and persistently, speaks out of turn. We meet neither heroes nor villains, merely gradations of villainy, stupidity, folly. Shakespeare's own allegiance seems to remain unfocused; when he sympathizes, his interest is reserved for the weak, unworthy Troilus, victim of a violent obsession that lends his personality a distorted strength. Both from the reader's and from the spectator's point of view, *Troilus and Cressida* wants light and shade; or, rather, it is a chequerwork of murky tones, lacking the moral chiaroscuro that we expect in a poetic tragedy. Numerous are the critics it has puzzled or offended. The poet, observes Dryden, appears to have begun to write 'with some fire; the characters of Pandarus and Thersites are promising enough; but after an entrance or two he lets them fall: and the latter part of the tragedy is nothing but a confusion of drums and trumpets, excursions and alarms'. Albeit 'more correctly written than most of Shakespeare's compositions,' remarks Johnson, 'it is not one of those in which either the extent of his view or the elevation of his fancy is fully displayed.' Its structure, says Hazlitt, is 'loose and desultory'; the drama 'rambles on just as it happens', overtaking, 'together with some indifferent matter, a prodigious number of fine things in its way'. But, particularly disconcerting to the ordinary reader, is Shakespeare's analysis of sexual love. Having exploded the 'Achillean virtues' celebrated in *Henry V*, he demolishes the romantic idealism of *Romeo and Juliet*. In Verona, love has a limitless scope: Juliet claims that she feels an 'infinite' affection. In Troy, it is the slave of chance, subject to the miserable limitations of the human mind and body:

> This is the monstruosity in love, lady—that the will is infinite and the execution confined; that the desire is boundless and the act a slave to limit

Troilus is a clear-sighted dupe, a romantic yet a natural cynic: Cressida, a sexual opportunist, born to love, betray and love again, for whom her own beauty is at once a weapon and a plaything, which she handles with half-amused indifference.

For each of them, love is primarily a raging appetite; and a student of Shakespeare's symbolism has noted that the images used to describe it are often connected with the sense of taste.[1] Desire arouses the idea of eating and drinking:

> I am giddy: expectation whirls me round.
> Th' imaginary relish is so sweet
> That it enchants my sense. What will it be
> When that the watery palate tastes indeed
> Love's thrice repured nectar?

Passion interrupted is like a spoiled feast:

> Injurious Time now with a robber's haste
> Crams his rich thievery up, he knows not how:
> As many farewells as be stars in heaven . . .

[1] Caroline Spurgeon, *op. cit.*

> He fumbles up into a loose adieu,
> And scants us with a single famished kiss,
> Distasted with the salt of broken tears.

All that is left of her love, after the beloved's infidelity, is compared
to the nauseous remnants of a meal:

> The fractions of her faith, orts of her love,
> The fragments, scraps, the bits and greasy relics,
> Of her o'ereaten faith are given to Diomed.

Images of hunger are coupled with images of disease. Under the
irritating influence of passion unsatisfied, Troilus' heart becomes a
rodent ulcer.

> I tell thee I am mad
> In Cressid's love. Thou answer'st she is fair;
> Pour'st in the open ulcer of my heart
> Her eyes, her hair, her cheeks, her gait, her voice . . .

Yet the lover's physical agonies have a spiritual counterpart.
Although his mistress may be a 'daughter of the game'—

> . . . Her wanton spirits look out
> At every joint and motive of her body.

—Troilus continues to demand of Cressida the 'winnowed purity' he
knows she cannot give: and from the resultant conflict he is forced
to seek refuge, either in romantic self-deception—

> If beauty have a soul, this is not she . . .

or, when his last illusion has evaporated, in the comforting hurly-
burly of a pitched battle. He leaves the stage with a farewell curse for
Pandarus, who lingers behind to deliver an unedifying epilogue on
the miseries that attend a bawd's career. We have returned to the
Bankside, its brothels and 'Winchester geese'.[1] Pandarus speaks of
the syphilitic's 'aching bones'; 'diseases' is his final word.

Such is the moral climate of Shakespeare's tragi-comedy, written
at the height of his powers, during a period of steadily increasing

---

[1] Prostitutes were known as 'Winchester geese' from the lodgings that many of them
occupied near the Bishop of Winchester's London residence.

fortune. In the next seven years, between 1601 and 1608, he was to produce no less than ten plays; and everything we can learn of his private circumstance would suggest that his outward life was calm and orderly. Yet beneath the surface there was evidently a profound disturbance, a seismic tremor, radiating from some unknown focus, which altered the whole landscape of his mind. It affected both his style and his subjects. Darkness gathers; everywhere a sense of claustrophobic oppression replaces the previous sense of freedom; old nightmares drift back to trouble him under new and far more terrifying shapes; and Richard of Gloucester, 'lost in a thorny wood', reappears as Thersites, enmeshed in his ferocious hatred of the world, trapped in an endless 'labyrinth of fury'. His characters cling with a horrified attachment to the objects that arouse their disgust or rage; their rancorous indignation frequently exceeds its aim: 'I do hate a proud man,' cries Ajax, 'as I do hate the engendering of toads.' Sexual love is often deeply suspect; and the poet who, in *Romeo and Juliet*, had paid an impartial tribute to the Heavenly and the Earthly Venus, substitutes for healthy desire a grotesque medieval demon, 'the devil luxury, with his fat rump and potato-finger . . .' It is significant, no doubt, that, in the year 1601, to a collection of verses entitled *Love's Martyr* Shakespeare should have contributed his beautiful threnody *The Phoenix and the Turtle*, 'allegorically shadowing the Truth of Love', and lamenting the death of married virtue. Historians have read into the poem a concealed political message—Shakespeare and his fellow contributors, who included Jonson, Chapman and Marston, were apostrophizing Southampton still imprisoned in the Tower. It seems more probable that the poem was an exercise on a theme, and that the Phoenix and his virgin bride stand for lost ideals of truth and goodness.

Shakespeare's 'Dark Period', in fact, may have had a double cause. He was shocked by the fall of Essex, a long-drawn tragedy that occupied the public stage from September 1599 to the close of February 1601; while some private catastrophe, some betrayal or failure of love, dealt him a second, and perhaps a graver, blow. *Troilus and Cressida* was closely followed by *Hamlet*. But before we examine this mysterious achievement as an index of its author's secret feelings, we must admit that, although the emotions that

coloured it appear to have been intensely personal, the basic outlines
of the drama are not in any way original. It is an old work magnificently refurbished. A play dealing with the Prince of Denmark was
already popular about 1589; in 1593, another version was performed
by the Lord Chamberlain's Men; and, in 1596, Lodge wrote of the
'foul lubber' who 'looks as pale as the visard of the ghost, which cried
so miserably at the theatre, like an oyster-wife, "*Hamlet revenge*".'
The early *Hamlet* was clearly a revenge-play, modelled on Kyd's
Spanish Tragedy; and Shakespeare's text has been described as a
'stratification', where petrified fragments of an old dramatic favourite
lie embedded in much newer writing. Can an exception be made for
the gloomy Prince himself? Well, Elizabethan audiences would
immediately have noted Hamlet's resemblance to an English 'malcontent'; and the malcontent was a recognized human type,
repeatedly discussed by physicians and psychologists.[1] Very often he
was a returned traveller, one of those Italianate Englishmen, who,
according to Nashe's *Pierce Penniless*, hung dejectedly around the
London streets. During their travels abroad, they had learned to
'walk melancholy with their arms folded', and their hats pulled down
across their eyes.[2] The malcontent was careful to proclaim his woes;
he was 'not affable in speech, or apt to vulgar compliment, but surly,
dull, sad, austere'; the hat that shaded his face usually wanted a
band; his hose were ungartered, and his cloak and doublet black or
drab. He avoided company and sought the deepest solitude. But,
although many of his kind were obvious ruffians, if they haunted
St Paul's preferring to skulk along the back aisles, their looks
'suspicious and heavy', rapiers '*punto reverso*', their right hands constantly fingering their daggers, some at least were persons of taste
and learning, men of 'a deep reach, excellent apprehension, judicious,
wise and witty'. But both classes were in open revolt against the
established social order; they felt that the times were out of joint, and
abominated the chaotic society that had failed to allow them their
appropriate due.

[1] Lawrence Babb, *op. cit.* John Marston's play *The Malcontent* was published in the
summer of 1604.
[2] Yet, I remember, when I was in France,
Young gentlemen would be as sad as night,
Only for wantonness. *King John*, Act IV Scene i.

S. *H. Excudit*

3 The Triumphal Arch erected for James I's entrance into London, 1603

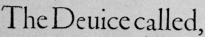

The Deuice called,

Noua fœlix Arabia, The new Arabia fœlix.

THIS *Pegme* prefented it felfe aboue the great Conduit in *Cheape:* and caried the name of the *New* vnder which title the whole Ifland of *Britannia* was figured.

This was beautified with a large Gate in the midft : On each fide was cut out a *Pofterne,* either of was —— foot wide, and —— foot high:before which *Pofternes* two *Portals* were built from the fame their fides open foure feuerall wayes, and feruing as *Pedeftals* (of *Rufticke*) to support two great *Py* whofe bafes were held vp with foure great *Bals,* and foure *Lyons.*

This *Mechanicke body* had other dead limmes, (which you may behold cut out on the other fide liuely and ftirring parts were thefe. *viz.*

In the moft eminent place was aduanced a perfon, reprefenting *Arabia Britannica,* and within a *Nefete* (beneath her *Fame.*

Directly vnder her, in a wide hollow fquare, were exalted fiue greene Mounts, the one fwelling aboue the othe which the fiue *Senfes,* (*Hearing, Seeing, Feeling, Smelling* and *Tafte,*) fate heauily drooping : before which Mounts, ar ciall *Lauer* was erected, called the Fount of *Vertue*; out of which (from fundry pipes) vpon his *Maiefties* approch wine very plenteoufly.

At the foote of this Fount lay *Detraction* and *Obliuion,* Sleeping till his Maiefties approch; but beeing arriued at the and the *Trompe of Fame,*ftarting vp the *Senfes,*they two likewife awaked, doing their beft, with clubs to beate downe the but were hindered by the *Senfes,* and a perfon reprefenting *Circumfpection.*

Vpon feuerall *Afcenfions,* (and clofe adioyning to the *Pyramids,*) were feated at one fide, the three *Graces,* and on th fide the three *Howres.*

The fpeakers were *Fame, Howres, Euphrofine* (one of the *Graces*) and *Circumfpection,* who was mounted on a Stag round about with *Pilaftres,* beeing drawne foorth fome thirtie foote in length from the other Building . And thus fe their voyces.

FAME.

TVrne into yce mine eye-bals whilft the found,
Flying through this brazen tromp,may back rebound,
To ftop Fames *hundred tongues , leauing them mute,*
As is an vntoucht bell, or ftringleffe Lute,
For Vertues Fount, which late ran deepe and cleere,
Dries : and melts all her body to a teare :
You Graces *: and you* Houres *that each day runne,*
On the quicke errands of the Golden Sunne,

Hereupon *Fame* founding her *Trumpet,* the *Sences* ftart vp,
cumfpection appeares, vttering thus much to the K ng.

Great Monarch of the Weft, whofe glorious Stem,
Does now fupport a triple Diadem,
Weying more then that of thy graund Graund-fire, (Brute,)
Thou that mayft make a King thy Subftitute,
And doeft befides the Red-rofe and the white,
With the rich flower of France, thy garland dight,
Wearing aboue kings now , or thofe of old,
A double Crowne, of Lawrell and of Gold,
O let my voyce paffe through thy Royall eare,
And whifper thus much, that we figure here.
A new Arabia, in whofe fpiced Neft,
A Phœnix liu'd, and dide in the Sunnes breft,
Her loffe made Sight, *in* Teares *to drowne her eyes,*

O fay ! to Vertues *Fount what has befell,*
That thus her Veines fhrinke vp.

GRACES — HOWRES.

We cannot tell.

EVPHROSINE.

Behold the fiue- fold guard of Senfe, *which keepes*
the facred ftreame, fits drooping : neare them fleepe,
Two horrid monfters: Fame, *fummon each fenfe,*
To tell the caufe of this ftrange Accidence.

Detraction and *Obliuion* awaken, and vanifh, while

The Eare *grew deaffe,* Tafte *like a Sick-man lyes,*
Finding no rellifh : Euery *other* Sence
Forgat his office, Worth *and excellence;*
Whereby this Fount of Vertue *gan to freeze,*
Threatned to be drunke vp by two enemies,
Snaky Detraction, *and* Obliuion,
But at thy glorious prefence both are gone.
Thou being that facred Phœnix, *that doth rife,*
From th'afhes of the firft; Beames from thine eyes
So vertually fhining, that they bring
To Englands new Arabia, *a new fpring :*
For Ioy whereof, Nymphes, Sences, Howre s *and* Fam
Eccho-loud Hymnes to his Imperiall name.

At the end of this fpeech, a fong (to an excellent Muficke) was deliuered, which being finifht, his Maieftie went on.

24 (*left*) The opening of a pageant-play, presented before the Arch of Triumph built to mark the King's arrival

25 Pages from the first Quarto of Hamlet, including a garbled version of the Prince's famous soliloquy

And so by continuance, and weakenesse of the braine
Into this frenfie, which now poffeffeth him:
And if this be not true, take this from this.

   King Thinke you t'is fo?

   Cor. How? fo my Lord, I would very faine know
That thing that I haue faide t'is fo, pofitiuely,
And it hath fallen out otherwife.
Nay, if circumftances leade me on,
Ile finde it out, if it were hid
As deepe as the centre of the earth.

   King. how fhould wee trie this fame?

   Cor. Mary my good lord thus,
The Princes walke is here in the galery,
There let *Ofelia*, walke vntill hee comes:
Your felfe and I will ftand clofe in the ftudy,
There fhall you heare the effect of all his hart,
And if it proue any otherwife then loue,
Then let my cenfure faile an other time.

   King. fee where hee comes poring vppon a booke.

      Enter Hamlet.

   Cor. Madame, will it pleafe your grace
To leaue vs here?

   Que. With all my hart.   *exit.*

   Cor. And here *Ofelia*, reade you on this booke,
And walke aloofe, the King fhal be vnfeene.

   Ham. To be, or not to be, I there's the point,
To Die, to fleepe, is that all? I all:
No, to fleepe, to dreame, I mary there it goes,
For in that dreame of death, when wee awake,
And borne before an euerlafting Iudge,
From whence no paffenger euer retur'nd,
The vndifcouered country, at whofe fight
The happy fmile, and the accurfed damn'd.
But for this, the ioyfull hope of this,
Whol'd beare the fcornes and flattery of the world,
Scorned by the right rich, the rich curffed of the poore?
                       The

The widow being oppreffed, the orphan wrong'd,
The tafte of hunger, or a tirants raigne,
And thoufand more calamities befides,
To grunt and fweate vnder this weary life,
When that he may his full *Quietus* make,
With a bare bodkin, who would this indure,
But for a hope of fomething after death?
Which pufles the braine, and doth confound the fence,
Which makes vs rather beare thofe euilles we haue,
Than flie to others that we know not of.
I that, O this confcience makes cowardes of vs all,
Lady in thy orizons, be all my finnes remembred.

   Ofel. My Lord, I haue fought opportunitie, which now
I haue, to redeliuer to your worthy handes, a fmall remembrance, fuch tokens which I haue receiued of you,

   Ham. Are you faire?

   Ofel. My Lord.

   Ham. Are you honeft?

   Ofel. What meanes my Lord?

   Ham. That if you be faire and honeft,
Your beauty fhould admit no difcourfe to your honefty.

   Ofel. My Lord, can beauty haue better priuiledge tha
with honefty?

   Ham. Yea mary may it, for Beauty may transforme
Honefty, from what fhe was into a bawd:
Then Honefty can transforme Beauty:
This was fometimes a Paradox,
But now the time giues it fcope.
I neuer gaue you nothing.

   Ofel. My Lord, you know right well you did,
And with them fuch earneft vowes of loue,
As would haue moou'd the ftonieft breaft aliue,
But now too true I finde,
Rich giftes waxe poore, when giuers grow vnkinde.

   Ham. I neuer loued you.

   Ofel. You made me beleeue you did.

                           E   Ha

26 Ben Jonson: 'a great lover and praiser of himself, a contemner and scorner of others . . . passionately kind and angry. . . .'

Shakespeare accepted the type, subtilized, enlarged, developed it and gave it a peculiarly individual turn. He adopted the same method with the other personages of the old play. Much of the action, however, he left unchanged. There Hamlet had pretended madness in order to disarm the King's suspicions. Shakespeare's Hamlet begins by following this lead, and instructs the devoted friend who has shared his vision of the Ghost, that, although his future be-haviour may at times be strange and puzzling—

> As I perchance hereafter shall think meet
> To put an antic disposition on

—Horatio must studiously refrain from hinting that he understands his motives. In fact, Hamlet's simulated madness merely excites the suspicions it is meant to lull; and at length, when the gentle and scholarly young prince, darting his sword through the arras, kills a harmless old courtier, we become aware that the distraction he had once assumed has now the strength of genuine frenzy. Hamlet's object is still to assassinate the King; but his hatred of the usurping monarch and his determination to avenge his father's death are dwarfed, in Shakespeare's re-writing, by his fierce obsession with his mother's guilt[1]; he detests Gertrude, not only because she had betrayed his father, but because, by succumbing to physical appetite, she has destroyed his own conception of her motherly virtue. She has proved unfaithful to father and son alike; and, pausing from his mission of revenge, he excoriates her sexual frailty:

> Nay, but to live
> In the rank sweat of an enseamed bed,
> Stewed in corruption, honeying, and making love
> Over the nasty sty . . .

Hamlet does not quite forget his role; the Ghost re-sharpens his 'almost blunted purpose'. But ending the King's life is a less signi-ficant task than cutting short the Queen's pleasures.

Shakespeare alone could have unified Hamlet; and even he did not completely succeed in unifying the entire play. Amid the craggy ruins of the antiquated melodrama, its elegant, if slightly dishevelled,

---

[1] A marriage to a deceased husband's brother ranked at the time as incestuous.

hero, a gold chain around his neck from which dangles the late King's portrait,[1] pursues a somewhat lonely course. He is a modern man; the court he inhabits is the creation of a former epoch—his story was derived from an *Historia Danica*, written towards the end of the twelfth century. Ovid surrounded by the Goths, a cultivated product of the Renaissance thrown back into the Middle Ages, he seems to have lost his way in space and time. His actions do not accord with his circumstances, nor do his reflections always suit his actions. At one moment, he is pensive and philosophic: at another, impetuous and even savage. He thinks and behaves on completely different planes. Hamlet, remarks a well-known poet and critic, is 'dominated by an emotion which is inexpressible' since it is 'in *excess* of the facts as they appear'; and the play itself, 'like the Sonnets, is full of some stuff that the writer could not drag to light, contemplate, or manipulate into art'. The primitive drama, no doubt, was horrid; Shakespeare's work, at its best and worst, is horrible; and 'under the compulsion of what experience he attempted to express the inexpressibly horrible' his readers cannot ever know.[2] But Essex's fall, may have supplied the impetus; for *Hamlet* is a tragedy of irresolution, and irresolution was Essex's dominant weakness. His, too, was a learned and sensitive mind; he, too, in his dealings with women had often shown a touch of cruelty. Each hero attempted to shoulder a task that just exceeded his individual powers; each hesitated upon the verge of action, and, when he felt that his nerve was failing him, relapsed into deep neurotic gloom.[3] Two strains are combined in Hamlet's character. First, he is the typical malcontent; secondly, he incorporates Shakespeare's observations of a fascinating contemporary he had admired and studied. Essex, like Hamlet, was a man of many parts—

[1] When Hamlet confronts Gertrude with his father's likeness, and insists she should compare it with her present husband's, he is evidently showing her the miniature portrait he wears.

[2] T. S. Eliot: 'Hamlet and his Problems', *The Sacred Wood*, 1920. 'Probably more people,' writes Dr Eliot, 'have thought *Hamlet* a work of art because they found it interesting than have found it interesting because it is a work of art. It is the "Mona Lisa" of literature.'

[3] For a more extended comparison of Hamlet and Essex, see John Dover Wilson, *op. cit.* According to the author, 'Hamlet is not Essex; he is Shakespeare's effort to understand Essex . . .'

> The courtier's, soldier's, scholar's, eye, tongue, sword,
> Th' expectancy and rose of the fair state . . .

But, whereas Essex was a forceful prose-writer, Hamlet is a passionately gifted poet; and it is with the help of his own eloquence—although he professes to despise words—that Shakespeare brings his character to life. Here as elsewhere, the dramatist does not produce a characterization and then match it with appropriate speeches, so much as allow a character to emerge out of the rich development of verbal patterns.[1] Thus Hamlet, a master of the monologue, draws his self-portrait in a long poetic reverie, which ranges from savage indignation and helpless disillusionment to glum acedia or resigned despair.

The creative poet is a natural egocentric; and, if we except his feeling for Horatio, whom he loves and who loves him, and who pronounces the farewell lines that speed him on the way to silence, Hamlet has very few affections. Did he seduce, or attempt to seduce, Ophelia? Certainly, she is the source of irritating memories; and the moral repulsion inspired by his mother's conduct soon extends to the girl he had once desired. He abandons her with little compunction—she has already faded into the background of his life; and the death of Polonius behind the arras is dismissed in a short and scornful phrase. They are shadows, and must return to the realm of shadows; for Hamlet, only Hamlet exists—the Self and its corroding fears and hatreds, its visions and its evil dreams. Hence his enthusiastic adoption by poets and prose-writers of the nineteenth century. Werther and Childe Harold are closely allied to him; so are Chateaubriand's René and Musset's Rolla; towards the end of the century, under the direction of Jules Laforgue, he is resuscitated, in *Moralités Légendaires*, as a protagonist of the Symbolist Movement and a post-Romantic *âme bien née*.

Very different was the welcome he received from seventeenth- and eighteenth-century audiences. Regarded through their eyes, Shakespeare's complex, thought-laden tragedy was a superbly stirring melodrama. On September 5th, 1607, William Keeling, captain of a merchantman named the *Dragon*, which traded with the East Indies,

---

[1] In Shakespeare's works, remarked Bernard Shaw, ideas arise from the words, not the grasp of words from the commerce of ideas.

held a party aboard his ship, 'where we gave the tragedy of *Hamlet*';
and next year, on March 31st, 'I invited Captain Hawkins to a fish
dinner, and had *Hamlet* acted aboard me: which I permit to keep my
people from idleness and unlawful games, or sleep'. In such performances, the Prince of Denmark must have been represented as a
resourceful avenger and expert duellist, rather than as a pensive
solitary. *Hamlet* 'pleased all', wrote Anthony Scoloker in 1604,
praising 'friendly Shakespeare's' work; and the contemplation of the
Prince's madness, whether real or feigned, at a period when visiting
Bedlam was still a popular amusement, did not necessarily excite
horror. 'The pretended madness of Hamlet,' observes Johnson,
'causes much mirth'; but Johnson adds that it seems to lack a motive;
'for he does nothing which he might not have done with the reputation of sanity.' Here and there, the critic agrees he is puzzled; after
Hamlet 'has, by the strategem of the play, convicted the king, he
makes no attempt to punish him; and his death is at last effected by
an incident which Hamlet has no part in producing'. The view of
Hamlet as the victim of his own native irresolution was completely
foreign to these early critics; and, while the English Augustans were
prepared to accept the drama as the imperfect achievement of a man
of genius, which gifted actors, from Betterton to Garrick, had
exalted and refined upon, the author of *Sémiramis*, in 1748, attacked
it with ferocious gusto: '*C'est une pièce grossière et barbare,*' writes
Voltaire, '*qui ne serait pas supportée par la plus vile populace de la
France et d'Italie.*' Everything about it shocked and disgusted him:
'*Hamlet y devient fou au seconde acte, et sa maîtresse folle au troisième;
le prince tue le père de sa maîtresse, feignant de tuer un rat . . . On
croirait que cet ouvrage est le fruit de l'imagination d'un sauvage ivre.*'

In every generation, Hamlet is re-born; and, with each re-birth
he acquires a fresh vitality. That renewed vitality is shared by his
fellow personages. As a Victorian critic has pointed out, Polonius
and Ophelia remain minor characters;[1] but they lead entirely separate
lives, and demand continuous reappraisal. Is Polonius merely the
portrait of a talkative, self-satisfied old minister of state? Shakespeare
may have had Burghley in mind—the aged statesman had also drawn

---

[1] '. . . All the persons in *Hamlet* except the hero are minor characters, who fail to rise
to the tragic level'. A. C. Bradley: *Shakespearean Tragedy*, 1904.

up a series of weighty admonitions for the benefit of his son Robert. But, if Polonius is meant to be ridiculed, why does he round off his catalogue of prosy advice with a single sentence of inspired wisdom?—

> This above all, to thine own self be true
> And it must follow as the night the day
> Thou canst not then be false to any man.

Similarly, if Ophelia is a modest and innocent virgin, accustomed to holding Hamlet at bay and quietly deflecting his improper jokes, why from the depths of her grief-troubled consciousness does there drift a plaintive bawdy song? Her ditty describes a seduction. Is it a seduction she has herself experienced, or the figment of some hidden longing? Does she reveal her desires under the influence of melancholy, as patients under an anaesthetic are supposed to babble out their darkest secrets? Melancholy, the Elizabethan believed, often had a fatal end. Some of the victims of love, like the maid-servant whom Desdemona recalls, would slip away into a slow decline; others were tempted to 'self-slaughter'; and in the annals of the Stratford neighbourhood was the story of a love-lorn girl who had committed suicide by drowning. All great artists seem to be endowed with prodigious powers of recollection; their memories preserve innumerable fragments, which, during the disturbances that attend the creative process, suddenly reappear upon the surface of the mind. From such a fragment, a tale he remembered hearing at Stratford, Shakespeare may have perhaps derived his picture of the doomed Ophelia, clambering fantastically garlanded among the riverside willows and plunging down towards a 'muddy death'. But the original episode was immensely enlarged and ennobled; Ophelia becomes a tutelary goddess of the stream, accompanied by strains of rippling water-music.

Hamlet is Shakespeare's most various play; though the tragedies that followed it are considerably better balanced, nowhere else does the dramatist's imagination cover quite so wide a field; and, to increase its richness and complexity, it includes a series of elaborate topical references. It hits, for example, at the contemporary stage and the thunderous declamatory mode of acting popularized by Edward Alleyn:

Speak the speech . . . [Hamlet begs the players] as I pronounced it to you, trippingly on the tongue, but if you mouth it as
many of your players do, I had as lief the town-crier spoke my
lines. Nor do not saw the air too much with your hand thus, but
use all gently, for in the very torrent, tempest, and as I may say
whirlwind of your passion, you must acquire and beget a temper-
ance that may give it smoothness. O, it offends me to the soul, to
hear a robustious periwig-pated fellow tear a passion to tatters,
to very rags, to split the ears of the groundlings, who for the most
part are capable of nothing but inexplicable dumb-shows and
noise . . .

This is Shakespeare himself, supervising a rehearsal at the Globe.
Earlier, Rosencrantz has mentioned a new theatrical development by
which the Chamberlain's Company were then troubled:

. . . There is, sir, an aery of children, little eyases,[1] that cry out on
the top of the question, and are most tyrannically clapped for 't:
these are now the fashion, and so berattle the common stages . . .
that many wearing rapiers are afraid of goose-quills . . .

Rosencrantz's remark and Hamlet's caustic reply allude to the
newly formed companies of boy-actors, choristers of St Paul's and
the Chapel Royal, who, since the end of 1599 and the beginning of
1600, had given performances, respectively in the cathedral precincts and at the old Blackfriars Theatre, where John Lyly had once
staged his shows. This amusing novelty had had a very kind
reception:

I saw the Children of Paul's last night,
And troth they pleased me pretty, pretty well.
The apes in time will it handsomely.

—declares a character in one of Marston's plays;[2] and his friend adds
that the room the boys used was a far more agreeable place of resort
than any vulgar, draughty open playhouse:

. . . I like the audience that frequenteth there
With much applause. A man shall not be choked

[1] Young hawks, newly taken from the nest.
[2] *Jack Drum's Entertainment*, performed by the Children of St Paul's in June, 1600.

With the stench of garlic: nor be pasted
To the barmy jacket of a beer-brewer.

An additional attraction was the Boys' involvement in the so-called
'Stage War', which provided their performances with a stimulating
controversial background. Jonson and Marston had recently fallen
out—it was a question both of private antipathy and of serious literary
differences;[1] both poets were working for the Boys' theatres, Jonson
for the Children of the Chapel, Marston for the Paul's Boys; and each
of them used the plays he wrote to hurt and humiliate his odious
rival.

Greatly delighting the *cognoscenti*, whom it drew away from older
playhouses, this battle of wits continued throughout the years 1600
and 1601; and it did not reach its end until Jonson, always a violent
dangerous adversary, had beaten Marston—or so he claimed—and
triumphantly carried off his pistol. As the chief dramatist of the most
famous adult company, Shakespeare had remained aloof; but,
indirectly, he felt the effects of the war, since the juvenile actors
were profiting at the expense of the Globe; and he must also have
noted that the vogue of the closed, or 'private', theatre, where a
fashionable audience, protected against sun or rain, could watch a
drama by candlelight, now threatened the popularity of his 'wooden
O'. His financial position, however, suffered no immediate setback;
and, as before, he chose to invest his earnings in the purchase of
landed property around Stratford. Having restored and redecorated
New Place, he acquired on May 1st, 1602, from William Combe of
Warwick and John Combe of Old Stratford, over a hundred acres of
arable land and twenty acres of pasture that the Clopton family had
once owned. The acquisition cost him 'three hundred and twenty
pounds of current English money'. That same autumn, he added to
the New Place property by purchasing the lease of an adjacent
cottage; and, three years later, in July 1605, he eventually branched
out into local tithes, buying for £440 half the corn and hay tithes of
Old Stratford, Welcombe and Bishopton, 'together with the small
tithes of the whole parish'.[2] Records also show him prosecuting

---

[1] Jonson objected to Marston's use of the word 'humour' and ridiculed his heavily
pedantic style.

[2] For a more detailed account of this complicated transaction, see E. K. Chambers,
op. cit.

lawsuits, to recover money he had lent, either in London or in Stratford. The sums concerned were never very large—£7 owed by the Londoner John Clayton, £1 19s. 10d., by a fellow Stratfordian named Philip Rogers.

More and more of the time he could spare from work seems now to have been passed in Warwickshire. Towards the end of the year 1603, he is listed among 'the principal tragedians', headed by Richard Burbage, who had enacted Jonson's play *Sejanus*; but after that date he does not appear in any surviving actors' list; and it is thought he had at last abandoned a career that, to judge from the evidence of the *Sonnets*, he had always found a little irksome. Henceforward, he was content to write and direct, and could spend the leisure he gained as a provincial gentleman at New Place. His father had died in September 1601; but Mary Shakespeare, heiress of the Ardens, lived on another seven years. By 1603, Shakespeare's daughters, Susanna and Judith, were marriageable young women of twenty and eighteen; the poet himself was thirty-nine; and his wife was forty-seven. Meanwhile, he had changed his London lodgings. Weary, no doubt, of the bohemian Bankside and the unpleasant neighbourhood of the Bear Garden, he had moved northwards back across the river; and, about 1602, he lodged above the shop of Christopher Mountjoy, at the corner of Silver and Monkwell Streets, near St Olave's Church, Cripplegate, where Mountjoy, a French Huguenot refugee, earned his living as a tire-maker, a manufacturer, that is to say, of women's pearl-sewn and jewelled head-dresses, which he sold to fashionable ladies of the Court and also to the new Queen. The Mountjoys had an only child, Mary, and a young French apprentice, Stephen Belott; they liked and respected their apprentice and noted 'a show of goodwill' between the young people; and Mistress Mountjoy, who especially favoured Stephen, 'did send and persuade . . . Mr. Shakespeare that lay in the house' to encourage him to ask for Mary's hand. Her husband promised that, among other benefits, he would recive £50 as marriage portion.

The marriage was celebrated in August, 1603. But the Mountjoy and Belott families were a somewhat dissipated crew—'*tous deux père et gendre debauchés*, noted the London Huguenots' religious leaders; Mountjoy's wife died and he took a concubine; he and Stephen very soon quarrelled; and, in May 1612, Belott brought a suit against Mountjoy, alleging that the dowry had not yet been paid. The assistance of 'friendly Shakespeare' was then invoked, and his depositions written down.[1] He was a gentleman of Stratford-upon-Avon; his age was forty-eight; and he had known the plaintiff and defendant, 'as he now remembreth, for the space of ten years or thereabouts'. The former he had known as servant to the latter; and 'during the time of his the complainant's service . . . he . . . to this deponent's knowledge did well and honestly behave himself; but to this deponent's remembrance he hath not heard the defendant confess that he had got any great profit and commodity by the service of the said complainant'. The defendant and his wife, however, had often said and reported 'that the said defendant was a very honest fellow'; and Mistress Mountjoy had solicited and entreated him 'to move and persuade the said complainant to effect the said marriage'. True, Mountjoy had promised to give Belott a 'portion in marriage . . . but what certain portion he remembreth not . . .' Again, we recognize Shakespeare's native caution; he was not to be betrayed into a possibly inaccurate statement, but did his best by both parties. We gather that he had esteemed his landlord, and taken an affectionate interest in Mary's feelings. It has been suggested that, when he was writing *Henry V* and describing the courtship of Henry and Katharine, he may have reproduced her broken English.

[1] Shakespeare's signature on this deposition is the earliest of the six surviving examples of his indifferent penmanship.

S

CHAPTER XI

Othello and Antony

WHETHER OUR SUBJECT be the author of *Hamlet*, *The Decline and Fall*, *Don Juan*, *La Comédie Humaine* or *A la Recherche du Temps Perdu*, a writer's private and literary selves are very often hard to reconcile. Those two selves are closely allied, yet, at first sight, strangely independent; for, although anything that happens in a writer's life may contribute to the progress of his art, the dignity that he achieves through art is seldom reflected by his private character. While Shakespeare was busily acquiring land, recovering the money his neighbours owed him, frequenting the Mountjoy's middle-class circle, conferring with the tradesman and his wife, or gossiping with Mary Mountjoy as she threaded pearls and twisted gold wire, he was also exploring the dark universe of his most tremendous later tragedies. *Hamlet* was followed by *Othello*, originally entitled *The Moor of Venice* and, under that title, performed in the Banqueting House, Whitehall, on November 1st, 1604. It bears little resemblance to its enigmatic predecessor. The theme is simple, the treatment lucid; it rushes towards its tragic conclusion with steadily increasing power and speed. Perhaps because it raises so few problems, many readers have found it intellectually less stimulating, emotionally far less satisfying, than both earlier and later plays. There is no complication of the main issue, not a digression or a sign of hesitation. Its hero is a unified personage: indeed, the unity and simplicity of his nature help to bring about his total ruin; and present-day critics, therefore, have sometimes denied him true dramatic dignity, alleging that Othello was a bogus great man—

great only in his own deluded view—and that he cherished 'an obtuse and brutal egotism', which soon degenerated into the 'ferocious stupidity' of an 'insane and self-deceiving passion'.[1]

Even his celebrated farewell speech has been said to strike a false note; he is 'cheering himself up',[2] we are told, when he should be submitting to the pattern of his fate and merging the sense of his personal identity in a 'transcended human whole'.[3] Such critics appear to ignore his background. During the Elizabethan Age, every eminent courtier and soldier was also an accomplished self-dramatist, fond of voicing in eloquent words the determination he expressed in glorious deeds. The Moor's last speech is a magnificent apology: his suicide, a calculated *coup de théâtre*. But then, the valedictory gestures of Essex and Ralegh show very much the same spirit: they, too, dramatized their farewells and attempted to stage a death-scene that accorded with their lives. Their efforts were generally applauded: contemporary Englishmen valued grandiloquence as much as they admired nobility. None of their heroes was in any way self-effacing, or content to rely upon the record of his actions; that record must be boldly proclaimed with the help of melodious and stately language; the hero's existence was a romantic framework that served to enclose his individual merits. Of all Shakespeare's doomed adventurers, Othello is endowed with the most romantic setting. Poetry is the element in which he moves; and, whenever he speaks of his soldierly past or of his royal parentage beneath a blazing African sky, the images he evokes, though remote and elusive, have a powerful incantatory charm. Nothing about him is common or trivial; his personal possessions partake of his own poetic quality—the fatal handkerchief, 'an antique token', that his father had once given to his mother—

> . . . There's magic in the web of it:
> A sibyl, that had numbered in the world
> The sun to course two hundred compasses,
> In her prophetic fury sewed the work . . .

or the Spanish rapier he leaves lying in his room:

[1] F. R. Leavis: *The Common Pursuit*, 1952
[2] T. S. Eliot: *Shakespeare and the Stoicism of Seneca*, 1927.
[3] John Bayley: *The Characters of Love*, 1961.

It was a sword of Spain, the ice brook's temper—
O, here it is . . .
          Behold, I have a weapon;
A better never did itself sustain
Upon a soldier's thigh . . .

Othello, an unusually perceptive commentator has pointed out, is planned on somewhat operatic principles;[1] and, as often as the hero makes his appearance, he is accompanied by a melody that belongs to him alone. Its effect, momentarily, is to arrest the movement of the drama, to command a hush and clear a space around him. Thus, in the second scene, where Brabantio, egged on by Iago and the foolish gentleman Roderigo, is hurrying through the alleys of Venice, clamouring for his lost daughter, Othello meets them with an opening phrase that has been described as 'one of Shakespeare's miracles',[2] so cold and compelling is its music after the hubbub of the angry, impatient crowd:

Roderigo: Signior, it is the Moor.
Brabantio: Down with him, thief.
Iago: You, Roderigo! come sir, I am for you.
Othello: Keep up your bright swords, for the dew will rust them.

We can always recognize Othello's voice; and it never fails to impose a sudden calm, when he is checking the riot aroused by Cassio's tipsy squabble:

          Silence that dreadful bell; it frights the isle . . .

—or while he stands at bay, among his judges and persecutors, beside the curtained bed that holds his wife's corpse. There, for the last time, he asserts his sovereign energy:

Lodovico: You shall close prisoner rest,
           Till that the nature of your fault be known

---

[1] 'The unique indicative function of the poetry is indeed comparable with the *aria*: Verdi's *Otello* is the most successful of all operas based on poetic drama, and the greatest performance of Othello was given by Salvini, an actor whose voice and bearing were trained in opera'. John Bayley, *op. cit.*

[2] A. C. Bradley, *op. cit.* Like many Shakespearian phrases, it has an early prototype: 'Your sword is bright, sir, put it up again'. *King John*, Act IV Scene iii.

To the Venetian state. Come, bring away.
Othello: Soft you; a word or two before you go.
I have done the state some service, and they know't.
No more of that. I pray you, in your letters,
When you shall these unlucky deeds relate,
Speak of me as I am . . .

It is ironic—and an intentional stroke of irony—that Othello, who has fallen a victim both to deceit, coupled with misunderstanding, and to his previous ignorance of his own temperament, should thereupon provide an analysis of his character that explains succinctly how he was betrayed and ruined. The end is in sight when he at last achieves self-knowledge: lack of self-knowledge has been his damning weakness. Here, despite his allegedly foreign descent—he is a native of 'Barbary' or Mauretania, a Berber nobleman, though on the Jacobean and Caroline stage he seems usually to have been portrayed as a 'thick-lipped' negro prince—Othello, as Shakespeare exhibits him, reveals some oddly English traits. Compared with other European races, we have earned a reputation for maturing slowly: we are said to remain incorrigible adolescents; and *Othello* is a tragic account of tardy beginnings and delayed awakenings. The Moor is not fully awakened until his opportunities have all been lost and spoiled. He has awoken slowly to the idea of love; indeed, as he confesses, he had become aware of love only when first he saw it reflected in Desdemona's virgin eyes; and he adds, with a frankness that might appear discreditable were candour and honesty not so important to his 'open nature', that his mistress had supplied the decisive hint upon which, at length, he spoke and acted.

Othello has been surprised by love, just as later he will be surprised by jealousy. Unlike Romeo, he is a novice in passion, at least in romantic and exalted passion; no dark Rosaline has ever troubled his sleep; and Desdemona, for all her quietness and innocence, in knowledge of the heart and its power is plainly the more experienced of the two. Not, of course, that this hardened campaigner has led a chaste, unspotted life: when he imagines Desdemona as the inhabitant of a brothel, he demonstrates, clearly and cruelly enough, that he knows his way around there. During his youth, he has enjoyed the usual soldierly diversions and paid some routine visits to the stews. But romantic love has remained outside his compass, not because he despises those vagrant feelings, but because—a remarkably English trait—he has been too busy, too happily and excitingly engaged, to have the leisure to indulge them. When love descends, it comes as a dazzling, unlooked-for reward, a fabulous jewel dropped into his lap:

> If heaven would make me such another world
> Of one entire and perfect chrysolite,
> I'ld not have sold her for it.

And, when that treasure has been received and embraced, his contentment is absolute and his satisfaction unbounded:

> If 'twere now to die,
> 'Twere now to be most happy; for I fear
> My soul hath her content so absolute
> That not another comfort like to this
> Succeeds in unknown fate.

Othello may have had his share of egotism; but it could scarcely be described as 'brutal egotism'. The limitations of his character correspond to his most endearing qualities. He is young in mind as he is young in heart—younger even than the schoolgirl he has married; and his arch-adversary is the kind of human being who seems never to have known youth. Certainly, Iago, at the age of twenty-eight,[1] has learned to harness all the adult vices.

Elsewhere, I have suggested that the crafty ancient was a recognizable Elizabethan type—the envious and rancorous outsider, who feels that his place in the established system is not the place that he deserves, and who works on a trusting employer's mind, as his steward, the Machiavellian Henry Cuffe, is said to have worked on that of Essex. How many accomplished villains were drawn by Elizabethan and Jacobean dramatists from this intermediate social class! If the Court was a nursery of intrigue, so, in a lesser degree, were most aristocratic English households; each had its circle of

---

[1] 'I have looked upon the world for four times seven years . . .' Act I Scene iii.

courtiers and promoted the same secret rivalries. Iago first confronts us as a disappointed man; although 'three great ones' have pleaded his suit, Othello has refused him the promotion that he claims. He is still the General's ancient, or ensign; while Michael Cassio, the bookish Florentine—

> That never set a squadron in the field,
> Nor the division of a battle knows,
> More than a spinster . . .

has been dubbed lieutenant in his stead. And not only is Cassio the native of a foreign city, an 'arithmetician' and a 'counter-caster'; but Othello makes it tactlessly plain that he regards him as a social equal. Iago is merely 'honest Iago', which conveys the General's appreciation but carries with it a certain touch of patronage; when Othello addresses Cassio, he prefers to use his first name. Finally, from among his other grievances, Iago produces a vague suspicion that Othello has seduced his wife, whom Desdemona, at her husband's request, has taken as her gentlewoman, Emilia, a sophisticated offspring of Venice, skilled in the amatory lore of that luxurious city. Iago's suspicion has not the smallest basis—it is a minor part of his complex pattern of resentment; and, whenever the ancient drags it up again, it always fails to ring true.

Since there is an obvious disproportion between the wrongs that Iago declares he has suffered and the passionate hatred that has become fixed in his mind, Shakespearian critics, for at least a century and a half, have been trying to hunt down some more abstruse motive. Coleridge's explanation is particularly striking. Iago, he assures us, has no tangible motive, apart from a deep-rooted love of evil, and his ingenious efforts to afford us a clue to his conduct merely exhibit 'the motive-hunting of motiveless malignity'. William Hazlitt, however, chose to see him as a crazy aesthete, an example of 'diseased intellectual activity, with the most perfect indifference to moral good or evil, or rather with a decided preference of the latter, because it falls more readily in with his favourite propensity, gives greater zest to his thoughts and scope to his actions . . . He is an amateur of tragedy in real life; and instead of employing his invention on imaginary characters . . . he takes the bolder and more desperate course of getting up his plot at home . . . and rehearses it in down-right earnest, with steady nerves and unabated resolution.' But the aesthete is inspired by some positive emotional impulse; and Bradley, nearly a hundred years later, mentions Iago's 'extraordinary deadness of feeling'. Passion, he remarks, is easily detected. 'And what vestige of it, of passion unsatisfied or of passion gratified, is visible in Iago? None: that is the horror of him. He has *less* passion than the ordinary man . . .' He exists at the centre of a moral and emotional vacuum. Emotionally, he is dead: perhaps he has always been dead. The chief object of his furious machinations is somehow to persuade himself that he is triumphantly alive.

If we are to follow Shakespeare towards the heights of his genius, it is often illuminating to begin our survey with the lowest possible assumptions and, before we consider his actual achievement, to try to unearth his original design. Let us assume, then, Shakespeare had once intended to present Iago as a typical Italianate villain, just such a fascinating, alarming, damnably adroit rogue as the early-seven-teenth-century audience relished, the arch-intriguer who advances to the front of the stage and, from behind his hand, provides a whis-pered commentary on the credulous behaviour of his future victims. But Iago grew: he rapidly increased his height; and very soon, through his connection with Othello, who, in his turn, was swiftly developing and arising, the rancorous, black-hearted ancient became a major tragic shape. As Hazlitt observes, Iago is a 'philosopher', an expert analyst of human thoughts and feelings, a cynical solipsist who believes that every man, like himself, is completely circum-scribed by his own immediate impressions, his own transitory desires and needs; that no standard of value can be said to 'make sense' that does not conduce to our personal advantage. Beyond self-interest, all is self-deceit '. . . Since I could distinguish betwixt a benefit and an injury,' he tells the bewildered, unhappy Roderigo, who is half mad with love for Desdemona, 'I never found a man that knew how to love himself . . . Virtue! a fig! 'tis in ourselves that we are thus or thus. Our bodies are gardens; to the which our wills are gardeners; so that if we will plant nettles or sow lettuce, set hyssop and weed up tine, supply it with one gender of herbs or distract it with many, either to have it sterile with idleness or manured with industry—why, the power and corrigible authority of this lies in our wills.'

As for love, he proceeds, 'we have reason to cool our raging motions, our carnal stings . . . whereof I take this, that you call love, to be a set or scion'. Roderigo submits: he accepts Iago's comforting promise that, given money and patience, he will obtain the freedom of Desdemona's bed—'she must change, she must . . . if sanctimony and a frail vow betwixt an erring barbarian and a supersubtle Venetian be not too hard for my wits . . . thou shalt enjoy her'—and goes his way with hopes restored. Roderigo, of course, is a fool; but it is not Roderigo alone who relies on Iago's worldly judgement. Othello, too, esteems his subordinate wise:

> This fellow's of exceeding honesty,
> And knows all qualities, with a learned spirit,
> Of human dealings

—and Iago agrees that none of his companions has a steadier, more realistic view of life. In his belief that he always sees clearly, he takes refuge from a sense of material failure. Whereas Othello enjoys the pride of success, coupled with instinctive pride of birth, Iago nurses the intellectual vanity of a clever, disappointed man. There is his consolation; there his ultimate defence. But, unluckily for Iago, carefully though he has studied him and thoroughly though he professes to understand him, there remains something in Othello's character that his private philosophy cannot quite absorb. He is as infuriated by its mysterious persistence as a scientist whose experiments are perpetually thrown into confusion by some factor that he cannot name or place. Othello, he is determined to believe—on this point, we have been wittily reminded, Iago's opinion anticipates that of the General's twentieth-century detractors[1]—is a bogus hero, arrogant, stupid and insensitive. But not only has he deceived his companions: Othello has successfully deceived himself—and to such good effect that he produces an air of harmony and natural dignity that Iago misses in his own existence. Even Cassio, with his nervous, excitable temper and his ridiculous attachment to a local courtesan, possesses the same maddening gift. If Desdemona's affections *were*

[1] John Bayley, *op. cit.*

to turn from Othello, it is in Cassio's arms, not in Iago's, that she
would seek another haven:

> He hath a daily beauty in his life
> That makes me ugly . . .

And the malevolent outsider likes to exacerbate his malice, now by
imagining that Othello may have cuckolded him, now by pretending
—rather half-heartedly, it is true: he knows he has little genuine
passion—that he has begun to lust after the General's consort:

> . . . I do love her too,
> Not out of absolute lust—though peradventure
> I stand accountant for as great a sin—
> But partly led to diet my revenge . . .

From the depths of his own inward deadness, he gazes up furiously
at the graceful, uncomplicated movements of an Othello or a Cassio.
Their spontaneity throws into harsh relief the awkward automatism
of his barren and limited nature.

Thus he opens his campaign against his simple-minded enemy by
suggesting that few situations or human relationships are really as
simple as we might at first suppose. No human being is exactly
what he seems:

> Men should be what they seem;
> Or those that be not, would they might seem none!

—and no imagination, his own included, is entirely devoid of dark
and lawless thoughts. No man, however honest and upright, can
afford to disclose every shadow that may cross his fancy:

> Good my lord, pardon me . . .
> Utter my thoughts! Why, say they are vile and false—
> As where's that palace whereinto foul things
> Sometimes intrude not? who has a breast so pure,
> But some uncleanly apprehensions
> Keep leets and law-days, and in session sit
> With meditations lawful?

Once this breach has been made through the ramparts of his victim's

optimistic and romantic candour, the 'uncleanly apprehensions',
of which Iago speaks, are soon enabled to find a free passage—and
circulate all the more freely because their intrusion is so unaccustomed. Now the sexual imagery in which Iago deals can find a way
into Othello's speeches. Hitherto the opponents have been clearly
distinguished, on the plane of speech as on the plane of action.
Othello is the romantic poet, enlarging and glorifying every subject
that he touches: Iago, with perverse artistry, borrows his compari-
sons from the realm of animals. Thus, Brabantio is aroused by a
voice beneath his casement, telling him that a brute beast is just then
covering his virgin daughter:

> Even now, now, very now, an old black ram
> Is tupping your white ewe . . .

And, again, in a burst of alliterative prose, Iago likens Othello to a
rampant African stallion. After a certain moment, it is safe to employ
these images when he is speaking in Othello's presence. The tormented husband has demanded 'satisfaction'; with masochistic zeal,
he insists on visual proof. Iago refuses him satisfaction, but simultaneously whets his victim's appetite:

> What shall I say? Where's satisfaction?
> It is impossible you should see this,
> Were they as prime as goats, as hot as monkeys,
> As salt as wolves in pride . . .

Presently, Othello adopts Iago's style and, being the more imaginative
man, allows his fancy yet more violent licence. Iago's comparison
has stuck in his mind; it returns to his lips while he is interviewing
the Venetian envoy who has arrived on an official mission. Having
horrified Lodovico by insulting and striking his wife, who, to
increase the brutality of the gesture is Lodovico's kinswoman, he
makes a last miserable, ineffective effort to play his public role with
proper dignity:

> Sir, I obey the mandate,
> And will return to Venice.—Hence, avaunt!—
> [Exit Desdemona]

> Cassio shall have my place. And, sir, tonight,
> I do entreat that we may sup together.
> You are welcome, sir, to Cyprus.—Goats and monkeys!

Critics, who have differed about Othello's pigmentation, also differ as to the effect that his African blood, his own consciousness of it, and the mistrust it perhaps inspired, may have had upon his character. The Elizabethans, knowing comparatively little of any country beyond Europe, would seem, apart from some ugly freaks of anti-Semitism, to have avoided the grosser forms of racial prejudice. Even in *The Merchant of Venice*, although the villain is a Jew, among Portia's suitors is a Moorish princeling; and Othello deals on equal terms with the arrogant Venetian nobles.[1] Both the General himself and his Italian enemies refer at times to the dusky colouring of his skin, which, before the tale he told had made its mark, is said to have affrighted Desdemona; but there is no suggestion that it had ever stood in his way, or that the Venetian senators had hesitated to employ him because his face was dark and strange. Yet, since Iago has taught him to believe that we can none of us fully understand our fellows, the fact that he is a member of a foreign race, and Desdemona 'a supersubtle Venetian', weighs heavily upon his spirits. He has made a dangerous choice, Iago reminds him:

> I know our country disposition well;
> In Venice they do let heaven see the pranks
> They dare not show their husbands; their best conscience
> Is not to leav't undone, but keep't unknown.

And from this point of view it is an easy step to the belief, not only that most Venetian women are naturally promiscuous, but that every woman is a creature of uncontrollable, incalculable whims, whom no lover should expect to understand and no husband need hope to possess entirely. Venetian husbands may be versed in compromise:

---

[1] While this section of the book was being written, the author happened to see in the Jamaican *Gleaner*, a daily newspaper with a large coloured readership, an account of a lecture delivered by Mr Philip Mason, Director of the Institute of Race Relations in London, which describes racial prejudice as one of the most important themes of Shakespeare's play: Iago is 'just the kind of person who is a racialist'.

such an admission of defeat revolts Othello's frank 'barbarian' mind:

> O curse of marriage
> That we can call these delicate creatures ours,
> And not their appetites! I had rather be a toad,
> And live upon the vapour of a dungeon,
> Than keep a corner in the thing I love
> For others' uses.

Iago's habits of thought, like his zoological imagery, have now begun to creep into Othello's language. No human being, however deep the love he professes, can safely say that he comprehends his fellow. Do these 'delicate creatures' comprehend themselves, since they are the sport of vagrant appetites that defy detection and refuse control? Iago's victim has now become his pupil; and when, at the close of a scene, Iago leaves him with the ambiguous declaration, 'I am your own for ever', though the sentence is framed as a declaration of loyalty, we feel that he is ratifying their infernal contract. Henceforward Iago is Othello's *doppelgänger*, the sinister reflection that sometimes haunts a neurotic during the preliminary stages of a mental breakdown.

In an earlier passage, I have attributed Othello's tragedy to his emotional youthfulness and unpreparedness, and have suggested that we should do well to consider him against the background of the poet's age. Particularly Elizabethan is the hero's view of love, in which sensuality and romantic sensibility seem to wage incessant warfare. Never have English writers been more involved with their senses, more exquisitely alive to the satisfactions of hearing, smelling, tasting, touching. Francis Bacon, we are told, as often as he retired to meditate, would have musicians playing in a nearby room; he planned his gardens so that the scent of flowers should 'come and go like the warbling of music'; blossoms and sweet herbs were strewn across his table; and none of his servants, Aubrey informs us, 'durst appear before him without Spanish leather boots'; for, should they wear ordinary boots, 'he would smell the neat's leather which offended him'. Othello, too, has a refined and exacting taste; and twice he dwells, with lingering, nostalgic relish, on Desdemona's natural fragrance:

> O thou weed,
> Who art so lovely fair and smell'st so sweet
> That the sense aches at thee . . .

—and later, as the agent of vengeance and death:

> When I have plucked the rose,
> I cannot give it vital growth again,
> It must needs wither: I'll smell it on the tree.
> O balmy breath, that dost almost persuade
> Justice to break her sword! . . .

It is Othello's voluptuous hyper-sensitiveness, and the tormenting memory of the pleasures he has once enjoyed, that at length goad him into desperate action. But, among Shakespeare's contemporaries and dramatic descendants, a delight in the sensuous world often co-existed with a fear and hatred of the flesh. They dreaded lust as much as they adored love; and for Othello, during the final crisis of his jealousy, the love he had known is merely lust disguised. Hence his masochistic impulse to reduce his remembered passion to the proper level. He pretends that his wife's bed-chamber is a room in a bawdy-house, where Desdemona is the whore and Emilia sits at the receipt of custom:[1]

> You, mistress,
> That have the office opposite to Saint Peter,
> And keep the gate of hell!
>   [Re-enter Emilia]
> You, you, ay, you!
> We've done our course; there's money for your pains:
> I pray you, turn the key, and keep our counsel.

Before he can destroy Desdemona physically, he must first destroy her in his own mind.

Othello, which Shakespeare derived from a French translation of an Italian novel, *Il Moro di Venezia*, by Giraldi Cinthio, is the picture of an ill-matched love: each protagonist has experienced love, but under a different form and presumably a different stage.

---

[1] Not long ago, in Orson Welles' production of *Othello*, this scene was omitted as too painful for a modern audience.

Shakespeare's next study of romantic passion describes a relationship in which like meets like. Both his chief characters are greedy, amorous and violent, true pagans, unselfconscious hedonists, totally unaffected by a modern sense of sin. The love that unites them may well be a shared illusion; but, so far as they themselves are concerned, it is an illusion that puts reality to shame:

> Eternity was in our lips and eyes,
> Bliss in our brows' bent; none our parts so poor
> But was a race of heaven . . .

Yet neither forgets their terrestial origins: they are still products of 'our dungy earth'; and one of the play's most extraordinary features is the dramatist's mingling of earthy and heavenly images. Now he lifts his lovers into the poetic empyrean, now plunges them back into the realm of discord, where Antony is a coarse-grained Roman soldier and his mistress a swart and hoydenish gipsy. It has been said that Shakespeare, having the bisexual temperament peculiar to many great artists, had fallen in love with his splendid Roman soldier;[1] but his portrait of the Egyptian Queen also displays a lover's sharpened insight. He does not pretend that she is a regularly beautiful woman, according to Elizabethan standards. Weathered by the Egyptian sun, now almost middle-aged,[2] she has so little regard for her feminine dignity that, when a frolic mood suddenly descends, she will 'hop forty paces through the public street'. Yet, even there, dishevelled and panting, Cleopatra makes 'defect perfection'. Once a man has begun to desire a woman as much for her defects as for her beauties, he has passed the sexual point of no return; and Antony has passed that point and is rapidly drifting far beyond it. All that concerns him is to remain in his present state of doubt and anxiety and longing and intermittent blessedness; to cherish the illusion that he knows to be an illusion, but that has become more precious than the whole of truth. Under the spell of their absorbing lust and love, Antony believes, as Cleopatra herself believes, that they have entered a universe in which Time has lost its power.

[1] Wyndham Lewis: *The Lion and the Fox*, 1927.
       Think on me,
  That am with Phoebus' amorous pinches black
  And wrinkled deep in time? Act I Scene v.

Although *Antony and Cleopatra* was produced after *King Lear* and *Macbeth*, between 1606 and 1607, Shakespeare's choice of subject— a passionate infatuation which betrays a great and generous man— prompts us to place the play beside *Othello*. But not only does the poet approach the subject differently: he employed, in composition, a very different method. From Cinthio's novel, he had taken his basic plot: while he wrote his second Roman drama, he was constantly dipping into North's *Plutarch*, borrowing entire passages which he enlarged and enriched, as the episodes the historian describes came to life again in his imagination.[1] A famous example is the use that Shakespeare made of Plutarch's brief description, translated by North, of Cleopatra sailing down the Cydnus:

> . . . she disdained to set forward otherwise, but to take her barge in the river of Cydnus, the poop whereof was of gold, the sails of purple, and the oars of silver, which kept stroke in rowing after the sound of flutes, hautboys, cithern, viols. . . she was laid under a pavilion of cloth of gold of tissue . . . her ladies and gentlewomen . . . were apparelled like the nymphs Nereides . . . some steering the helm, others tending the tackle and ropes of the barge, out of which there came a wonderful passing sweet of perfumes, that perfumed the wharf's side . . .

In Shakespeare's text, this sumptuous nautical pageant is re-created as an apotheosis of the Queen; her barge burns on the water; beneath her pavilion, hung with cloth-of-gold, Cleopatra is a supernatural visitant, a Venus or an Amphitrite:

> Her gentlewomen, like the Nereides,
> So many mermaids, tended her i'th'eyes,
> And made their bends adornings: at the helm
> A seeming mermaid steers: the silken tackle
> Swell with the touches of those flower-soft hands,
> That yarely frame the office. From the barge
> A strange invisible perfume hits the sense
> Of the adjacent wharfs.

[1] For an analysis of Shakespeare's method, see John Middleton Murry: *Countries of the Mind*, 1931.

Less often remarked is the characterization of Antony's pleasures. As the dolphin reveals his back above the water, Antony, Plutarch had written, rose superior to the unworthy pleasures of his life. Shakespeare adopted and transfigured the simile:

> . . . His delights
> Were dolphin-like, they showed his back above
> The element they lived in . . .

For Shakespeare's contemporaries, the lines had a double significance: the dolphin was one of the kings of nature, and belonged to the family of royal beasts that also included the eagle and the lion. Antony, too, is a natural sovereign; he had inherited Caesar's overwhelming magnitude:

> His legs bestrid the ocean: his reared arm
> Crested the world: his voice was propertied
> As all the tuned spheres, and that to friends;
> But when he meant to quail and shake the orb,
> He was as rattling thunder.

To ensnare this demi-god—and there seems no doubt that Shakespeare intends we should regard Antony as a genuinely great man—it needs the fascination of a demi-goddess. But, although Cleopatra is 'a most triumphant lady', a hunter worthy of her prey, who entangles the victim 'in her strong toil of grace', her feet are still upon the earth. However puissant her attractions, they are those of ordinary flesh-and-blood; and the poet emphasizes her terrestrial origins with an odd and homely image, drawn not from the banks of the Nile but from the water-meadows through which the Avon flows. When she deserts her lover during the battle of Actium, she is likened to 'a cow in June', driven wild by summer gadflies; and Antony, 'the noble ruin of her magic', is the 'doting mallard', as the dramatist must often have watched it, scudding after its elusive mate.

These words, of course, are spoken by Scarus, Antony's disappointed friend; but, whatever their context, they would have appeared intolerably 'low' to any poetic dramatist of a later period.

T

In Shakespeare's tragedy, which makes no attempt either at strict historical accuracy or at classical correctitude, they render an important service. His noble protagonists, despite the momentous roles that fate has allotted them, share our ordinary human appetites and failings. Cleopatra's earthiness is an essential part of her charm —none of the poet's other heroines is depicted in such realistic detail; and, only when she knows that death is approaching does she assume the habiliments of tragic dignity. Her suicide is a primitive ritual sacrifice;[1] she immolates herself on the tomb of the hero whom she has helped to drag down; and in her spiritual metabolism—the elemental pattern that, according to Elizabethan psychologists, formed the basis of every human character—she then feels a corresponding change, as air and fire, the highest and subtlest elements, symbols of mind and spirit, begin to prevail over their less exalted fellows:

> Give me my robe, put on my crown, I have
> Immortal longings in me. Now no more
> The juice of Egypt's grape shall moist this lip . . .
> I am air and fire; my other elements
> I give to baser life. So, have you done?
> Come then and take the last warmth of my lips.

'Of all Shakespeare's historical plays,' decided Coleridge, *Antony and Cleopatra* was 'by far the most wonderful'; and its achievement was 'greatly owing to the manner in which the fiery force is sustained throughout, and to the numerous momentary flashes of nature counteracting the historic abstraction'. Hazlitt's tribute is equally appreciative: 'Shakespeare does not stand reasoning on what his characters would do or say, but at once *becomes* them, and speaks and acts for them.' Coleridge adds that, if a reader wishes to understand 'the judgement as well as the genius of Shakespeare', he should 'compare this astonishing drama with Dryden's *All for Love*'. The comparison is undoubtedly worth making—not, however, because it exposes Dryden's weakness, but because his accomplishment in one field underlines Shakespeare's triumph in another. *All for Love* is among the finest efforts of post-Shakespearian tragic literature.

---

[1] See Wyndham Lewis: *op. cit.*

What it lacks is Shakespeare's 'fiery force', his unending richness and variety and the splendid irregularity—irregular as life itself—of his assimilative and creative imagination. First performed in 1678, *All for Love* is a notably well-balanced play. The intricacies of the older dramatist's plot, borrowed from Plutarch and transferred to the stage, Johnson complained, 'without any sort of connection or care of disposition', have been firmly, neatly ironed out. The characters have been stripped of their superfluous trappings; and neither hero or heroine ever gives utterance to an unexpected or provokingly incongruous phrase. They are invariably eloquent and dignified; but, although their speeches may suggest rhetorical set-pieces—masterly re-creations of what, in the circumstances that confront them, such characters *ought* to think and say—their eloquence reaches an impressive level. Dryden's Antony is a literary romantic, obsessed by visions of his own past:

> I was so great, so happy, so beloved,
> Fate could not ruin me; till I took pains,
> And worked against my fortune, chid her from me,
> And turned her loose; yet still she came again.
> My careless days, and my luxurious nights,
> At length have wearied her, and now she's gone,
> Gone, gone, divorced for ever.

At the same time, he dwells on the recollections of an unqualified, untroubled love:

> Think we have had a clear and glorious day
> And Heaven did kindly to delay the storm,
> Just till our close of evening. Ten years' love,
> And not a moment lost, but all improved
> To the utmost joys,—what ages have we lived?

As for Shakespeare's inconstant Queen, she becomes a woman of heroic temper. There is no talk of parleying with Octavius; it was not she, but her treacherous sailors, who deserted from Antony's line of battle; and no sooner has she lost her love than she prepares to welcome death:

'Tis sweet to die, when they would force life on me,
To rush into the dark abode of death,
And seize him first . . .[1]

'In my style,' wrote Dryden, 'I have professed to imitate the
divine Shakespeare'; yet the effect of his imitation was merely to
demonstrate how little he understood his great original. *All for Love*
is an admirably constructed drama, interspersed with fine poetic
passages: Shakespeare's play is somewhat ill-planned—the progress
of the love-story is frequently interrupted by the 'drums and trumpets, excursions and alarums', that Dryden deplored in *Troilus and
Cressida*; but its poetry is organic, a natural product of the poet's
theme. Dryden brings his personages to life by re-creating their
most salient moods; while Shakespeare seems to live through them,
and gradually re-live their whole existence. He knows that love,
however powerful, does not necessarily cast out baser feelings.
Antony may be vulgarly abusive—he denounces his mistress as 'a
boggler'. When Enobarbus, in a whispered aside, hints that the
great orator is playing to the gallery:

Cleopatra: What does he mean?
Enobarbus: To make his followers weep.

—Cleopatra does not reprove him for his facile sneer. But the two
Antonys have an important point in common: each speaks of human
experience as a dream. Dryden's hero awakens regretfully:

. . . My whole life
Has been a golden dream of love and friendship.

Shakespeare's great man finds himself and his fortunes reflected in
the dream-like procession of the clouds:

Eros, thou yet behold'st me?
Eros: Ay, noble lord.
Antony: Sometime we see a cloud that's dragonish,
A vapour sometime like a bear or lion,
A towered citadel, a pendant rock,

[1] Then is it sin
To rush into the secret house of death,
Ere death dare come to us? *Antony and Cleopatra* Act V Scene i.

A forked mountain, or blue promontory
With trees upon't, that nod unto the world . . .
That which is now a horse, even with a thought
The rack dislimns, and makes it indistinct
As water is in water.

Eros: It does, my lord.

Antony: My good knave Eros, now thy captain is
Even such a body: here I am Antony,
Yet cannot hold this visible shape, my knave.

All Shakespeare's great tragic figures, and many of his lesser personages, seem to be haunted, during moments of crisis, by a sense of individual unreality. It is significant how often the word 'dream' occurs in Shakespeare's plays and sonnets. A man of the world, who adored the visible world, which he described more appreciatively, vividly and minutely than any other English poet, he was also fascinated by images of evanescence, by cloud-shapes, the movement of the tides or the curling eddies of an inland flood. Evidently he loved to stare at water; maybe he had acquired the habit at Stratford, his elbows on the parapet of Clopton Bridge. In *Henry IV, Part II*, he had already written of the tide 'that makes a still-stand, running neither way'; and Antony, referring to his injured wife, employs a variant of the same metaphor:

Her tongue will not obey her heart, nor can
Her heart inform her tongue—the swan's down-feather,
That stand upon the swell at fall of tide
And neither way inclines.

In the imagery of Shakespeare's later plays, not least in *Antony and Cleopatra*, we observe this constant alternation—between images that express strength and solidity and size and a rival group derived from those aspects of Nature which suggest transience and mutability. It is doubtful if he had ever studied the Ephesian philosopher Heraclitus; but Heraclitus' belief that there was no lasting reality except the reality of change, and his declaration that 'Everything flows'—life into death, and non-existence into life again—recalls Antony's speech on the passage of the clouds and his comparison of his own personality to a mass of shifting and dissolving vapours. Although Shakespeare was a Renaissance humanist, beneath his regard for the dignity of the individual lurked doubts that grew more and more obsessive.

Yet the universe in which we half believe, momentarily may be as pleasing and stimulating as a world that we wholeheartedly accept. Shakespeare's personal balance appears to have remained unshaken; perhaps, like Keats, he had decided that 'the only means of strengthening one's intellect is to make up one's mind about nothing', and that, instead of seeking to exorcize doubt, the poet should welcome it and learn to live with it. Under the surface there may have been darkness and confusion; so far as we can judge from existing records, his quotidian life ran smoothly forward. We cannot tell whether the sexual catastrophes described in *Othello* and *Antony and Cleopatra* were based on any real experience; but his attitude towards love and passion, so cautious when he was writing *Venus and Adonis*, so lyrical in *Romeo and Juliet*, had clearly suffered a profound change. Why this change occurred, we need never hope to know; a couple of anecdotes, however, have been handed down to us that indicate that Shakespeare was an active lover and had possibly earned some reputation as a rake. On March 13th, 1602, a Templar named John Manningham heard an amusing and mildly scandalous tale which he committed to his diary. While Burbage was playing Richard III, he noted, an ill-behaved citizen's wife, who desired the handsome tragedian, 'before she went from the play . . . appointed him to come that night unto her by the name of Richard III. Shakespeare overhearing their conclusion went before, was entertained, and at his game ere Burbage came. Then message being brought that Richard III was at the door, Shakespeare caused return to be made that William the Conqueror was before Richard III.' Such anecdotes, mostly apocryphal, are told of every well-known man; but the story shows that his gossiping contemporaries credited the poet with an amorous and adventurous nature. Four years later, according to a seventeenth-century report, he became the father of an illicit child.

The putative father was John Davenant, a vintner of Oxford, 'a very grave and discreet citizen', who kept the Crown Tavern in

Cornmarket.[1] The vintner's wife is said to have been 'a very beautiful woman, and of a very good wit and of conversation extremely agreeable ... Mr. William Shakespeare was wont to go into Warwickshire once a year, and did commonly in his journey lie at this house ... where he was exceedingly respected.'[2] The Davenants' son William, afterwards Poet Laureate and knight, a popular personage at Court, despite a humiliating mishap which had deprived him of his nose,[3] was born in the year 1606; and 'Sir William would sometimes, when he was pleasant over a glass of wine ... say that it seemed to him that he writ in the very spirit' of Shakespeare, 'and seemed contented enough to be thought his son'. The tradition was current at the beginning of the next century: Shakespeare, Thomas Hearne informs us, was William Davenant's god-father: ' 'tis further said that, one day going from school, a grave Doctor in Divinity met him, and asked him, "Child, whither art thou going in such haste?" To which the child replied, "O, Sir, my god-father is come to town, and I am going to ask his blessing." To which the Doctor said, "Hold, child, you must not take the name of God in vain."' Davenant was an exquisite minor poet—the songs that he wrote for Court court-masques are among the loveliest products of his age; and, although imaginative genius is rarely transmitted, it is likely enough that William Davenant may have inherited a small allowance of his father's talent, and that the rivulet of inspiration that glorifies his work he owed to his distinguished ancestry. None of his brothers and sisters, we are told, resembled him; nor did he resemble his supposed begetter. John Davenant, Anthony Wood heard, 'was of a melancholy disposition, and was seldom or never seen to laugh ...'

On his way to and from Stratford, Shakespeare continued to take an affectionate interest in the fortunes of the Davenant children; and Robert, who became a Fellow of St John's College and an erudite divine, used to claim that, during visits to the Crown Tavern, his parents' celebrated friend had given him 'a hundred kisses'. The poet was not a man who neglected his obligations; and, a year after William Davenant's christening, he probably attended the wedding

[1] For a photograph of John Davenant's Painted Chamber at No. 3 Cornmarket, see E. K. Chambers: *op. cit.*
[2] From the manuscript material collected by John Aubrey for his *Brief Lives*.
[3] For a more detailed account of this disaster, see John Aubrey: *Brief Lives*.

at Stratford parish church of his elder daughter, Susanna, whom on June 5th, 1607 he married off to Dr John Hall. It was a worthy match. Hall, a thirty-two-year-old medical practitioner with Puritan sympathies, had a considerable reputation among their Warwickshire neighbours; and, during the course of the following February, Susanna bore her only child, Elizabeth. That autumn, early in September, Elizabeth's great-grandmother, Mary Shakespeare, died. She, had lived long enough to see the restoration of her family; William now 'a gentleman of worship', had achieved a position as comfortable and secure as her husband's state had been precarious;[1] while the New Place recalled the dignified surroundings of Robert Arden's Wilmcote manor. Shakespeare would appear to have loved New Place, and to have enjoyed building, gardening and entertaining. But until 1613 he owned no London house; and much of his leisure time he must have spent in general company—for example, at the Mermaid Tavern, Bread Street, which, since the beginning of the new reign, when William Johnson had acquired the lease from his former employer William Williamson, had become a favourite resort of urban wits. Under its sign, just off Cheapside, assembled on the first Friday of every month a 'worshipful fraternity of sirenaical gentlemen', including such luminaries as Jonson, Drayton, the melodious lyricist Thomas Campion and John Donne, still an unpublished poet, though his Songs and Sonnets had already been written and, in manuscript, widely circulated and admired. Shakespeare must certainly have read them, and have met their strange tormented author.[2] At the Mermaid, too, about the year 1608, he would have encountered a pair of rising dramatists, John Fletcher and Francis Beaumont, both fashionable and well-born young men who possessed a glib poetic talent; and it was Beaumont who later reminded Jonson of those happy Mermaid evenings:

[1] The poet's brothers were considerably less successful. Gilbert, who at one time inhabited London where he worked as a haberdasher, is said to have lived to 'a patriarchal age'; but Richard, who apparently remained at home, died in February, 1613; and the youngest Edmund, who became a player and begot a 'base-born' child, predeceased Mary Shakespeare, dying in December, 1607.

[2] Born in 1572, Donne had accompanied Essex to Cadiz and on the less triumphant Islands Voyage. Later, he had joined the household of Lord Keeper Egerton, but had been disgraced and imprisoned after the discovery of his secret marriage with Egerton's young niece by marriage.

What things have we seen
Done at the Mermaid! heard words that have been
So nimble, and so full of subtle flame,
As if that every one from whom they came
Had meant to put his whole wit in a jest . . .

Some of the wit that flashed at the Mermaid was no doubt supplied by Shakespeare, with Jonson as his chief antagonist; and Thomas Fuller's *Worthies of England*, published in 1662, contains a famous account of how they joined battle, 'like a Spanish great galleon and an English man-of-war; Master Jonson . . . was built far higher in learning, solid, but slow in his performances. Shake-spear . . . lesser in bulk, but lighter in sailing, could turn with all tides, tack about and take advantage of all winds . . .' Shakespeare's renown as a dazzling light-weight—the brilliant opportunist whose achievement had enraged Greene—survived the production of his greatest tragedies.

CHAPTER XII

'Unaccommodated Man'

AGAIN WE ARE faced with the disconcerting contrast between an artist's personal and his literary character. Shakespeare was evidently a gregarious man; yet through his tragedies, and indeed through many of his comedies, runs the theme, lengthily developed and diversified, of individual isolation. All his tragic heroes are somehow cut off: Brutus and Cassius by their common failure, which at once unites them and divides them; Hamlet by his sense of moral infirmity and intellectual superiority; Othello and Antony by their obsessive passions; Macbeth by the accumulation of guilt; Lear by the descent of madness; Coriolanus—

> Like to a lonely dragon that his fen
> Makes feared . . . more than seen

by his insensate egotism and overwhelming pride. For each of them, the Self is a citadel and a prison; he is condemned to a solitude that grows increasingly claustrophobic as the tragedy pursues its course. Nor can captive communicate with captive. Macbeth has had a devoted partner and accomplice; but, when his fate is closing in upon him, and Lady Macbeth has receded into the world of nightmare, he feels that he stands utterly alone. Although the hero's isolation may be heightened by, it does not necessarily result from, his individual wrong-doing: his misdeeds merely provoke the crisis that teaches him to comprehend his plight. He is lonely: he has always been lonely. For, whereas every other form of tragedy presupposes a Divine Law and hints at the possibility, however remote, of reconciliation and atonement, Shakespeare, in his tragic vision of human life, seems to have dispensed with the idea of God. Few poets, brought up under a Christian civilization, are so little indebted to the Christian ethos. Marlowe was a rebel and an alleged atheist; but Faustus, in his agony, invokes the blood of Christ.[1] Shakespeare, conservative and agnostic, makes only the most perfunctory references to Christian imagery or Christian doctrine. His tragic personages live and die without hope of supernatural succour.

In *Macbeth* and *King Lear*, a mood that we can trace back into Shakespeare's past, perhaps as far back as *Richard III* and *King John*, suddenly reaches a volcanic climax. Yet, at the time, the eruption went unnoticed. It did not occur to Shakespeare's contemporaries that the dramas he produced during the first decade of the seventeenth century were in any way different from those he had written during the previous ten years; and, until modern criticism had re-assessed his work, there was no talk of a 'Dark Period', when his plays, hitherto lyrical or majestic, reveal an excruciating inward conflict. But this type of criticism may over-simplify the facts. Before we discuss 'Macbeth and the metaphysic of evil'[2], we should remember that *Macbeth*, probably composed in 1605 or 1606 and based on a story derived from Holinshed, was intended to entertain a special audience: the King's Men were favourite performers of the Court— during the Revels of 1604 to 1605, they presented eleven plays, eight of them by Shakespeare, out of a grand total of twenty-two; and whatever material they provided must be carefully suited to their employers' tastes. Appropriate subjects were discussed with court dignitaries, as we learn from a letter that, in January 1605, the Chamberlain of the Exchequer addressed to Robert Cecil on the vexatious problem of arranging new amusements:

I have . . . been [he announces] all this morning hunting for players, jugglers and such kind of creatures, but find them hard to find; Wherefore, leaving notes for them to seek me, Burbage is come, and says there is no new play that the Queen hath not seen, but they have revived an old one, called *Love's Labour Lost*, which

---

[1] 'See, see, where Christ's blood streams in the firmament!
    One drop would save my soul . . .'
[2] G. Wilson Knight: *The Wheel of Fire*, 1930.

for wit and mirth, he says, will please her exceedingly. And this is appointed to be played tomorrow night at my Lord of South-ampton's, unless you send a writ to remove the corpus cum causa to your home in Strand. Burbage is my messenger, ready attending your pleasure.

Although it was thought that a comedy would please 'the dancing Queen', her husband had more serious interests. Learned, yet pro-foundly superstitious, James was devoted to the investigation of the Black Arts, and in 1597 had himself published an erudite volume on demonology, upholding the real existence of warlocks and witches against the deplorably sceptical views expressed by Reginald Scot. Some strange experiences had reinforced his convictions. He was fond of personally examining witches; and, towards the end of February 1592, a suspected witch named Agnes Sampson was brought into his presence at Holyrood House. At first, she had denied everything; but, having been taken away and 'grievously tortured with a rope thrawen around her head' and the Devil's secret mark brought to light 'upon her privities', she 'confessed that, on Hallowe'en last, she, with a great company of other witches, to the number of two hundred, had gone to sea, each one in a riddle or sieve, drinking and making merry as they sailed, until they came to the Kirk of North Berwick in Lowthian, where they landed and danced a reel, Geillis Duncan going before them playing on a small trumpet, called a "Jew's trump" . . .' The King next interrogated the warlock Duncan, who, apparently delighted to display his skill, 'played this dance upon the trumpet'. James retorted that they were both liars; but Agnes Sampson, 'taking him a little aside . . . declared the very words which had passed between him and his Queen at Upslo in Norway the first night of their marriage, with their answers one to the other; whereat the King wondered greatly and swore by the living God that he believed all the devils in Hell could not have discovered the same . . .'[1]

Here, then, was an odd and dramatic subject that, particularly if it were adorned with some references to his ancient lineage, was

---

[1] *Newes from Scotland*, 1591.

certain to amuse the monarch. Shakespeare adopted the sieve-sailing witches, their grotesque ceremonies and barbarous doggerel rhymes; but how literally he believed in witches and witchcraft is a question almost impossible to answer. During the sixteenth and seventeenth centuries, few Englishmen felt any doubts as to the real existence of the supernatural world; the scientist was often an occultist; and the celebrated Dr Dee himself, though he had accepted the Copernican theory, excelled in mathematics and made momentous improvements in the art of navigation, was also an adept of the 'secret sciences', who, assisted by the 'skryer', or clairvoyant, Edward Kelley, daily conversed with disembodied spirits. These beliefs Shakespeare presumably accepted, as he accepted the other opinions of his day; but apparently they did not reach the deepest levels of his imagination. His ghosts—even the ghost of Hamlet's father, a 'majestical' rather than a horrific presence, whose fluent delivery of over eighty lines of resounding blank verse defeats all the modern producer's attempts to give it an appropriately wraith-like air—are descendants of the same loquacious family that Thomas Kyd had once brought on to the English stage. So long familiar with the spectres and portents that lurk in the darkened regions of the human mind, Shakespeare needed no supernatural incentive to arouse his poetic sense of mystery. Hamlet is a far more mysterious personage than his father's mailed and visored shadow; Macbeth's witches are harmless anachronisms besides the population of his teeming private hell.

Such a hell Marlowe had already envisaged, when he described the plight of Mephistophilis;[1] and, to evoke the atmosphere of Macbeth's prison house, his creator employs a complex literary symbolism, in which every image is designed to strengthen the effect of darkness, claustrophobic solitude and incommunicable nervous dread. 'It is certainly indicative,' writes the analyst of his imagery, 'that there are only two plays in which the word "love" occurs so seldom as in *Macbeth*, and no play in which "fear" occurs

---

[1] Faustus: Where are you damn'd?
Mephistophilis: In hell.
Faustus: How comes it, then, that thou art out of hell?
Mephistophilis: Why, this is hell, nor am I out of it.
The Tragical History of Doctor Faustus, c. 1588.

so often . . .'[1] Shakespeare's contemporaries feared and hated night; and nocturnal imagery dominates the whole drama. Now that, for himself, Macbeth has 'murder'd sleep', the hours of night are doubly dreadful. Their approach is alarming to good and bad alike, as the 'shard-borne beetle' whirrs through the dusk, 'the crow makes wing to the rooky wood' and, against the western horizon, glimmering with 'streaks of day', the belated traveller spurs towards his inn. Since night brings a suspension of healthy activities, it was thought to propagate both vice and sickness. In *Macbeth*, images of disease are almost as numerous as those of terror. Macbeth's criminality is an infection, soon transferred to the entire realm:

> Foul whis'prings are abroad: unnatural deeds
> Do breed unnatural troubles: infected minds
> To their deaf pillows will discharge their secrets . . .

He appeals to the Doctor for a drastic purgative that will restore his invaded kingdom to 'a sound and pristine health', and, earlier, in a much more celebrated passage, for some drug that will palliate his wife's misery:

> Canst thou not minister to a mind diseased,
> Pluck from the memory a rooted sorrow,
> Raze out the written troubles of the brain,
> And with some sweet oblivious antidote
> Cleanse the stuffed bosom of that perilous stuff
> Which weighs upon the heart?

Himself he rejects all medicine—

> Throw physic to the dogs, I'll none of it.

For, although *Macbeth* recalls the state of morbid distraction in which every sight or sound seems to confirm the sufferer's own anxieties and fears, its hero overcomes his neuroses—his 'terrible dreams' and the restless 'torture of the mind'—and thrusts them away from him with a wild display of courage. Except for Coriolanus, he is Shakespeare's last attempt to depict an indubitably great man. Brave, determined, eloquent, passionate, he has a large allowance of

[1] Caroline F. E. Spurgeon, *op. cit.*

the heroic qualities that moved a sixteenth- or seventeenth-century audience. They move us today; but towards the crime he commits we are bound to adopt a somewhat different point of view. It is the result of his crime that interests us—the rapid brutalization that overtakes an admirable character. We are less concerned with the nature of the crime; whereas for Shakespeare's contemporaries the killing of Duncan was not only a cruel and treacherous, but a savagely sacrilegious, act. Duncan, in whose face, while he lies asleep, Lady Macbeth thinks that she distinguishes a resemblance to her own father, may be a prosy, talkative old fellow mortal. At the same time, he is the Lord's Anointed; and his murder, like Henry's deposition of Richard and Essex's revolutionary intrigues, threatens the law of proportion and degree. Shakespeare must emphasize the sovereign's sanctity—James I, Duncan's descendant, lived in perpetual terror of assassination—and endow the spectacle of the butchered monarch with a solemnly impressive colouring:

> Here lay Duncan,
> His silver skin laced with his golden blood . . .

To underline the importance of the message, he put the words into Macbeth's mouth.

In its context, this archaic picture of the Dead King seems curiously ill-placed. Macbeth's real tragedy is not that he has committed sacrilege, but that, as he goes on from violence to violence, he feels an insuperable barrier building up between himself and mankind. In the early scenes, fear is the keynote of the drama—the hammering at the castle-gate suggests the frightened knocking of a heart;[1] in later episodes, apprehension gradually gives way to despair, disgust and overwhelming weariness. Having ceased to be terrible, life is unbearably tedious; and the dramatist repeats the burden of Lewis the Dauphin's speech in *King John*:

> Life is as tedious as a twice-told tale . . .

Worse than the horror of life is its unending monotony—

---

[1] Although this wonderful scene inspired one of the most imaginative flights of nineteenth-century Shakespearian criticism, De Quincey's *On the Knocking at the Gate in Macbeth* (1823), Coleridge was gravely offended by 'the disgusting passage of the Porter', which he believed to be the players' own gratuitous interpolation.

> To-morrow, and to-morrow, and to-morrow,
> Creeps in this petty pace from day to day,
> To the last syllable of recorded time . . .

The 'twice-told tale' has become a player's mouthings, or a tale—

> Told by an idiot, full of sound and fury,
> Signifying nothing.

Even before his wife's death, Macbeth has decided that he must continue to drive forward merely because to go back would be insufferably wearisome:

> . . . I am in blood
> Stepped in so far that, should I wade no more,
> Returning were as tedious as go o'er . . .

His only refuge is in a self-destructive resolution, that promises at least the comfort of mental excitement and intense physical activity:

> They have tied me to a stake; I cannot fly,
> But bear-like I must fight the course.[1]

And, like a Russian bear, pulled down by English mastiffs, at Dunsinane he fights and dies.

While, in Macbeth, sudden explosions of colour—usually the colour of blood—and metallic coruscations of light—the light reflected by an imaginary dagger-blade—shine against a dark background, the colour-scheme that pervades *King Lear* has been described as cold and dim and gloomy.[2] The drama that Shakespeare took from Holinshed, who had extracted it from Geoffrey of Monmouth's twelfth-century *Historia legum Britanniae*, belongs to an almost prehistoric past. 'Leir, the son of Balderd', had ruled over the primitive Britons 'at what time Joas reigned as yet in Juda'. So early chroniclers believed; but, according to students of Celtic mythology, his origins can be traced into the world of legend, where he reigned as Lir, the blue-tressed Celtic Poseidon, and had three daughters, goddesses of the winds, Regan and Goneril, the winds

---

[1] Shakespeare never hesitated to repeat an effective image. See *King Lear*, Act III Scene vii: 'I am tied to th' stake, and I must stand the course.'
[2] A. C. Bradley, *op. cit.*

that vex and destroy, Cordelia the bland and gentle breeze. This derivation cannot have been known to Shakespeare; but, in his picture of daughterly ingratitude, he gives the old king, his two un-kind children and the evil subordinates they attract a violent, elemental quality. The landscape of the drama is vague and chaotic, swept by merciless storms, often blotted out by fog, which lifts now and then to disclose a terrifying natural prospect—the 'horrible steep' near Dover, whence, the length of ten masts below, Edgar pretends that he can distinguish the surge chafing 'on th' unnumb'red idle pebble' and the samphire-gatherer pursuing his vertiginous trade, as he dangles in mid-air among the circling crows and choughs.

King Lear, then, has the rugged outlines of a legend—the monarch's decision to break up his realm is the kind of episode that early storytellers loved. Yet, despite his ancestry, Lear himself emerges as the least heroic of all Shakespearian heroes. In some ways, he is the most pathetically human. Othello, Antony, Macbeth at least *begin* as great men, natural sovereigns of creation; and their air of greatness never quite vanishes. Lear, on the other hand, is only splendid in his ruin, like a building that does not achieve dignity until the fabric has been half destroyed by time. For Shakespeare, even while he was writing the *Sonnets*, the prospect of growing old seems to have held unusual terrors; and Lear is old age personified —the winter of existence at its darkest and its worst, its irritability and its childish petulance, its preoccupation with the glories of past years and its insecure, somewhat grudging attachment to the meagre benefits of the present day. Old age seldom removes our failings, but often throws them into fresh relief; and in Lear it emphasizes a strain of restless, self-tormenting egotism hitherto partly satisfied by his enjoyment of his own power. Once he has ceased to rule, his appetite for authority becomes a passion that corrodes his heart and mind. He demands gratitude, clamours for reverence and affection, and, now that he can no longer dominate through strength, attempts to rule through a display of weakness. Just as *Othello* was to inspire an unequalled opera, *Lear* would contribute the germ of an extra-ordinarily moving short novel. *A Lear of the Steppes* is a masterpiece directly descended from a masterpiece; and, if Shakespeare's hero is the scion of an ancient Celtic god, Turgenev's tremendous prota-

V

gonist, Martin Petrovitch Harlov, is the offspring of a Russian folk-demon. Both are foolish, misguided, yet immensely formidable beings, whose wrath and self-pity shake the frame of Nature.

In Shakespeare's play, the elements respond. Lear's outcries recall the lamentation of the wind amid a labyrinth of ruined masonry; and they are accompanied by the uproar of the storm, which, when *King Lear* was first produced, either at the Globe or 'before the King's majesty at Whitehall upon Stephen's Night', December 26th, 1606, the players must have imitated with the help of trundled cannon-balls, or 'rolled bullets'. The world itself is tottering and collapsing; Lear's private universe has already fallen; and from its wreckage arise a host of phantoms that run riot around the old King's head. There is the fantastic demonology evoked by Edgar in the borrowed character of 'Poor Tom', one of the ragged, moon-struck waifs who then haunted English lanes and highroads:[1]

> Five fiends have been in poor Tom at once: as Obidicut, of lust; Hobbididence, prince of darkness; Mahu, of stealing; Modo, of murder; Flibbertigibbet, of mocking and mowing. . . .[2]

But, for Shakespeare's audience, there would have been something not altogether unamusing about Tom's demented monologue—harmless madmen often aroused laughter; and much more dreadful are the apparitions conjured up by Lear himself. They adopt, many of them, a strangely sexual guise. Lear associates Goneril's malice with ideas of his own fleshly failings:

> . . . Thou art my flesh, my blood, my daughter—
> Or rather a disease that's in my flesh,
> Which I must needs call mine. Thou art a boil,
> A plague-sore, or embossed carbuncle,
> In my corrupted blood.

Parenthood is the penalty he has paid for desire; the devils who

---

[1] 'The country gives me proof and precedent
Of Bedlam beggars who, with roaring voices,
Strike in their numbed and mortified bare arms
Pins, wooden pricks, nails, sprigs of rosemary . . .'
                                        Act II Scene iv
[2] Shakespeare derived these names from a *Declaration of egregious Popish Impostures*, published in 1603.

surround and torment him are projections of remembered lust; and Lear pictures the whole world, human or animal, as the playground of unbridled appetite, on which, once again a sovereign, he imagines that he sits in judgement:

> I pardon that man's life. What was thy cause?
> Adultery?
> Thou shalt not die. Die for adultery? No!
> The wren goes to't, and the small gilded fly
> Does lecher in my sight.
> Let copulation thrive: for Gloucester's bastard son
> Was kinder to his father than my daughters . . .

It is for the Female Principle he reserved his deepest loathing; and here his imagery suggests the grotesque inhabitants of an inferno created by Pieter Bruegel:

> Behold yond simp'ring dame,
> Whose face between her forks presages snow . . .
> The fitchew[1] nor the soiled horse goes to't
> With a more riotous appetite.
> Down from the waist they are centaurs,
> Though women all above.
> But to the girdle do the gods inherit,
> Beneath is all the fiend's.
> There's hell, there's darkness, there is the sulphurous
>   pit;
> Burning, scalding, stench, consumption; fie, fie, fie,
> pah, pah! Give me an ounce of civet, good apothecary,
> to sweeten my imagination . . .

Faced with the old king's explosions of horror and hatred, critics have sometimes conjectured that Lear's tirades may afford us an insight into Shakespeare's personal tragedy. The dramatist must have been close, they assert, about the year 1606, to physical or mental breakdown; a theory is even advanced that he may have contracted a disease, possibly syphilis, the 'great pox', which, having now reached its terrible tertiary stage, was beginning to affect the balance

---

[1] Polecat.

of his brain. No such explanation, however, is needed. Through all Shakespeare's adult dramas we find evidence of the same anarchic mood—a horror of life that is opposed and held in check by a naturally sanguine and creative spirit; and to the resultant conflict, waged on a gigantic scale, we owe the character of his poetic genius. Against the dramatist who feared and hated the world was matched a poet who, more deeply perhaps than any other English poet, understood what Charles Baudelaire would call 'the ecstasy of living'.[1] Later, in *Timon of Athens*, Shakespeare voiced an unrelieved pessimism; but, while the disabused Timon remains an embittered social satirist, Lear's theme, once he has transcended his immediate grievances, is not the current evils of society but the basic condition of mankind at large. To draw our first breath is probably as irksome an experience as to make our final exit:

> Thou must be patient. We came crying hither;
> Thou know'st the first time that we smell the air
> We wawl and cry.

In flashes of lucidity that penetrate his darkest delirium, Lear sees Man, the decorative social being, stripped bare of his adventitious trappings and reduced again to his essential nakedness:

> Thou art the thing itself. Unaccommodated man is no more but such a poor, bare, forked animal as thou art. Off, off, you lendings! Come, unbutton here!

So speaking, he attempts to tear off his clothes—a gesture that is primarily realistic, but here possesses a symbolic value.[2] Lost travellers, we are told, threatened with death from thirst or exhaustion, very often cast away their garments. Lear does his best to abandon them—that he may finish his journey alone and unprotected, like the 'poor, bare, forked animal' he is. Previous Shakespearian heroes had gone to meet their death in royal state: the sole dignity the dramatist allows Lear is that of self-appointed destitution.

The King and his fellow victims sometimes speak of 'the gods', but usually as ingenious ministers of vegeance. Divine 'justice' is

---

[1] *Journaux Intimes*: 'Tout enfant, j'ai senti dans mon coeur deux sentiments contra-dictoires: l'horreur de la vie et l'extase de la vie.'

[2] It may be compared to Harlov's frenzied destruction of his house.

measured by its cruelty; neither on this nor on any other plane are the gods expected to bring help and comfort; and, while in *Hamlet* 'the rest is silence', in *Lear* the end is universal darkness. Cordelia has vanished beyond hope of recovery:

> Thou'lt come no more,
> Never, never, never, never, never!

Life, in retrospect, has been a long punishment; death is welcome merely as a relief from pain:

> Vex not his ghost: O, let him pass; he hates him,
> That would upon the rack of this tough world
> Stretch him out longer[1]

And so distressing was the effect upon Christian sensibility that, until he came to edit the play, Johnson informs us, having as a young man been shocked by Cordelia's death, he was not sure he had ever summoned up the necessary resolution to re-read the last scenes. Thus he applauded—at least, he refused to condemn—the well-meant efforts of Nahum Tate, who, in 1680, gave the old-fashioned tragedy a happy ending, which shows the king replaced on his throne and Cordelia married to the high-minded Edgar. No 'triumph of persecuted virtue'—no suggestion, indeed, of such a possibility—could have been reconciled with Shakespeare's tragic plan. Yet some cold comfort Edgar allows us, throwing it out lightly, almost casually, during the course of an engagement between the two camps. Blind Gloucester is reluctant to follow him:

> No further, sir; a man may rot even here.
> Edgar: What, in ill thoughts again? Men must endure
> Their going hence, even as their coming hither;
> Ripeness is all . . .

Every attempt to describe a poet's 'philosophy' is apt to involve some misconception of the nature of creative genius. Shakespeare

[1] As Dr Spurgeon remarks, *Lear* abounds in images of torture, of which the most celebrated—

> I am bound
> Upon a wheel of fire, that mine own tears
> Do scald like molten lead

has given its title to Professor G. Wilson Knight's well-known essay.

had not a philosophic mind: his task was to absorb the raw material of experience and re-create it in beautifully significant forms, rather than investigate its hidden 'meaning' or seek to impose an intellectual pattern. But Edgar's speech certainly encourages the belief that, if the poet had adhered to an existing school of philosophy, Zeno would have been his master. It is classical Stoicism that Edgar preaches; the virtues he recommends are endurance and fortitude, unsupported by any trust in a system of divine rewards and penalties. Among modern masters, Shakespeare was surely indebted to the great French essayist, whom John Florio, Southampton's learned protégé, had translated only three years earlier. The first edition of Montaigne's essays had appeared in 1580; in 1576, when he was forty-two, he had caused to be struck his famous medal with its characteristic inscription: '*Que scais-je?*' Like the dramatist, he was not a pedant or a scholar, but a man who preferred to dip into the books he handled; he, too, was both conservative and agnostic, attached to the sensuous pleasures of the world, but dominated by a restless, inquisitive mind that would let no accepted opinion pass untried. Again, he made a cult of friendship, and felt that masculine friendship, such as the devotion that had bound him to Etienne de la Boétie, was a far more precious gift than love between the sexes. Finally, the 'ripeness' that Montaigne aimed at was derived from inward harmony and self-knowledge: 'That is an exquisite life,' he wrote in his essay *Of Repenting*, 'which even in its own private keepeth itself in awe and order. Everyone may play the juggler, and represent an honest man upon the stage; but within . . . where all things are lawful, where all is concealed, to keep a due rule or formal decorum, that's the point.'[1] Here we recollect Polonius' advice to his son. Unlike the dramatist in his darkest period, the essayist did not despair of mankind; but Shakespeare must have studied Montaigne and admired his subtle self-portrait—the record of a man who enjoyed his passage through the world but had early come to terms with the idea of leaving, who hoped above all else, he told his readers, that he would die 'quietly and constantly.'[2]

[1] Florio's translation. For a more literal rendering, see the English version by J. M. Cohen, 1958.

[2] From the essay entitled 'That we should not judge of our happiness until after our death.'

In *Lear*, indeed in the whole corpus of the later tragedies, Edgar's speech has no exact parallel. For once Shakespeare appears to be voicing a conviction, something that moralists might almost call a 'message'. It is very brief; it appears oddly timed—around the speaker a disastrous battle is raging; but its unexpectedness underlines its gravity. Was it inserted by Shakespeare to relieve the desperation of the last scenes; and, if that be so, did it fulfil its purpose? *Hamlet* is said to have been an attempt 'to express the inexpressibly horrible'; and in *Lear* there is a burden of horror difficult to resolve into dramatic shape. Edgar advises Gloucester that we must 'endure'; but Lear's hardly-bought resignation brings him little real comfort: when he dreams of finding some peace with Cordelia, his precarious haven is at once demolished. Oedipus never reaches Colonus; as the drama closes, we are looking forward into a chasm, and back across an old exhausted world that, Gloucester prophesies, will soon 'wear out to nought'. The effect is too disturbing to be completely satisfying. Shelley, however, acclaimed *Lear* as 'the most perfect specimen of the dramatic art', and Hazlitt, as 'the best of all Shakespeare's plays, for it is the one in which he was the most in earnest'. That it is technically perfect, we should scarcely claim today. Cordelia is a piece of obstinately tactless virtue; Regan and Goneril are indistinguishable serpents, hatched from the same ill-omened egg. And, although Coleridge asserted that Edgar's pretended madness helped to take off 'part of the shock which would otherwise be caused by the true madness of Lear', their simultaneous presence in the storm scene, where they are accompanied by the Fool, a congenital zany, is apt to divide the modern reader's interest. Edgar's lunacy is fantastic and imaginative; yet the demon rout he conjures up around him threatens to overshadow the old King's *danse macabre*.

Compared with *Lear*, Shakespeare's last great tragic production, written about 1607 or 1608, is a singularly well-shaped play.[1] *Coriolanus* has as distinct an outline as *Othello*, and moves at the same rapid pace. Again the characters are few; there is no complication of the central drama, which, for the last time, seems to be clearly connected with the dramatist's impressions of the fall of Essex. Not that

[1] It has been classed by T. S. Eliot with *Antony and Cleopatra* as 'Shakespeare's most assured artistic success'.

the insolent Roman general bears a detailed resemblance to the English leader. Coriolanus had despised the plebeians: Essex wooed the London mob. But each was a proud and irritable spirit, constantly fretting against the limitations his circumstances imposed on him, who had something excessive in his temperament that defied all attempts at self-mastery. Like Essex, Coriolanus had been the skilful agent of his ruin; and it is Volumnia's fate not only to love and admire —he has inherited her stubborn patrician arrogance—but, reluctantly, to understand her son:

> You might have been enough the man you are,
> With striving less to be so . . .

He is also understood by an old enemy; and, after Coriolanus has defected to the Volscians and mounted an attack on Rome, Aufidius pays him an unwilling tribute:

> I think he'll be to Rome
> As is the osprey to the fish, who takes it
> By sovereignty of nature. First he was
> A noble servant to them, but he could not
> Carry his honours even. Whether 'twas pride,
> Which out of daily fortune ever taints
> The happy man; whether defect of judgement,
> To fail in the disposing of those chances
> Which he was lord of . . .

Essex's inability to 'carry his honours even', coupled with his lack of judgement, had certainly provoked his downfall. No great literary personage, however, is the detailed portrait of an individual; and, although Coriolanus doubtless embodies Essex, Shakespeare used a familiar source-book and frequently consulted Plutarch's narrative. 'He was a man too full of passion and choler,' runs the text in North's rendering, 'and too much given over to self-will and opinion . . . that remembered not how wilfulness is a thing of the world, which a governor of a commonwealth, for pleasing, should shun, being that which Plato called "solitariness" . . .' In Shakespeare's tragedy, the hero's solitariness, the sense of isolation that governs his character, is the origin of all his other failings. He cannot

27 Five examples of Shakespeare's signature

Church   Peter Church   Guildhall   Albertines of greate   S. Laurents Poultney   the Royal Exchange   S. Michaels

The 3 Cranes   Stilliard   Old Swan

T H A M E S I S   F L U V I

Southwarke

28 The City and Bankside in 1647. To the left, seen across the garden of the Bishop of Winchester's palace, rise the Bear Garden and the second Globe. The artist has transposed their positions; and the Globe was probably octagonal in shape

1. Gray-Church   5. Dunston in the East   3. Alhallows barking

Lyon key   Billings gate

THE BRIDGE

29 London Bridge seen from Southwark

communicate: he is walled in by his pride: the gestures that he makes towards his fellow human beings, unless they convey an order or a threat, have the air of distant ineffective signals. Yet that egocentricity, so long as it remains unshaken, is also the basis of his individual power; and, once he has begun to abandon his solitude, he feels that he is losing his hold upon his own identity:

> Like a dull actor now
> I have forgot my part . . .

The part he has hitherto been playing is the only part that he knows how to play. A single touch of compassionate irresolution, and the whole fabric of his authority dissolves. The Volscian wolf-pack gathers around for the kill; Aufidius derides his human weakness and brutally denounces him as a 'boy of tears'.

Coriolanus is a monolithic tragedy, less complex than *Hamlet*, less exalted than *Antony and Cleopatra*, planned on a less ambitious scale than *Macbeth* or *Lear*. It is the most classical of Shakespeare's Roman dramas; but the lyric element is not entirely banished. Indeed, its touches of lyricism are all the more effective in that austere and solemn setting. Thus, Coriolanus, during the hour of his greatest triumph, having received his mother's loud congratulations, notices his young wife standing mutely by, and reaches out towards her with a sudden flash of love:

> My gracious silence, hail!
> Wouldst thou have laughed had I come coffined home,
> That weep'st to see me triumph?

Although the characters are simply, severely drawn, they are illuminated by brilliant naturalistic touches. Coriolanus begs Cominius for a poor man's life, but, wounded and battle-weary as he is, finds that he cannot recollect his name:

> Larius: Marcius, his name?
> Coriolanus: By Jupiter, forgot!
> I am weary; yea, my memory is tired.
> Have we no wine here?

Cominius: Go we to our tent:
                 The blood upon your visage dries; 'tis time
                 It should be looked to: come

Menenius, the blustering Falstaffian senator—'one that loves a cup
of hot wine with not a drop of allaying Tiber in't . . . one that con-
verses more with the buttock of the night than with the forehead of
the morning'—when Coriolanus rejects his self-confident plea,
shrinks to the dimensions of a lost, pathetic old man; but, like
Falstaff rejected by the 'son' he has cherished, he rises above his
humiliation and displays a cool, ironic fortitude. Coriolanus has done
and said his worst. 'You keep a constant temper', Menenius replies;
and, to the derisive Volscians who encircle him: 'I neither care for
th' world nor your general . . . He that hath a will to die by himself
fears it not from another . . .' At which, he turns away, leaving the
man of action to execute his stupid, suicidal vengeance.

We do not know where *Coriolanus* was first presented—whether
before their Majesties at Whitehall, or in the more spacious surroundings of the Globe; but, during August 1608, the King's Men
had acquired a new playhouse. The Blackfriars Children, having
produced two plays that offended authority, had fallen into official
disgrace and been disbanded by the government; and the lease of the
theatre in the ancient monastic building had been surrendered to the
landlord. A company of seven was thereupon organized, including
the Burbage brothers, Shakespeare, Heminge and Condell, which
took over the Blackfriars Theatre—with lucrative results as it turned
out: the dividend they drew from Blackfriars was soon far larger
than their profits at the Globe. The former was a private playhouse,
a fashionable candle-lit room, suited to a prosperous audience and
the showier type of modern play. Given this novel background,
Shakespeare accepted the prevailing taste. What the seventeenth
century demanded was not so much dramatic excitement as graceful
poetic entertainment. New writers had begun to earn fame—
Beaumont and Fletcher, for instance, whose tragi-comedy *Philaster*
appeared between 1608 and 1610. Two clever, ambitious young men,
they shared lodgings on the Bankside, 'one wench', (according to
Aubrey) and 'the same clothes and cloak, etc.'; and the plays that they
wrote, either separately or in collaboration, combined pretty speeches

and facile poetic eloquence with a vein of mild salacity. Whereas the Elizabethans had applauded the tremendous hubbub of a *Tamburlaine*, a *Spanish Tragedy*, a *Titus Andronicus* or a *Richard III*, played in daylight beneath the open sky, the Jacobeans preferred a more intimate drama, in which several forms of dramatic amusement were lightly and expertly mixed, and particularly appreciated the kind of ingenious stage-craft familiarized at Whitehall by the designs of Inigo Jones.

Shakespeare's later productions, written for the Blackfriars, seem as a group to reflect this general tendency: he encourages the stage-designer to display his skill, but limits the opportunities of the great tragedian. His penultimate period has often troubled his admirers; but, just as certain Egyptologists have succeeded in convincing themselves that the plan of every Egyptian sanctuary symbolizes a magical idea, and that all its irregularities must have been purposefully arranged to indicate some hidden truth, so Shakespearian critics have discovered an explanation for the oddities and incongruities of his last plays. He cannot, they feel, have been merely careless or hurried: if the structure of a work is imperfect, its imperfections must have a secret meaning. Lytton Strachey, however, writing in 1906, adopted a more cynical, or more realistic, line. Shakespeare, he suggested, was now a tired man—and not only tired, but bored and disillusioned, 'bored with people, bored with real life, bored with drama, bored with everything except poetry and poetical dreams'.[1] Although Strachey may have overstated his case, it is certainly less unconvincing than the popular Victorian theory, which showed the poet emerging serene and triumphant from the dark struggle that had produced *Macbeth* and *Lear*. Tired Shakespeare may well have been. During the opening decade of the seventeenth century, he wrote some twelve or thirteen plays, six of them the tragic masterpieces in which his powers of feeling and gift of poetic invention were simultaneously at full stretch. The great tragedies absorbed his genius: for slighter productions he was apt to employ his talent; and his talent he sometimes used sparingly, often eking it out with the help of other men's efforts. In 1612 or 1613, Fletcher may have been the prosaic versifier who contributed to the drafting of *King Henry VIII*;

[1] From an essay first published in 1906, reprinted in *Books and Characters*, 1922.

and, in the same year, Shakespeare may have assisted Fletcher to
frame a rather feeble play, *The Two Noble Kinsmen*, based upon
Chaucer's story of Palamon and Arcite.[1]

So much for the question of workmanship; there remains a more
engrossing problem. How can we explain Shakespeare's choice of
subjects, the manner in which he handled his subjects, and the
cumulative impression we receive of satiety and contemptuous
distaste? The bitter residue of the tragedies would appear to have
overflowed into the lesser dramas. All these plays—from *All's Well
that Ends Well* and *Measure for Measure*, written in the first five years
of the century, to *Cymbeline*, produced about 1609 or 1610—strike
an obscurely jarring note. Plays with elaborate 'happy endings' fail
to convey a mood of genuine happiness: plays that depict romantic
passion give the theme of love and desire an ugly, disconcerting
twist. Shakespeare still climbs into the realms of the highest poetry;
but either his personages elude him or he has begun to lose his
original interest in the fascinating vagaries of human character. *All's
Well that Ends Well* is probably a revised version of one of his earlier
successes; it is odd, however, that he should have undertaken to
revise a work both so defective and so strangely unattractive. Nothing
could be better than Helena's soliloquy, describing her hopeless love
for the callous and snobbish Bertram:

> 'Twas pretty, though a plague,
> To see him every hour, to sit and draw
> His arched brows, his hawking eye, his curls,
> In our heart's table; heart too capable
> Of every line and trick of his sweet favour.
> But now he's gone, and my idolatrous fancy
> Must sanctify his relics.

Yet there is something radically wrong about a youthful heroine who
is promised the husband she desires because she has cured an old
king of a fistula, and, when her reluctant husband refuses to con-

---

[1] *The Two Noble Kinsmen* was originally published in 1634, when its authorship was
attributed to 'Mr. John Fletcher and Mr. William Shakespeare'. Coleridge had 'no doubt
whatever that the first act and the first scene of the second act . . . are Shakespeare's'.
If so, they do him comparatively little credit, although they do not lack charm. The play
contains a sub-plot coloured by recollections of Ophelia's death.

summate the marriage and leaves France for an Italian battlefield, manages to smuggle herself into his bed by occupying the place of a more seductive girl. Bertram reveals himself as a mendacious opportunist, but at length recognizes his middle-class wife and is dismissed to live happily ever after, and the complacent Helena enjoys her modest triumph. Shakespeare borrowed his story from Boccaccio; but it is equally difficult to understand why he should have selected the tale, and why Coleridge should profess to regard Helena as the 'loveliest creation' of his fancy. *Measure for Measure*, derived from George Whetstone's *History of Promos and Cassandra*, published in 1578, is a considerably less unpleasing work; but, although this tragi-comedy has a memorable prelude—the study of a secretly lecherous magistrate who, during his master's absence, gives Isabella the painful choice between submitting to his unwanted embraces and seeing her brother Claudio die—the latter part is weak and awkward. The 'Duke of dark corners' suddenly returns to his dukedom and, by means of a series of intricate manoeuvres, exposes villainy and rescues helpless virtue.

Before he had wound up his plot, Shakespeare seems to have been growing weary. During the earlier scenes, lust and the fear of death still quicken his imagination. As in the *Sonnets*, desire is a poisoned bait:

> Our natures do pursue,
> Like rats that ravin down their proper bane,
> A thirsty evil . . .

Claudio at the outset is prepared to make a gallant end:

> If I must die,
> I will encounter darkness as a bride,
> And hug it in mine arms.

Then the prospect becomes intolerably dreadful, and he rejects his sister's desperate pleadings:

> Ay, but to die, and go we know not where,
> To lie in cold obstruction, and to rot,
> This sensible warm motion to become
> A kneaded clod; and the delighted spirit

> To bathe in fiery floods, or to reside
> In thrilling region of thick-ribbed ice,
> To be imprisoned in the viewless winds
> And blown with restless violence round about
> The pendent world; or to be worse than worst
> Of those that lawless and incertain thoughts
> Imagine howling—'tis too horrible!

But the devious machinations of the eccentric and ill-advised Duke are presented on a very different level; and, after the haunting song with which the fourth act opens—

> Take, oh take those lips away,
> That so sweetly were forsworn,
> And those eyes, the break of day,
> Lights that do mislead the morn . . .

—the interest of the drama gradually declines.

Timon of Athens and *Pericles*, which are believed to have succeeded *Coriolanus*, are yet stranger and more uneven works. For *Timon*, Plutarch's 'Life of Antonius' afforded a preliminary hint; and Shakespeare may also have re-embellished the fabric of an old play. Coleridge describes it as a lingering vibration of *Hamlet*, and its protagonist as 'a Lear of the satirical drama; a Lear of domestic or ordinary life;—a local eddy of passion on the high road of society . . .' *Timon*, remarks Hazlitt, is 'the only play of our author in which spleen is the predominant feeling of the mind . . . Timon is tormented with the perpetual contrast between things and appearances, between the fresh, tempting outside and the rottenness within, and invokes mischiefs on the heads of mankind proportioned to the sense of his wrongs and of their treacheries'. The effect is social rather than universal, splenetic rather than deeply tragic. It wants action: invective is piled on invective, tirade added to eloquent tirade. Satire may furnish the stuff of poetry, but not until it has been subtilized and transformed; and *Timon* reaches a poetic height only in occasional unrelated passages, as when the hero speaks of his tomb and delivers his last message to a world that he despises and detests:

> Come not to me again, but say to Athens,
> Timon hath made his everlasting mansion

Upon the beached verge of the salt flood,
Who once a day with his embossed froth
The turbulent surge shall cover; thither come,
And let my grave-stone be your oracle.

As for *Pericles, Prince of Tyre*, it is the dramatist's worst and weakest drama. A quarto was published in 1609, bearing Shakespeare's name and describing it as a 'much admired play . . . divers and sundry times acted by his Majesty's Servants, at the Globe on the Bankside'; but it was omitted from the First and Second Folios; and Jonson in 1630 dismissed it as 'a mouldy tale', which seems a not unfitting epitaph. Yet, awkward and old-fashioned though it is, *Pericles* includes a few Shakespearian passages, notably two references to the sea, which had always delighted the contemplative Midland poet—Pericles' invocation of the deity of the storm:

Thou god of this great vast, rebuke these surges,
Which wash both heaven and hell . . .
        The seaman's whistle
Is as a whisper in the ears of death . . .

and, after her supposed drowning, his passionate lament for Lychorida:

A terrible childbed hast thou had, my dear;
No light, no fire: th'unfriendly elements
Forgot thee utterly; nor have I time
To give thee hallowed to thy grave, but straight
Must cast thee, scarcely coffined, in the ooze;
Where, for a monument upon thy bones,
And e'er-remaining lamps, the belching whale
And humming water must o'erwhelm thy corpse,
Lying with simple shells.

If *Pericles* is an antique melodrama, with *Cymbeline* we return to the landscape of a fairy tale. Shakespeare adopts the fairy-tale convention—an injured princess and a pair of young princes, brought up among the mountains by a devoted old retainer; but he makes no effort to reform its crudities. Faults of construction are accompanied by at least one curious psychological error. Because he has purloined his rival's clothes, Imogen mistakes the headless body of the gross and boorish Cloten for that of her charming and accomplished husband:

> A headless man? The garments of Posthumus?
> I know the shape of's leg; this is his hand;
> His foot Mercurial; his Martial thigh . . .

And the mistake somehow spoils our impression of her sensitive but passionate character. Shakespeare, we feel must have inserted the episode merely to please his Jacobean audience. His Elizabethan comedies are often improbable; but they produce an atmosphere in which improbability and absurdity are blended into a beguiling poetic scheme. The plot of *Cymbeline* is inescapably absurd; its pattern is fragmentary and ill-achieved. The poetry is imposed on the story; it is no longer a pervasive influence; we enjoy the poetic passages as a series of anthology-pieces that redeem the indifferent quality of much of the surrounding text. In *Cymbeline*, we are told, Shakespeare was experimenting with a new technique, and moving away from realism towards a more symbolic method.[1] But it is hard to resist the conclusion that he was growing tired of his work, and was sick of the stage and its exasperating demands.

This view is supported by his next move: during 1611, he disposed of the shares he held in the Blackfriars Theatre and the Globe. Presumably, he contemplated retirement; and, according to the tradition preserved by Nicholas Rowe, not long afterwards he withdrew to New Place. 'The latter part of Shakespeare's life,' Rowe informs us, 'was spent, as all men of good sense will wish theirs may be, in ease, retirement, and the conversation of his friends.' London, however, was to draw him back again; and the year 1613 proved an especially busy period. In January and February, when, amid 'triumphs, pastimes, and sundry devices', the King's daughter, the Princess Elizabeth, was betrothed and married to the Elector Palatine, eight of his plays were produced at Whitehall. On March 10th, he purchased the old Blackfriars Gate House, a venerable fragment of medieval architecture now adapted as a modern dwelling,

---

[1] E. M. W. Tillyard: *Shakespeare's Last Plays*, 1938.

expended 'the sum of one hundred and forty pounds of lawful money of England', and, in the vexatious contemporary fashion, immediately took out a mortgage. Later that month, as ever versatile, he designed an *impresa*, or emblematic card-board shield, which Richard Burbage caused to be made and painted, for Lord Rutland to carry at a tilting match held on the anniversary of the King's accession.

Then Shakespeare's company suffered a sharp reverse. On the afternoon of June 29th, during a performance of *Henry VIII*, a flaming wad, discharged from a stage cannon, set fire to the thatched roof of the Globe, and the blaze involved the whole theatre. The audience promptly took to their heels:

> Out run the knights, out run the lords,
> And there was a great ado;
> Some lost their hats, and some their swords;
> Then out run Burbage too . . .

related a ballad-monger of the day. No lives were lost, though the theatre was destroyed. 'This,' recorded Sir Henry Wotton, 'was the fatal period of that virtuous fabric, wherein yet nothing did perish but wood and straw, and a few forsaken cloaks; only one man had his breeches set on fire, that would perhaps have broiled him, if he had not by the benefit of a provident wit put it out with bottle ale.' As we know, the 'virtuous fabric' was re-built, and continued its existence in an even nobler and more impressive shape; but, before the work of re-building was under way, an unpleasant domestic scandal must have summoned Shakespeare home to Stratford. Susanna Hall had been married since 1607;[1] and she was now accused by a slanderous neighbour, named John Lane, of having 'been caught with Rafe Smith at John Palmer's'. She defended herself against the charge of adultery by bringing an action in the Worcester Consistory Court; and, as Lane did not produce a defence—he was a Catholic and alleged to be a drunkard—Susanna Hall won her case and her adversary suffered excommunication. Clearly, her good-natured

[1] Susanna Hall, who died at New Place, where during the Civil Wars she once entertained Queen Henrietta Maria, on July 11th, 1649, was reputed to be both pious and, according to her epitaph, 'witty above her sex'.

W

father took her part; in his will, she would be generously remembered. After all, only through Susanna's five-year old daughter, Elizabeth, could he yet hope for the continuance of his line.[1]

It is to the tranquil happiness they imagine him enjoying at this period of his later life that some biographers have attributed the serene wisdom they think they distinguish in his last two comedies. Shakespeare, they assure us, was now at peace, amid the dignified surroundings he had chosen and the people whom he most loved—walking the gardens of New Place side by side with the learned Dr Hall, daily pleased by the sight of his pretty grandchild and basking in the spring sunshine of his unmarried daughter's beauty. Perdita and Miranda are peculiarly attractive girls. May not they have been portraits of Judith Shakespeare, for whom he felt a special tenderness? The storms had blown out; his doubts had evaporated. Having at last achieved 'the serene self-possession he had sought with such persistent effort',[2] Shakespeare could look down on humanity from a calm Olympian height. Unfortunately, that comforting vision is based on very little evidence. Neither *The Winter's Tale* nor *The Tempest* suggests that it was written in entirely tranquil spirits. True, they are much more enjoyable plays than their immediate predecessors; but each has its dark and devious aspect, and includes many poignant references to the cruelty and uncertainty of human life. Written in the early months of 1611, *The Winter's Tale* was seen by Simon Forman at the Globe on May 15th, 1611,[3] on November 5th was performed before the King, and later revived as one of the tragedies and comedies presented in 1613 to mark the marriage of the Princess. Sexual jealousy provides the mainspring of the plot—the obsessive, unreasonable jealousy suffered by Leontes King of Sicilia when he has too confidently promoted an affection between his wife Hermione and his old friend Polixenes, the Bohemian monarch. In 1609, the *Sonnets* had been published; and *The Winter's Tale* also tells the story of an emotional masculine friendship that runs aground upon the shoals of passion. Hermione, as it happens, is entirely innocent; and, after sixteen years—during

---

[1] Judith was to bear three sons, all of whom predeceased her. Susanna's daughter Elizabeth died without issue in 1670.
[2] Edward Dowden: *Shakespeare, his Mind and Art*, 1875.
[3] *Book of Plaies*, 1511.

which time she is successfully concealed in a private house by the 'grave and good Paulina'—she is re-discovered as a living statue behind the curtain her devoted guardian draws. Here is a strategem that must have appealed to the Jacobean stage-designer, with his liking for dumb-shows, transparencies and other ingenious scenic whims. The spectacle of Hermione, first statuesque and immobile, then slowly coming to life, would have given the designer just the pretext that he needed.

The framework of *The Winter's Tale* is thus deliberately artificial; but its characters—particularly Mamillius, Leontes' little son, Autolycus, pedlar and sneak-thief, and the enchanting Perdita, Hermione's long-lost child—are drawn with naturalistic skill. The literary atmosphere is that of a fairy-tale; yet in *The Winter's Tale*, unlike *Cymbeline*, it is a fairy-tale that completely carries us away. Even its absurdities and incongruities persuade. Why, for the purposes of the tale, should not Bohemia have a sea-coast? The celebrated stage-direction, *Exit, pursued by a bear*, leaves us with the agreeable conviction that Antigonus' assailant is not a flesh-and-blood predator and unlikely to do him any real harm.[1] No less illusory are all the other details. 'This is fairy gold, boy,' exclaims the shepherd, 'and 'twill prove so: up with't, keep it close . . .' After a grim and darkling introduction, the spirit of happiness re-asserts itself, as Autolycus sings of his life on the road and remembers the bleaching sheets that incautious housewives, English or Bohemian, hang out along the country hedges:

> When daffodils begin to peer,
> With heigh! the doxy over the dale,
> Why, then comes in the sweet o' the year:
> For the red blood reigns in the winter's pale.

> The white sheet bleaching on the hedge,
> With heigh! the sweet birds, O how they sing!
> Doth set my pugging[2] tooth on edge,
> For a quart of ale is a dish for a king.

---

[1] It has been suggested, however, that a tame bear, well-known to the audience, may perhaps have been brought on.
[2] Thievish.

The lark that tirra-lyra chants,
With heigh! with heigh! the thrush and the jay:
Are summer songs for me and my aunts,[1]
While we lie tumbling in the hay.

The sheep-shearing feast, held at the shepherd's cottage, is a precious fragment of 'the golden world'; and Perdita, youth and gaiety incarnate, recalls the Elizabethan passion for the dance as a reflection of the divine harmony that rules the spheres:

. . . When you do dance, I wish you
A wave o' th' sea, that you might ever do
Nothing but that; move still, still so;
And own no other function . . .

Yet, in Shakespeare's play, even among carefree peasants lurk reminders of futurity and death, from which physical oblivion is the only sure refuge. 'Beating and hanging,' confesses Autolycus, 'are terrors to me: for the life to come, I sleep out the thought of it.' By a similar route, the disillusioned shepherd wishes he could have escaped the pains of adult memory: 'I would,' he sighs, 'there were no age between ten and three-and-twenty, or that youth would sleep out the rest; for there is nothing in the between but getting wenches with child, wronging the ancientry, stealing, fighting . . .' It must have been about the age of twenty-three or twenty-four that Shakespeare first came up to London.

Oddly enough, the germ of *The Winter's Tale* was extracted from a popular novel, *Pandosto: The Triumph of Time*, published in 1588 by Shakespeare's old detractor Robert Greene. More mysterious are the sources of *The Tempest*, enacted by the King's players at White-hall on Hallowmas Night, November 1st, 1611, and revived, among fourteen other plays, in May 1613, 'for presenting before . . . the Lady Elizabeth and the Prince Palatine Elector'. One of the books that Shakespeare probably consulted was *A Discovery of the Barmudas* an account of a stormy voyage to the 'still-vexed Bermoothes' issued in the year 1610; he also borrowed from Montaigne, Golding's *Metamorphoses*, Eden's *History of Travayle*, which gave him the name

[1] Mistresses.

'Setebos', and Heywood's *Hierarchie of the Blessed Angels*, which introduces Ariel, 'the earth's great lord' mentioned by 'the Hebrew Rabbins'. Naturally, he suited his play to the prevalent dramatic taste, including a series of masques and shows that brought on 'strange Shapes', dancing 'with gentle actions of salutation', the goddesses June, Ceres and Iris, 'Reapers, properly habited', nymphs and 'divers Spirits, in shape of dogs and hounds'. Ariel's songs were probably set to music by Johnson, a composer then employed at Court,[1] and he, too, may have provided the snatches of 'solemn and strange music' that haunt Prospero's enchanted island. For the contemporary audience, Shakespeare's fantasia was merely another delightful scenic entertainment of a kind to which they were already well accustomed; and we know that it offended the author of *Bartholomew Fair*, who remarked that, being a sober realist, he was 'loath to make nature afraid . . . like those that beget Tales, Tempests, and such like Drolleries!' Not until the Victorian Age did critics conjecture that the play might have some deeper import: that Prospero was the dramatist himself, a benevolent magician bidding the world goodbye, drowning his book, discarding his magic robes and, having written off his mundane concerns, retiring to Milan or Stratford.

Later critics have rejected this view. Prospero, they point out, is undoubtedly erudite; but he is not by any means benevolent. Indeed, he is 'self-opinionated and sour . . . his gravity is often another name for pedantic severity, and . . . there is no character in the play to whom, during some part of it, he is not studiously disagreeable'.[2] His treatment both of Ariel and of Caliban is marked by sudden violent explosions of cruelty and ill-temper: Caliban hates and fears him. Ariel—denounced as 'malignant thing' and 'dull thing', and threatened with twelve winters' imprisonment, pegged in the entrails of a knotty oak—cringes miserably before his master's rage. Prospero is also a suspicious Puritan, and has a puritanical horror of the flesh. If the great magician is a dramatic self-portrait, Shakespeare portrays his ageing self in an unconscionably harsh light.

[1] R. Johnson, a musician in the service of the King's elder son, Prince Henry, also composed the music for Middleton's *Witch*. His scores are preserved in a collection of *Cheerful Ayres or Ballads*, 1660.

[2] Lytton Strachey, *op. cit.*

Beyond Prospero's cell lies a 'filthy-mantled pool'; and his mind encloses many dark crevices. Of his companions, the most vividly described is 'a savage and deformed slave'; and Caliban is at once a repellent, and a tragic and imposing, figure. For Caliban is untutored humanity, Primitive Man with his poetic sense of wonder, his brutal instincts and his superstitious fears. Under Prospero's sway, he has learned the use of language; but he expresses the ingrown resentment felt by every backward people on whom European civilization has once conferred its doubtful blessings:

> You taught me language, and my profit on't
> Is, I know how to curse.

When he curses, however, the down-trodden slave becomes a poet:

> As wicked dew as e'er my mother brushed
> With raven's feather from unwholesome fen
> Drop on you both . . .

Nor does he lack an inherited self-esteem. He is proud of 'Sycorax my mother', the god Setebos whom she followed, and the riches and wonders of the island he believes he has inherited. Finally, he joins forces with the 'drunken butler' and his friend, who appear to him in the guise of democratic liberators, and who represent the brutal idiocy of modern civilization as opposed to the innocent savagery of so-called 'uncivilized' races.

Like *A Midsummer Night's Dream*, Shakespeare's last comedy is a waking dream, made up of many separate visions. Prospero is dreaming of power and knowledge: Miranda and Ferdinand, of love: Stephano and Trinculo, of their new-found kingdom: the conspirators, Sebastian and Antonio, of treachery and self-advancement. Antonio is yet another of Shakespeare's solipsistic rogues; and once again we hear Iago's whisper:

> Sebastian: But, for your conscience?
> Antonio: Ay, sir: where lies that? if 'twere a kibe[1]
>   'Twould put me to my slipper: but I feel not
>   This deity in my bosom . . .

[1] A sore on the heel.

> Here lies your brother,
> No better than the earth he lies upon.
> If he were that which now he's like—that's dead—
> Whom I with this obedient steel—three inches of it—
> Can lay to bed for ever . . .

Presently, each of them awakes, and awaking finds his real identity—
'in a poor isle . . . where no man was his own'; but meanwhile
Prospero has reminded Ferdinand that the whole universe may be
an 'insubstantial pageant', and we, too, the illusory creatures of a
dream:

> Our revels now are ended. These our actors,
> As I foretold you, were all spirits, and
> Are melted into air, into thin air,
> And, like the baseless fabric of this vision,
> The cloud-capped towers, the gorgeous palaces,
> The solemn temples, the great globe itself,
> Yea, all which it inherit, shall dissolve,
> And, like this insubstantial pageant faded,
> Leave not a rack behind: we are such stuff
> As dreams are made on; and our little life
> Is rounded with a sleep. Sir, I am vexed.
> Bear with my weakness, my old brain is troubled . . .

Here, at least, Prospero's voice is that of his author; but the doubt
he expresses was not peculiar to the poet's mind. 'Life is as it were a
play and a dream', had written St John Chrysostom during the
fourth century, 'for as on the stage when the curtain is closed the
shifting shadows are dissolved, and as with the flashing light dreams
are dispelled, so in the coming consummation all things will be
dissolved and will vanish away'.[1] The idea that the world is a
stage constantly recurs in Elizabethan and Jacobean literature; and,
some nine years before the composition of *The Tempest*, William
Alexander, subsequently Earl of Sterling, published *The Tragedy of
Darius*, which contains a passage that, despite its clumsiness, may
possibly have caught Shakespeare's notice:

[1] Quoted by Anne Righter: *Shakespeare and the Idea of the Play*, 1962.

Let greatness of her glassy sceptres vaunt:
Not sceptres, no, but reeds, soon bruis'd, soon broken:
And let this worldly pomp our wits enchant.
All fades, and scarcely leaves behind a token.
Those golden palaces, those gorgeous halls,
With furniture superfluously fair:
Those stately courts, those sky-encountering walls
Evanish all like vapours in the air.

The difference between talent and genius, and the use that genius may make of talent, have seldom been more clearly illustrated. Prospero's speech does not conclude the play, and is not its moral and didactic climax. The lines are not a rhetorical essay on a theme; they occur as the momentary reflections of an ageing magician whose 'old brain is troubled'. Their effect is spontaneous; they are almost casually delivered; but we re-read them with that indescribable sensation—'a shiver down the spine', accompanied by 'a constriction of the throat and a precipitation of water to the eyes'—which, according to A. E. Housman,[1] is provoked only by the highest flights of verse.

The Tempest, Hazlitt decided, was 'one of the most original and perfect' of Shakespeare's productions, in which he exhibited the full 'variety of his powers'. The magician who summons up earth-shaking storms can also evoke heavenly music. He has explored the depths of misery and infamy; and sometimes he turns on mankind like Prospero reviling Caliban. Yet through Miranda's eyes he looks out on to a 'brave new world', peopled by comely and surprising shapes: 'How beauteous mankind is!' she cries. Prospero, it is true, does not share his daughter's illusions; and 'Poor worm, thou art infected!' is his acid comment, when he perceives that earthly love has touched her heart. Shakespeare's own attitude is far less censorious—or his sympathies are much more evenly divided; he remains as sensitive to the beauty of existence as to its undertones of gloom and horror. He is still the poetic humanist, still the master of words, who loves his medium for its own sake; and so completely has he mastered it that he varies his tempo with bewildering celerity and ease, either producing a strongly dramatic image:

[1] The Name and Nature of Poetry, 1933.

> Their understanding
> Begins to swell, and the approaching tide
> Will shortly fill the reasonable shores
> That now lie foul and muddy.

—or evoking an exquisite impression of fragility and evanescence:

> Ye elves of hills, brooks, standing lakes, and groves,
> And ye, that on the sands with printless foot
> Do chase the ebbing Neptune, and do fly him
> When he comes back . . .

For many images, he calls on his recollections of the sea; but it is from the thatched roof of a Warwickshire cottage he takes his picture of the old courtier:

> His tears run down his beard, like winter's drops,
> From eaves of reeds.

Memory, said to be the Mother of the Muses, serves him as faithfully in *The Tempest* as in all his earlier work.

Again we admire his miraculous gift of compression. Within a single elliptical phrase—

> Now in the waist, the deck, in every cabin
> *I flamed amazement* . . .

> She that is queen of Tunis: she that dwells
> *Ten leagues beyond man's life* . . .

> The sole drift of my purpose doth extend
> *Not a frown further.*

—he packs an unlooked-for density of meaning. Particularly in the most ambitious speeches, blank verse has become a kind of free verse; the rhythm is deliberately fractured; and the flow of the verse is no longer circumscribed by orthodox prosodic rules. Thus, in Prospero's threnody, a line concludes with 'and'; while poetic eloquence is artfully married to the cadences of ordinary speech. There are three pauses; and each not only provides a breathing-space but marks a stage in the unfolding pattern of ideas. 'Our revels now are ended'—Prospero makes a plain statement. More mysteriously, he draws the audience's attention to the disappearance of the spirit-actors, finishing with an evocative repetition: 'melted into air, into thin air'. His third paragraph begins on a subdued note, but rapidly gathers emphasis and passion, as we see the solid universe fading and melting—not in a Christian Day of Judgement, but in a pagan dream-chaos where reason and identity dissolve. Nothing is more characteristic of Shakespeare than his magnificently noncommittal grace. He rarely labours a dramatic point, and never seeks to ram his genius home. His finest melodies are almost thrown away. He rouses his audience, engages its human sympathies, stirs its poetic imagination, then bids it farewell with a light and easy gesture:

> Good morrow masters, put your torches out.
> The wolves have preyed, and look, the gentle day,
> Before the wheels of Phœbus, round about
> Dapples the drowsy east with spots of grey:
> Thanks to you all, and leave us. Fare you well.[1]

The Tempest, since it was Shakespeare's last comedy, has a particularly quiet and nostalgic ending. In 1612 or 1613, he may have returned to London for a few months' work; but, as an independent creative artist, he had now pronounced his valediction.

He was not inspired, however, by his fellow magician's example. Prospero looks forward to a life of studious seclusion, where 'every third thought shall be my grave': Shakespeare continued to engage in business and to share in the prosaic concerns of his middle-class Stratfordian neighbours. On September 11th, 1611, he had been listed among the seventy-one citizens who had contributed 'towards the charge of prosecuting the Bill in parliament for the better repair of the highways and amending divers defects in the Statutes already made'; and, in 1614, he was chosen to entertain a visiting preacher, receiving from the Stratford corporation a quart of sack and a quart of claret that had cost them twenty pence. During the September of that same year, he became involved in the troublesome question of the Welcombe enclosure. A certain Arthur Mainwaring, steward to

---

[1] *Much Ado about Nothing* Act V Scene iii.

Lord Ellesmere, had originally proposed the scheme and had gained the support of other Warwickshire capitalists. Such undertakings encouraged the use of more scientific agricultural methods and consequently enriched the landlord; but they were opposed by villagers who had been accustomed to till the medieval open-strip fields, gather turf and firewood from the adjacent common and graze their animals upon its rough grass. The Stratford Corporation was inclined to mistrust the plan; and Thomas Greene, the Town Clerk, frequently consulted Shakespeare. During November, they were both in London, Greene preparing a petition to the Privy Council; and, on November 17th, he recorded that, 'at my cousin[1] Shakespeare coming to town, I went to see him how he did' and discussed the problems that enclosure raised—'he and Mr. Hall say they think there will be nothing done at all'; and, on December 25th, that he had written Shakespeare a letter signed by various interested persons, and despatched 'a note of the inconveniences would grow by the enclosure'. The scheme eventually miscarried; but, while it was still under discussion, Shakespeare seems to have pursued his customary line, safeguarding his position as a landlord, but generally preferring to remain aloof. Greene's references to the part that Shakespeare played conclude with a somewhat enigmatic entry: 'W. Shakespeare's telling J. Greene I was not able to bear the enclosing of Welcombe'. Here apologists like to assume that Greene wrote 'I' when he intended to write 'he', and that Shakespeare, a champion of the cottagers' rights, was deeply outraged by the whole proposal.

The conversation that Greene reports appears to have taken place in September 1615; and, early next year, Shakespeare's thoughts were engaged by a more cheerfully domestic subject. Judith Shakespeare, now thirty-one years old, was betrothed to Thomas Quiney, a tavern-keeper, then aged twenty-six, son of the Shakespeares' family friend Richard. They were married on February 10th; and, before the ceremony, Shakespeare instructed Francis Collins, a lawyer practising at Warwick, to draft his last will and testament, which, after prolonged revision, he eventually signed on March 25th. The executors appointed were John and Susanna Hall, to whom he bequeathed the residue of his estate, 'goods, chattels, leases, plate,

---

[1] The exact degree of Greene's relationship to Shakespeare has never been established.

jewels and household stuff', while to Susanna went his landed property. Judith was to have £150, and his 'broad silver-gilt bowl'; his sister Joan Hart, £20, 'all my wearing apparel' and 'the house with the appurtenances in Stratford wherein she dwelleth for her natural life'; Joan's three sons, £5 each. To Thomas Combe, he left his sword; to the poor of Stratford, £10; among those who were to receive the sum of £1 6s. 8d. apiece to 'buy them rings', he named his fellow players John Heminge, Richard Burbage and Henry Condell. A single mention of Anne Shakespeare is inserted on the third sheet: 'I give unto my wife my second-best bed with the furniture.' No doubt she was otherwise provided for; and, under English common law, his widow would have been by no means destitute.[1] Authorities have suggested that Anne may have claimed the bed because it had a sentimental value, and that, when she was married thirty-four years earlier, she had brought it with her from her old home.

We do not know how Shakespeare disposed of his library; and anti-Stratfordians have therefore argued that New Place must have been wholly bookless. But most seventeenth-century testaments, even wills made by modest yeomen farmers, enumerate a few favourite volumes; and it is reasonable to assume either that Shakespeare's collection was included among the goods, chattels and household stuff that he bequeathed with New Place, or that there had long been an understanding in the family that the poet's books should go to Dr Hall. Did they include any of his own works, quartos good and bad, or perhaps a copy of the unauthorized *Sonnets*? Shakespeare was now severing the link that bound him to his literary past. Unlike Jonson, he produced no collected edition; nor is there the slightest evidence that he attempted to revise his plays. He had abandoned them as firmly and conclusively as Prospero rejected his magic lore. Half the dramas he had written were still unpublished; his interest in them had been sold outright; and probably the manuscripts remained in London. '*Je ne m'occupe plus de ça*', declared Arthur Rimbaud, when he was questioned by Delahaye on the subject of his early poems; and Shakespeare, too, may have regarded his poetic existence as a curious episode now best forgotten.

[1] See E. K. Chambers: *op. cit.*

But with his old colleagues he did not lose touch. He rode up to revisit his London haunts, or they rode down to see him in the country; and during the spring of 1616, noted John Ward, vicar of Stratford from 1662 to 1681, 'Shakespeare, Drayton and Ben Jonson had a merry meeting, and it seems drank too hard, for Shakespeare died of a fever there contracted . . .' He died on April 23rd, and was buried on the 25th, in Stratford's parish church beside the Avon. A Warwickshire stone-cutter carved a doggerel epitaph, pronouncing a solemn curse on any avaricious sexton who, to make room for some unknown newcomer, should cast his mortal remains into the adjacent 'bone-house'. The grave itself, beneath the broad, cold light of the chancel window, is said to have been seventeen feet deep.

BIBLIOGRAPHY

Akrigg, G. P. V.: *Jacobean Pageant, or The Court of King James I*, 1962.
Auerbach, Erna: *Nicholas Hilliard*, 1961.

Babb, Laurence: *The Elizabethan Malady: A Study of Melancholy in English Literature*, 1951.
Bayley, John: *The Characters of Love*, 1961.
Bradbrook, M. C.: *The School of Night*, 1936.
Bradley, A. C.: *Shakespearian Tragedy*, 1904.
Brandes, George: *William Shakespeare*, 1916.
Brown, Ivor: *Shakespeare*, 1949.
Boyd, Morrison Comegys: *Elizabethan Music and Musical Criticism*, 1940.

Chambers, E. K.: *William Shakespeare: A Study of Facts and Problems*, 1930.
Cooper, Duff: *Sergeant Shakespeare*, 1949.
Cunnington, C. Willett and Phyllis: *A Picture History of English Costume*, 1960.

Devereux, Walter Bourchier: *Lives and Letters of the Devereux, Earls of Essex*, 1853.
Dodd, A. H.: *Life in Elizabethan England*, 1961.
Dowden, Edward: *Shakespeare, his Mind and Art*, 1875.
Dunlop, Ian: *Palaces and Progresses of Elizabeth I*, 1962.

Gibson, H. N.: *The Shakespeare Claimants*, 1962.
Gillet, Louis: *Shakespeare*, 1930.
Granville-Barker, H.: *Prefaces to Shakespeare*, 1927.

Halliday, F. E.: *Shakespeare in his Age*, 1956.
Halliday, F. E.: *Shakespeare and his Critics*, 1958.
Halliday, F. E.: *The Life of Shakespeare*, 1961.

335

Harbage, Alfred: *Shakespeare's Audience*, 1941.
Harrison, G. B.: *The Life and Death of Robert Devereux, Earl of Essex*, 1937.
Harrison, G. B.: *The Elizabethan Journals*, 1938.
Harrison, G. B.: *Introducing Shakespeare*, 1939.
Harrison, G. B.: *Elizabethan Plays and Players*, 1940.
Harrison, G. B.: *Shakespeare's Tragedies*, 1950.
Hearsey, John E. N.: *Bridge, Church and Palace in Old London*, 1961.
Henslowe's Diary, edited by Walter W. Greg, 1904.
Henslowe Papers, edited by Walter W. Greg, 1907.
Hentzner, Paul: *Travels in England*, 1844.
Herbert of Cherbury, Lord: *Autobiography*, edited by Sidney L. Lee, 1886.
Hodges, C. Walter: *The Globe Restored*, 1953.
Holmes, Martin: *Shakespeare's Public*, 1960.
Hotson, J. Leslie: *The Death of Christopher Marlowe*, 1925.
Hotson, J. Leslie: *Shakespeare versus Shallow*, 1931.
Hotson, J. Leslie: *I, William Shakespeare*, 1937.
Hotson, J. Leslie: *Shakespeare's Sonnets Dated*, 1949.
Hotson, J. Leslie: *Shakespeare's Motley*, 1952.
Hotson, J. Leslie: *The First Night of Twelfth Night*, 1954.
Hotson, J. Leslie *Shakespeare's Wooden O*, 1959.
Hurstfield, Joel: *Elizabeth I and the Unity of England*, 1960.

Jenkins, Elizabeth: *Elizabeth and Leicester*, 1961.

Knight, G. Wilson: *The Wheel of Fire*, 1930.

Leavis, F. R.: *The Common Pursuit*, 1952.
Lee, Sidney: *A Life of William Shakespeare*, 1908.
Leishman, J. B.: *Themes and Variations in Shakespeare's Sonnets*, 1961.
Lewis, Wyndham: *The Lion and the Fox*, 1927.
Loseley Manuscripts, The, edited by John Kempe, 1835.

Mattingley, Garrett: *The Defeat of the Spanish Armada*, 1959.
Morris, Helen: *Elizabethan Literature*, 1953.
Murry, John Middleton: *Countries of the Mind*, 1922.

Neale, J. E.: *Queen Elizabeth*, 1934.

Pitcher, Seymour M.: *The Case for Shakespeare's Authorship of 'The Famous Victories'*, 1962.

Read, Conyers: *Lord Burghley & Queen Elizabeth*, 1960.
Righter, Anne: *Shakespeare and the Idea of the Play*, 1962.
Rowse, A. L.: *The England of Elizabeth*, 1950.

Salisbury Papers: Historical Manuscripts Commission, 1906.
Shaw, G. B.: *Shaw on Shakespeare*, edited by Edwin Wilson, 1961.
Sitwell, Sacheverell: *British Architects and Craftsmen*, 1945.
Smith, Logan Pearsall: *On Reading Shakespeare*, 1933.
Southern, Richard: *The Seven Ages of the Theatre*, 1962.
Spurgeon, Caroline F. E.: *Shakespeare's Imagery*, 1935.
Steiner, George: *The Death of Tragedy*, 1961.
Steward, J. I. M.: *Character and Motive in Shakespeare*, 1949.
Stoll, Elmer Edgar: *Art and Artifice in Shakespeare*, 1933.
Stopes, Charlotte Carmichael: *The Life of Henry Third Earl of Southampton*, 1922.
Strachey, Lytton: *Books and Characters*, 1922.
Sydney Papers, edited by Arthur Collins, 1746.

Tillyard, E. M. W.: *Shakespeare's Last Plays*, 1938.
Tillyard, E. M. W.: *The Elizabethan World Picture*, 1943.
Tillyard, E. M. W.: *Shakespeare's History Plays*, 1944.

Weston, William: *The Autobiography of an Elizabethan*, translated by Philip Caraman, 1955.
Wilkinson, L. P.: *Ovid Recalled*, 1935.
Wilson, John Dover: *The Essential Shakespeare*, 1932.
Wright, Louis B.: *Middle-class Culture in Elizabethan England*, 1935.
Wythorne, Thomas: *Autobiography*, edited by James M. Osborn, 1961.

X

INDEX

In this index S = Shakespeare

abdication, a dangerous topic, 198, 235
Achillean virtues, in *Henry V*, 211, 261
Achilles (in *Troilus and Cressida*), 259, 260
acting style, 44, 90, 148, 269–70
action, men of: in conflict with irresolute, 197; portrayal of their secret inconsistency, 201
actors—*see* players
Adam (in *As You Like It*), S's playing of, 185
Admiral's Men, 42, 44, 46, 159 n.; reformed by Alleyn, 147–8
aestheticism, Elizabethan, 97
Alarm to England (Rich), 54 n.
Alexander, William, 327
All for Love (Dryden), 290–2
All's Well that Ends Well, 316–17
allegory, 95, 96
Allen, Giles, 219
Allen, William, 67
Alleyn, Edward, 46, 51–2, 122, 154, 192, 220; acting style, 44, 148, 269; forms new Admiral's Men, 147–8
Amores (Ovid), 97
Amoretti (Spenser), 121
anachronisms, 259, 323
anarchic mood, of S's adult dramas, 308
ancient, crafty, a recognized type, 233–4, 278–9
Andersen, Hans, 172
Antony, 111; his funeral oration over Caesar, 256–7; S's alleged love for, 287; as a demi-god, 289; compared with Dryden's Antony, 291, 292–3; isolated by passion, 298
Antony and Cleopatra, 111, 311 n., 313; and 'Dark Lady', 132; romantic love in, 287, 288, 294; imagery of, 287, 289, 293; sources of, 288–9, 291; compared with *Othello*, 288; Coleridge and Hazlitt on, 290; 'fiery force' of, 290, compared with Dryden's *All for Love*, 290–2
apprentices, 25, 156
Apuleius, 171
architecture, Elizabethan, 86, 92, 95, 252
Arden, Mary—*see* Shakespeare, Mary

Arden, Robert (grandfather), 17, 18, 296
Arden, Forest of, 17–18, 183
Ariosto, Ludovico, 58
aristocracy, in the romantic comedies, 167–8
Aristotle, and Three Ages of Man, 183–4
Armado (in *Love's Labour's Lost*), identified with Ralegh, 142–3
Armin, Robert, 187, 254
Arte of English poesie, The (Puttenham), 121 n.
arts, Elizabethan, 88–92
As You Like It, 18 n.; Marlowe the 'dead shepherd' in, 50, 97 n.; lyricism of, 168; S shown as 'social climber' in, 168; sources of, 180; popularity of, 183; moralizings of, 183, 185; an amoral comedy, 184–5; S thought to have played Adam, 185
Ascension Day mummers, 25
Ashton, Thomas, 245
aspiration, in Elizabethan temperament, 81
Astrophel and Stella (Sidney), 121
atheism, 48–9, 50, 94, 299
attitudes, dramatic, emotions signified by, 84
Aubrey, John, 22, 65, 160, 182, 193, 285, 295 n., 314
audiences, Elizabethan, 40, 43, 53, 57–8, 60, 156–7
Auerbach, Erna, 91 n.
Autolycus (in *Winter's Tale*), 323–4

Babb, Lawrence, 191 n., 264 n.
Bacon, Anthony, 108, 112, 113 n., 175, 227
Bacon, Francis, 31, 36, 215, 285; and Essex, 111–12, 224; prosecutor in Essex trial, 232, 243, 244
Bacon, Lady Nicholas, 113
Bagot, Anthony, 107
Baines, Richard, 48
Baldwin, T. W., 156 n.
Bandello, Matteo, 180
Bankside, 35, 51, 159, 220, 262, 272, 314
Barnes, Barnabe, 116, 121
Barnfield, Richard, 114 n., 214

339

Bartholomew Fair (Jonson), 58 n.
Baudelaire, Charles, 19 n., 130 n., 308
bawdiness, Elizabethan, 151
Bayley, John, 275 n., 276 n., 281 n.
Bear Garden, 220–1
bear-baiting, 220–1
Beard, Thomas, 49
'beards, Cadiz', 224
Beatrice (in *Much Ado*), 181–2
Beaumont, Francis, 36, 296–7, 314
Bedford, third Earl of, 248
beggars, 67
Belott, Stephen, 272–3
Benedick (in *Much Ado*), 181–2
benefit of clergy, 192
Benson, John, 134
Berners, John Bourchier, second Lord, 171
Berowne (in *Love's Labour's Lost*), 142;
  his 'whitely wanton', 131, 145; as a
  literary misogynist, 143–6; on female
  organism, 145; on love's authority, 146
Betterton, Thomas, 21 n.
Biron, Maréchal de, 142
Blackfriars Theatre, 270, 314, 315, 320
Blackwell, Father George, 68
blood-sports, 220–1
Blount, Sir Christopher, 229, 230, 233,
  234, 239–40, 244, 247
Boccaccio, 317
Bottom (in *Midsummer Night's Dream*),
  173–4, 182
boy-actors, 180; companies of, 42–3,
  270–1, 314; female parts played by, 59,
  181, 185
Boyd, Morrison Comegys, 88 n.
Bracciano, Don Virginio Orsino, Duke of,
  71, 180
Bradbrook, M. C., 75 n., 80 n.
Bradley, A. C.: on *Hamlet*, 268; on
  Othello, 276, 280; on *King Lear*, 304
Brandes, George, 211 n.
Bretchgirdle, John, 24
Bridges, Robert, 151
Brien, Alan, 168 n.
Brooke, Arthur, 149–50
Brown, Ivor, 132 n.
Bruno, Giordano, 31
Brutus, 256–7, 258, 298
Bull, John, 88
bull-baiting, 221
Burbage, Cuthbert, 219
Burbage, James, 148, 165
Burbage, Richard, 148, 160, 165, 188,
  254, 272, 294, 299–300, 314, 321; as
  Shylock, 176; part-owner of Globe,
  219; S's bequest to, 332
Burghley, William Cecil, Lord, 108, 111,
  112, 116, 118, 175, 228, 252; feud with
  Essex, 224; possible model for Polo-
  nius, 268

business dealings, Elizabethan love of,
  219
Bussy d'Ambois (Chapman), 145 n.
Byrd, William, 88

Cadiz, Essex expedition to, 223–4, 229,
  296 n.
'Cadiz beards', 224
Calderon, Don Pedro, 172
Caliban (in *Tempest*), 325; as Primitive
  Man, 326
Camden, William, 191
Campion, Thomas, 296
Capell, Edward, 185 n.
Case is Altered, The (Jonson), 158 n.
catastrophe, prohecies of (1588), 32
Catholic priests, persecution of, 67–8
Catullus, 150
Caxton, William, 258
Cecil, Robert (later Earl of Salisbury),
  70, 79, 108, 109, 111, 112, 114, 117,
  175, 227, 247, 248, 252, 253 n., 299;
  feud with Essex, 224, 225, 231, 234,
  237, 245, 260
Chamberlain, John, 228
Chamberlain's Men, 41, 42, 147, 188,
  221, 264; re-formed, 148; S in, 148,
  166; Jonson joins, 191–2; present
  Richard II for Essex faction, 235, 250;
  become King's Men, 254; and boy-
  actors, 270–1
Chambers, E. K., 19 n., 31 n., 42 n.,
  195 n., 196 n., 215 n., 255 n., 271 n.,
  295 n., 332 n.
Chapel Royal, Children of, 42, 270–1
Chapman, George, 48, 129, 144–5, 188,
  263; ponderous style, 97; nocturnal
  imagery, 142; compared with S, 179;
  his *Iliad*, 211, 258
Charlecote, 23
Chateaubriand, Vicomte de, 267
Chaucer, Geoffrey, 96, 171, 178 n., 258
  316
Cheerful Ayres or Ballads, 325 n.
Chettle, Henry, 62, 64, 120, 137, 250
childhood and children, 19–20, 153, 161–2
Chomley, Richard, 48
Chorus, S's use of, 213
Christianity, rarely mentioned by S, 299
Chronicle (Hall), 199
Chronicles (Holinshed), 54, 55, 197
Chronicles of England (Stow), 200
Cinthio, Giraldi, 286, 288
class system, 163
classical legend, 95–8, 101
Clayton, John, 272
Cleopatra: terrestrial origins, 287, 289;
  as a demi-goddess, 288–9, 290; her
  suicide a ritual sacrifice, 290; com-
  pared with Dryden's Cleopatra, 291

Clifford, J. L., 21 n.
Clopton, Sir Hugh, 22
clothing, 86-7, 117
clowns, dress of, 187
Cobham, Lord, 164, 204, 214 n.
Coke, Sir Edward, 232
Coleridge, S. T., 55 n., 316; on quarrel scene in *Julius Caesar*, 256 n.; on Iago, 279; on *Antony and Cleopatra*, 290; on *Macbeth*, 303 n.; on Helena in *All's Well*, 317; on *Timon of Athens*, 318
Colin Clout's Come Home Again (Spenser), 60
colours: emotions signified by, 84-5; contrasting schemes of *Macbeth* and *Lear*, 304
Combe, John, 271
Combe, Thomas, 332
Combe, William, 271
Comedy of Errors, The, 58, 149, 188, 215
'common man', rare in S, 174
Compton, Lady, 143-4
Condell, Henry, 188, 254, 314, 332
conservatism, Elizabethan, 83-4
Constable, Henry, 114 n., 121
Constance (in *King John*), on loss of child, 161-2
convention, in drama, 84-5
Copernicus, 82
copyright, absence of, 216
Coriolanus: isolated by pride, 298, 312-3; S's last attempt to create great man, 302
Coriolanus, 210, 302; Essex link with, 311-2; 'a monolithic tragedy', 313; lyricism of, 313; naturalistic touches, 313-4
costume, players', 160, 187
Cotton, John, 21
Court: influence on drama, 38-9; criticism of, 39; Chamberlain's men perform at, 41, 42, 250; 'popish' practices, 69; restlessness, 70-1; magnificence of, 71, 78, 92; rivalry at, 76; support of players, 77-8, 188, 250, 299; Essex's plan to seize, 230, 234, 241; his dismissal from, 231
Cowell, William, 103, 214
Cowley, Richard, 182, 254
Cressida, a sexual opportunist, 261-2
Croce, Benedetto, 169
Croft, Sir James, 72
Crosse, Henry, 157
Cuffe, Henry, 234, 278
Cult of Love, 144
Curtain playhouse, 35, 155, 159, 219
customs dues, farming of, 232 n., 254
Cymbeline, 316; fairy-tale convention, 319, 323; psychological error in, 320; symbolic method, 320

dancing, 25, 73, 89-90, 93, 324
Daniel, Samuel, 53 n., 121, 127
Danvers, Sir Charles, 231, 234, 248
Darius, The Tragedy of (Alexander), 327-8
'Dark Lady', 130-2, 145
Dark Lady of the Sonnets, The (Shaw), 131 n.
Davenant, John, 294
Davenant, Robert, 295
Davenant, Sir William, 41, 166, 295
David's Tears (Hayward), 85 n.
Davies, Sir John, 89
Davies, John, 36, 114 n.
Davies, Richard, 29
De Quincey, Thomas, 303 n.
De Revolutionibus Orbium Coelestium (Copernicus), 82
Dead Term, The (Dekker), 34 n.
death, Elizabethan preoccupation with, 25, 38, 317-18, 324
Deburau, Charles, 187
decay, 25
Declaration of egregious Popish Impostures, 306 n.
Dee, Dr John, 82, 301
'deed of darkness', 145
'degree', medieval theory of, 83-4, 85, 303
Dekker, Thomas, 34, 156, 158, 159
Delia (Daniel), 121, 127
demonology, 169-71, 306
Derby, Ferdinando Lord, 48
Derby, William Earl of, 168
Desdemona (in *Othello*), 269, 277, 279, 281, 286
Devereux, Walter Bourchier, 243 n.
Devil's Advocate: Falstaff as, 206, 260; in *Troilus*, 260
devotional poetry, 94
Diana (Constable), 121
Dido, Tragedy of (Marlowe), 46
Digges, Thomas, 82
Discovery of the Bermudas, A, 324
Discovery of Witchcraft, The (Scot), 169-70, 171
Dr Faustus (Marlowe), 81, 299, 301 n.
Dodd, A. H., 20 n., 33 n.
Dogberry, origin of, 182
Dolman, John, 53
Donne, John, 36, 94, 296
Dowden, Edward, 322 n.
Dowland, John, 88
drama: Elizabethan, resemblance to Japanese, 39; versatility, 40; development of, 42-3; revolutionized by *Spanish Tragedy* and *Tamburlaine*, 42, 43; conventional symbolism in, 84-5; comedy of 'humours', 188, 189, 190-1; Jonson's concepts of, 189-90, 212, 325; new Jacobean type of, 314-5, 325

dramatic sense, Elizabethan, 38, 53, 275
dramatists, Greene's diatribe against,
　62–4
Drayton, Michael, 54 n., 121, 127, 128,
　130, 297, 333
'dream', frequent occurrence of word,
　293
Droeshout, Martin, portrait of S, 65
Drummond of Hawthornden, 191, 194
Dryden, John: on Marcutio, 152; on
　Falstaff, 204; on Troilus and Cressida,
　260; his All for Love compared with
　Antony and Cleopatra, 290–2
Duff Cooper, Sir Alfred (Lord Norwich),
　28 n.
Duncan, Geillis, 300

Earl, John, 34
'ecstasy of living', S's understanding of,
　308
Eden, Richard, 324
Edmunds, Pearse, 118
education, Elizabethan, 20–1, 96 n., 156;
　popularizing of, 53–4
Edward II (Marlowe), 46, 198
Egerton, Sir Thomas, 227, 231, 232,
　296 n.
El Dorado, 79
elements, 82; in man, 85, 290
Eliot, T. S.: on Marlowe, 50; on Hamlet,
　266; on Othello, 275; on Coriolanus,
　311
Elizabeth I, 31, 36, 53, 54, 66, 168, 180;
　entertained at Kenilworth, 23–4; at
　Tilbury, 33; Court of, 38–9, 41–2, 69,
　71–8, 92, 116; religious practice, 69;
　and Parliament, 69–70; her progresses,
　71–2, 74, 87, 92; entertainment, love
　of, 73; character, 72–5; devotion
　aroused by, 75–6; kingship, concep-
　tion of, 76–7, 199; Hilliard's portrait
　of, 90; and Essex, 107–9, 110–11,
　114–15, 198, 223, 224–6, 228, 230–1,
　235; 'mortal moon', 126; haunted by
　fall of Richard II, 198, 248; alleged
　desire to see 'Falstaff in love', 209;
　appearance, 225; and Essex rebellion,
　238, 241, 248–9; last days and death,
　248–50
Elizabeth, Queen of Bohemia, 320, 322,
　324
England's Mourning Garment (Chettle),
　250
entertainments, 23–4, 25–6, 73, 220–1
Erasmus, 93
Essex, Robert Devereux, second Earl of,
　38, 53, 87, 116, 117, 171 n., 180; his
　tragedy reflected in S's tragic dramas,
　33, 254–6, 258, 260, 266–7, 275,
　311–12; S attracted to, 106–7, 115,

147, 250, 254, 256; and Elizabeth,
　107–9, 110–11, 114–15, 144, 198, 223,
　224–6, 228, 230–1, 233; rivalry with
　Ralegh, 107–8, 142, 144, 223, 231, 234,
　243; military exploits, 109–10, 127,
　142, 211, 222–3, 296 n.; political
　intrigue, 112, 147, 198; character,
　112–13, 222–3, 312; literary gifts,
　114–15; and Lopez case, 175, 177;
　Henry V designed to please, 211, 222;
　and Irish rebellion, 222–3, 226, 228–
　30; Apology, 227, 231; in custody,
　231–2; his own rebellion, 234–42;
　surrender, 242–3; trial and death,
　243–6, 250–1, 263; compared with
　Hamlet, 266
Essex, Frances, Lady, 109, 113
Essex, Lettice Knollys, Lady, 23, 107,
　171 n.
Essex House, 113–15, 231, 233, 234, 236,
　240–3
Essex's Last Goodnight, 246
Essex's Players, 30
Every Man in his Humour (Jonson), 78 n.,
　188, 189–90
Every Man out of his Humour (Jonson),
　163
exercise, Elizabethan need for, 88
exploration, 79–80

Faerie Queene (Spenser), 81 n.
fairies, 170–1
fairy-tale convention: in Cymbeline, 319–
　20; in Winter's Tale, 323–4
Falkland, Lucius Cary, second Viscount,
　193
Fall of the late Arian, The, 48 n.
Falstaff, Sir John: origins of, 200, 204;
　at ease with himself and the world,
　203, 205; the spirit of unbelief, 204,
　206; as Devil's Advocate, 206, 260;
　Johnson on, 204–5; his wit, 205; Hazlitt
　on, 205, 211; more than a symbol, 206;
　and illusion of youth, 206; rejected by
　Henry, 206, 210–11, 314; comic
　portrait of English Gentleman, 206–8;
　a lord of language, 208–9; resurrected
　in Merry Wives, 209; a 'runaway
　character' to be killed off, 211; be-
　comes 'real' personage, 214
Famous Victories of Henry V, The, 200–1
　204
fashion, 86–7, 117
Fastolfe, Sir John, 204
fatalism, 25
fear, the keynote of Macbeth, 301–2, 303
female parts, played by men and boys, 39,
　59, 181, 185
Female Principle, 102; Lear's loathing
　for, 307

Ferreira, Esteban, 175
Ferrex and Porrex (Norton and Sack-
ville), 36, 42
festivities, country, 25
Field, Nathan (boy-actor), 180
Field, Richard, 30-1, 32, 34, 100; *Venus
and Adonis* and *Rape of Lucrece* printed
by, 97, 103
Fitton, Mary, 131, 228
flesh, fear and hatred of, 286
Fletcher, John, 296, 314, 315-16
Fletcher, Lawrence, 254
'Floating World', 39
Florio, John, 114 n., 116, 143, 310
Ford, John, 84, 114 n.
Forman, Simon, 322
Fortune Theatre, 154, 155, 219
free will, 85
Frezer, Ingram, 49
Fuller, Thomas, 297
furnishings and decoration, Elizabethan,
87, 252

gain, Elizabethan lust for, 79, 81, 86, 94,
219, 251
Gardiner, William, 30 n., 164-5
Gascoigne, George, 23, 24, 58
Gentleman, English, Falstaff a comic
portrait of, 206-7
Gentleman Pensioners, 72 n.
gentry, increasing power of, 163
Geoffrey of Monmouth, 304
Gerard, Father John, 68
ghosts, in Elizabethan drama, 43, 301
Gibbons, Orlando, 88
Gide, André, 197
Gillet, Louis, 27 n.
Globe Theatre, 155-6, 235, 270, 271,
306, 312, 322; building of, 219-20;
S disposes of share in, 320; burnt
down, 321
Golden Ass, The (Apuleius), 171 n.
Golding, Arthur, 36, 96, 324
Goldingham, Harry, 173
Goliards, 96
Goodman, G., 144 n.
Gorboduc (Norton and Sackville), 36, 42
Gosson, Stephen, 158, 160 n., 174
grandiloquence, Elizabethan love of, 275
Gray's Inn, 36, 149
Greene, Robert, 42, 55 n., 324; death,
61-2; resentment of S, 63-4
Greene, Thomas, 331
Greene's Groatsworth of Wit, 62-4
Greenwich Palace, 149, 168
Grendon, original Dogberry at, 182
Greville, Fulke, 31, 223
Grey de Wilton, Lord, 234, 243
groundlings, 156, 159
guilds, 156

Gull's Hornbook, The (Dekker), 34 n.,
156 n.

Hall, Edward, 199, 258
Hall, Elizabeth (S's grand-daughter), 296,
322
Hall, Dr John (S's son-in-law), 296, 322,
331, 332
Hall, Joseph, 188
Hall, William, as 'W.H.', 123-4
Hamlet: a 'malcontent', 264, 266; his
madness, 265, 268; a modern man,
266; Eliot on, 266; Essex and, 266-7;
irresolution of, 266, 268; poet and
egocentric, 267; his speech to the
players, 269-70; isolation of, 298
Hamlet, 309, 311, 313; S as Ghost in,
148; Essex link in, 254, 266-7; dating
of, 255; sources for, 264, 265, 266; a
tragedy of irresolution, 266, 268;
regarded as melodrama, 267-8; Voltaire's attack on, 268; all minor characters except Hamlet, 268 n.; S's
'most various play', 269; references
to contemporary stage in, 269-70
Harbage, Arthur, 156 n.
Harbert, William, 103 n.
Hardwick Hall, 86
Harington, Sir John, 74-5, 233, 249
harmony, inward, 191; Falstaff's achievement of, 203, 205
Harriot, Thomas, 48
Harrison, G. B., 63 n., 188 n.
harvests, poor, 67, 169, 218
Harvey, Gabriel, 62, 102, 214
Harvey, William, 103 n.
Hathaway, Anne: marriage, 26-7; birth
of children, 27, 29; possible character
of, 27-8; gets 'second-best bed', 332
Hathaway, Richard (S's father-in-law),
26, 27
Hatton, Sir Christopher, 74
Hayward, Sir John, 85 n.
Hayward, Dr John, 231, 235
Hazlitt, William: on *Venus and Adonis*
and *Rape of Lucrece*, 104; on Shylock,
176; on S's blank verse, 179; on
Falstaff, 205, 211; on *Troilus and
Cressida*, 261; on Iago, 279-80; on
Antony and Cleopatra, 290; on *Lear*,
311; on *Timon of Athens*, 318; on
Tempest, 328
Hearne, Thomas, 295
Hearsey, John E. N., 33 n.
Heine, Heinrich, on Shylock, 177
Helena (in *All's Well*), 316-17; Coleridge
considers S's 'loveliest creation', 317
hell, 301
Heminge, John, 188, 219, 254, 314, 332
Heneage, Sir Thomas, 124

Henri of Navarre, 76, 110, 142
Henry IV, 20 n., 87 n., 196, 216, 293; sources for, 199–201; 'rammed with life', 201; S satisfies popular patrons with, 201–2; unequal verse, 202; preoccupation with time, 202–3; superlative character of Falstaff in, 203–11; rejection theme in, 210; popularity of, 213–14
Henry V, 196, 220, 273; a disappointing work, 211–12; hero a 'commonplace man', 212; Chorus in, 213; popularity of, 213; Essex addressed in, 222
Henry VI, 58, 196; reference to forced marriage, 28; sources for, 55; immaturity, 55; S's so-called 'political awareness' in, 56–7; immediate success, 60; Greene's parody of line in, 63
Henry VII, 54
Henry VIII, 115, 196, 315, 321
Henslowe, Philip, 35, 159, 188, 192; career of, 50–1; theatre interests, 51, 53, 59, 60 n., 154, 155, 191; builds Fortune, 219; manages Bear Garden, 220
Hentzner, Paul, 38 n., 79 n., 87 n., 93 n., 221, 253 n.
Heraclitus, 293
Herbert of Cherbury, Lord, 72, 90, 94
Hero and Leander (Marlowe), 97, 100–1
Herrick, Robert, 25
Hervey, Sir William, 124, 125–6; as 'Mr. W. H.', 125
Heywood, Thomas, 325
Hierarchie of the blessed Angels (Heywood), 325
hierarchy, society and, 83–4
Hilliard, Alice, 90, 91
Hilliard, Nicholas, 81, 90–2
Historia Britonum (Geoffrey of Monmouth), 304
Historia novellamente retrovata di duo nobili amanti (de Porto), 149 n.
historical plays, popularity of, 54–5, 147, 196, 201
History of Travayle (Eden), 324
History of the World (Ralegh), 83 n.
Holinshed, Raphael, 53–4, 55, 197, 199, 258, 304
Hollar, Wenceslaus, 220
Holofernes (in *Love's Labour's Lost*), 143
homme moyen sensuel, Falstaff as, 205
homosexuality: Marlowe and, 47; Southampton and, 117–18, 134; in S., 132–4, 256, 287
Hooker, Richard, 36
Horace, 195
horror, burden of, in *Hamlet* and *Lear*, 311

Hotson, T. Leslie, 30 n., 49 n., 71 n., 121 n., 154 n., 155 n., 165 n., 180 n., 187 n.
houses, great, 86, 88, 92, 95, 252–3
Housman, A. E., 328
Humorous Day's Mirth, An (Chapman), 188
'humours', bodily, 85; comedy of, 188 189, 190–1
Hunks, Harry (Russian bear), 221
Hunsdon, George, Lord, 41 n., 48, 164
Hunsdon, Henry, Lord, 41, 164
Hunt, Simon, 21
Hunter, G. K., 183 n.
Huon of Bordeaux (Berners), 171
Hurstfield, Joel, 69 n.
Hymn of Heavenly Beauty (Spenser), 83 n.

Iago: recognized type of crafty ancient, 278; suggested motives, 279–81; Coleridge and Hazlitt on, 279–80; his 'deadness of feeling', 280; a major tragic figure, 280; a 'philosopher', 280–1; campaign against Othello, 281–5; sexual imagery from animal realm, 283; Othello's *doppelganger*, 285
Idea's Mirror (Drayton), 54 n., 121, 127, 128
Iliad (trans. Chapman), 211, 258
illiteracy, 20, 156
'in the round' staging, 154
Inner Temple, 36
Inns of Chancery, 36
Inns of Court, 36–7, 149
'interludes', 42
Ireland, rebellion in, 222–3, 226, 228–30, 234
irresolution: in Richard II, 197; *Hamlet* a tragedy of, 266, 268; Essex's weakness, 266; in Coriolanus, 313
Isam, Mistress, 62
Isle of Dogs, The (Jonson and Nashe), 189, 192
Itinerary (Moryson), 143 n.

Jack Drum's Entertainment (Marston), 270 n.
James I, 70, 234, 243, 252–3, 303; patronage of players, 254, 299; interest in witchcraft, 300
Japan, drama of, resemblances to Elizabethan, 39
Jaques, moralizings of, 183–4
jealousy: in *Othello*, 282–3, 285–6; in *Winter's Tale*, 322
Jenkins, Elizabeth, 24 n.
Jenkins, Thomas, 21
Jew of Malta, The (Marlowe), 46, 47, 174, 175 n.

John Chrysostom, St, 327
Johnson (or Janssen), Gerard, bust of S by, 65
Johnson, R. (musician), 325
Johnson, Samuel, 21 n., 193; on Falstaff, 204–5; on Troilus and Cressida, 261; on Hamlet, 268; on All for Love, 291; on Lear, 309
Jones, Inigo, 86, 315
Jonson, Ben, 21, 40, 43, 58 n., 163, 220, 263, 272, 296, 297, 319, 332, 333; tribute to S, 64; on playgoers, 158; his dramatic concepts, 189–90, 212, 325; career, 191–2; character, 193, 194; his circle, 193; contrasted with S, 194; as critic of S, 194–5; in 'Stage War', 271
Joyce, James, 27, 203 n.
Julia (in Two Gentlemen), earliest of S's comic heroines, 59–60
Julius Caesar, 237 n.; dating of, 254–5; Essex link with, 255; quarrel scene in, 256–7; nobility of characters, 257, 258; powerful imagery, 257–8; a tribute to humanity, 258; sources for, 258; anachronisms, 258–9

Kabuki drama, 39
Kean, Edmund, as Shylock, 176, 177
Keats, John, 135
Keeling, William, 267–8
Kelley, Edward, 301
Kempe, William, 148, 160, 187, 219
Kenilworth Castle, 22–4; Elizabeth entertained at, 23–4, 171, 173
Keymis, Lawrence, 48
Kindheart's Dream (Chettle), 64
King John, 216, 264 n., 299; reference to loss of son in, 161–2; source of, 196–7; and tediousness of life, 303
King Lear, 299; 'colour-scheme' of, 304; sources of, 304–5; Turgenev novel inspired by, 305–6; elements and apparitions, 306–7; and S's personal tragedy, 307–8; Tate's happy ending for, 309; S's 'message' in, 309–10, 311; Edgar's Stoicism, 309, 310, 311; burden of horror in, 311; imperfections, 311
King's Men, 324; James I's patronage, 254, 299; at Blackfriars Theatre, 314
kingship, 76–7, 198–9, 235
Knight, G. Wilson, 299 n., 309 n.
'Knight's Tale' (Chaucer), 171
Knollys, Lettice, 23, 107, 171 n.
Kyd, Thomas, 43, 48–9, 264, 301

Laforgue, Jules, 267
Lamb, Charles, on Malvolio, 186
Lambarde, William, 248

Lane, John, 321
Langley, Francis, 164–5
language, Elizabethan love of, 53, 275
law-students, support for players, 36
law-suits, 219
Lear: isolated by madness, 298; least heroic of S's heroes, 305; old age personified, 305; his sexual phantoms, 306–7, 311; and basic condition of mankind, 308–9; self-appointed destitution, 308
Lear of the Steppes, A (Turgenev), 305–6, 308 n.
Leavis, F. R., 275 n.
Lee, Anne, 165
Lee, Sidney, 72 n., 123 n., 132 n.
Legend of Good Women, A (Chaucer), 178 n.
Leicester, Robert Dudley, Earl of, 22–3, 28, 33, 87, 107, 111, 171 n.
Leicester's Players, 30
Leishman, J. B., 127 n., 134 n.
Leontes (in Winter's Tale): tenderness with son, 161; jealousy, 322
Leveson, Sir John, 238, 239
Lewis, Wyndham, 287 n., 290 n.
Lie, The (Ralegh), 39 n.
Lincoln, Lord, 248
literature: Renaissance influence on, 86; Classical influence on, 95–8, 101; Elizabethan attitude to purpose of, 120–1
Lloyd, David, 31 n.
Lodge, Thomas, 42, 62, 180, 264
London: plague in, 25, 51, 52, 61, 105, 141; S's arrival in, 32, 40; 16th-c., 33–40, 54; City, 33–4, 78; playhouses, 35, 36, 38, 51, 78, 147, 154–9, 164–5, 219–20, 314; Inns of Court, 36–7, 38, 149; St Paul's 33–4, 36, 93; Bear Garden, 220–1; Essex rebellion in, 234–42; S's lodgings in, 272; Mermaid, 296–7
loneliness, theme of, 57, 177, 181, 186, 201, 298–9, 312–3
Longueville, Duc de, 142
Lopez, Dr, 174–5, 177
Lorenzo (in Merchant), poetic speeches of, 177–9
Love, Cult of, 144
love, Elizabethan attitude to, 143–6, 151, 285
love, romantic: Venus and Adonis and, 100, 149; in Romeo and Juliet, 149, 151, 261, 263, 277, 294; in Midsummer Night's Dream, 169; Othello and, 277, 278, 285–6; in Antony and Cleopatra, 287
love, sexual: in Marlowe's Hero and Leander, 100–1; in Troilus and Cressida,

love, sexual: *contd.*
  261–2, 263; in *Othello*, 286; in *Measure for Measure*, 317
Love's Labour's Lost, 50 n., 58, 84 n., 215, 301; references to Marlowe in, 97 n.; and 'Dark Lady', 131, 145; perhaps intended for private audience, 141–2; satirical strokes at Ralegh, 142–3; theme of battle of sexes, 143–6, 181; pastoral ditty in, 146–7
Love's Labour's Won, 216
Love's Martyr, 263
Low Countries, campaign in, 110, 191, 212 n.
Lucy, Sir Thomas, 23, 29–30, 218
'Lucy Negro', 131
Luddington chapel, 27
Luther, Martin, 32
Lydgate, John, 258
Lyly, John, 42–3, 248, 270

Macbeth: isolated by guilt, 298, 303; his private hell, 301, 302; S's last attempt to create great man, 302; his rapid brutalization, 303; and monotony of life, 303–4
Macbeth: origin of, 299–301; supernatural in, 301; symbolism of darkness and disease, 301–2; fear the keynote, 301, 303; killing of Duncan a sacrilege, 303; knocking at the gate, 303; 'colour-scheme' of, 304
Machiavelli, 47, 97
Madre de Dios (Spanish ship), 66, 79
Mainwaring, Arthur, 330–1
Maisse, Hérault de, 224–5
malcontent: Hamlet as, 264, 266; a recognized type, 264–5
Malcontent, The (Marston), 264 n.
maltsters, profiteering, 218, 256
Malvolio, 84; a tragic character, 185–6; link with Richard III, 186; self-love, 186; Lamb on, 186
Manningham, John, 188, 294
Markham, Gervase, 114 n., 115–16
Marlowe, Christopher, 43, 55 n., 62–3, 80–1, 174, 301; 'aspiring mind', 44; self-portraits, 44–5; compared to S, 46, 50, 100–1, 137; 'mighty line' of, 46, 198; homosexuality, 47; atheism, 47, 48, 299; in secret service, 47–8, 49; and 'School of Night', 48; mysterious death, 49–50; 'dead shepherd' in *As You Like It*, 50, 97 n.; Ovidian influence, 97; influence on S, 97, 198
marriage, forced, references to, 28–9
Marston, John, 36, 188, 214, 263, 264 n., 270–1
'Martin Marprelate' tracts, 43, 68
Mary Queen of Scots, 70, 76, 115

Masefield, John, 212 n.
Mason, Philip, 284 n.
masques, 323, 325
Mattingly, Garrett, 32 n.
May-day revels, 25
Mayne, Duc de, 142 n.
Measure for Measure, 221 n., 316, 317–18
melancholy, Elizabethan, 191, 269
Melancthon, 32
Menaechmi (Plautus), 58, 188
Menenius (in *Coriolanus*), 210, 314
Merchant of Venice, The, 216, 284; view of universe in, 82, 180; raw material for, 174–6; mastery of blank verse in, 174, 179; musical quality of poetry in, 177–9; boy-actors as Hermia and Helena, 181
merchant-class, 78–9
Mercutio (in *Romeo and Juliet*), 145, 260; based on a London wit, 93–4, 152; 'genial obscenities' of, 151; has to be killed off, 152, 211
Meres, Francis, 49, 122, 161; tribute to S, 215–16
Mermaid Tavern, 296–7
Merry Wives of Windsor, 21, 30, 211
Metamorphoses (Ovid), 96, 100, 324
Meyrick, Sir Gelly, 234, 248
Micro-cosmographie (Earle), 34 n.
Middle Temple, 36; *Twelfth Night* at, 188
Middleton, Thomas, 325 n.
Midland landscape, 22
Midsummer Night's Dream, A, 23, 216; rhetoric parodied in, 104–5; lyricism of, 168; composition and sources of, 168–70, 171; dream-like atmosphere, 169, 172–3, 326; theme of illusory romantic love, 169, 172; tributes to Elizabeth in, 171; 'rude mechanicals', 173–4
Mirror of Martyrs (Weever), 255 n.
misogyny, poetic, 143
Modena, Nicholas da, 92 n.
monopolies, sale of, 70
monotony of life, theme of, 162, 303–4
Montaigne, 310, 324
moral realism, Jonson's aim of, 189, 190, 325
Moralités Légendaires (Laforgue), 267
morality plays, 42, 206
Morley, Thomas, 88
Moro di Venezia, Il (Cinthio), 286, 288
Morris, Helen, 80 n.
Moryson, Fynes, 143 n.
Mountjoy, Charles Blount, Lord, 113, 234, 245
Mountjoy, Christopher, 272–3
Mountjoy, Mary, 272, 273, 274

Much Ado About Nothing, 330 n.;
lyricism of, 168; sources of, 180;
battle of sexes in, 181-2; clowns in, 182
mummers, 25
Murry, John Middleton, 288 n.
Musaeus, 97
music, 88-9, 93
Musset, Alfred de, 267
'My Picture Left in Scotland' (Jonson),
192 n.
mythology, 95, 96, 98, 101

Napper, Edward (or Edmund), 138
Nashe, Thomas, 25 n., 42, 60, 61, 62, 64,
116, 132 n., 157, 188-9, 264
Neale, J. E., 76 n.
'New Learning', 42
New Place, Stratford, 22, 163, 166, 167,
271, 272, 296, 320, 321 n., 322, 332
Newes from Scotland, 300 n.
Night: Elizabethan fondness for apostro-
phizing, 104; fear of, 302; imagery of,
142, 302
noblemen: support of players, 36, 78;
decline of, 163
noise, Elizabethan love of, 93 n.
Nonsuch Palace, 72, 92, 230, 255 n.
Norden, John, 37 n., 220 n.
North, Sir Thomas, 258, 288, 312
Northumberland, Earl of, 48
Norton, Thomas, 36
Nottingham, Lord Howard of Effingham,
Earl of, 223, 225, 237, 240, 242-3
Nurse (in *Romeo and Juliet*), 151; illus-
trates S's comprehensive sympathy,
152-3

Oberon (in *Midsummer Night's Dream*),
23, 171; 'charged with life', 173
Ocean's Love to Cynthia, The (Ralegh), 75
old age, personified by Lear, 305
Oldcastle, Sir John, 204, 214 n.
Oliver, Isaac, 92
Ophelia (in *Hamlet*), 268, 269
Orchestra, or a Poem of Dancing (Davies),
89
Orinoco river, 79
Otello (Verdi), 276 n.
Othello: a unified personage, 274;
criticized as 'bogus great man', 274-5,
281; his farewell speech, 275; poetic
quality, 275-7, 283; lack of self-
knowledge, 277, 285; English traits,
277, 278; slow awakening to love,
277-8; young in mind, 278, 285;
Iago's campaign against, 281-5; natural
dignity and harmony, 281, 282; effect
of African blood, 284; his voluptuous
sensitiveness, 285-6; isolated by
passion, 298

Othello: power and unity of, 274, 311;
romantic setting, 275; poetry of,
275-6; operatic qualities, 276, 305;
a 'tragic account of tardy beginnings',
277; animal imagery of, 283, 285;
racial prejudice, 284; sexual love in,
286, 294; source of, 286, 288; compared with *Antony and Cleopatra*, 288
outsider, a recognized type, 233-4, 278-9
Ovid, 21, 100, 158, 171; attraction for
Elizabethans, 95-7, 98
Oxford, 116, 294-5
Oxford, Edward de Vere, seventeenth
Earl of, 117, 216 n.

pageants, 23-4, 33, 171
Painter, William, 149 n.
painting, Elizabethan, 90-2
Palladis Tamia (Meres), 49, 215-16
Pandarus (in *Troilus*), 260, 262
Pandosto: The Triumph of Time (Greene),
324
Paris Garden, 51, 164
Parliament, power of, 69-70
Parma, Duke of, 33
Parsons, Robert, 48
Parthenophil and Parthenope (Barnes),
121
Passionate Pilgrim, The, 122
patriotism, 54
Patroclus (in *Troilus*), 259, 260
Paulet, Sir Amias, 76
Peacham, Henry, 160
Peele, George, 42, 55 n., 116
Pembroke, William Herbert, Earl of, 123,
228
Pembroke's Men, 188
Percy, Sir Charles, 214, 235
Percy, Sir Joscelyn, 235
Perfit Description of the Celestial Orbes
(Digges), 82
Pericles, Prince of Tyre, 318, 319
Petruchio (in *Taming of the Shrew*),
blustering eloquence of, 58
Philaster (Beaumont and Fletcher), 314
Philip II of Spain, 32, 223
Phillips, Augustine, 219, 254
Phoenix and the Turtle, The, 263
'picture stage', 154
Pierce Penniless (Nashe), 264
Pilgrimage to Parnassus, 215
piracy, 66, 79
Pitcher, Seymour M., 200 n.
plague, 24-5, 52, 61, 105, 141, 147,
218
Platter, Thomas, 255
Plautus, 58, 188
play-going, 53, 157, 159
play-writing, Elizabethan methods,
59

players: City antagonism to, 35, 157–8, 164; support from noblemen and law-students, 36, 78; re-formation of, 147–8; bohemian life, 148–9, 160; Puritan opposition, 157–8, 160; costumes, 160; changed status, 160, 163; James I's patronage, 253, 254, 299–300

players, touring: at Stratford, 24, 30, 32; life of, 51–2

playhouses, 35, 36, 38, 51, 78, 147; structure and stages of, 154–6, 213, 219–20, 271; audiences, 156–7, 158–9; objections to, 157–8, 160, 164; 'notable beauty' of, 159; S on restrictions of, 212–13; closed private type, 271, 314; stage-craft, 315, 323, 325

plays, printing of, 216

Plays Confuted in Five Actions (Gosson), 160 n.

Plume, Thomas, 19 n.

Plutarch, 258, 288, 289, 312, 318

Poetaster (Jonson), 158 n., 195

Poley, Robert, 49

Polonius (in *Hamlet*), 310; perhaps based on Burghley, 268–9

Pope, Thomas, 219

population, 33

popularizing, educational, 53–4

Porto, Luigi da, 149 n.

portrait-painting, 90–1

Practicall Musicke (Morley), 88

priests, Catholic, persecution of, 67–8

Primitive Man, Caliban as, 326

privacy: Elizabethan lack of, 88; modern insistence on, 93

Proctor, John, 48 n.

Promos and Cassandra (Whetstone), 317

Prospero (in *Tempest*): on forced marriage, 28–9; as S, 29, 325, 327; recollects daughter's infancy, 161; disagreeable character, 325; on the illusory universe, 327–8; cynicism, 328

Puritans, 68–9, 70; opposition to theatre, 157–8, 160; and royal authority, 198, 226, 233; opposition to bear-baiting, 221; Essex allied to, 226, 233

Puttenham, George, 121

Queen's Players, 24, 30, 41

Quiney, Adrian, 217

Quiney, Richard, 217, 218

Quiney, Thomas, 217, 331

Rabelais, 208

racial prejudice: in *Merchant*, 175, 176–7; in *Othello*, 284

Rainsford, Lady, 128

Ralegh, Sir Walter, 36, 38, 39, 87, 126, 227, 275; his 'School of Night', 48, 142, 147; adoration of Queen, 75–6;

as explorer, 79–80; religion of, 94; rivalry with Essex, 107–8, 112, 142, 144, 223, 231, 234, 243, 246; Armado identified with, 143; in Tower, 254

Rape of Lucrece, 50, 109, 214, 215; dedicated to Southampton, 101; Hazlitt on, 104; rhetoric in, 104, 105

religion, 67–8, 94, 299

Renaissance, 81, 86

Repentance of Robert Greene, The, 63 n.

Return from Parnassus, The, 160 n., 163 n., 215

revenge, tragedies of, 43, 58, 264

Reynolds, William, 118

rhetoric, 104–5

Rich, Barnabe, 54

Rich, Lady Penelope, 27, 113–14, 121, 232, 242

Richard II: effigy of, 198; Elizabeth obsessed by fall of, 198, 248; a Marlovian personage, 198–9

Richard II, 53, 93 n., 197–9, 216; Essex shown in, 106–7; abdication theme in, 198–9

Richard III: tirades of, 56, 57; and prison of Self, 57, 186; Alleyn's portrayal of, 148; link with Malvolio, 186, and with Thersites, 263

Richard III, 57, 58, 196, 216, 299

Richardson, John, 26

Richmond Palace, 250

Righter, Anne, 327 n.

Rimbaud, Arthur, 332

Rogers, Philip, 272

Romeo, 277; and 'Dark Lady', 131, 145, 151; transcendent passion of, 151

Romeo and Juliet, 34 n., 87 n., 146, 214, 216; stylized passions of, 146; and romantic love, 149, 151, 261, 263, 277, 294; sources of, 149–50; dominating image of light in, 150; bawdy wit, 150–1; secondary characters in, 151–3; mastery of rhythms of common speech in, 153; staging of, 154

Rosalind (in *As You Like It*), 183; her view of love and marriage, 184; Shaw on, 184–5

Rosalynde (Lodge), 180

Rose playhouse, 35, 51, 60 n., 148, 159, 219

Rowe, Nicholas, 21, 29–30, 148, 166, 176, 188, 320

Rowse, A. L., 33 n., 38 n., 163 n.

Rutland, Roger Manners, fifth Earl of, 229, 248, 321

Sackerson (Russian bear), 221

Sackville, Thomas, 36

St Paul's Cathedral, 33–4, 93; choristers, 42, 43, 270–1; Churchyard, 34, 38

Salvini, Tommaso, 276 n.
Sampson, Agnes, 300
Sandells, Fulk, 26
scenic entertainments, 325
School of Abuse (Gosson), 158
'School of Night', Ralegh's, 48, 50, 142
Scienza Nuova (Vico), 203 n.
Scoloker, Anthony, 268
Scot, Reginald, 169–70, 171, 191, 300
Sejanus (Jonson), 272
self-dramatization, of courtiers and soldiers, 275
Seneca, dramatic method of, 42
senses, delight in, 285, 286
Seven Ages of Man, 183–4
Seven Deadly Sins of London (Dekker), 159 n.
Shadow of Night, The (Chapman), 142 n.
Shakespeare, Ann (sister), 18
Shakespeare, Edmund (brother), 18, 296 n.
Shakespeare, Gilbert (brother), 18, 296 n.
Shakespeare, Hamnet (son), 27, 29, 32; effect of death on S, 160–2
Shakespeare (later Hart), Joan (sister), 18, 332
Shakespeare, John (father), 17–19, 21, 22, 28; claims grant of arms, 18; misfortunes of, 18–19, 21; gets grant of arms, 160, 162–3, 164, 166; death, 272
Shakespeare (later Quiney), Judith, 27, 29, 32, 272, 322, 331–2
Shakespeare, Mary (mother), 17–18, 272; 'a superior soul', 17, 19; death, 296
Shakespeare, Richard (brother), 18, 296 n.
Shakespeare (later Hall), Susanna (daughter), 27, 272, 296, 321–2, 331–2
Shakespeare, William: birth and parentage, 17–19; childhood, 19–22; education, 21–22; thrust into marriage, 26–7; supposed work as schoolmaster or lawyer's clerk, 28; as a soldier, 28, 213; leaves Stratford, 29–30, 32; deer-stealing story, 29–30, 47; links with literary and dramatic circles, 30–1, 34, 39; possible patron in Fulke Greville, 31; professional beginnings, 41, 50; joins Strange's Men, 41, 42; writes first historical plays, 54–7; early comedies, 58–60; earliest reference to growing popularity, 60; Greene's invective against, 63–4; more favourable tributes to, 64–5; his attitude to Elizabeth, 77; influenced by Marlowe, 97; publishes *Venus and Adonis*, 97; inferences about life and tastes, 98–101; chooses Southampton as patron, 102–3, 106, 115; meets Southampton and Essex, 106–7; begins to compose

sonnets, 118, 120–2, 126; spokesman in them for Southampton's family, 119, 124–5; his feelings for patron, 128–9, 131–4, 210; and 'Dark Lady', 129–32; growing reputation, 137–8, 140; smooth professional progress, 147; in control of Chamberlain's Men, 148, 160; death of son, 160–2; buys New Place, 163, 166; in Swan Theatre squabble, 165; changes London lodgings, 165, 220; helped by Southampton, 166–7, 250; acts in *Every Man in his Humour*, 188; Jonson's tribute, 194–5; as a celebrated writer, 214–6; invests in native county, 216–7, 218, 271; strengthens Stratford ties, 217–8, 271–2, 296, 330–1; affected by fall of Essex and Southampton, 250–1, 254–6, 263; 'Dark Period', 263, 294, 299, 307–8; buys more property, 271; gives up acting, 272; amorous exploits, 294–5; family affairs, 296, 321–2, 331–2; adapts work to taste for scenic entertainment, 314–15; tires of work and stage, 315, 317, 320; contemplates retirement, 320, 325; buys Blackfriars Gate House, 320–1; retires to Stratford, 330; busy in local affairs, 330–1; his will, 331–2; death, 333
Imagery: alternation of solidity and transience, 293; of animals, 98–9; of bear tied to stake, 304; of birds, 100; bold and expansive, 135–6, 257–8; of 'buzzing night-flies', 202; of claustrophobia, 301–2; of clouds, 202, 292–3; country, 329; of disease, 262, 302; of dolphin, 289; of evanescence, 293; homely, 136–7, 289; of hunger, 261–2; of hunted hare, 99; incomparable, 202; Lear's, of women, 307; of leviathan, 202; of light, 150, 172; of night, 302; of sea, 319, 329; sexual, from animals, 283, 285; of snail, 99, 146; of sport, 98–9; of stallion, 98–9; of taste, 261–2; of water, 55, 293; of 'wet sea-boy', 202
Literary characteristics: anarchic mood in adult dramas, 308; antithetical stanzas, 105; audience, readiness to please, 57–8, 209, 212, 320; bawdy, 150–1; blank verse, mastery of, 174, 179, 185, 328–30; borrowing of plots, 58, 149, 174, 180, 196, 199–200, 258, 264, 288, 317, 324–5; character, method of portraying, 185, 208, 267; childhood references, 19–20, 161–2; Chorus, use of, 213; clowns, 173–4, 182; comic technique, 58–9; compression, gift of, 329; country background, 59, 98, 146–7, 183; descriptive passages, 105, 288–9; 'dream' frequency,

Shakespeare, William: contd.
292–3, 326, 327; extravagant style,
early, 104–5; fairy-tale convention,
319, 323; 'fiery force', 291; heroines,
comic boyish, 59–60, 91, 167, 181, 184;
imagery—see separate entry; improvization, 194; language, use of, 180, 185,
267, 328–30; lost interest, signs of, 135,
317, 320; lyricism, 59, 168, 177–9, 313;
manuscripts, carelessness over, 193,
194, 216, 332; monotony of life,
theme of, 162, 303–4; music, frequent
references to, 89; non-committal grace,
330; past, endowment of characters
with, 152–3, 172–3; political 'message',
263; private life, subjects drawn from,
147, 201; realism, move from, to
symbolism, 320; speech, common,
mastery of rhythms of, 153, 208;
vitality, 195, 201, 291; wit, 141, 150–1,
152; working methods, 59, 144
Personal characteristics: acting ability,
148, 185; agnosticism, 299; amiability,
65, 140; aristocracy, fondness for, 151,
167, 168; assimilative talents, 86, 167,
200, 291; attractive appearance, 65;
business acumen, 162–4, 166, 216–19,
330–1; 'civility', 64, 120; company,
love of, 296–7, 298, 333; conflict in
character, 162, 308; conservatism, 84,
147, 299; experience, appetite for, 137;
generosity, 188; 'gentle', 64, 140;
'good honest fellow', 19; homosexuality, alleged, 132–3, 134, 256,
287; 'honey-tongued', 215; horror of
life, 308; 'ideas', supposed lack of,
185; interest in work, loss of, 135, 317,
320; lassitude, 135, 137; love of life,
162; as a lover, 294–5; man of the
world, 137, 293; opportunism, 57, 63,
121, 325; pessimism, 162, 308;
philosophy, probable, 310, 311; 'political awareness', lack of, 56–7, 201,
263; romantic love, little early interest
in, 100–1, 149; sanguine temperament,
162, 308; scholarship, alleged meagre,
195; 'sweetness', 64–5; wit, 295
Shallow, Mr Justice (in Henry IV), 211,
214; based on Sir Thomas Lucy, 30;
Falstaff's treatment of, 207–8; and
bear-baiting, 221
Shaw, Bernard, 267 n.; on S's bawdy,
151; on As You Like It, 184–5;
resentment of S, 185 n.
Shaw, Robert, 189
Shelley, P. B., on Lear, 311
Shepherd's Calendar (Spenser), 86
Shoreditch Theatre, 148
Shottery, 26
Shrove Tuesday revels, 25

Shylock (in Merchant): outruns S's
intention, 176, 211; speaks for Jewry,
176; 'spiritual disproportion' between
persecutors and, 176–7; Kean as, 176,
177; a lonely being, 177
Sidney, Sir Philip, 31, 110, 113, 121,
132 n.
Sidney, Sir Robert, 240, 241–2
sin, Elizabethan sense of, 38
Sixtus V, Pope, 73
Skialetheia (Guilpin), 107 n.
Slender (in Henry IV), 30 n.
Sly, William, 254
Smith, Sir Thomas, 163
Snitterfield, 17
Snow Queen, The (Andersen), 172
Soer, Dorothy, 165
sonnet-writing, 121
Sonnets, 143, 272, 317; Southampton
depicted in, 118–19, 124–5, 132, 134,
167; dating of, 121–2, 126–7; published, 122, 322; dedication, 122–4;
derivative elements, 127–8; 'Dark
Lady' of, 129–32, 145; 'monument to
homosexual love', 132–4; double en-
tendres in, 133; transience of youth
and love their real subject, 134;
contemporary popularity, 134; later
attitude to, 134–5; unevenness, 135;
imagery of, 135–7; reveal S's mind in
early middle age, 137, 210
Southampton, Thomas Wriothesley, first
Earl of, 115
Southampton, Henry, second Earl of,
115–16
Southampton, Henry Wriothesley, third
Earl of, 114, 141, 147, 222, 260;
Venus and Adonis dedicated to, 64,
102–3; ancestry, 115–16; S's first
meeting, 106; character, 106, 117–19,
134; appearance, 117, 247; 'cherisher
of poets', 114, 116, 143, 167; S's
sonnets and, 118–19, 123, 124–5, 132,
134, 167; urged to marry, 118–19, 124–
5; as 'Mr. W. H.', 123; S helped by,
166–7, 250; humiliated at Court, 227;
marries, 227–8; and Irish rebellion,
229, 230; and Essex rebellion, 241–3,
244; sentenced to life imprisonment,
247, 250, 263; released, 253–4
Southampton, Elizabeth Vernon, Lady,
118, 214, 227–8
Spanish Armada, 32–3, 66, 124, 126, 127
Spanish Tragedy (Kyd), 40, 43–4, 58, 264
Speculum Britanniae (Norden), 37 n.
Spencer, Gabriel, 189, 192
Spenser, Edmund, 60, 81, 83, 86, 121
Spurgeon, Caroline F. E., 150 n., 261 n.,
302 n., 309 n.
Stafford's Players, 30

stage, idea of world as, 327–8
stage, Elizabethan, 154–5, 156, 213, 219–20
stage-craft, 154, 155, 315, 323, 325
stage properties, 159–60
'Stage War', 271
Standen, Anthony, 39
stars, influence of, 82, 85
Steevens, George, 134
Steiner, George, 257 n.
Stewart, J. I. M., 210 n.
Stoicism, of Edgar in *Lear*, 310
Stone, Lawrence, 78 n., 144 n.
Stopes, Charlotte Carmichael, 124 n.
Stow, John, 199–200
Strange's Men, 41, 52, 147
Strachey, Lytton, 315, 325
Stratford: John S's house in, 17, 18, 28; school, 20–1; Elizabethan 22, 25; plague in, 24–5; New Place, 22, 163, 166, 167, 271, 272, 296, 320, 321 n., 322, 332; S's birth in, 24; mummers in, 25; S leaves, 29–30; London players at, 30, 32; S's periodic visits to, 160; S buys property in, 163, 166, 167, 271; decline of, 218; S's increasing time at, 271–2; his daughter's wedding at, 296; his retirement to, 320, 321–2, 330–3; his death and burial at, 333
Street, Peter, 154
Sturley, Abraham, 217, 218
summers, rainy, 67, 169, 218
superstition, 25, 32, 169–71, 301
Suppositi, I (Ariosto), 58
Surrey, Henry Howard, Earl of, 86, 96, 121
Swan Theatre, 154, 159, 164–5
symbolism: conventional, 84–5; S's move from realism to, 320
Symbolist Movement, 267

talk, Elizabethan love of, 93–4
Tamburlaine the Great (Marlowe), 43, 44–5, 80–1
Taming of the Shrew, The, 58–9, 181
Tarlton, Dick, 187
taste, Elizabethan, 86, 88, 92
Tate, Nahum, his happy ending for *Lear*, 309
Tears of the Muses (Spenser), 60
Tears of Fancy (Watson), 121
temperament, Elizabethan, 81, 86, 88–90, 92–4, 97, 191, 251
Tempest, The, 322; reference to forced marriage, 28–9; sources of, 324–5; as scenic entertainment, 325; as S's farewell, 325, 330; 'a waking dream', 326–7; S's mastery of words in, 328–30; imagery, 328–9; gift of compression in, 329

Temple Grafton, 26, 27
theatre: dominated by business men, 50–1; Greene's diatribe on, 62–4
Theatre playhouse, 35, 155, 159, 165, 219
Theatre of God's Judgments (Beard), 49
Theobalds, 252–3
Thersites (in *Troilus*), 260, 263
Thorpe, Thomas (publisher of S's sonnets), 122–3, 125
Throckmorton, Elizabeth, 75
Tilbury, 33
Tillyard, E. M. W., 56 n., 83 n., 84 n., 85 n., 320 n.
Timber (Jonson), 194
time, preoccupation with, 202–3
Timon of Athens, 251; pessimism of, 308, 318; Coleridge and Hazlitt on, 318; 'spleen' in, 318
Titania, 169; derivation of name, 171; 'charged with life', 173
Tichfield, 141
Titus Andronicus, 58, 60, 139, 216; costumes for, 160
touring players, 24, 30, 32, 51–2
Traversi, Derek, 59 n.
Treatise on the Arte of Limninge, A (Hilliard), 91
Treatise of the Soul (Ralegh), 80
Troilus and Cressida, 254; theory of 'degree' in, 83; Essex link with, 258, 260; sources for, 258; unpleasantness of, 259–60; unpopularity, 260–1; sexual love analysis, 261–3; imagery of, 261–2
Troilus and Cressida (Chaucer), 258
Troublesome Reign of John, King of England, The, 196
Turgenev, Ivan S., 305
Twelfth Night, 185–8; first performance, 71, 180, 188; S shown as 'social climber' in, 168; sources of, 180; unedifying effect, 185; nonsense-poem in, 186–7
Two Gentlemen of Verona, The, 146, 215; source of, 58; S's 'most tedious play', 59; his earliest comic heroine in, 59–60
Two Noble Kinsmen, The, 316
Tyrone, Hugh O'Neill, second Earl of, 228, 229, 230

Ulysses (in *Troilus*): and 'degree', 83; on Achilles, 259–60
unemployment, 67
Unfortunate Traveller (Nashe), 116
universe, theories of, 71, 82–4, 180, 301
'University Wits', 42
unreality, sense of, in S's tragic figures, 293

Van Doren, Mark, 135 n.

Vaughan, Henry, 94
Vautrollier, Thomas, 31
Venus and Adonis, 36, 50, 96–100, 101–3, 141; dedicated to Southampton, 64, 102–3, 107; published, 97, 102; rustic imagery in, 98–100, 146; and romantic love, 100, 149, 294; as an erotic poem, 100; popularity of, 102, 105, 214, 215; Hazlitt on, 104
Vere, Lady Elizabeth, 118, 168
Vernon, Elizabeth (Lady Southampton), 118, 214, 227–8
Vice (or Tempter), Falstaff as, 206, 260
Vico, Giovanni Batista, 203
Vida es sueño, La (Calderon), 172
Virgil, 195
Virtue's commonwealth, 157 n.
Voltaire, on *Hamlet*, 268

Wakeman, Roger, 138
Walsingham, Sir Francis, 47, 49, 109, 112, 174, 175
Walsingham, Sir Thomas, 47
wandering scholars, 96
Ward, Rev. John, 333
Warwick Castle, 23
Watson, Thomas, 121, 135
Wayte, William, 30 n., 164–5
Weever, John, 215, 255
Welcombe, 271, 330–1
Welles, Orson, 286 n.
Wentworth, Peter, 68
Weston, William, 249–50
'W. H., Mr', 123–4, 125
Whateley, Anne, 26
Whetstone, George, 317

Whitehall Palace, 37–8, 72, 87, 180, 235, 241, 306, 312, 320, 324
Wilkinson, L. P., 96 n.
Williams, Sir Roger, model for Fluellen, 212
Willobie His Avisa, 137–9
Willoughby, Ambrose, 227
Willoughby, Henry, 138
Wilmcote, 17, 32, 296
Wilson, John Dover, 167 n., 255 n., 256 n., 266 n.
Winter's Tale, The: tribute to childhood in, 20, 161; theme of sexual jealousy, 322; fairy-tale atmosphere, 323; spirit of happiness, 323–4; sources of, 324
Witch, The (Middleton), 325 n.
witchcraft, 170, 171, 300–1
Witt, Johannes de, 154, 155 n., 159, 164
women, increasing authority of, 143–4
Wood, Anthony, 295
Woodward, Joan (Alleyn), 51, 52
Worcester, Earl of, Players, 24
Worthies of England (Fuller), 297
Wotton, Sir Henry, 234 n., 321
Wright, Louis B., 54 n.
Wyatt, Sir Thomas, 86, 96, 121
Wythorne, Thomas, 53, 78–9, 84–5

Yedo (now Tokyo), resemblances to Elizabethan London, 39
yeomanry, rise of, 163
Yong, Bartholomew, 114 n.
Young, G. M., 36 n.

Zeno, 310